Intelligent Souls?

TRANSITS:
LITERATURE, THOUGHT & CULTURE, 1650–1850

Transits is a series of scholarly monographs and edited volumes publishing beautiful and surprising work. Without ideological bias the series seeks transformative readings of the literary, artistic, cultural, and historical interconnections between Britain, Europe, the Far East, Oceania, and the Americas during the years 1650 and 1850 and as their implications extend down to the present time. In addition to literature, art, and history, such "global" perspectives might entail considerations of time, space, nature, economics, politics, environment, gender, sex, race, bodies, and material culture and might necessitate the development of new modes of critical imagination. At the same time, the series welcomes considerations of the local and the national, for original new work on particular writers and readers in particular places in time continues to be foundational to the discipline.

Since 2011, sixty-five *Transits* titles have been published or are in production. For a list of recent titles in the series, see the last page in the book.

TRANSITS

Intelligent Souls?

FEMINIST ORIENTALISM IN EIGHTEENTH-CENTURY ENGLISH LITERATURE

SAMARA ANNE CAHILL

Bucknell UNIVERSITY | UNIVERSITY PRESS

Library of Congress Cataloging-in-Publication Data

Names: Cahill, Samara Anne, author.
Title: Intelligent souls? : feminist orientalism in eighteenth-century English literature / Samara Anne Cahill.
Description: Lewisburg : Bucknell University Press, [2019] | Series: Transits: literature, thought & culture, 1650–1850 | Includes bibliographical references and index.
Identifiers: LCCN 2018058747| ISBN 9781684480982 (cloth : alk. paper) | ISBN 9781684480975 (paperback. : alk. paper) | ISBN 9781684480999 (e-pub) | ISBN 9781684481019 (web PDF) | ISBN 9781684481002 (mobi)
Subjects: LCSH: English literature—18th century—History and criticism. | English literature—Women authors—History and criticism. | Orientalism in literature. | Soul in literature. | Women in literature.
Classification: LCC PR448.W65 C34 2019 | DDC 820.9/3522—dc23
LC record available at https://lccn.loc.gov/2018058747

A British Cataloging-in-Publication record for this book is available from the British Library.

♾ The paper used in this publication meets the requirements of the American National Standard for Information Sciences—Permanence of Paper for Printed Library Materials, ANSI Z39.48-1992.

www.bucknell.edu/UniversityPress

Distributed worldwide by Rutgers University Press

Manufactured in the United States of America

Deo gratias.

To my parents, who came from different worlds,
and to the fellow travelers who showed me others.

CONTENTS

Introduction: Foreign Intelligence 1

1 The Negative Ideal 15

2 Minding the Gap 53

3 The Canal of Pleasure 100

4 A “Foreign and Uninteresting” Subject 142

5 The “Mahometan Strain” 167

Epilogue: Save Our Souls? 199

Bibliography 205

Index 223

Intelligent Souls?

INTRODUCTION

Foreign Intelligence

> His wife, if you look at his wife, she was standing there. She had nothing to say. She probably—maybe she wasn't *allowed* to have anything to say.
>
> —Donald J. Trump

DONALD J. TRUMP'S ASSESSMENT OF GHAZALA Khan's appearance with her husband, Khizr, at the 2016 Democratic National Convention shows that a professed concern for Muslim women may easily be used to frame a discussion of national security. At that convention, Hillary Rodham Clinton became the first female presidential candidate in U.S. history to be nominated by a major party. It was a historic event rendered even more memorable by Khizr Khan's speech, in which he argued that Trump's proposed immigration policies would have prevented his son Humayun—a soldier killed by a suicide bomber in Iraq in 2004 and posthumously awarded a Purple Heart—from entering the United States as a child immigrant.

By focusing on Mrs. Khan's silence rather than her son's heroism or her husband's eloquence, Trump leveraged two seemingly mutually exclusive anti-Muslim stereotypes: Muslim men oppress women and Muslim women do not have anything to say. For Trump, either Mr. Khan was oppressing Mrs. Khan (a woman who had something to say) or Mrs. Khan had no position on the death of her son. Invoking these logically exclusive stereotypes while adopting a posture of uncertainty ("probably," "maybe") enabled Trump to malign Muslim men and Muslim women simultaneously, to frame the interpretive choices as limited to ones in which Muslim gender relations are necessarily less civilized, modern, and egalitarian than gender relations among other populations, and to present himself as a powerful man who is generously attentive to women's voices and position in society. Trump's response to Mrs. Khan shows that a powerful eighteenth-century trope—that Muslim men oppress Muslim women by preventing them from developing their intelligence—is still highly effective in the twenty-first-century public sphere.

This would be a much shorter book if anti-immigration presidential candidates were the only ones who used the trope. But Trump is not alone, and the reasons for the rhetorical power of the trope go beyond (while certainly including) Islamophobia. *Intelligent Souls?* examines how non-Muslim women, in using the trope that Islam denies women's intelligence, sought to reposition themselves in English (and, after the Act of Union in 1707, British) society between 1696 and 1792. These dates mark the beginning of a sea change in Englishwomen's professional writing—the 1695–96 theater season was an unprecedented *annus mirabilis* for women playwrights—and the publication of the cornerstone of Western feminism, Mary Wollstonecraft's *A Vindication of the Rights of Woman*. The trope, which I call "misogynistic mortalism," projected patriarchal oppression onto a variety of religiopolitical others, but predominantly followers of Islam, in order to align Trinitarian orthodoxy with women's education, spiritual equality, and intelligence. Why would such an alignment have been useful in English culture? The answer can be found in the political centrality of the Church of England (Anglican Church) and its doctrine. Trinitarian orthodoxy—the belief that Jesus Christ is fully human, fully divine, and a member of the Trinity alongside God the Father and the Holy Spirit—was enshrined in English legislation. Anglican ministers had to subscribe to the Thirty-Nine Articles of Religion, the official statement of Anglican doctrine, in which Trinitarian orthodoxy was preserved. King William issued *Directions to our Arch-Bishops and Bishops for the Preserving of Unity in the Church, and the Purity of Christian Faith, Concerning the Holy Trinity* in 1696; the Blasphemy Act of 1697 penalized non-Trinitarian belief; and, in Scotland in 1697, the allegedly anti-Trinitarian Thomas Aikenhead became the last person to be burned as a heretic in Great Britain. In 1792, the prominent Whig statesman Charles James Fox failed to have the penalties on non-Trinitarian belief lifted. Religious nonconformity to Trinitarian orthodoxy was penalized until the Doctrine of the Trinity Act was passed in 1813. Those who denied the Trinity could not hold public office, serve as Anglican clergymen, or receive a degree from Oxford or Cambridge.[1] Neither could women. This mutual exclusion gave women a fulcrum point to argue for improvements in their own status, particularly in regard to education. Ultimately, women leveraged Trinitarian orthodoxy to align the English religiopolitical establishment with the argument that women's intelligence should be recognized. This is one of the reasons why Islam—which rejects the Christian Trinity—became a "negative ideal" for eighteenth-century Englishwomen. By affirming Trinitarian orthodoxy while displacing their critiques of patriarchy onto Islam, women were able to characterize their intelligence as foundational to English (and ultimately British) identity. The displacement could only work if Islam truly prevented women from cultivating their intelligence. But it is not immediately clear why denying the Trinity should also entail denying women's intelligence. I argue that through a series of propagandistic rhetorical moves in the late seventeenth century—rhetoric targeting non-Trinitarian Christians rather than Muslims or women—Trinitarian Christians came to associate Islam with the denial of women's immortal souls. This is how misogynistic mortalism became conventional: the assertion that Islam denied women's immortality would also mean that it denied women's intelligence. For most Christians, and certainly for seventeenth- and eighteenth-century Anglicans, the soul was the divine element that distinguished humans from animals: only humans are *imago Dei*, that is, in possession of the intelligence that makes a creature an image of God. Human identity is, uniquely, intelligent and immortal. Thus, to deny that women had souls would be to deny them intelligence (and human identity), too. In short, for women to leverage Trinitarian orthodoxy, it was necessary to believe that Muslim men oppressed women by denying their immortal souls and their intelligence and that Muslim women must therefore be oppressed and unable to develop their intelligence.

My argument, though attending to a very different historical period, largely coincides with that of Miriam Cooke, who coined the term "Muslimwoman" to describe a particular stereotype of Muslim women. The "Muslimwoman" is veiled, submissive, silent, and often secluded in the harem. It is a stereotype "created for Muslim women by outside forces, whether non-Muslims or Islamist men. Muslimwoman locates a boundary between 'us' and 'them.'"[2] The "Muslimwoman" is the ultimate victim, and as long as she exists, so, too, does the fantasy that others need to save the "Muslimwoman" from Muslim men. Numerous scholars, including Cooke, have pointed to the particular popularity of the "Muslimwoman" in Western media after 9/11.[3] But cognate tropes existed much earlier. Indeed, Joyce Zonana argues that the phenomenon she has coined "feminist orientalism"—the displacement of "the source of patriarchal oppression onto an 'Oriental,' 'Mahometan' society, enabling British readers to contemplate local problems without questioning their own self-definition as Westerners and Christians"—arose with Wollstonecraft's *A Vindication of the Rights of Woman*.[4] Yet the displacing mechanism at the heart of feminist orientalism predates this formulation, too. If we bracket the anachronism of the *terminology*—neither "feminism" nor "orientalism" (in Edward Said's modern sense) existed before 1792—and focus on the *mechanism* of displacement, then the roots of feminist orientalism are evident almost a century before Wollstonecraft railed against the "Mahometan strain."[5] Further, the displacement is evident in a variety of literary genres that contributed to the development of that quintessential genre of modernity, the novel.

It has been widely, if not uniformly, accepted that Edward Said, building on Ian Watt's classic account of the "rise" of the novel, is correct in claiming that "the novel, as a cultural artefact of bourgeois society, and imperialism are unthinkable without each other."[6] Gayatri Chakravorty Spivak supports this conclusion while focusing specifically on the leverage that imperialism gave women authors and characters in the process of "soul making." For Spivak, nineteenth-century British heroines had to carve out a space for themselves between "childbearing" (which defined women in terms of sexual reproduction and the nuclear family) and "soul making"—thinking about individual women in terms that go "beyond 'mere' sexual reproduction."[7] If, as Bonnie Latimer has argued, the "marital imperative is a crucial one" for women in eighteenth-century British fiction and culture, then the attraction of "soul making" would have been powerful for women writers.[8] Equally powerful would have been the rhetorical restrictions on politically (and often economically) disenfranchised women as eighteenth-century British fiction came to be characterized by a "prescriptive realism" that increasingly shunned "foreignness" and which had a powerful "ability to *exclude*" (and particularly to exclude "Muslim characters").[9] In other words, women authors were caught between the "soul making" of British heroines and a cultural imperative to exclude Muslims. Increasingly, Islam was excluded by British women for precisely its supposed denial of women's "soul making" ability.

Brean Hammond and Shaun Regan have argued that the eighteenth-century British novel arose out of an "amniotic fluid" that was characterized more by "certain kinds of discourses with particular ideological agendas" than by "specific formal features associated with genre."[10] And since the "gradual domestication of the literary agenda" entailed the increasing marginalization of Muslim characters, it is necessary to go beyond the Saidian (and Wattian) understanding of the novel to understand how this anti-Islam trope developed, particularly for certain kinds of women. The women who contributed most to the perpetuation of the misogynistic mortalism trope—and thus to the origins of feminist orientalism—tended to be intellectual, morally didactic writers, women like Elizabeth Singer Rowe and Penelope Aubin and the circle of women who associated with or were otherwise influenced by Samuel Richardson and Samuel Johnson (including the Bluestockings and Mary Wollstonecraft). Why these women should have been predisposed to perpetuate an Islamophobic trope goes to the heart of why reading Said's critique of orientalism back into the seventeenth and eighteenth centuries is misleading. (Said himself specifically characterized the "modern" orientalism he critiqued as beginning with Napoleon's 1798 invasion of Egypt.[11])

It is not my intention to excoriate women like Rowe, Aubin, the Bluestockings, and Wollstonecraft. Indeed, the project out of which *Intelligent Souls?* grew was in large part motivated by the desire to defend Wollstonecraft from the charge that, as the mother of Western feminism, she was singularly responsible for initiating feminist orientalism. What the research increasingly showed, however, was that, while Wollstonecraft was not singularly responsible, she and many women writing in the century before her had uncritically received an Islamophobic rhetorical trope. Why generations of women who prized intelligence and discernment should, essentially, have failed to do their homework puzzled me, until it became clear that they were working within very specific cultural constraints that went beyond (but certainly included) cultural bias. These constraints had little to do with Islam and everything to do with a bizarre conjunction of Anglican religiopolitical authority, seventeenth-century polemic, and the place of the soul in women's education arguments.

In other words, "misogynistic mortalism" was a contribution to what Hammond and Regan have called the ideological "amniotic fluid" from which the patchwork genre of the novel evolved. Most eighteenth-century references to misogynistic mortalism occur outside of prose fiction. But to understand the trope's function *within* fiction, it is necessary to look at its circulation in the ideological amniotic fluid that Hammond and Regan identify. For this reason, I survey not just prose fiction but also plays, religiopolitical polemics, histories, educational treatises, poetry, and personal letters.

For instance, seventy-five years before Wollstonecraft invoked the "Mahometan strain," Alexander Pope and Lady Mary Wortley Montagu already believed that Islam denied women immortal souls and, thus, intelligence. Tellingly, this belief was firmly rooted in book knowledge rather than in actual experience—it was the product of an imagined geography. According to Edward Said, this imagined geography arose from a "textual universe" that enabled a "free-floating mythology of the Orient."[12] An enamored Pope wrote to Montagu about her impending journey to the Ottoman Empire as the wife of the British ambassador. His tone is light and flirtatious, but his use of the trope is no less serious for all that. He tells her,

> I expect to hear an exact account, how, and at what places, you leave one Article of Faith after another as you approach nearer to Turkey. . . . At every Christian Virtue you lost, at every Christian Habit you quitted, it will be decent for me to fetch a holy Sigh, but still I shall proceed to follow you. How happy will it be, for a gay young Woman, to live in a country where it is a part of Religious worship to be giddy-headed? I shall hear at Belgrade, how the good Basha receivd the fair Convert with tears of joy, how he was charm'd with her pretty manner of pronouncing the words Allah, and Muhammed, and how earnestly you joind with him in

> exhorting Mr Wortley to be circumcised. . . . Lastly I shall hear how the very first Night you lay at Pera, you had a Vision of Mahomet's Paradise, and happily awaked without a Soul. From which blessed instant the beautiful Body was left at full liberty to perform all the agreeable functions it was made for.[13]

Pope draws on a number of important representations used in British self-construction. He alludes, first, to the instability of religious and bodily integrity (underscored by the possibility of Mr. Wortley's circumcision, a common concern of sailors in early modern "Turk" plays); second, to the equally conventional representation of eroticized religious seduction of Christian women by Muslim leaders; third, to the notion that the only allegiance Christian women have to their religious beliefs is their lack of "liberty" (opportunity, that is); fourth, to the assumption that Islam is particularly appealing to women because it is not based in reason but rather approves of their being "giddy-headed"; fifth and last, and most important, to the assumption that Islam holds that women do not have souls that will be held accountable in the afterlife. With this last point he bridges the gap between his own Catholicism and Montagu's Anglicanism by contradistinguishing them, as fellow Christians, from Islam.

Pope was a marginalized Roman Catholic who used the leverage of an imagined Muslim alterity—specifically gendered to exclude only women from moral agency—to bridge the religious gap between himself and Montagu while cheekily imagining a time when her chastity would not be in his way. Pope's vision of the journey to Pera is the imagined geography that Montagu will ultimately reject: it is a pilgrim's progress in reverse, in which the Christian husband becomes mutilated and unmanned and the Christian wife becomes soulless and sexually available.

Crucially, Montagu's attitude to what she and Pope believed to be Islam's position on female immortality changed as their shared imagined geography was replaced by her personal experience. In one of her first letters written from within the Ottoman Empire, sent from Adrianople and dated April 1, 1717, she wrote to her sister Lady Mar that the "threatened punishment of the next [world]" is used to discipline the chastity of English wives but that such a doctrine is "never preached to the Turkish damsels."[14] When she first reached the Ottoman Empire, in other words, she agreed with Pope's assessment. But almost a year later, in February 1718, she assured the Abbé Conti that "'tis certainly false, though commonly believed in our parts of the world, that Mohammad excludes women from any share in a future happy state."[15] Montagu does not specify that she used to be one of those who believed it to be true, but the fact that she was able to use the trope—and understand Pope's use of it—meant that it was indeed "commonly believed" in England and Europe by 1717.

But how did it come to be "commonly believed"? To answer that requires a foray into the rhetorical quagmire of the Trinitarian Controversy of the 1690s, a quagmire that encompassed the fast-and-loose deployment of pejoratives by a number of parties including "Latitudinarians" (an imprecise but useful umbrella term for Anglicans who favored Protestant ecumenism); Socinians (Christians or freethinkers who rejected the Trinity); Roman Catholics (like Anglicans, they believed in the Trinity; unlike Anglicans, they also believed in transubstantiation—the belief that bread and wine could mystically become Christ's body and blood); and High Church Anglicans (who felt, in the late seventeenth and early eighteenth centuries, that the Church of England was in danger precisely because of the moderation of the Latitudinarians). What was the connection between Trinitarian orthodoxy and women's immortality? To make the stakes clearer: the connection is really between Christ's humanity (is he fully human or is he also fully divine and therefore part of the Trinity?) and women's humanity (are they human moral agents because they have immortal souls?). The two issues became rhetorically associated due to a controversial anti-Socinian pamphlet published in 1595 that became widely disseminated in Europe by the end of the eighteenth century. I examine the influence of the pamphlet more extensively in chapter 1, but to follow this capsule version of the argument of *Intelligent Souls?* it is necessary to know that the anonymous author (often identified as Valens Acidalius) satirized Socinian exegesis by arguing that, using the same methods by which Socinians concluded that Christ was not divine, he could also conclude that women were not human. The gauntlet was thrown down: either Christ was part of the Trinity or women were not fully human. Since Trinitarian orthodoxy was central to Anglican religiopolitical authority, the pamphlet's method of attacking Socinianism gave women powerful sociopolitical leverage in establishing themselves as moral agents—as immortal, human, and intelligent.

But that leaves the question of how Islam figured in all of this. There were a number of factors in play, which I discuss in chapter 1. Most crucially, however, Islam considers Christ to be a prophet—not the son of God. If Christ is not God, then there can be no Trinity. Islam and Socinianism shared a common anti-Trinitarian stance. For this reason, even a leading Latitudinarian like Gilbert Burnet associated and rejected both Islam and Socinianism in his influential *An Exposition of the Thirty-nine Articles* (1699). But *did* Islam deny women souls? The interpretation of holy texts can always be co-opted by extremists, of course, but misogynistic mortalism is not Muslim doctrine. In the Qur'an, sura 3 ("The House of 'Imran"), verse 195, the Lord declares:

> I disregard not the works of any who works among you,
> Be they male or female,
> The one is like the other.[16]

In sura 4 ("Women"), verse 57, it is written, "Those who believe and do good deeds We shall lead into Gardens beneath which rivers flow, abiding therein for ever. In it they shall have pure spouses, and We shall lead them into an overspreading shade." This vision of paradise certainly includes women, because, in verse 124, it is declared, "Whoso does good deeds, whether male or female, and has faith, shall enter the Garden and will not be wronged one fleck." The statement is repeated, with slight modifications, in sura 40 ("Forgiver") and sura 48 ("Victory"). True, women inherit less property than men (4:11), husbands are permitted to hit their wives (4:34), and men are legally responsible for women (4:34), but these are historical practices common to both Christian and Muslim societies. Amina Wadud, in her book on Muslim feminist exegesis, devotes an entire chapter to the Qur'anic position on women in the afterlife.[17] While there is interpretive latitude in understanding the allegory of the garden promised to the faithful, the Qur'an is clear that women as well as men will be rewarded in the afterlife.[18]

So, misogynistic mortalism is not part of Muslim doctrine. More troublingly, any eighteenth-century reader who wanted to investigate Muslim doctrine could have consulted even the unsympathetic 1649 English translation of the Qur'an (republished in 1688) and, later, the more evenhanded translation of George Sale (1737) to verify that misogynistic mortalism was not enjoined by Islam's holy text. The origin and continuation of the Islamophobic misogynistic mortalism trope is puzzling, until it is seen as part of a larger network of concerns—including women's professional writing (and education), ecclesiastical authority, and political preferment—that beset England in the 1690s. Islam was not just a straw man. It was also a stand-in for enemies closer to home: the anti-Trinitarian Socinian and, more generally, the freethinker, libertine, and atheist.

The only requirement for misogynistic mortalism to work was the sleight of hand by which the limited knowledge of Muslim women conveyed through (predominantly male) Western travel accounts became knowledge of Muslim women's "real" experience. The geographic distance between England and the Ottoman Empire subtended this enabling fiction and expedited the absorption of feminist orientalism into the canon of Western feminism. Put most simply: British women who relied on the trope represented themselves as *currently* in the possession of intelligence that Muslim women *currently* did not have but would be *able* to cultivate (with a proper education and conversion from Islam, of course). The assumption was that the religious and spatial context of Muslim women—and here the fantasized space of the harem looms large—would have to change in order for them to cultivate the intelligence that the Christian woman had already cultivated (or was in the process of cultivating).[19] Of course, this singular possession of intelligence was an enabling fiction used by women who were only too aware of the limits and precariousness of their own educational access. But by demonizing Muslim doctrine and the imagined space of the harem this way, it was possible to envision the consequences of treating women as objects of bodily pleasure rather than as moral agents capable of intellectual pleasure. Part of the fiction was that the harem appealed to the baser, physical pleasures of both men (sexual pleasure) and women (pleasures of the body and senses, including a delight in food, clothing, gossip, and other unintellectual "feminine" accomplishments). Within this narrative, only Christian women *could* cultivate intellectual pleasure. Thus, the denial of intelligence to Muslim women was premised not on their natural inferiority but on the assumption that different, hierarchically organized pleasures were afforded by different religious contexts. Women's bodies could be pleased and pleasing in the imagined space of the harem, but their minds could never be educated. Thus, an investment in Christian superiority; anxiety that women be recognized as intellectual agents and therefore fully human subjects; the geographic distance between English and Muslim women during the eighteenth century (most travelers were male); and a failure to be curious about the actual experiences of Muslim women across that distance solidified into the trope that Islam denied intelligence to women by denying that they had immortal souls. In short, the Islamophobic version of misogynistic mortalism affirmed that a woman could not *have* intelligence while *being* Muslim.

Bernadette Andrea identified 1696 as the starting point of feminist orientalism because the 1695–96 theater season in London was a milestone of output by women authors, many of whom wrote about Islam or used Muslim settings. Not all of these representations were negative.[20] Humberto Garcia has demonstrated the influence of Islamic republicanism on English and British political theorists of the "long" eighteenth century.[21] British attitudes to Islam were varied and complex. My argument is indebted to the pioneering work of both Andrea and Garcia, but where I diverge from them is in tracing the development of feminist orientalism from a very specific politicized trope that, I argue, only *became* Islamophobic in the 1690s. Misogynistic mortalism sprang forth at the crossroads of the Renaissance *querelle des femmes* (a sprawling debate about the status of women) and the post-Reformation concern about non-Trinitarian exegesis that was at the heart of toleration debates after the English Revolution of 1688. Indeed, scholars of tolerationist discourse in seventeenth-century England have identified a "Trinitarian controversy of the 1690s."[22] The controversy was essentially an exercise in policing the boundaries of English (and later British) identity. A wide variety of groups was vilified, including freethinkers; anti-Trinitarians; Anglicans who supported, or who were accused of supporting, heterodox interpretations of the Bible or of Anglican doctrine; and non-Christians. However, the publication (or republication) in the 1680s and 1690s of a variety of works pertaining to Islam—the republication of the 1649 English translation of the Qur'an; the Ottoman histories of Sir Paul Rycaut (partly based on the compendious and influential history of Richard Knolles); and a variety of propaganda pieces intended to cast the prophet Muhammad as an impostor—meant that Islam became a convenient "negative ideal" with which to castigate-by-association rival Christian groups. Misogynistic mortalism yoked the recognition of women's intelligence to Trinitarian orthodoxy. Rhetorically, one entailed the other and both required the rejection of Islam.

Intelligent Souls? is organized thematically within a broadly chronological frame. Chapter 1 charts the establishment of Islam as the "negative ideal" in English society from the 1690s onward by surveying the connection between mortalism, Trinitarianism, and biblical exegesis established by the anti-Socinian pamphlet *Disputatio Nova Contra Mulieres* (1595). The *Disputatio* contributed to the demonization of Socinianism and explains why Islam would have been useful in the anti-Socinian Trinitarian Controversy of the 1690s. Establishing Islam as the "negative ideal" enabled the simultaneous demonization of Socinians, deists, and other freethinkers while offering them an opportunity to forsake the radical anti-Trinitarian otherness of Islam. Lancelot Addison and Humphrey Prideaux are central to the construction of "Christian" pleasures of the mind being superior to "Muslim" pleasures of the body and thus to the characterization of Islam as irreconcilable with English and British identity.

Chapter 2 addresses women's particular investments in the use of spiritual intelligence to negotiate the problem of national identity as it was constructed in terms of distance from others (with respect to both geography and religion). Further, while focusing initially on Katherine Philips and Margaret Cavendish—seventeenth-century writers influenced by the neoplatonic allegiances of King Charles I's consort Queen Henrietta Maria—the chapter shows that women writers were perfectly capable of writing about distant places, including the Ottoman Empire, without resorting to feminist orientalism. Philips and Cavendish throw into sharp relief the reliance of early eighteenth-century women novelists on misogynistic mortalism. The contrast suggests that there was indeed a shift in the 1690s: before that, even women writers concerned with women's souls could write about them without resorting to Islamophobic misogynistic mortalism. After the 1690s, it was far more likely for women writers to rely on the trope. Elizabeth Singer Rowe, Penelope Aubin, and Jane Barker draw on the trope implicitly and explicitly.

Chapter 3 considers the hierarchizing of different pleasures and argues that women adopted the alignment of Christianity with intellectual pleasures and Islam with sexual pleasures consolidated by writers during the Trinitarian Controversy. An important subsection of chapter 3 is women's responses to the development of the "Platonic Lady" stereotype. This stereotype, which traded in hostility to the foreignness of Queen Henrietta Maria, marginalized single intellectual women by associating them not only with Roman Catholicism and libertinism but also with stereotypical "Muslim" pleasure. The Platonic Lady is an important component of how feminist orientalism developed, for the trope essentially turned the discourse of the soul against women. The Platonic Lady talks a great deal about her soul, but ultimately she lacks the intelligence necessary to preserve the chastity upon which Christian integrity depended.

Chapter 4 discusses the problem of curiosity and, specifically, the increasing tendency in fiction to present Muslim lands—particularly the extensive territory of the Ottoman Empire—as not worth knowing about. Yet there is a tension within this representational tradition. Samuel Johnson dismissed the Ottoman Empire as a "foreign and uninteresting" subject, but he was nevertheless exercised by its cultural difference. If he flirted with misogynistic mortalism, he also insisted to his companion (and, later, biographer) James Boswell that "Mahometan" civilization was a source of profound knowledge. Johnson and one of the leading novelists of mid-century, Samuel Richardson, both used Islam as a foil to think through the characteristics and behavior of a well-educated Christian woman. Their influence on a younger generation of women writers would have profound consequences for women and their writing about Muslim empires as sources of knowledge and objects of pleasurable attention. The chapter concludes with an analysis of Charlotte Lennox's *The Female Quixote*, the final chapter of which may have been written by Johnson. *The Female Quixote* was the death knell of the British heroine's curiosity about Muslim experience. After 1752, the "soul making" that Spivak describes meant the rejection of Muslim influence.

Chapter 5 partly turns away from fiction to consider the broad sweep of misogynistic mortalism in women's education arguments from the 1730s to the 1790s before addressing Mary Wollstonecraft's writing. The chapter examines vindications of women's intelligence beginning with the anonymous "Sophia" essays published in 1739 and 1751. In the 1750s, the Bluestockings—women who promoted a life of the mind through sociability—also used misogynistic mortalism to think through issues of women's education. Finally, I trace the links between the immortal soul and women's intelligence in Wollstonecraft's fiction and in her *A Vindication of the Rights of Woman*. The concept of the intelligent soul was central to Wollstonecraft's argument for women's education; she thus repeatedly relied on misogynistic mortalism. Feminist orientalism had arrived.

I conclude with an epilogue that situates the eighteenth-century legacy of misogynistic mortalism in terms of Wollstonecraft's nineteenth-century transatlantic legacy and contemporary problems within global feminist dialogue. A continuing assumption of cultural superiority—the enlightenment of the secular West over and against the supposed benightedness of Islam—jeopardizes feminist dialogue even in the twenty-first century. Inquiry, curiosity, pleasurable interest in the "negative ideal" may be the best way forward. In the twenty-first century will the crafting of a global community be characterized more by inquiry or exclusion?

NOTES

Epigraph: Donald J. Trump, interview by George Stephanopoulos, *This Week with George Stephanopoulos*, ABC, July 31, 2016, quoted in Amy Davidson Sorkin, "What Donald Trump Doesn't Get about Ghazala and Khizr Khan," *New Yorker*, August 1, 2016, http://www.newyorker.com/news/amy-davidson/what-donald-trump-doesnt-get-about-ghazala-and-khizr-khan. Sorkin characterized Trump's interview, in which he discussed the Khans' appearance at the Democratic National Convention, as Trump wavering "between the dismissal of the idea that Ghazala might have a thought in her head and the opportunity to insinuate that Khizr was a domestic crypto-Sharia tyrant." For the full interview, see ABC News, "'This Week' Transcript: Donald Trump, Vice President Joe Biden, and Ret. Gen. John Allen," July 31, 2016, http://abcnews.go.com/Politics/week-transcript-donald-trump-vice-president-joe-biden/story?id=41020870.

1. Wilfrid Prest, "Law, Lawyers and Rational Dissent," in *Enlightenment and Religion: Rational Dissent in Eighteenth-Century Britain*, ed. Knud Haakonssen (Cambridge: Cambridge University Press, 1996), 171, 173.
2. Miriam Cooke, "Deploying the Muslimwoman," in "Roundtable Discussion: Religion, Gender, and the Muslimwoman," *Journal of Feminist Studies in Religion* 24, no. 1 (Spring 2008): 91.
3. See particularly Lila Abu-Lughod, *Do Muslim Women Need Saving?* (Cambridge, Mass.: Harvard University Press, 2013) and the volume *Muslim Women, Transnational Feminism and the Ethics of Pedagogy: Contested Imaginaries in Post-9/11 Cultural Practice*, ed. Lisa K. Taylor and Jasmin Zine (New York: Routledge, 2014).
4. Joyce Zonana, "The Sultan and the Slave: Feminist Orientalism and the Structure of *Jane Eyre*," *Signs: Journal of Women in Culture and Society* 18, no. 3 (Spring 1993): 593. See also Kevin Berland's argument that in Samuel Johnson's *Rasselas*, and other eighteenth-century orientalist romances, "the author of an ostensibly oriental tale has borrowed the exotic detail of eastern storytelling to dress up an otherwise western narrative and system of values." Kevin Berland, "The Paradise Garden and the Imaginary East: Alterity and Reflexivity in British Orientalist Romances," *Eighteenth-Century Novel* 2 (2002): 149. And in the same volume, M. O. Grenby focuses on "the way in which conservatives and radicals differently chose to deploy these Oriental allegories" in eighteenth-century political critiques. See M. O. Grenby, "Orientalism and Propaganda: The Oriental Tale and Popular Politics in Late-Eighteenth-Century Britain," *Eighteenth-Century Novel* 2 (2002): 216. Grenby con-

cludes that for "both radicals and conservatives, the Other was already within, and it was faced not with complacency, but with apprehension and disquiet" (235). For a recent extension of this argument, one that focuses on the orientalism of Romantic writers like Shelley and Byron, see Gerard Cohen-Vrignaud, *Radical Orientalism: Rights, Reform, and Romanticism* (Cambridge: Cambridge University Press, 2015).

5. Mary Wollstonecraft, *"A Vindication of the Rights of Men" and "A Vindication of the Rights of Woman,"* ed. Sylvana Tomaselli (Cambridge: Cambridge University Press, 2001), 87.
6. Edward Said, *Culture and Imperialism* (New York: Vintage Books, 1993), 70–71.
7. Gayatri Chakravorty Spivak, "Three Women's Texts and a Critique of Imperialism," *Critical Inquiry* 12, no. 1 (Autumn 1985): 244, 248.
8. Bonnie Latimer, *Making Gender, Culture, and the Self in the Fiction of Samuel Richardson: The Novel Individual* (Farnham: Ashgate, 2013), 153.
9. Margaret Anne Doody, *The True Story of the Novel* (New Brunswick, N.J.: Rutgers University Press, 1996), 292–293.
10. Brean Hammond and Shaun Regan, *Making the Novel: Fiction and Society in Britain, 1660–1789* (Houndmills: Palgrave Macmillan, 2006), 16–25.
11. Edward Said, *Orientalism* (New York: Vintage Books, 1979; reprint, with a new afterword, New York: Vintage Books, 1994), 87.
12. Said, *Orientalism*, 52–53.
13. Alexander Pope, *The Correspondence of Alexander Pope*, vol. 1, *1704–1718*, ed. George Sherburn (Oxford: Clarendon Press, 1956), 368–369.
14. Lady Mary Wortley Montagu, *The Turkish Embassy Letters*, ed. and annotated by Malcolm Jack, with an introduction by Anita Desai (1994; repr., London: Virago, 2009), 71.
15. Montagu, *Turkish Embassy Letters*, 109. With some qualifications, Alexander Bevilacqua argues that the European "tradition of research and the effort at charitable reinterpretation of Islam" dated from the seventeenth and eighteenth centuries when "global commerce brought Europeans into increased contact with the peoples, goods, languages, beliefs, and customs of Asia." Alexander Bevilacqua, *The Republic of Arabic Letters: Islam and the European Enlightenment* (Cambridge, Mass.: Belknap Press of Harvard University Press, 2018), 2.
16. *The Qur'an*, trans. Tarif Khalidi (London: Penguin Classics, 2009). I also consulted *The Qur'an*, trans. M. A. S. Abdel Haleem (Oxford: Oxford University Press, 2010).
17. Amina Wadud, "The Equity of Recompense: The Hereafter in the Qur'an," chap. 3 in *Qur'an and Woman: Rereading the Sacred Text from a Woman's Perspective* (New York: Oxford University Press, 1999).
18. I consulted Ustaz Zhulkeflee Bin Haji Ismail regarding how to interpret the Qur'an's position on women's immortality. The Ustaz explained that in the Qur'an itself (Aali 'Imran 3:7), the Qur'an is described as composed of two different kinds of verses: *aayat muhkamat* ("verses basic or fundamental [of established meaning]") and *aayat mutashaabihat* ("verses not of well-established meaning [allegorical]"). The same verse explains that "those in whose hearts is perversity follow the part thereof that is not of well-established meaning . . . seeking discord, and searching for its interpretation." Later, the Qur'an expressly insists on its use of parables and metaphors: "Verily We have displayed for mankind in this Qur'an all manner of similitudes [*min kul-li-ma-tsal*], but man is more than anything contentious" (Qur'an: Kahfi: 18:54). The Ustaz further explained that most descriptions pertaining to God and the afterlife "can only be conveyed allegorically. . . . Those who insist upon literal understanding of these *aayat mutashaabihat* usually chose to ignore, or perhaps they are unaware of, the guideline given by the author of the Qur'an." Thus, descriptions of the garden of the afterlife—including descriptions of material goods like clothing, food, and, most famously, the reward of a community of virgins (houris)—are allegorical. Further, the Ustaz identified a Hadith reported by Muhammad ibn Ismail al-Bukhari in which the

Prophet states that Allah told him that the reward for pious followers in the afterlife was one that no eye had ever seen. (Hadith are holy sayings of the Prophet not included in the Qur'an. Exegetes evaluate them according to the authority of the source; al-Bukhari is considered extremely reliable.) The Ustaz also explained that in the Qur'an male and female were created from a single soul (*nafsun waahid*) and from this a mate was created (*zaw-jaha*) (Qur'an: An-Nisa: 4:1). Finally, he pointed out that the garden of the afterlife, even though it is described allegorically, certainly included women. The Qur'an says as much: "Whoso doeth an ill-deed, he will be repaid the like thereof, while whoso doeth right, whether male or female, and is a believer, (all) such will enter the Garden, where they will be nourished without stint" (Qur'an: Ghafir: 40:39–40). See Zhulkeflee Bin Haji Ismail, "Principles in Tafsir al-Qur'an in the Name of Allah, the Most Compassionate, Most Merciful. How the Qur'an Explains Itself regarding Interpretation of Its Verses," slides presented in clarifying questions posed by Samara Anne Cahill, School of Humanities and Social Sciences, Division of English, Nanyang Technological University, Singapore, October 19, 2016, @ Wisma Inda, SlideShare. Warmest gratitude to the Ustaz (may he rest in peace), to his family for their hospitality (and for the apples), and to Nurul Wahidah Binte Mohd Tambee for bringing us together. I would also like to thank the students who, with great candor and generosity, shared with me their experiences as believing Muslim women. Ultimately, I did not use specific excerpts from our interviews, but I appreciated our conversations very much, and their perspectives certainly informed the writing of this book.

19. Much has been written on the use of inaccurate, fantastical, and eroticized imaginary constructions of the harem (the sequestered space for women within the home) in Western literature. The diversity of harems, as Ruth Bernard Yeazell argues, was often collapsed by associating "the harem" with the Grand Seraglio of the Ottoman sultans. Yeazall's study is a useful survey that complicates my argument about negative representations of the harem and underscores that, while Islamophobic misogynistic mortalism was highly conventional, it was not uncontested. See Ruth Bernard Yeazell, *Harems of the Mind: Passages of Western Art and Literature* (New Haven, Conn.: Yale University Press, 2000). As Yeazell argues of the first travelers to have a sustained exposure to real harems, "The very fact that nineteenth-century travelers repeatedly recorded their disenchantment with actual harems, announcing over and over again how little the reality of Eastern domestic life met their expectations, testifies to the continuing power of the imaginary harems they had inherited" (2).
20. Bernadette Andrea, ed., *Delarivier Manley and Mary Pix: English Women Staging Islam, 1696–1707,* with an introduction by Bernadette Andrea, The Other Voice in Early Modern Europe: The Toronto Series, 17 (Toronto: Iter Inc. and Centre for Reformation and Renaissance Studies, 2012). For a complementary account of Delarivier Manley and Mary Pix, see Ros Ballaster, *Fabulous Orients: Fictions of the East in England, 1662–1785* (2005; repr., Oxford: Oxford University Press, 2007), 83–90.
21. For a discussion of "Islamic republicanism," the influence of the Hungarian Revolution on English tolerationist discourse in the seventeenth century, and the Whig oppositional use of Ottoman precedent to argue for religion toleration (and the resulting backlash), see Humberto Garcia, *Islam and the English Enlightenment, 1670–1840* (Baltimore: Johns Hopkins University Press, 2012), 26, 109. For a discussion of England's negotiation of its changing transnational power position in the early modern world vis-à-vis the Ottoman Empire, see Emily M. N. Kugler, *Sway of the Ottoman Empire on English Identity in the Long Eighteenth Century* (Leiden: Brill, 2012), 86–89.
22. Ann Thomson, *Bodies of Thought: Science, Religion, and the Soul in the Early Enlightenment* (Oxford: Oxford University Press, 2008), 40, 103; Martin Greig, "Heresy Hunt: Gilbert Burnet and the Convocation Controversy of 1701," *Historical Journal* 37, no. 3 (1994): 569.

1

THE NEGATIVE IDEAL

THE ISLAMOPHOBIC USE OF MISOGYNISTIC mortalism—the accusation that Islam denies that women have immortal souls and, therefore, intelligence—became useful in the English (and later British) context as a way of rhetorically fabricating a Protestant unity that could never exist. This assertion of unity was important in the face of a series of exegetical, doctrinal, and political controversies. Among them was the Trinitarian Controversy of the 1690s in which the language of Trinitarianism ("substance," "person") came under such intense pressure that it threatened to collapse. The concept of the Trinity mattered because it was foundational to Anglican identity and was enshrined in English law. The Trinitarian Controversy has been extensively discussed, most thoroughly by Philip Dixon, and my concern in this chapter is not so much to rehearse the controversy itself as to lay out the circuitous route by which the exclusion of Islam became central to defenses of Anglican orthodoxy in the 1690s. In the next chapter I discuss how women writers drew on this rhetorical framework in their arguments for women's intelligence after the 1690s. But to understand this rhetorical context requires some background on the antagonism felt by several groups—including Roman Catholics, High Church Anglicans, Socinians, and Dissenters—toward the set of ecumenically minded Anglican ministers known as the "Latitudinarians." A very brief overview of the religiopolitical background of this antagonism will help to clarify why Anglicans, and particularly those known as "Latitudinarian" Anglicans, would have had an investment in excluding Islam from English identity.

THE PURITY OF CHRISTIAN FAITH

King Charles II ascended the English throne in 1660. After the upheaval of the Civil Wars, it seemed that religious uniformity, or at least a Church of England that could encompass all English Protestants, would reinforce social stability. But including all Protestants within the Church of England proved difficult. The result was the Clarendon Code, a series of acts that penalized those Protestants who could not accept the Book of Common Prayer or what it contained—the Thirty-Nine Articles of Religion, the Church of England's statement of doctrine. Those Protestants who could not approve of the Thirty-Nine Articles came to be known as Dissenters (or nonconformists).

Part of the Clarendon Code, the Act of Uniformity of 1662 required the Church of England's Book of Common Prayer to be used in religious services. "Institutionalised Dissent" commenced with the ejection of "ministers, university dons and schoolteachers who refused to accept the Book of Common Prayer."[1] The Act of Uniformity thus informed the "literary culture aligned with Protestant dissent" that included writers like John Milton, John Bunyan, and Daniel Defoe.[2] The marginalization of Dissent was enforced until the repeal of the Corporation and Test Acts in 1828. In short, between 1662 and 1828, "Anglican exclusiveness and resentment triumphed over Protestant ecumenicism."[3] The Church of England was bulwarked by state power, but it did not represent all English Protestants. Nor did it represent English Catholics, who hastened to point out any inconsistencies between Trinitarian orthodoxy (which Roman Catholics and Anglicans shared) and the departures of Anglicanism from Roman Catholic doctrine. For instance, in the "rule of faith" controversy of the 1680s, English Catholics charged the Latitudinarians with Socinianism because they had defended the use of reason in scriptural interpretation.[4] I discuss Socinianism at length below, but, very broadly speaking, it was identified with an exegetical tradition that denied Christian mysteries, particularly Christ's identity with God the Father. Socinianism therefore, and most significantly for this argument, rejected the Trinity. It had this in common with Islam, which considers Jesus Christ a prophet, but denies that he is consubstantial with the Father or that he died to atone for human sin. In the 1680s, then, Catholics were using Trinitarian orthodoxy to challenge defenses of Protestant exegesis.

A further complication of English Protestantism occurred in 1688–89 when the Roman Catholic king James II, who had come to the throne after the death of his brother, fled (or abdicated) from England. His Protestant daughter and her husband, Mary and William of Orange, ascended the throne. They soon issued what is now commonly referred to as the Act of Toleration (1689); it granted limited concessions to Protestants outside of the Church of England. But the Act of Toleration left in place two of the most discriminatory pieces of legislation, the Corporation Act (1661) and the Test Act (1673), which regulated access to "'offices of trust,' whether civil or military, under the Crown." To hold such offices required "receiving the sacrament of holy communion according to the rites of the Church of England."[5] Though some Church of England ministers mobilized a "comprehension" scheme—by which they intended "modifying liturgy and discipline . . . to allow reincorporation of some moderate Dissenters or leaving most Dissenters free to worship as they would"—this project ultimately failed.[6] Circumscribed "toleration" and legal marginalization of Dissenters were the norm for the entirety of the eighteenth century. The "Occasional Conformity" debate, which resulted in the passing of the Occasional Conformity Act in 1711, derived from the practice of those who were not members of the Church of England occasionally (at least once a year) taking communion according to its rites so that they could qualify for these employments. The Occasional Conformity controversy effectively ended in 1717 when George I, the first of the Hanoverian kings, prorogued Convocation. This was a crucial decision, for Convocation was the official assembly of bishops and clergy and the main instrument by which certain Anglicans tried to assert an ecclesiastical authority independent of the Crown. Meetings of Convocation were merely formal from 1717 until the nineteenth century. Parliament repealed the Occasional Conformity Act in 1719.

This is a very broad portrait of the legal status and frustrations of Protestants who did not accept the Book of Common Prayer. But there were profound divisions even among those Protestants who did accept it. After William and Mary came to the throne in the "Glorious Revolution" of 1688, the Church of England clergy were required to take an oath of loyalty that recognized William and Mary as England's monarchs. Those bishops and clergy who refused to swear the oath (nonjurors) were deprived of their sees in February 1690 and new ministers were ultimately consecrated in their stead. The ejection of the nonjurors left ecclesiastical power in the hands of the so-called Latitudinarian ministers. It also "transformed the whole tenor of counter-revolutionary Anglicanism," resulting, ultimately, in a "church in danger" polemic in the late seventeenth and early eighteenth centuries.[7] High Church Anglicans (who favored liturgical ritualism and a more conservative model of ecclesiastical authority) tried to wrest power away from the "Latitudinarian" Anglicans by accusing them of being inadequate shepherds of their Christian flock—of giving *too much* latitude on questions of Anglican orthodoxy and, therefore, of imperiling the Protestant identity of England. After England and Wales merged with Scotland to become the United Kingdom (1707) the "Church of England" was increasingly referred to as the Anglican Church. In short, among

Roman Catholics, Dissenters, High Church Anglicans, and—ultimately—deist freethinkers, the Latitudinarian Anglicans were the beleaguered but nevertheless dominant religious group in England. But who were these men?

"Latitudinarian" is a useful but notoriously imprecise term that belies the complexity and diversity of thought among the men generally identified as such. But, very broadly speaking, "Latitudinarian" usually suggested an inclination to see the relationship of reason and religion as one of cooperation rather than antagonism and to approve of religious toleration (of non-Anglican Protestants). Influential ministers would include Archbishop John Tillotson; his successor Archbishop Thomas Tenison; Edward Stillingfleet, bishop of Worcester; Simon Patrick, bishop of Ely; and Gilbert Burnet, bishop of Salisbury. Burnet was the author of *An Exposition of the Thirty-nine Articles of the Church of England* (1699), often called the "manifesto of the latitudinarian party."[8] There were also political and geographic associations: Latitudinarians were "prominent London divines who opposed James II and received advancement under his successors."[9] The Latitudinarians were at the center of the Trinitarian Controversy.[10]

The reasons for this were multiple. First, Trinitarian orthodoxy was enshrined in the Thirty-Nine Articles, which codified the doctrine of the Church of England and to which all clergy of the Church of England had to subscribe. Along with the Athanasian Creed, the Thirty-Nine Articles were enforced "on clergymen when taking orders, and on undergraduates either on taking their degree (at Cambridge) or in order to matriculate (at Oxford)."[11] This meant that Trinitarian orthodoxy was enforced by the state on clergy, officeholders, and those who wished to attend university.

Second, the Latitudinarians were particularly close to William of Orange and were in a position to ask for his intervention when defending themselves against those (like the nonjurors and High Church Anglicans) who felt excluded by the Revolution Settlement. Indeed, Archbishop Tenison asked King William to intervene in the Trinitarian Controversy, which resulted in the issuance of *Directions to our Arch-Bishops and Bishops for the Preserving of Unity in the Church, and the Purity of Christian Faith, Concerning the Holy Trinity* (February 3, 1696). This was followed in 1697 by the Blasphemy Act, which "prescribed three years imprisonment for those convicted of anti-trinitarian belief."[12] The Blasphemy Act, though rarely used, was not amended until the Doctrine of the Trinity Act (1813). In Scotland, which had passed an earlier Blasphemy Act, Thomas Aikenhead, who had allegedly scorned the Trinity, became "the last person to be executed for heresy in the British Isles" in 1697.[13]

Third, the Latitudinarians came under attack specifically for their supposed heterodoxy and had to defend themselves—against charges of Socinianism—by distancing themselves not only from the Church of Rome but also from the charge of free thinking. Scholars have widely acknowledged the fast-and-loose deployment of religious pejoratives in this period, pejoratives that were often highly inaccurate. The Latitudinarians were a prime target of such pejoratives and often returned the rhetoric in kind.[14] The historically situated development of this rhetorical quagmire is how Islam came to be excluded from the British political establishment (which was officially Trinitarian) and extolled by certain political theorists as an alternate legislative model.[15]

Islam and Socinianism were linked because of their shared rejection of the Christian Trinity, which associated them with the Christological disputes and the Trinitarian Controversy of the early church.[16] But the association was more complicated than that. Anglican thinkers, in their refutations of Roman Catholic dogma, often turned to the doctrines of the early church. Roughly speaking, the "early church" refers to Christianity before it received the official sanction of temporal power by coming under the protection of the Roman emperor Constantine. Constantine called the Council of Nicaea (325 CE) from which came the foundational Nicene Creed. Further, Reformation writers used the tensions between the Eastern and Western Christian churches following the Council of Chalcedon (451 CE), during which the Arian heresy figured prominently, as a precedent for how valid differences between Christians had been marginalized by the increasing domination of the "Church of Rome."[17] However, the use of this precedent had ominous implications for the representation of Muslims. The divisions of the church post-Chalcedon set a precedent for thinking through the divisions of Christendom after the Reformation. Further, post-Reformation writers saw a parallel between the rise of Islam after the Council of Chalcedon (Muhammad lived ca. 570–632 CE) and the rise of the Ottoman Empire (most shockingly epitomized by the conquest of Constantinople in 1453) just before the Reformation. In this way, Islam (and particularly its successful military expansion) came to be seen as the transhistoric scourge of God upon a disunited Christianity.[18] Deists, freethinkers, and Socinians themselves vaunted Islam at the expense of Anglican orthodoxy.[19]

Prominent Latitudinarian Gilbert Burnet's *An Exposition of the Thirty-nine Articles* (1699) makes clear the connections that the Latitudinarians saw between the splintering of post-Chalcedon Christianity into the "Eastern" and "Western" churches, the corruption of Roman Catholicism, and the military power of Islam. While the *Exposition* is squarely aimed at refuting the points of Roman Catholic doctrine from which the Church of England had departed (most notably transubstantiation), it also explicitly, though mildly, rejects Socinianism and includes several references to Islam. Burnet saw a logical, historical connection between Muslim military expansion and the corruption of the "bishops of Rome." In his exposition of Article 37, Burnet points out that as late as "the middle of the Fifth Century" there was no superiority of the bishop of Rome over other sees (including Constantinople, Alexandria, and Antioch) and that the "*African* Churches" likewise at "that time knew nothing of any Superiority the Bishops of *Rome* had over them."[20] Most crucially, in his exposition of Article 28 ("The Supper of the Lord"), on the profound difference between Anglican and Roman Catholic positions on transubstantiation (whether there is a Real Presence of Christ in the Eucharist), Burnet at one point claims that the corruptions of the Church of Rome were able to take root in part because of Islam. Of the divisions within fifth-century Christianity, Burnet laments the "state that the world fell in" when "Vast Swarms out of the North over-run the Roman Empire"; invaders included, in "the West, the Goths . . . [and] the Saracens and Turks in the East," who "made Havock of all that was polite or learned; by which we lost the chief Writings of the first and best Times."[21] These invasions led to "dark and ignorant Ages. All fell under much oppression and misery; and Europe was so over-run with Barbarity and Ignorance, that it cannot be easily apprehended." Yet these were "not only times of Ignorance, but they were also times of much Corruption" including the "scandalous unconstancy of the Councils of those Ages." Burnet draws a historical connection between the Goth and Muslim invasions, the decline of learning, and ages of darkness and ignorance that enabled the corruption of an increasingly powerful "Bishop of Rome" to flourish.

Yet, alongside this rhetorical tradition by which Muslim military successes ushered in Roman Catholic corruption, it is crucial to hold in view the related but distinct rhetorical tradition that associated Islam with deists, freethinkers, and Socinians. This second rhetorical tradition was particularly important when set against the backdrop of the Deist Controversy that commenced, after the lapsing of the Licensing Act in 1695, with the publication of John Toland's *Christianity not Mysterious* (1696). Deism was, in some sense, more dangerous than Roman Catholicism because it posed an internal threat. Indeed, Robert G. Ingram has described deist freethinking as the "greatest threat to the established Church" and also "the greatest threat to English Christianity in general." This threat was "not thought to be refuted successfully by the orthodox until the mid 1730s when . . . Joseph Butler published his *Analogy of Religion* (1736)."[22] In other words, due to a network of associations linking Roman Catholicism, deism, and Socinianism, Islam continued to be positioned against the Trinitarian orthodoxy of the Anglican establishment throughout the eighteenth century. It remains to show how this associative network produced the claim that Islam favored physical pleasure over intellectual pleasure and how it came to be associated with the denial of immortality to women. It is one of history's great ironies that a famous and long-lasting Islamophobic trope initially had nothing to do with Islam.

"NOR FINDE WEE THAT GOD BREATH'D A SOULE IN HER"

Around 1610, a young John Donne wrote a poem to the Countess of Huntingdon in which he yoked the naturalness of women's subjection to the problems of post-Reformation biblical exegesis. His speaker tells her: "Man to Gods image, *Eve*, to mans was made, / Nor finde wee that God breath'd a soule in her."[23] Donne's speaker not only provocatively denies that women are the image of God, or *imago Dei* (effectively denying them human status), he also justifies this denial in terms of an omission in the Book of Genesis: "wee," the people of the book, do not find that God breathed a soul into Eve as He did into Adam. Donne's statement could be read as either conventional misogyny or intellectual play, or perhaps both. But clearly the poem was not Donne's final position on women's status as human beings. Twenty years later, in his capacity as an Anglican clergyman, Donne sermonized, "Some men out of a petulancy and wantonesse of wit, and out of the extravagancy of Paradoxes, and such singularities, have called the faculties, and abilities of women in question, even in the roote thereof, in the reasonable and immortal soul . . . ; no author of gravity, of piety, of conversation in the Scriptures could admit that doubt, whether woman were created in the Image of God, that is, in possession of a reasonable and immortall soul."[24] Either Donne had changed his mind since 1610 or his poetic speaker did not speak for him. Yet Donne was aware that women's possession of immortal souls could be and had been questioned on scriptural grounds. Here was an ambiguity in the very fabric of Christian identity: If the intelligent soul is the marker of human identity, then why does the Book of Genesis mention only Adam's soul? Are men's and women's souls not equal? Or not equally intelligent? And is it scripture or church tradition that clarifies the matter?

The question of women's immortality thus went to the heart of exegetical conflicts between Roman Catholicism and the diverse groups categorized by George Huntston Williams as members of the "Magisterial Reformation" and the "Radical Reformation."[25] These groups struggled, in their different ways, to reconcile the importing of a Hellenic "immortal soul" into the Judaic tradition that gave birth to Christianity. Was man naturally immortal (possessed of an immortal soul), or was his immortality only *conditional* upon God's grace? The Book of Genesis (the creation myth of all three Abrahamic faiths—Judaism, Christianity, and Islam) says nothing explicitly about Eve, or any woman, having a soul, even though women's immortality was considered undebatable according to Roman Catholicism and, later, Anglican doctrine. This conflict—between scriptural evidence and magisterial teaching—explains, at least in part, the gap between John Donne's playful assurance to the Countess of Huntingdon that the Book of Genesis says nothing about women's souls and his later position, as an Anglican minister, that women must indeed have them.

Donne's sermon shows that at stake in discussions of women's souls was the question of whether they were truly human, a condition that assumed three traits: being capable of reason, having an immortal soul, and being made in the image of God. In Roman Catholicism and Anglicanism this traditional trinity of characteristics distinguished humans from the rest of creation. The immortal soul necessarily brought with it considerations of women's ability to exercise reason (and to respond to education), to experience salvation or damnation in eternity (to possess moral agency and accountability), and to belong to the human community created in God's image. To deny souls to women was—in the Roman Catholic and Anglican views—to deny them reason, immortality, and humanity. These three were inextricably linked. Also linked in exegetical debates were the status of women, the status of Christ, and the authority of Trinitarian Christianity.

A problem with the alignment of human identity and the reasonable, immortal soul arose when considering women, who had, historically speaking, been considered less rational than, and therefore logically subordinate to, men. Christian scripture reinforced women's subordinate status: man must be the head of woman and she must submit to him (Genesis 3:16; Ephesians 5:23; Colossians 3:18; 1 Timothy 2:11–12; 1 Peter 3:1, 3:5–6). How can this be if women and men, being equally human, must also be equally capable of reason? Or is there some essential difference between the souls of men and those of women that renders women "human" but subordinate? Clive Hart, whose monograph follows the debate on women's souls from the writings of Saint Augustine to the nineteenth century, identifies a lingering ambiguity in discussions of women's souls. Early Christian disagreement about women's souls intersected with classical arguments that women were naturally inferior to men. The rediscovery of Aristotle's works in the thirteenth century reinforced the idea that women might have souls, but perhaps not the rational souls that conferred immortality.[26] Aristotle, after all, claimed that there were three kinds of soul: the vegetable or nutritive (having the power to grow and to reproduce) the sensible (having sense perception), and the rational (having an intellectual nature). Thus, women's subjection to men might derive not simply from women's greater physical weakness but also from an inherent rational incapacity. In this context, for a woman to claim that she had an intelligent (that is, rational) soul was to declare a position on women's ontological status within the terrain of Christian exegesis. Women's "intelligence" in this scenario becomes crucial to evaluating not only their status as humans but also their "natural" relationship to men. Their status also became implicated in the contest over biblical exegesis between Socinians and Trinitarian Christians.

SOCINIANISM, MORTALISM, AND THE *DISPUTATIO NOVA CONTRA MULIERES*

Founded by Faustus Socinus (1539–1604), Socinianism rejected what most members of the Magisterial Reformation considered fundamental: the Christian Trinity and, therefore, the divinity of Christ.[27] For the Socinians, there was no scriptural evidence that Christ was consubstantial with God the Father. The Socinians were often conflated with a variety of other heterodox Christian thinkers who fell under the umbrella term of "mortalists." To use the term "mortalist" requires some explanation, since it represents a set of controversial and often misrepresented positions in Christian thought.

Between the Council of Florence (1438–45) and the Fifth Lateran Council (1512–17), the Roman Catholic Church made official the long-standing belief that the soul was naturally immortal and that the soul could consciously experience the period between death and resurrection. This position enabled the church to theorize the existence of purgatory and, therefore, to justify the issuance of indulgences, one of the major targets of the Reformation. Some Reformers shared the orthodox Christian position on the natural immortality of the soul, while others saw it as a Platonic (pagan) import that was inconsistent with both scripture and the Christianity of the primitive (pre-Constantine) church. This last group occupied a spectrum of beliefs regarding what the soul's experience would be after the death of the body. Some believed that the soul slept, while others believed that it died with the body but could be resurrected on the Day of Judgment.

"Christian mortalism" is thus a shorthand term for a range of beliefs regarding how to think of the soul if it is not naturally immortal. Christian mortalism does not assert that the soul is not resurrected, but rather asserts that the resurrection of the soul is *conditional* upon God's grace and that its immortality is not an essential, "natural" quality. In other words, Christian mortalism is "an alternative Christian hope" to be distinguished from strict mortalism or annihilationism, the belief that the soul and body are never resurrected.[28] The opponents of the Christian mortalists, however, rarely made this distinction and often played on the assumption that Christian mortalists were atheists or libertines.

The propagandistic value of the slipperiness of "mortalism" partially explains the enduring attention given to the treatise *Disputatio Nova Contra Mulieres* (*A New Argument Against Women*, 1595). Though earlier texts had aligned "Infidelitie" with the denial of women's immortal souls, it was the *Disputatio* that really turned misogynistic mortalism into a post-Reformation rhetorical weapon.[29] The anonymous author (identified by some scholars as Valens Acidalius) satirically attempted to debunk Socinian exegesis by demonstrating that, using the same analytical tools the Socinians used to conclude that Jesus Christ was not the Son of God, he could prove that women had no souls.[30] A few excerpts will suffice to show the *Disputatio*'s provocative pairing of exegetical refutation and misogynistic humor. The author puts his case bluntly enough: "Since in Sarmatia, as though it were a region of virtually total licence, it is allowed to believe and teach that, together with the Holy Ghost, Jesus Christ, the Son of God, savior and redeemer of our souls, is not God, I believe I may also freely believe and teach something much less serious—to wit, that women are not man and what follows as a consequence: that Christ did not suffer for them and that they will not be saved."[31] Defending the orthodox doctrine of the Trinity is clearly the author's aim, but his methodology is an exegetical *reductio ad absurdum* of the material implications of denying the Trinity without also questioning the Christian orthodoxy of sexual relations. He brings this point home in Thesis 16 when, of the scriptural statement that man and woman shall be one flesh (Genesis 2:24), the author argues that "the Anabaptists [by which he means Socinians] themselves give no other interpretation of this passage, although they contradict themselves, believing that in marriage two people are one man while they deny it to be possible that in the Trinity three persons may be one God."[32] In the concluding thesis, the author reaffirms that his real target is the exegesis of Socinians (and, ironically, Roman Catholics). But he concludes, with an edge of misogynistic humor, "I have proved . . . that woman is not man, nor is to be saved. Which if I have not achieved, I have nevertheless shown to all the world how the heretics of these times, especially the Anabaptists and Papists, usually explain sacred scripture and what method they use for the establishment of their execrable dogmas. Enough to the wise. I nevertheless plead with the unwise little women that with the benevolence and love which they possessed in former times they may embrace me; which if they do not so wish, may the beasts perish for all eternity."[33] The narrative persona acknowledges that women have souls but threatens to withdraw the acknowledgment if he does not receive sexual favors. In the author's conclusion, the tension is clear between the magisterial assertion that women have immortal souls and the androcentric heterosexual desire for women to exist as *machines de plaisir*.

Thus the exegetical tug-of-war after the Reformation laid the foundation for the seventeenth-century discourse surrounding women's souls, a discourse complicated by debates circulating during the Renaissance *querelle des femmes* regarding women's status as reasonable creatures.[34] Very few Christians in early modern Europe would have claimed to believe that women did not have souls.[35] But after the *Disputatio*, the belief that someone, somewhere, believed it became a politicized trope. Misogynistic mortalism thus took root amid the religious controversies of late sixteenth-century Europe. It was a useful polemical tool that rarely represented an opponent's actual position on women. More disturbingly, it enabled religiopolitical opponents to displace their own problematic treatment of women onto each other.

The *Disputatio* proved to be very popular among continental Protestants, including those who chose to refute it, as Simon Gediccus (1551–1631) and Arcangela Tarabotti (1604–1652) did, or those who chose to discredit rival confessions by attributing the belief to them.[36] Protestant writers such as Johannes Leyser, a Lutheran pastor, accused the Roman Catholic Church of questioning whether women had souls. Manfred P. Fleischer points out that in subsequent translations "the dispute was popularized in Germany in Catholic disguise, perhaps by a Protestant plagiarist."[37] But how could Roman Catholics come to stand in for Socinians? Roman Catholics could be targeted with misogynistic mortalism because some polemicists misrepresented an account in Gregory of Tours's *History of the Franks*. In the original account a council of bishops had debated whether women could be included in biblical uses of the term *homines* (Latin for "human being," but with the secondary meaning of "men").[38] The ambiguity of the term *homines* in relation to women was raised as an issue by a single bishop, and the council settled the matter in favor of acknowledging that women were human and endowed with souls. But that context did not prevent the "myth"—that the Roman Catholic Church had at some point denied that women have souls—from being perpetuated across Europe for centuries to come.

Pierre Bayle (1647–1706) praised Acidalius's intellectual abilities as a Latin scholar and mentioned the pamphlet in his *Dictionnaire historique et critique* (1697).[39] As Clive Hart has shown, the rhetorical soullessness of Christian women had become proverbial by the seventeenth century, though he argues that after the early seventeenth century it was mostly used in jest rather than in "serious creative literature."[40] In contrast, I argue that it shifted to a quite serious Islamophobic discourse. Nevertheless, Hart sums up the influence of the *Disputatio* best when he observes that although "writers frequently debated these propositions in the spirit of a social or scholarly game," the "energetic refutations" showed "how disturbing [the *Disputatio*'s] arguments could be."[41] Disturbing, too, were debates about the Real Presence of Christ in the Eucharist, the relationship between the human body and the human soul, and, ultimately, Christendom's relationship with God. These debates show how misogynistic mortalism was related to a variety of wider anxieties about infidelity and heresy in the Reformation and post-Reformation periods. The rest of the chapter charts the Islamophobic transition of misogynistic mortalism from post-Reformation concerns regarding the integrity of Christendom to the Trinitarian context of the 1690s.

THE CHRISTIAN COMMONWEALE

Richard Knolles's influential *The Generall Historie of the Turkes* (1603) is an exemplary instance of Christian unity being figured as inversely proportional to the military power of Islam. Knolles saw the military victories of the Ottoman Empire as proof that God was punishing European princes for the disunity of Christendom—both in the early church and during the Reformation. The parallel of the rise of Islam during the splintering of the early Christian church and the rise of the Ottoman Empire during the Reformation would be picked up by the Trinitarian controversialists at the end of the seventeenth century. Knolles attributed the Ottoman Empire's military success in part to "the small care the Christian princes . . . have had of the common state of the Christian Commonweale: whereof even the verie greatest are to account themselves but as the principall members of one and the same bodie, and have or ought to have as sharpe a feeling one of anothers harmes, as hath the head of the wrongs done unto the feet."[42] Knolles figured the Ottoman triumph in terms of the failure of Christian military powers to live according to their shared Christian identity. Christendom ought to function as a united body extending from the head to the feet. Knolles used Islam as a "negative ideal" in order to bulwark the unity that Christendom ideally ought to have.

But Christendom was not united, and this disunity played out as much on the printed page as on the battlefield. Scriptural exegesis became a particularly contentious arena of Reformation debate, and, given the geopolitical developments of the early modern period—the Conquest of Constantinople (1453), the Conquest of Granada (1472), the expulsion of the Moors and Jews from Spain, and the beginning of the Columbian Exchange (1492)—these exegetical debates gradually incorporated nascent cultural hierarchies slowly established across Europe, the Ottoman Empire, and the New World.[43] As Jonathan Sheehan has demonstrated, the exegesis of the Enlightenment Bible enshrined the binary of "East" and "West" and co-opted modernity for the "West."[44] The Qur'an, too, was used to negotiate what the "West" meant. Ziad Elmarsafy has trenchantly argued that "the history of the translation of the Qur'an is bound inextricably with conflicts within the West rather than between the Muslim world and the West. In this the history of translations is moving in line with the major trend that made *confessional rivalry the primary motor of cultural change in Europe by the mid-seventeenth century*."[45] The Qur'an was often used to marginalize undesirable Christian denominations or political opponents by associating them with Islam as the "negative ideal"—as titles such as *Alcoran of the barefote friars* (1550), *Luther's Alcoran* (1642), *The Alcoran of the Franciscans* (1679), and *The Alcoran of Lewis XIV* (1707) demonstrate. Mortalists were often grouped together as one of those undesirable groups.

The doctrine of the Church of England wavered or seemed to waver on whether mortalism of any kind ought to be explicitly rejected. Archbishop Cranmer's Forty-Two Articles of Faith (1553) explicitly rejected mortalism, because it was associated with Anabaptists (Article 40), but the Thirty-Nine Articles (1563) removed this explicit rejection. In the view of some English Protestants, well into the eighteenth century, this removal kept alive an "old controversy" about whether the Anglican Church had sufficiently distanced itself from the taint of "popery" and its pagan, Platonic corruption of the pure tenets of the Primitive Church.[46] In an effort to defend Anglican orthodoxy from mortalist charges of papist corruption, Anglican writers turned increasingly to Islam as a "negative ideal" to shore up Christian unity.[47]

Further, Unitarians (Socinians) or Unitarian sympathizers such as the polemicist Stephen Nye established a link between Islam and heterodox Christianity (whether mortalist or anti-Trinitarian) that was particularly provocative in the debates regarding the toleration and comprehension of nonconformists between the Act of Uniformity (1662) and the stymying of High Church leadership after the proroguing of Convocation (1717). Whig Latitudinarian Anglicanism became dominant.[48] Misogynistic mortalism was thus a handy way of negotiating increasing concerns about confessional pluralism, toleration, and the stability of the Anglican state. The structural problem of having a state church that did not represent all members of the body politic made it expedient to deploy a "rhetoric of controversy" to fabricate a coherent national identity.[49] It is important to recognize that hostility to Islam was embedded in a network of exclusions meant to delineate and to bulwark a workable Protestant national identity the uniformity of which could never be a reality. As Peter Lake has argued, prejudice is a context-bound narrative that addresses a "real" experience while constituting identities from discursive materials ready to hand.[50]

Many scholars have become increasingly wary of using hard-and-fast categories to discuss the complexities of religiopolitical identity in seventeenth- and eighteenth-century England. While noting the "insularity of Anglicanism," John Walsh and Stephen Taylor also outline a number of debates among the "major schools of churchmanship" in the Georgian period (that is, High Church, liberal or Latitudinarian, and Evangelical).[51] Brent Sirota's analysis of the Anglican revival of the early eighteenth century, set amid "the high-church and Tory charge that the Church of England was in danger," shows that there were "wildly contradictory assessments of the fortunes of the established church."[52] So polarized were these assessments that they indicate the Church of England had become "incomprehensible to itself. The parties of high and low church were not simply speaking past one another; they were speaking what increasingly seemed to be mutually unintelligible languages of churchmanship."[53] More optimistically, William J. Bulman has argued that the state church of "later Stuart England" "teemed with creativity": the English Enlightenment was not simply a struggle between freethinkers and a hidebound clergy, between "innovators" and "ossifiers."[54] Nor would it be fair to set up simplistic categories of those "for" and "against" religious liberties since "hardly anyone in the period seems to have been willing to consistently countenance them." Rather, the "conflicts of the later Stuart era . . . were struggles among rival visions of modernity."[55] Thus, it makes sense for Ben Lazare Mijuskovic to argue that in the background of ongoing Enlightenment debates about "immortality," "unity of consciousness," and "personal identity" was "Epicurean materialism and the mortalist heresy, the latter philosophically emphasizing the inseparability of soul and body."[56] The nature of the soul, the nature of the Trinity, and the authority of the Anglican Church were all interconnected and all part of the terrain in which "rival visions of modernity" were negotiated. The English Enlightenment would not have been possible without these intra-Christian disputes regarding the nature of the soul.

These disputes informed and were informed by the New Science and its focus on clarity of expression. B. W. Young points out that as anti-dogmatism diffused throughout the intellectual ferment of eighteenth-century England the notion of the Trinity was sacrificed for "intellectual clarity and philosophical rather than theological respectability."[57] Young's point coincides with Paul C. Davies's focus on the diversity within Anglican thought indicated by the tension between more Augustinian thinkers and the progressive "dulcification" of the "doctrine of future rewards and punishments in the afterlife."[58]

There is a further tension, not just in the diversity of thought, but in the changing of cultural frames over the eighteenth century, too. As Franklin Perkins has observed, in his analysis of the Eurocentrism of Enlightenment philosophy, natural theology—"knowledge that can be had 'naturally,' without the aid of revelation"—gradually gained an ascendance over other lenses that could be used to know other cultures.[59] These other lenses include the *prisca theologia* (ancient theology) of the Renaissance, a syncretic method of finding Christian truths in pagan traditions that was related to the hermetic tradition and which declined in the seventeenth century. In other words, the increasingly outmoded *prisca theologia* looked outward to other cultures; the increasingly dominant natural theology concerned itself with homegrown reason.

Thus, an array of approaches to cultural and religious diversity in the late seventeenth century was gradually, but not uniformly, marginalized. One approach was genuine attention to, and interest in, cultural difference—this would be represented by the eminent orientalist Edward Pococke the elder, whose death in 1691 marked a precipitous decline in Arabic learning in England.[60] Another approach was appreciating cultural difference as the road not chosen; this was represented by Stephen Nye, Henry Stubbe, and other freethinkers who saw Islam, alongside other cultural alternatives such as China, as legislative exemplars. Another alternative, one that would become dominant, if not universal, was cultural chauvinism of the kind that sees any marker of cultural difference in terms of hierarchy. The final approach, and the object of this study, was displacement of internal difference onto cultural difference. Feminist orientalism was part of this last approach.

Early modern polemic was both vertiginously malleable and oversimplified, collapsing differences among very different groups. Samuel C. Chew, for instance, has noted of early modern continental polemic that Roman Catholics combined attacks upon Islam with attacks upon Lutherans and Calvinists, while Protestants could in turn "associate Rome and Islam together as partners in iniquity."[61] And as Benedict S. Robinson has pointed out, in the seventeenth century Islam was seen as taking up the mantle of enthusiasm and religious frenzy that began with the Greek Platonists, thus setting up an "intimate relationship between Islam and the radical Protestant sectaries" that begins the "long history of enthusiasm, from Locke to Kant to Hegel and beyond."[62] Islam was also associated with Protestant sectarianism in the histories of the early church published in the late seventeenth and early eighteenth centuries because it was the sectarianism alongside the "superstition and clerical self-advancement" that was the "state of Christianity against which Mahomet was to introduce his renovation."[63] Thus the contest in the 1690s between Socinian and Trinitarian Christians known as the Trinitarian Controversy took place in an extremely complicated forum of multiple identifications, ideological cross-hatchings, and outright misrepresentation.

According to Martin Greig, the Trinitarian Controversy of the 1690s originated in a "pamphlet war on idolatry" that pitted Roman Catholic apologists against Anglican Latitudinarians.[64] Philip Dixon has shown in his extensive survey of the Trinitarian Controversy that arguments about the Trinity in the midst of the civil and confessional disputes of the 1640s prefigured the stakes of Trinitarian discourse in the 1690s and that, in both cases, an attack on the doctrine of the Trinity was seen as an attack on the "established civil order."[65] Indeed, John Walsh and Stephen Taylor identify the "doctrine of the Trinity" and the related matter of subscription to the Thirty-Nine Articles as two of the debates that each served as a "polemical focus for group identity" in the tensions between High Church and Latitudinarian Anglicans after the mid-century point.[66] This is why Islam continued to be discursively useful as a marker of extreme cultural difference. As a discursive entity, "Islam" could serve as the site to which all disputes about domestic heterodoxy could be displaced.

Into this mix came Socinian or freethinking texts like Stephen Nye's *A Brief History of the Unitarians* (1687; republished 1690); John Toland's *Christianity not Mysterious* (1696); Toland's examination of early Christianity, *Nazarenus* (1718); Matthew Tindal's attack on the clergy *The rights of the Christian church* (1706); and William Whiston's *Primitive Christianity Reviv'd*, a defense of subordinationism (the belief that Christ is not co-equal with the Father) in 1711.[67] These contributions to the canon of Enlightenment freethinking were joined in 1719 by the *Traité des trois imposteurs*, a notorious text that had been circulating since the 1670s and which claimed that Jesus as well as Muhammad and Moses were impostors who fabricated their religions in order to gain political power.[68] Latitudinarian Anglicans thus had a very narrow field of maneuver: High Church Anglicans could accuse them of privileging reason like the Socinians; anti-Trinitarians could accuse them of privileging tradition over scripture, like the papists.

Polemical analyses of Muslim belief proliferated in the years leading up to the Trinitarian Controversy. Lancelot Addison's work was particularly influential in the development of Islamophobic misogynistic mortalism. Addison's *The First State of Mahumedism* (1679) was republished in 1687. Noting that the "Alcoran" says that "GOD . . . created seven Habitations, each of which is called a Paradise," he dwells on the sensuous imagery—"*Silks*, Purples, *Tapestries*, Tissues, Brocado's"—before turning to the *ne plus ultra* of Muslim sensuality, the "*Horhin*" (houris). Describing them as "Virgins" who "live recluse" and "are made on purpose to entertain the *Musulmin*," he demurs from going into greater detail, for "here he [Mahumed] speaks such uncouth filthiness, as may not with due modesty be named to an *ingenuous Reader*. But, I confess, so great is the naughtiness of the things to be met with in *Andreas Maurus* his account of Mahumed's Paradises, that I had rather the curious Reader should consult this Author." He concludes the chapter, "among all the Luxuries provided for the men, not one word is spoken of any entertainment provided for the women; which the converted *Alfaqui* notes for a singular defect (amid all the accomplishments) of *Mahumed's future state*."[69] The "Andreas Maurus" Addison refers to must be Johannes Andreas Maurus. According to the title page of the translation of his "The Confusion of Muhamed's Sect," he was a Muslim "Bishop" before converting to Christianity.[70] Addison, drawing on, but also subtly revising Maurus's earlier work (1652), concludes that Islam promises no paradise to women. In the English translation of Maurus, however, though the houris are "not of humane race," nevertheless there is a "feast which God will make to the men and women in Paradise."[71] In other words, while Maurus's version of paradise is certainly sensual, it *does* include human women in addition to the celestial *houris*. Addison thus seems to be an initiator, though by no means the only one, of the Islamophobic turn in the misogynistic mortalism trope.

One would expect an English translation of the Qur'an itself to follow suit. But the only English version of the Qur'an available in seventeenth-century England was the 1649 translation (usually attributed to Alexander Ross) of André du Ryer's French translation. The translation begins with a prefatory "THE TRANSLATOR TO THE Christian Reader" that is contemptuous of Islam. But the translation itself nevertheless renders the Qur'anic account of paradise fairly: "man" is "Male and Female" and an "account shall be required of his actions."[72] No misogynistic mortalism in this translation, then. The translation of du Ryer's French version was the only English translation available in seventeenth-century England, though Latin versions were in circulation.

The misogynistic mortalist turn is, however, evident in the fictionalized political commentary *Letters Writ by a Turkish Spy* (first translated into English in 1687) and its 1691 continuation. Written by Giovanni Paolo Marana, a Genovese employed by an ambassador to France, the *Turkish Spy* was ostensibly a series of letters about European political intrigues from the pious, intellectual Turkish spy Mahmut to various figures in the Ottoman court at Constantinople. The letters focus particularly on the machinations of Cardinal Richelieu and the French court between the years 1637 and 1682. It shares many similarities to Charles Montesquieu's *Lettres persanes* (1721), which centers on the Persian traveler Usbek and the increasing instability of his seraglio back home in Ispahan. But, as Ros Ballaster points out, each of the two texts "delivers different insights into the gendered dynamics of looking and speech."[73] Both texts focus on the French context and so are not directly related to my argument about the English context, but they do help shed light on the escalation of misogynistic mortalism in commentary about Islam and Muslims. The famous episode of Anais told by Zulema in *Lettres persanes* clearly, and subversively, shows an astute, courageous, philosophical Muslim woman enjoying all the sexual pleasures of immortality conventionally believed to be reserved for Muslim men.[74] Anais is murdered by her jealous husband when she tries to negotiate between him and her browbeaten companions in the seraglio. But after dying, she enjoys several days of inexpressible sensory and sexual delight with the equivalent of an all-male harem before recollecting herself and sending one of her companions to impersonate her husband, displace him, and rule more graciously in his stead. The story of Anais is a story of consensus, female agency, and the importance of graciousness in a ruler, whether political or domestic.

The 1687 edition of the *Turkish Spy* more extensively engages the problem of Muslim women's immortality.[75] Mahmut veers back and forth between religious triumphalism—he emphasizes that the sterility of Christian kings makes them weak in comparison to the sultan (who is not limited to one wife)—and personal vulnerability (24–25). Mahmut is anguished to be alone in the midst of unbelievers who believe the Qur'an to be "only a parcel of Lyes" (226). But while he addresses Christian scorn of the Muslim paradise—one Jesuit scoffs that Muhammad "makes a Paradise to consist of Beautiful Women, where one may abandon himself to all sorts of Pleasure and Debauchery, and that he hath not foreseen a Hell, where he, and all his Followers, ought to suffer the Pains due to their Crimes"—he believes himself destined for the garden of paradise and describes it in terms that coincide with the Qur'anic description of the celestial garden (123). After his love interest Daria disappoints him, he comforts himself with the frailties of women and celebrates the "Laws" of Constantinople that prevent men there from "falling into the like Irregularities" such as monogamy (314). He further assures himself that "our Religious Arabians have spoken yet more Elegantly, when they wrote, That God made a particular Paradise for them [women], because, say they, should they enter into that of Men, they would soon change it into a Hell." Interestingly, Mahmut uses the biblical rather than the Qur'anic creation myth in explaining that "Eve plaid her part so well when she was seduced by the Serpent in the Terrestrial Paradise, that she deceived her Spouse also, that he might lye under the like Condemnation. But however, this Sex having amongst so many Defects something that is amiable; let us love them at least, because of their Usefulness for continuing the Species, but not for their Beauty; whose Enchantments corrupt the Mind, and hinder all the excellent Operations of it" (315–316). Mahmut's rejection by Daria and his reaction to it—situating it in terms of men's intellectual agency, identifying women with reproduction and sin, and suggesting that polygamy protects men from vulnerability and emotional deterioration—suggest a complex imbrication of cultural difference, gender difference, personal disappointment, and political theorization. It also registers how personal vulnerability might motivate arguments about domestic and political organization. In the 1687 edition, then, Muslim women are immortal, but their paradise is separate from that of men.

The 1691 edition emphasizes Ottoman military might relative to the weakness of European powers, while Mahmut frets that Europeans believe that a sultan "indulging himself in Female Pleasures" would not "have discovered such a martial and Active Spirit, in asserting the Honour of the Ottoman Empire."[76] In keeping with the European convention of associating Ottoman might with Christian disunity, he praises the "Divine Providence" that has, "out of the Discords of Christian Princes" drawn "Occasions to enlarge the Sacred Empire of the Mussulmans; and to spread the Ottoman Conquests o'er the Western World" (49). He also enters the fray of the Trinitarian Controversy in proclaiming that

> Mussulman Heroes . . . know, that when they march against the Infidels, 'tis in Vindication of the Eternal Unity: And therefore, instead of endeavouring to shun, they court a Death so glorious, as that which will immediately transport them to the Bosom of our Holy Prophet, and to the Inexpressible Delights of the Gardens of Eden. Where this Truth is firmly rooted, there is no Room for Fear to plant it self. But, the Case is otherwise with Infidels, who blaspheme that purest Undivided Essence. They assert and believe a Plurality of Gods, and therefore in Time of Danger, amongst so many Deities, they know not whom to address or whom to confide in. (50–51)

Mahmut takes the position shared by Muslims and anti-Trinitarians that to consider Christ and the Holy Spirit as part of the Godhead is really to be polytheistic rather than monotheistic. There is one God, He is an "Eternal Unity," and He has no associates. Mahmut's position goes to the heart of the Trinitarian Controversy: Can one talk of a mysterious Trinity without understanding how three persons can be one Godhead? And if Christ is not God, what is his relationship to humanity? Can he be said to have atoned for the sins of humanity? Or was he merely a prophet—a good man, a moral example, but certainly not God? The 1691 edition of the *Turkish Spy* shows that the Trinitarian Controversy had already entered popular literature written by men. By 1696, the same could be said of literature by women. It is easy to see why. Not only does Mahmut conventionally construe Ottoman military vigor as an analogue of reproductive capability (thus linking sexual access to women to military might), but he also criticizes women's relative social liberty in Europe: "The Stupidity of the Nazarenes [Christians] provokes my Pen, who allow their Women all the uncontroulable Freedom and Opportunities, that commonly give Birth to the most irregular Amours, and yet believe 'em Innocent. They are perfect Idolaters of that Sex; not having learned, with the illuminated

Mussulmans, That Women are of a Creation Inferior to that of Men, have Souls of a lower Stamp, and consequently more prone to Vice; and, that they shall never have the Honour to be admitted into Our Paradise" (72). The 1691 edition is getting closer to what women will use in the feminist orientalist tradition: Islam is presented as believing that women's souls are inferior to those of men, of being of a "lower Stamp." Mahmut tells his addressee, Useph Bassa, that he should "not suffer thy Reason to be blinded by the Enchantments of these deluding Fair Ones; but so love Women, as still to remember thou art a Man, which is something more Sublime" (72). The 1691 edition of the *Turkish Spy* shows that there was already a connection between, on the one hand, the Trinitarian Controversy about the nature of Christ and, on the other, the polemical tradition of claiming that Muslims (or Protestant minorities or Roman Catholics or Jews) distinguish women's souls from men's souls.

Islamophobic misogynistic mortalism did not, then, derive from seventeenth- or eighteenth-century English translations of the Qur'an but rather was fabricated from fictional reportage and polemical commentaries on Muhammad that characterized him as an impostor and Islam as a military threat. The Islamophobic turn occurred because the Trinitarian Controversy coincided with concerns about Socinianism alongside new work on Islam and Muhammad, a republication of the English translation of the Qur'an, and newly republished histories of the Ottoman Empire.

"THOSE BESTIAL ENJOYMENTS OF LUST AND SENSUALITY": THE ISLAMOPHOBIC TURN

The *Disputatio* had yoked together an explicit rejection of Socinian exegesis and a tacit rejection of misogynistic mortalism. One entailed the other. To disbelieve women's immortality was to read the Bible and its depiction of Christ's relation to the human community the way a Socinian would read it; to be a Socinian was to challenge the most basic relationships—between God and man and between man and woman. To assert that women had souls was to reject Socinian exegesis. This was the convention from the time of the publication of the *Disputatio* to the beginning of the Trinitarian Controversy. The Islamophobic turn of misogynistic mortalism arose because of several converging factors: the perceived decline of the Ottoman Empire after the defeat at Vienna (1683) and the Treaty of Karlowitz (1699); the alignment of Socinianism with Islam in the writings of Henry Stubbe and Stephen Nye; and the proliferation of anti-Muslim and orientalist publications that marked a departure from the Arabic learning exemplified by Edward

Pococke the elder.[77] Further, even the real experiences of, and encounters with, Muslim men had to vie with the polemical use of the "Mahometan" straw man in intra-Christian disputes.[78] P. M. Holt particularly cites Humphrey Prideaux's *The True Nature of Imposture Fully Display'd in the Life of Mahomet* (1697) as a product of the "Trinitarian Controversy."[79] Islam was used associatively: atheists, deists, and Socinians were marginalized because of an asserted similarity to Islam. In Prideaux we can see the formulation of an alignment of Christian spiritual pleasures against Muslim sensual pleasures that would become central to feminist orientalism.

Prideaux's *True Nature of Imposture* included a prefatory letter to the reader, the "Life of Mahomet [Muhammad]," the "Letter to the Deists," and an extensive description of his sources. The structure is important because Prideaux's denigrating biography of Mahomet is crucial to his refutation of deist arguments about the imposture of Christianity. Tellingly, the "Life" is almost as long as the "Letter." Prideaux's prefatory "To the Reader" explains the genesis, structure, and goal of his work: initially planning to write a history of the "ruin" of the Eastern church, he was diverted by his concerns about the rise of infidelity in England and, particularly, of the tendency to see Christianity as an imposture. He explains that, in order to address those who have forsaken their Christian faith, he intends to give them a rubric of what properly constitutes "imposture." The best way was to contradistinguish Christianity from the true imposture: Islam. Prideaux's treatment of Mahomet, in other words, is ground-clearing for his real target: English deists. He thus intends to describe Mahomet "in the foulest Colours I am able."[80] So, unlike Knolles, who saw Islam as the scourge of God upon a guilty Christendom, or writers like Addison and Rycaut, who used Islam as a pretext to discuss intra-Christian disputes such as the Civil Wars or the Exclusion Crisis, Prideaux shored up Christianity against deism by deflecting imposture—its "marks and properties"—entirely onto Islam.[81] Like the oriental tale, Prideaux's *Imposture* showed that the ostensibly distant was really a discussion of domestic concerns.

Borrowing from earlier sources, Prideaux argued that Islam was the scourge of God, a punishment of the eastern provinces of the Roman Empire for their schism. Further, he pointed out that controversialists tend to be those who most quickly abandon the true faith. The rise of Islam, associated with the ruin of the Eastern church, is a warning from God to all other Christians "against the wickedness of Separation and Division."[82] Christendom and Islam figured as opponents in this zero-sum game: any power in Islam was evidence of Christian weakness and particularly of weakness born of schism and disunity. Conversely, the weakness of the Muslim empires would be confirmation of Christian integrity and God's approval. Women figured in this zero-sum game because Muslim military power was linked to the supposed sensual rewards of the houris in heaven and the permission to have multiple wives and concubines.[83] This zero-sum game was trans-historical: just as the Eastern Christian Church had collapsed, in Prideaux's view, from internal disagreements and in concert with the rise of Islam, so, too, "are not our Divisions now brought to much the same height with theirs, which drew down from the just hand of God this terrible destruction upon them."[84] And, in case there might be any ambiguity about the analogy, he posited that "God may in the same manner raise up some Mahomet against us for our utter confusion" (xiii). The problem with this trans-historical argument by analogy is that it displaced the events of another time and place, causing Islam to look like a more direct threat than it actually currently was. To read Prideaux uncritically would be to assume that England and the Ottoman Empire did not have an ongoing diplomatic and trade relationship from the reign of Elizabeth I until the Ottoman-German alliance of 1914. It would also be to forget that, with its presence in the Mediterranean and in eastern Europe, the Ottoman Empire was often an asset, if not an official ally, to England and other Protestant powers in diverting the military focus of the powerful Hapsburg Empire.[85] Prideaux's excoriation of Islam ignored his geopolitical reality.

Prideaux portrayed Islam as a present threat by positing it as a historical archetype functioning in a narrative of impending doom. This enabled him to cast Islam and Christian minorities—"the Plague is already begun among us" of the "Socinian, the Quaker, and the Deist"—in a narrative for which there was no empirical evidence except the bare fact of Christian division.[86] But since men need examples, not exhortations, to be "contented with that blessed Establishment of Divine Worship and Truth" that God "hath in so great purity given unto us," Prideaux began his attack on deism and sectarianism with "the deluge of Mahometan Tyranny and Delusion" (xiv–xv). Prideaux believed his excoriation of Islam to be particularly timely given "those disturbances that hapnd [*sic*] about the Doctrine of the Trinity" which he felt had enabled the atheist, deist, and Socinian to gain ground in the public sphere (xvi).

Prideaux was not alone in using the disunity of the early Christian church to discuss controversies in the seventeenth century. In fact, John Selden's partial translation of Eutychius's work on the early church (1642), which he used to show that Presbyterianism existed in antiquity, later made its way into Edward Pococke's full translation, which aroused the concern of Edward Stillingfleet, who sought to attack the "Erastian disenfranchising of the church for which Selden so earnestly advocates."[87] The oriental scholar Johann Heinrich Hottinger also referred to Eutychius in his *Historia Orientalis* (1651) as part of his attempt to dispute the Socinian charge that "Trinitarian dogma . . . had been the main source of long-lasting disagreement and dissent in the early Eastern Christian community."[88] Hottinger instead used references in the Qur'an to show that the Trinity was *not* a late addition to Christian doctrine. That the disunity of the early Christian church had enabled, or had been punished by, the rise of Islam was a contention of seventeenth-century English scholars from Richard Knolles to Humphrey Prideaux.

Prideaux saw the audience of *True Nature* as the deists whom he hoped to persuade away from their error; he explicitly did not address atheists or "Epicurean" deists whom he believed denied first principles.[89] Prideaux makes an influential contribution to a line of thought that would have profound consequences for the representation of Muslim women: atheists and Epicurean (by which he means materialist) deists, like Muslims, are not motivated by human reason. Rather, they have given themselves up "without fear of future Judgment, to all those Bestial Enjoyments of Lust and Sensuality which their corrupt Hearts carry them after"; it is "the Brutal Appetite of the Beast" that motivates them—they are beneath human reason (xx). Prideaux's subsequent characterization of Mahomet will emphasize, repeatedly, the stereotypical alignment of the pleasures of the flesh, a fixation on collecting women, bestial appetites, and the contribution of all of these to the fabric of the ultimate imposture: Islam.

Prideaux listed seven marks of imposture, but the three that are most influential in the history of feminist orientalism are the following: imposture has a carnal interest as its end; its founder is characterized by wickedness; and it must be backed by "Force and Violence."[90] Prideaux's "Life of Mahomet" is almost as long as the "Letter to the Deists," and this was because his hope to persuade the deists that Christianity was not an imposture depended on showing that Christ was not like "Mahomet": Christ did not institute Christianity for a carnal end, he was not wicked or interested in temporal power, and he did not rely on force or violence. For Prideaux, Mahomet's religion, in contrast, *must* be an imposture because he believed it was characterized by all three. Prideaux's defense of Christianity against deism depended on his character assassination of Mahomet. Prideaux was not the first polemicist to align Islam with sensual pleasures—in fact, it is no surprise that, like Addison, he borrowed extensively from Andreas Maurus. But the popularity of *True Nature* and its direct commentary on the Trinitarian and toleration debates make it a keystone in establishing the cultural frame used by women who aligned Islam with physical pleasure while identifying Christianity with intellectual and spiritual pleasures.

Prideaux consistently emphasized what he took to be the intellectual confusion and sensuality of Mahomet's life. Islam is a "Medley made up of *Judaism*, the several *Heresies* of the *Christians* then in the *East*, and the old *Pagan* Rites of the *Arabs*, with an Indulgence to all Sensual Delights."[91] This was of a piece with Mahomet's life, which was "very licentious and wicked." Of course, it was not simply the fear that schism of the kind that characterized the ancient Eastern Church would destroy the Church of England that provoked Islamophobic rhetoric. Socinians, Unitarians, deists, and freethinkers from Stubbe to Nye to Toland were quite ready to make the connection between non-Trinitarian Christianity (which was excluded from the Toleration Act of 1689) and Islam. Indeed, one argument for doing away with the mystery of the Trinity was that it prevented non-Christians from converting.[92] The Trinity was a central concept in articulating the limits of comprehension and toleration.

Prideaux also continued the post-Reformation polemical maneuver of conflating many different opponents, not just the Socinians and Muslims, but also Roman Catholicism. Like Hottinger before him and Burnet after him, Prideaux used Arabic history to debunk Roman Catholic authority.[93] For Prideaux, the corrupt worldly power claimed by the pope emerged simultaneously with the rise of Islam: Mahomet's initial successes in converting his family members occurred at the same time that the "Bishop of Rome" first began styling himself as the "Universal Pastor" and claiming "Supremacy" in the "Church of Christ."[94] Yet Prideaux also used this ancient history to take a dig at "our *Socinians*," who, even more silly than Mahomet, deny the Holy Trinity and the divinity of Christ while still accepting the "holy Scriptures . . . to be genuine and uncorrupted" (19–20). Prideaux was thus part of a concerted effort to displace Socinianism and Roman Catholicism from English identity by aligning them with the "negative ideal" of Islam.

Given this context, the supposedly sensual pleasures of Islam provided a welcome and convenient straw man to unite various opponents. It was not an innocent gesture for Prideaux to attribute the appeal of a sensual paradise to the "gust of the Arabians," who, "being within the Torrid Zone," were given to the excessive love of women (25, 108). The Arabians, and by extension all Muslims, were, in Prideaux's view, bound to the material world by their climatological identity; they were physically distinct from Europeans, and that distinction mapped onto their depraved preference for physical rather than spiritual pleasures. His argument extended to Muslim women. Dismissing the extreme youth of Ayesha ("full eight Years old") when her marriage to Mahomet was consummated, he reasoned, "it is usual in those hot Countries, as it is in all *India* over, which is in the same Clime with *Arabia*, for Women to be ripe for Marriage at that Age, and also bear children the year following" (52). Yet, as with Trump's comments about Khizr and Ghazala Khan, we must ask who is being targeted here. Is "Mahomet" a lecher because he abuses young girls, or do the young girls of Arabia and India lack the capacity to suffer the way Christian girls would? Prideaux argues that, born in the torrid zone, they cannot suffer in the same way as Christian girls: they are exotic fruit "ripe" for consumption. But his target is clearly the military might and religious alternative of Islam (and, ultimately, the Christian disunity caused by deism). Prideaux, like Trump, invokes two logically exclusive Islamophobic arguments (Mahomet is brutal to girls; Muslim girls are too "ripe" to suffer) to position Christian men as superior to both Muslim men and Muslim girls.

According to Prideaux, Mahomet's "two predominant Passions were *Ambition* and *Lust*," as demonstrated by the "course which he took to gain *Empire*" and "the multitude of Women which he had to do with" (137). But Prideaux also believed that for his argument about imposture to work, it was not enough for an impostor to be wicked; rather, the very nature of his wickedness had to be interwoven into the fabric of the imposture. For this reason, ambition and lust "run thorough the whole Frame of his Religion, there being scarce a Chapter in his Alcoran, which doth not lay down some Law of War and Bloodshed for the promoting of the one; or else give some liberty for the use of Women here, or some promise for the enjoyment of them hereafter to the gratifying of the other" (138). Not only is Mahomet violent and lecherous, but his religion is, too, and it thus attracts like-minded converts. Mahomet's "brutish Passion" is portrayed as so well known that leaders who wished for his attention knew that they must ply him with women (145). According to Prideaux, when Mahomet's wives protested his sleeping with a servant girl, "out comes a new Revelation to justify him in it" (147). Prideaux makes Mahomet's supposed lust the foundation of his revelations as well as his diplomatic relations. The revelation permitting men to sleep with servant girls is seen as welcome to his "licentious Followers," who "gladly laid hold of the liberty which he had granted; and ever since it has been an establish'd *Law* among all of that *Sect*, besides their Wives, to keep as many Women Slaves for their Lust, as they shall think fit to buy. . . . And the *Grand Signior*, who never marries, hath all his Women under this later Notion, that is, as his Slaves, and he keeps none but such in his *Seraglio*" (147). Here it is clear how female enslavement, stereotypically Muslim physical pleasure, and political rhetoric became imbricated: men dominated by physical pleasure were vulnerable to being bribed with beautiful women, were likely to enslave women for their sexual use, and were vulnerable to bogus "revelations" that appealed to their self-interest. Prideaux's "Letter to the Deists," in which he argued that Christ is not an impostor, derives its full weight from being juxtaposed with this "Life of Mahomet." Using his seven marks of imposture, Prideaux worked his way through each one to argue that Christ is characterized by none of the lust and ambition characteristic of "Mahomet." Prideaux highlighted what he wanted to be seen as Christ's truth by preceding it with his character assassination of Muhammad.

Indeed, Prideaux believed that if Christ had "offered at more of this World's interest . . . or if he had joined thereto, the enjoyment of carnal pleasure as Mahomet did, there might then have been some ground of charging him of differing from those Notions for the serving of his own interest."[95] Thus while Christ's suffering atonement was "the whole end and purpose" of his mission, the followers of "Mahomet," like Prideaux's contemporaries who denied the immortal soul, were only interested in "worldly pleasure."[96] Early Christians, by contrast, were persecuted because Christianity was "against the lusts and pleasures and other evil courses of this World" (42). "Empire and Lust"—and particularly the assertion that "Mahomet" desired to have as many women as he pleased—were the engines behind the founding, expansion, and continuation of Islam for Prideaux (55). This alignment of Islam with physical pleasure and the accumulation of multiple women for the sexual satisfaction of one man, contrasted with the alignment of Christianity with the spiritual pleasure of eternal reward, would deeply inform Englishwomen's writing about Islam. *The True Nature of Imposture* was so popular that it went through eight editions by 1723.[97] Its popularity indicates the profound distance imagined between Islam and English identity. This distance was also enshrined on the stage. Just as early Reformation morality plays used misogynistic mortalism to disentangle the "Infidelitie" of Roman Catholicism from English identity, so, too, did John Dryden adopt it to theorize the relationship between English identity and King William.

MAHOMETAN WILLIAMITES ON THE ENGLISH STAGE

After the Revolution of 1688 a disappointed, impoverished, and Roman Catholic John Dryden, stripped of his poet laureateship, wrote what has been praised as one of his greatest later plays: *Don Sebastian* (1689–90). Derek Hughes sees it as "exceptional among Dryden's later plays not only in its quality but in its resurrection of the dramatic medium which had most consistently stirred his originality and inventiveness: the heroic play."[98] Yet Hughes denies that it is "Part III of *The Conquest of Granada*," seeing it rather as illustrating a new "religious earnestness with which Dryden criticizes the heroic life."

But religious earnestness is only part of the distinction between *Don Sebastian* and *The Conquest of Granada*. This play provides an example of how a writer might use Islam to adapt to the shifting dispensation of the 1690s—and how Islam could be used to satirize religiopolitical opponents. Dryden, unlike most of the well-known female writers of the seventeenth century, whom I consider in the next chapter, published works both before and after the Revolution of 1688. Lady Mary

Wroth died circa 1651/3, Katherine Philips in 1664, Margaret Cavendish in 1673, and Aphra Behn in 1689, shortly after William and Mary came to the throne. Dryden is thus a rare instance of a writer who used misogynistic mortalism and who wrote both before and after the Revolution. His writing shows the changing discursive possibilities for the trope.

A noticeable, apparently Islamophobic shift is evident in Dryden's work from his pre-1690 to his post-1690 treatment of Islam. *The Conquest of Granada* (acted 1670; published 1672) depicted a contentious historical event in the *Reconquista* of Islamic Spain by Christian forces. If Dryden had been Islamophobic, it would have been logical for him to use misogynistic mortalism to characterize the Muslim characters. But he does not—in fact, there are Muslim characters of integrity and moral authority. In *Don Sebastian* (acted 1689, published 1690), however, the trope is repeatedly mentioned. Why this transition should have taken place makes little sense until Zonana's point about the displacement involved in feminist orientalism is taken into account. *Don Sebastian* is less about Islam, despite the North African setting, than it is about the Revolution of 1688. Just as in "Absalom and Achitophel" Dryden used ancient Jerusalem as a setting to critique the Earl of Shaftesbury's role in the Exclusion Crisis, so, too, in *Don Sebastian* Dryden used a foreign location to explore problems at home.

Indeed, David Bywaters argues that Sebastian "clearly resembles James [II], also the victim of a foreign usurper: the alteration of a few proper names would make this a Jacobite history of the Revolution and prophecy of its consequences."[99] Dryden's representation of Muslim doctrine in *Don Sebastian* differs strikingly from his treatment of Islam in the 1670s. In "Notes and Observations on *The Empress of Morocco*" (1674), co-written with John Crowne and Thomas Shadwell, the Dryden of the 1670s was condescending toward Islam but did not believe it denied women's immortality. In responding to Elkanah Settle's play, which they considered "a Rapsody of non-sense [*sic*]," they never questioned its depiction of Muslim women's immortality.[100] True, *The Empress of Morocco* does not present women in paradise, but it does show the villainous Queen Mother in hell, and this suggests that in a Muslim context women would be held morally accountable. While deriding the play for making "Mahometans believe a Purgatory," Dryden and his co-authors seemed to intend this comment to be of a piece with their other copious criticisms of Settle's confounding of real differences (in this case conflating Roman Catholics and Muslims).[101] Further, while they savaged Settle's "very liberall Mess"—specifically the passage in which the heroine Morena envisions souls being freed of the "grosser burden" of their bodies—they never question Settle's representation of a Muslim woman assuming that she has an immortal soul (105, 104). Finally, of the passage in which the villainous Queen

Mother avows that she despises divine punishment, they comment: "It is written like one that thinks without a Soul, as he makes his Queen Mother do" (130). This is not the sort of comment one makes if one believes that misogynistic mortalism is Muslim doctrine.

Some of the Muslim characters in *The Conquest of Granada* (1672) are rendered sympathetically, and in *Aureng-Zebe* (1676), set in Mogul India, Nourmahal, the Empress, defends her power bid by declaring: "Virtue's no slave of Man; no Sex confines the Soul: / I, for my self, th'Imperial Seat will gain."[102] The less ambitious but more sympathetic Melesinda promises her dying husband:

> Nor Fate, nor You, can my vow'd faith control;
> Dying, I'll follow your disdainful Soul:
> A Ghost I'll haunt your Ghost; and, where you go,
> With mournful murmurs fill the Plains below. (5.1.380–383)

Clearly neither Nourmahal nor Melesinda believes that the material body is the entirety of her identity.

Yet this representation of Muslim characters all changed in *Don Sebastian*. The tragedy depicts the (unwittingly) incestuous romance between the historical king of Portugal and his fictional sister, the half-Moroccan, half-Portuguese Christian convert Almeyda, Queen of Barbary. Further, while Bywaters considers Dryden's allegorical poem *The Hind and the Panther* (1687) to be "the last of Dryden's direct analyses of English politics," he argues that in *Don Sebastian*, Dryden's "first major work after the Revolution," the former poet laureate "is concerned with much the same set of political issues as in *The Hind and the Panther*, and he engages them by many of the same rhetorical strategies" including an "allegorical fable with a complex form of political parallel."[103] In fact, Dryden relied on the triangulations of the mortalist and toleration debates to portray Sebastian as James II, the Moors as Anglicans, Muley-Moloch the tyrant as William of Orange, and none other than Gilbert Burnet as the Mufti. Dryden clearly used the conflation of the Williamite Latitudinarians, of whom Burnet was one, with heterodox thinkers to imply that the entire Revolution Settlement was illegitimate. Tellingly, it is in an early dialogue between Muley-Moloch and the Mufti that Dryden inserts misogynistic mortalism. Shortly before the heroine Almeyda unveils herself to reveal her identity, the Mufti declares, "Our Law says plainly Women have no Souls," and the tyrannical Muley-Moloch assents, "'Tis true; their Souls are mortal."[104] Almeyda, a Christian convert, first identifies herself as "She whom thy Mufti tax'd to have no Soul"; later scorns the besotted Muley-Moloch, advising him to "take the Distaff, for thy Soul's my Slave"; and imagines her "Soul" being taken "home" after death (1.1.441, 2.1.452, 2.1.539). Dryden figures England as an injured lady whose integrity is doubted by the Williamite elite. Yet there were collateral consequences to Dryden's political critique of Burnet and William of Orange: it reinforced the alignment of Islam and tyranny, and it portrayed women as intellectually and morally oppressed by Muslim authorities. Thus, by 1689 misogynistic mortalism had taken the English stage. As we will see in the next chapter, by 1696 it had become part of women's arsenal in defending their intellectual and literary abilities.

NOTES

1. Knud Haakonssen, "Enlightened Dissent: An Introduction," in *Enlightenment and Religion: Rational Dissent in Eighteenth-Century Britain*, ed. Knud Haakonssen (Cambridge: Cambridge University Press, 1996), 10.
2. Penny Pritchard, "Studies in English Protestant Dissent and Literature after 1662," *Literature Compass* 15, no. 5 (2018): e12469, 1, https://doi.org/10.1111/lic3.12469.
3. Wilfrid Prest, "Law, Lawyers and Rational Dissent," in Haakonssen, *Enlightenment and Religion*, 170.
4. Brent Sirota, "The Trinitarian Crisis in Church and State: Religious Controversy and the Making of the Postrevolutionary Church of England, 1687–1702," *Journal of British Studies* 52 (January 2013): 31. Sirota sees the Trinitarian Controversy as a "disciplinary crisis" with political, not just theological, implications (27). Most politically significant was "the waning confidence among churchmen of all stripes in the ability of reason to successfully carry the day and the concomitant turn toward public authority to resolve the dispute" (30). Political interventions included "a royal directive to the episcopate" and a "parliamentary statute" (27) in support of Trinitarian orthodoxy. Martin Greig also argues that the Trinitarian Controversy began with Latitudinarian-Catholic hostilities but dates them from Edward Stillingfleet's pamphlet war with "catholic apologists" in the 1670s. See Martin Greig, "Heresy Hunt: Gilbert Burnet and the Convocation Controversy of 1701," *Historical Journal* 37, no. 3 (September 1994): 569. Though it began as anti-Latitudinarian polemic used by Catholics, it was soon "taken over by high churchmen . . . and nonjurors" (570).
5. Prest, "Law," 170–171.
6. R. K. Webb, "The Emergence of Rational Dissent," in Haakonssen, *Enlightenment and Religion*, 15. On the failure of comprehension, see also Isabel Rivers, "Religion and Literature," in *The Cambridge History of English Literature, 1660–1780*, ed. John J. Richetti (Cambridge: Cambridge University Press, 2005), 446. On the connection between the failure of comprehension and the Trinitarian Controversy, see Sirota, "Trinitarian Crisis," 37–48.
7. Brent Sirota, *The Christian Monitors: The Church of England and the Age of Benevolence, 1680–1730* (New Haven, Conn.: Yale University Press, 2014), 149–150, 172.
8. See Ann Thomson, *Bodies of Thought: Science, Religion, and the Soul in the Early Enlightenment* (Oxford: Oxford University Press, 2008), 34; but also see Robert E. Sullivan, *John Toland and the Deist Controversy: A Study in Adaptations*, Harvard Historical Studies (Cambridge, Mass.: Harvard University Press, 1982), 10.
9. Sirota, "Trinitarian Crisis," 33. According to Douglas Hedley, the term "has come to be used by scholars to denote a loosely knit group of Church of England men of liberal and moderately rationalistic temper whose intellectual roots lay in the irenic theology of the Cambridge Platonists." They felt that "the Act of Uniformity of 1662 . . . had been too draconian. . . . But the Latitudinarian interest in the growth of a genuinely national

Church and their opposition to the rigidity of the High Church party encouraged an atmosphere in which the Anti-Trinitarians could profit." Douglas Hedley, "Persons of Substance and the Cambridge Connection: Some Roots and Ramifications of the Trinitarian Controversy in Seventeenth-Century England," in *Socinianism and Arminianism: Antitrinitarians, Calvinists and Cultural Exchange in Seventeenth-Century Europe*, ed. Martin Mulsow and Jan Rohls (Leiden: Brill, 2005), 232, 229.

10. Erastianism is the doctrine that the state should be supreme (even over the church) in matters of ecclesiology. The "nonjuring church," on the other hand, "comprised, on the whole, a movement for ecclesiastical autonomy" that resulted in the Convocation Crisis. See Sirota, *Christian Monitors*, 154. Note also that the deprivation of the nonjuring clergy and consecration of new clergy in 1690–91 coincided with what Philip Dixon has identified as the opening salvo of the Trinitarian Controversy, the pamphlet war between Stephen Nye (author of *A Brief History of the Unitarians*, an anti-Trinitarian work published in 1687 but republished in 1690) and the hapless Trinitarian defender Dr. William Sherlock, later dean of St. Paul's Cathedral and author of *A Vindication of the Doctrine of the Holy and Ever Blessed Trinity and the Incarnation of the Son of God* (1690). According to Dixon, it was "Sherlock's inopportune use of the emergent category of 'consciousness' in relation to the persons of the Trinity that was to shatter the fragile unity of the trinitarian party" (110). In short, by using "consciousness" (which must pertain to an individual) rather than the traditional "substance" in describing the relation of the persons of the Trinity, Sherlock unwittingly argued for polytheism. The opponents of Trinitarian orthodoxy had a field day. See Philip Dixon, *"Nice and Hot Disputes": The Doctrine of the Trinity in the Seventeenth Century* (London: T & T Clark, 2003), 106–112. J. A. I. Champion has suggested that "the Socinian or Unitarian polemic of the 1690s was a crucial movement in the development of the Enlightenment idea of religion." J. A. I. Champion, *The Pillars of Priestcraft Shaken: The Church of England and Its Enemies, 1660–1730*, Cambridge Studies in Early Modern British History (Cambridge: Cambridge University Press, 1992; first paperback ed., 2014), 101.
11. B. W. Young, *Religion and Enlightenment in Eighteenth-Century England: Theological Debate from Locke to Burke* (Oxford: Clarendon Press, 1998; reprint, Oxford: Clarendon Press, 2001), 21.
12. Dixon, *"Nice and Hot,"* 134; see also Thomson, *Bodies of Thought*, 36; and Sullivan, *John Toland*, 105.
13. Dixon, *"Nice and Hot,"* 134–135.
14. For the recognition of how widespread was this rhetorical ploy, by which opponents were associated with other (sometimes opposed) groups, see Isabel Rivers, *Reason, Grace, and Sentiment: A Study of the Language of Religion and Ethics in England, 1660–1780*, vol. 1, *Whichcote to Wesley* (Cambridge: Cambridge University Press, 1991), 9. For a discussion of the earlier "competing religious conspiracy theories, based upon perceptions of a religio-political 'other'" and of the "polemical constraints under which English Protestants were required to work," see Anthony Milton, *Catholic and Reformed: The Roman and Protestant Churches in English Protestant Thought, 1600–1640* (Cambridge: Cambridge University Press, 1995; paperback ed., 2002), 2, 7. For the High Church charge that calls for "moderation" were the product of "an alliance of courtiers, Whigs, atheists, Scottish Presbyterians, and English fanatics," see Sirota, *Christian Monitors*, 170. For the way the term "Turk" was "used by many theologians even against theological opponents within Christianity" in the early modern period, see Dietrich Klein, "Hugo Grotius' Position on Islam as Described in *De veritate religionis Christianae, Liber VI*," in Mulsow and Rohls, *Socinianism and Arminianism*, 153. For Socinianism as a "stock part of the abusive rhetoric of much religious debate" in the seventeenth century, see Dixon, *"Nice and Hot,"*

39. On the use of "character types" and the "abiding preoccupation with the sorting and stabilizing of difference" that resulted in "binaries" being "perversely useful" (and continuing to be so), see Jayne Elizabeth Lewis, introduction to *Religion in Enlightenment England: An Anthology of Primary Sources*, ed. Jayne Elizabeth Lewis (Waco, Tex.: Baylor University Press, 2017), xviii, xxvii. For the "success of the High-Church party in giving their political campaign against the Revolution Settlement the specious appearance of a defense of orthodoxy," see Sullivan, *John Toland*, 76. On how "accusations of heresy and irreligion were used as a stick to beat one's political opponents and we should be careful about taking at their face value accusations of atheism, republicanism, fanaticism, or enthusiasm," see Thomson, *Bodies of Thought*, 31. Of an earlier characterization that was picked up during the Trinitarian Controversy, Nabil Matar has observed that early modern writers typically ignored "over half a millennium of the Arab-Islamic legacy" in the Mediterranean, ignoring "the 'Infidel' contributions to Christian civilization" in order to associate the Saracens (often grouped with the later Ottomans) with "the 'beast' imagery of Biblical apocalyptic texts." Nabil Matar, *Islam in Britain, 1558–1685* (Cambridge: Cambridge University Press, 1998), 158. Regarding how the "Anglican counter-polemic [in the 1690s] was not only strengthened by the identification of Socinian theology with Islamic, but also by their complicity as human impostures," see Champion, *Pillars of Priestcraft*, 112. I discuss the association of Socinianism and Islam below.

15. On "Islamic republicanism" as a legislative model for English Enlightenment thinkers, see Humberto Garcia, *Islam and the English Enlightenment, 1670–1840* (Baltimore: Johns Hopkins University Press, 2012), 4–12.
16. For the evolution of the Christology—specifically in regard to Arianism, between the Council of Nicaea (325 CE) and the Council of Chalcedon (451 CE)—through which seventeenth-century writers thought, see A. M. C. Waterman, "The Nexus between Theology and Political Doctrine," in Haakonssen, *Enlightenment and Religion*, 201–202. As Waterman notes, the "Book of Common Prayer . . . is replete with Trinitarian references" (202). For overviews of the early Christian "Christological Controversy" and "Trinitarian Controversy," see Richard A. Norris Jr., trans. and ed., *The Christological Controversy*, with supplemental material by Robert C. Saler (Minneapolis: Fortress Press, 1980); and William G. Rusch, trans. and ed., *The Trinitarian Controversy* (Minneapolis: Fortress Press, 1980). For the link, as early as the 1650s, between Arianism, Socinianism, and Islam, see Matar, *Islam in Britain*, 48. For the reliance of "Anglican apologetic" on proofs from the early church fathers in addition to an overview of the early Arian controversy to which they referred and to Samuel Clarke's use of mostly Greek (rather than Latin) patristic thinkers in his *Scripture-doctrine of the Trinity* (1712), which many of his contemporaries considered Arian, see Thomas C. Pfizenmaier, *The Trinitarian Theology of Dr. Samuel Clarke (1675–1729): Context, Sources, and Controversy* (Leiden: Brill, 1997), 102, 89–102, 103. As Pfizenmaier points out, the *Scripture-doctrine* "embroiled [Clarke] in controversy until his death" (2), and, according to Dixon, it "destroyed his chances completely" of becoming a bishop. See Dixon, *"Nice and Hot,"* 183.
17. Though it was not published at the time, Henry Stubbe's *An Account of the Rise and Progress of Mahometanism* circulated in manuscript copies. Stubbe maintained that "much of Mahomet's success lay in his revival of primitive (Arian) Christianity which had been lost sight of by this time because of the dominance among the Christian churches in many places of a corrupt Trinitarianism." See James R. Jacob, *Henry Stubbe, Radical Protestantism and the Early Enlightenment* (Cambridge: Cambridge University Press, 1983; first paperback ed., 2002), 65. See also Nabil Matar's argument that, while not a Socinian himself, Stubbe's generous "attitude toward Islam went beyond anything that even the Socinians proposed." Nabil Matar, introduction to *Henry Stubbe and the Beginnings of Islam: "The*

Originall & Progress of Mahometanism," ed. Nabil Matar (New York: Columbia University Press, 2014), 13.

18. See, for instance, P. M. Holt's overview of Humphrey Prideaux's rhetoric, in P. M. Holt, "The Treatment of Arab History by Prideaux, Ockley and Sale," in *Historians of the Middle East*, ed. Bernard Lewis and P. M. Holt (London: Oxford University Press, 1962; reprint, London: Oxford University Press, 1964), 291. See also Klein's observation that Martin Luther saw both Islam and the papacy as threats but that the Turkish threat should be seen as a "catalyst for repentance"; Hugo Grotius also saw Islam within "the framework of this purifying punishment from God." Klein, "Hugo Grotius' Position," 152, 155. The influential historian Richard Knolles, as I discuss below, also saw Islam as the scourge of God upon a divided Christendom.
19. See Champion, *Pillars of Priestcraft*, all of chap. 4, "'Historia monotheistica': Judaism, Islam and Christianity: Unitarian Polemic, 1671–1718" (99–132). See also Sullivan, *John Toland*, for Arthur Bury's claim that "monotheism . . . associated Christianity with Islam" (70); William Freke's claim that the unscriptural Athanasian Creed was the only thing that separated Islam and Christianity (99); and John Toland's claim that the Qur'an was "a plausible competitor for the title of God's revelation" (250). See also Nabil Matar, introduction to *Henry Stubbe and the Beginnings of Islam: "The Originall & Progress of Mahometanism,"* edited and with an introduction by Nabil Matar (New York: Columbia University Press, 2014), 1–48.
20. Gilbert Burnet, *An Exposition of the Thirty-nine Articles of the Church of England. Written by Gilbert Bishop of Sarum. The Third Edition Corrected* (London: Printed for Ri. Chiswell, at the Rose and Crown in St. Paul's Church-Yard, 1705), 382; also 334–335.
21. Burnet, *Exposition*, 334–335.
22. Robert G. Ingram, *Religion, Reform and Modernity in the Eighteenth Century: Thomas Secker and the Church of England*, Studies in Modern British Religious History (Woodbridge: Boydell Press, 2007), 27. But Ingram also notes that Butler's *Analogy* had "repulsed the deist threat, but it did not kill off theological heterodoxy itself. Beginning in the 1750s and crescendoing through the 1760s, a new wave of heterodox work loudly demanded reform in church and state. This time it was anti-Trinitarianism, rather than deism" (75).
23. John Donne, "To the Countess of Huntingdon" [ca. 1610], in *The Complete Poetry and Selected Prose of John Donne*, ed. Charles M. Coffin (New York: Modern Library, 2001), 170–171. For an analysis of this poem that addresses Donne's arguments about women's immortality, see Helen L. Gardner, "Notes on Donne's Verse Letters," *Modern Language Review* 41, no. 3 (July 1946): 318–321.
24. John Donne, *LXXX Sermons* (1640), 242. Preached on Easter Day, 1630.
25. George Huntston Williams, *The Radical Reformation*, 3rd ed. (Kirksville, Mo.: Truman State University Press, 2000). For Williams, the "Magisterial Reformation" has three branches: Lutheranism, the Reformed churches, and Cranmerian Anglicanism. The Radical Reformation—whose members espoused "the faithful restoration of the apostolic church as it existed in the age of the martyrs before it was prudentially supported by Constantine"—also had three branches: the Anabaptists, the Spiritualists, and the Evangelical Rationalists. See Williams, *Radical Reformation*, xxxii–xxxiv. The unique character of Anglicanism, as a state church, Williams describes as preserving "episcopacy on principle, but primarily as a constitutional necessity in the magisterial reformation of a national kingdom, with its lords temporal and lords spiritual in the upper house of its Parliament, interpreted as at once the national diet and national synod" (xxxii).
26. Clive Hart, *Treatise on the Question Do Women Have Souls and Are They Human Beings? "Disputatio Nova," with Translation, Commentary and Appendices by Clive Hart*, expanded and rev. ed. (Lewiston, N.Y.: Edwin Mellen Press, 1998), 1–3.

27. Socinians advocated rationality in religious belief, the separation of church and state, and simple, minimal dogma (for this reason, the term "Socinian" was used loosely as a common epithet to dismiss any kind of "free thinking"). Socinians believed that Christ was holy in his behavior, but not in his nature. Accordingly, they did not believe in the Trinity (or in the doctrine of Christ's satisfaction for the sins of humanity) and later called themselves Unitarians. See John C. Higgins-Biddle, introduction to *The Reasonableness of Christianity* (1695), by John Locke, ed. John C. Higgins-Biddle (Oxford: Clarendon Press, 1999), xv–cxv, especially xlii–lxxiv, "The Spectre of Socinianism."
28. Bryan W. Ball, *The Soul Sleepers: Christian Mortalism from Wycliffe to Priestley* (Cambridge: James Clarke, 2008), 20–21.
29. Predating the *Disputatio*, Lewis Wager's Reformation morality play *A new enterlude . . . entreating of the life and repentaunce of Marie Magdalene* (ca. 1565) is an early instance of misogynistic mortalism in Reformation England. Set in Jerusalem at the time of Jesus Christ, the play poses Infidelitie in "Jurie" (Jewry) against "Knowledge of Sin" to reclaim the soul of the vain and deluded Mary Magdalene. Infidelitie at one point assures Mary, "Women have no soules, this saying is not newe, / Men shall be damned, and not women which do fall." Lewis Wager, *A new enterlude, never before this tyme imprinted, entreating of the life and repentaunce of Marie Magdalene not only godlie, learned and fruitefull, but also well furnished with pleasaunt myrth and pastime, very delectable for those which shall heare or reade the same. Made by the learned clarke Lewis Wager* (Imprinted at London: by Iohn Charlevvood, dwelling in Barbican, at the signe of the halfe Eagle and the Key, 1566), 21.
30. Manfred P. Fleischer, "'Are Women Human?'—the Debate of 1595 between Valens Acidalius and Simon Gediccus," *Sixteenth Century Journal* 12, no. 2 (Summer 1981): 107–120.
31. Hart, *Treatise*, 47 (Thesis 1).
32. Hart, *Treatise*, 52.
33. Hart, *Treatise*, 70.
34. Tjitske Akkerman and Siep Stuurman, introduction to *Perspectives on Feminist Political Thought in European History: From the Middle Ages to the Present*, ed. Tjitske Akkerman and Siep Stuurman (London: Routledge, 1998), 9–10.
35. George Fox, in his travels around England in the 1640s, describes how he encountered "a sort of People, that held, *Women have no Souls*, (adding in a light manner,) *no more than a Goose*," but he "reproved them, and told them, that was not right: For *Mary* said, *my soul doth magnifie the Lord, and my Spirit hath rejoyced in God my Saviour*." His encounter suggests that misogynistic mortalism was possibly a heterodox minority perspective. George Fox, *A JOURNAL, or Historical Account of the Life, Travels, Sufferings, Christian Experiences and Labour of Love in the Work of the Ministry Of That Ancient, Eminent and Faithful Servant of George Fox; Who departed this Life in great Peace with the LORD, the 13th of the 11th Month, 1690. The First Part* (London: Printed and sold by J. Sowle in White-Hart-Court in Gracious-street, 1709), 35.
36. Michael Nolan, "The Myth of Soulless Women," *First Things* 72 (April 1997): 13–14. Nolan's article charts the continental development of the myth. Misogynistic mortalism is still associated with Roman Catholicism. See Kathleen Sprows Cummings, "Do Women Have Souls? Catholicism, Feminism & the Council of Mâcon," *Commonweal*, September 11, 2009, 20–23.
37. Fleischer, "'Are Women Human?,'" 110.
38. According to translator Ernest Brehaut, Gregory (538–594) completed the epilogue of *Historia Francorum* in 594, the year of his death. See Ernest Brehaut, introduction to *History of the Franks*, by Gregory Bishop of Tours (New York: W. W. Norton, 1969), xv.
39. Bayle, however, argued that Acidalius did not author the work: "On lui avoir imputé à tort un petit livre qui fut imprimé l'an 1595 dont le sujet étoit *que les femmes ne sont pas des*

animaux raisonnables" (People have wrongly imputed to him a small book, imprinted in the year 1595, of which the subject is, *that women are not reasonable animals*.—My translation). Bayle mentions nothing explicitly about women's souls. Pierre Bayle, *Dictionnaire historique et critique* (Rotterdam: R. Leers, 1697), 85. As in England, the attraction of the debate for French writers remained from the 1690s, the time when Bayle was writing, until almost the time of the French Revolution. Mirabeau mentions the Acidalius-Gediccus controversy in a letter from the 1780s: "Quand tu voudras, madame, je t' indiquerai une belle dissertation, où l' on prouve en forme, par cinquante témoignages de l' écriture, que les femmes ne font pas partie du genre humain" (When you like, Madam, I will show you a clever treatise where it is formally proved in fifty written instances that women are not a part of human kind.—My translation). Gabriel-Honoré Riquetti, comte de Mirabeau, *Lettres originales de Mirabeau* (Paris: Garnery; Strasbourg: Treuttel; London: De Boffe, 1792), 387.

40. Hart, *Treatise*, 14.
41. Hart, *Treatise*, 19.
42. Richard Knolles, "THE AUTHORS INTRODUCTION to the Christian Reader unto the Historie of the Turkes following," in *The Generall Historie of the Turkes* (London: Printed by Adam Islip, 1603), unpaginated.
43. On the formation of cultural hierarchies, see Carina L. Johnson, *Cultural Hierarchy in Sixteenth-Century Europe: The Ottomans and Mexicans* (Cambridge: Cambridge University Press, 2011); and Nancy Bisaha, *Creating East and West: Renaissance Humanists and the Ottoman Turks* (Philadelphia: University of Pennsylvania Press, 2004).
44. Jonathan Sheehan, *The Enlightenment Bible: Translation, Scholarship, Culture* (Princeton, N.J.: Princeton University Press, 2005), see particularly x–xiv.
45. Ziad Elmarsafy, *The Enlightenment Qur'an: The Politics of Translation and the Construction of Islam* (Oxford: Oneworld Books, 2009), 28–29 (my emphasis). Elmarsafy also provides a useful historical overview of Western translations of the Qur'an from Robert of Ketton's *Lex saracenorum* of the late twelfth century to Ludovico Maracci's Counter-Reformation translation (1698) to Frances Sale's English translation (1734). He also includes an overview of important texts in the history of "Arabic and Islamic studies." See Elmarsafy, chap. 1 ("Translators and Translations of the Qur'an"), 1–36.
46. Ball, *Soul Sleepers*, 56–62, 158–162.
47. Linda Darling uses the phrase "negative ideal" to describe British constructions of the Ottoman Empire in the seventeenth century. See Linda Darling, "Ottoman Politics through British Eyes: Paul Rycaut's *The Present State of the Ottoman Empire*," *Journal of World History* 5, no. 1 (1994): 92.
48. See also David Sorkin, *The Religious Enlightenment: Protestants, Jews, and Catholics from London to Vienna* (Princeton, N.J.: Princeton University Press, 2008), 29–30.
49. Rivers, *Reason, Grace, and Sentiment*, 1:7.
50. Peter Lake, "Anti-Puritanism: The Structure of a Prejudice," in *Religious Politics in Post-Reformation England*, ed. Kenneth Fincham and Peter Lake (Sussex: Boydell & Brewer, 2006), 87–88; Peter Lake, "Anti-popery: The Structure of a Prejudice," in *Conflict in Early Stuart England: Studies in Religion and Politics, 1603–1642*, ed. Richard Cust and Ann Hughes (London: Longman, 1989), 72–106.
51. John Walsh and Stephen Taylor, "Introduction: The Church and Anglicanism in the 'Long' Eighteenth Century," in *The Church of England c. 1689–c. 1833: From Toleration to Tractarianism*, ed. John Walsh, Colin Haydon, and Stephen Taylor (Cambridge: Cambridge University Press, 1993; first paperback ed., 2002), 15.
52. Sirota, *Christian Monitors*, 149–150.

53. Sirota, *Christian Monitors*, 150.
54. William J. Bulman, *Anglican Enlightenment: Orientalism, Religion and Politics in England and Its Empire, 1648–1715*, Cambridge Studies in Early Modern British History (Cambridge: Cambridge University Press, 2015), 5–6.
55. Bulman, *Anglican Enlightenment*, 6–7.
56. Ben Lazare Mijuskovic, *The Achilles of Rationalist Arguments*, International Archives of the History of Ideas, Series Minor, 13 (The Hague: Martinus Nijhoff, 1974), 27.
57. Young, *Religion and Enlightenment*, 11.
58. Paul C. Davies, "The Debate on Eternal Punishment in Late Seventeenth- and Eighteenth-Century English Literature," *Eighteenth-Century Studies* 4, no. 3 (Spring 1971): 257.
59. Franklin Perkins, *Leibniz and China: A Commerce of Light* (Cambridge: Cambridge University Press, 2004), 4.
60. For Pococke's central contribution to Arabic learning in England, and its decline after his death, see Gül A. Russell, ed., *The 'Arabick' Interest of the Natural Philosophers in Seventeenth-Century England* (Leiden: Brill, 1994); G. J. Toomer, *Eastern Wisedome and Learning: The Study of Arabic in Seventeenth-Century England* (Oxford: Oxford University Press, 1996); and Mordechai Feingold, "Learning Arabic in Early Modern England," in *The Teaching and Learning of Arabic in Early Modern Europe*, ed. Jan Loop, Alastair Hamilton, and Charles Burnett (Leiden: Brill, 2017), 33–56.
61. Samuel C. Chew, *The Crescent and the Rose: Islam and England during the Renaissance* (New York: Octagon Books, 1965), 101.
62. Benedict S. Robinson, *Islam and Early Modern English Literature: The Politics of Romance from Spenser to Milton*, Early Modern Cultural Studies, 1500–1700 (New York: Palgrave Macmillan, 2007), 174.
63. Champion, *Pillars of Priestcraft*, 124.
64. Greig, "Heresy Hunt," 569.
65. Dixon, *"Nice and Hot,"* 174.
66. Walsh and Taylor, "Introduction: The Church and Anglicanism," 46.
67. For more on Whiston's involvement in the Trinitarian Controversy, see Dixon, *"Nice and Hot,"* 31–32, 180–183.
68. Silvia Berti, Françoise Charles-Daubert, and Richard Popkin, eds., *Heterodoxy, Spinozism, and Free Thought in Early-Eighteenth-Century Europe: Studies in the "Traité des trois imposteurs,"* International Archives of the History of Ideas 148 (Dordrecht: Kluwer Academic Publishers, 1996), xv–xvi.
69. Lancelot Addison, *The First State of Mahumedism* (London: Printed for Will Crook, 1687), 120–121.
70. [Andreas Maurus] I. N., trans, *THE CONFUSION OF MUHAMED'S SECT, OR A Confutation of the Turkish ALCORAN. Being a Discovery of many secret Policies and practices in that Religion, not till now Revealed. Written Originally in Spanish by Johannes Andreas Maurus, who was one of their Bishops and afterwards turned Christian. Translated into English by I. N.* (London: Printed for h. Blunden, at the Castle in Cornhill, 1652). Apparently the passage that caused Addison such blushing is this: "The said Pages shall come, every one with a dish in his hand, and in the dish a Citron, and shall give to every male of the *Moores*, and as soon as the *Moores* shall smell to this Citron, one of the aforesaid Virgins shall issue out of it, most gallantly attired and beautifull, and shall embrace the *Moore*, and the *Moore* her, and so they shall continue in that Act of embracing each other the space of fifty years, without rising or separating from each others body, taking all manner of pleasure that a man can have with a woman" (162–163).
71. Maurus, *CONFUSION*, 159.

72. [Alexander Ross], *The Alcoran of Mahomet, Translated out of Arabick into French BY THE Sieur du Ryer, Lord of Malezair, and Resident for the French King, at ALEXANDRIA. And Newly Englished, for the satisfaction of all that desire to look into the Turkish Vanities* (London: Printed, and are to be sold by Randal Taylor, near Stationers Hall, 1688), chap. 75 ("The Chapter of the Resurrection"), 477.
73. Ros Ballaster, *Fabulous Orients: Fictions of the East in England, 1662–1785* (2005; repr., Oxford: Oxford University Press, 2007), 153.
74. Montesquieu, Charles de Secondat, Letter 141, in *Persian Letters*, trans. with an introduction by C. J. Betts, Penguin Classics (1973; repr., London: Penguin Books, 2004), 247–254.
75. [Giovanni Paolo Marana], *Letters Writ by a Turkish Spy, Who lived Five and forty Years, Undiscovered, at PARIS: Giving an Impartial Account to the Divan at Constantinople, of the most Remarkable Transactions of Europe; And discovering several Intrigues and Secrets of the Christian Courts, (especially that of France) from the Year 1637, to the Year 1682. Written Originally in Arabick, first Translated into Italian, afterwards into French, and now into English* (London: Printed by J. Leake, and are to be sold by Henry Rhodes, next door to the Swan-Tavern, in Fleet-street, 1687).
76. [Giovanni Paolo Marana?], *The Third Volume of Letters Writ by a Turkish Spy, Who lived Five and forty Years, Undiscovered, at PARIS: Giving an Impartial Account to the Divan at Constantinople, of the most Remarkable Transactions of Europe; And discovering several Intrigues and Secrets of the Christian Courts, (especially that of France) continued from the Year 1645, to the Year 1682. Written Originally in Arabick, Translated into Italian, and from thence into English by the Translator of the First Volume* (London: Printed by J. Leake, for Henry Rhodes, near Bride lane, in Fleet street, 1691), 26, 47.
77. For Pococke's influence on writers as diverse as Grotius, Stubbe, and Prideaux, see Justin J. Meggitt, *Early Quakers and Islam: Slavery, Apocalyptic and Christian-Muslim Encounters in the Seventeenth Century*, Studies on Inter-religious Relations 59 (Uppsala: Swedish Science Press, 2013), 35. Matar also shows that the translation by Pococke's son, Edward Pococke the younger, of the Islamic-Aristotelian allegory *Hayy Ibn Yaqzan* appealed both to advocates of "rational religion" and to Quakers like George Keith and Robert Barclay, "the architect of Quaker theology." Matar, *Islam in Britain*, 99–100. Keith passed an English translation to Henry More, who mentioned it to Anne Conway. Matar, *Islam in Britain*, 100. See also Bernadette Andrea, "Early Quaker Women, the Missionary Position, and Mediterraneanism," chap. 3 in *Women and Islam in Early Modern English Literature* (Cambridge: Cambridge University Press, 2007), 53–77.
78. Meggitt, *Early Quakers and Islam*, 33; Matar, *Islam in Britain*, 103; Holt, "Treatment of Arab History," 292.
79. Holt, "Treatment of Arab History," 291.
80. Humphrey Prideaux, *The True Nature of Imposture Fully Display'd in the Life of Mahomet with A Discourse annexed, for the Vindicating of Christianity from this Charge; Offered to the Consideration of the Deists of the present Age*, 2nd ed. corrected (London: Printed for William Rogers, at the Sun against St. Dunsten's Church in Fleetstreet, 1697), iv. Because the different sections of the work—prefatory letter, "Life of Mahomet," and "Letter to the Deists"—are not paginated continuously, I cite the prefatory letter as *True Nature* and specify "Life of Mahomet" or "Letter to the Deists" for all other quotations.
81. Sir Paul Rycaut, who issued a continuation of Knolles's *Historie* (completed in 1700), and published several of his own works on the Ottoman Empire, declared of Muslim women that they have "no principles of virtue of moral honesty or Religion, *as to a future state* relating to the rewards or punishments of their good or bad actions." Sir Paul Rycaut, *The present state of the Ottoman Empire* (London: Printed for John Starkey and Henry Brome,

1668), bk. 2, chap. 21 ("Of Marriages and Divorces, and how far Concubinage is indulged amongst the Turks"), 153 (my emphasis). Lady Mary Wortley Montagu thought not only that Rycaut was "commonly" mistaken but also that he was politically motivated. In a May 1718 letter, she scoffed, "The Armenians have no notion of transubstantiation, whatever account Sir Paul Rycaut gives them (which account I am apt to believe was designed to compliment our court in 1679), and they have a great horror for those amongst them that change to the Roman Religion." Lady Mary Wortley Montagu, *The Complete Letters of Lady Mary Wortley Montagu*, ed. Robert Halsband, 3 vols. (Oxford: Clarendon Press, 1965), 1:318, 411.

82. Prideaux, *True Nature*, viii, ix; xi.
83. Chew, *Crescent and the Rose*, 111.
84. Prideaux, *True Nature*, xi.
85. Cemil Aydin, *The Idea of the Muslim World: A Global Intellectual History* (Cambridge, Mass.: Harvard University Press, 2017), 29–31.
86. Prideaux, *True Nature*, xiv.
87. Reid Barbour, *John Selden: Measures of the Holy Commonwealth in Seventeenth-Century England* (Toronto: University of Toronto Press, 2003), 373. Echellensis also responded to Selden's use of Eutychius "in support of the Puritan opposition to episcopacy." See Jan Loop, "Johann Heinrich Hottinger (1620–1667) and the 'Historia Orientalis,'" *Church History and Religious Culture* 88, no. 2 (2008): 170n2.
88. Jan Loop, *Johann Heinrich Hottinger: Arabic and Islamic Studies in the Seventeenth Century*, Oxford-Warburg Studies (Oxford: Oxford University Press, 2013), 208. In fact, in Loop, all of chapter 5, "Islam and the History of the Church: Writing Church History," is useful for understanding the imbrications of Islam in late seventeenth-century Trinitarian disputes.
89. Prideaux, *True Nature*, xix.
90. Prideaux, "Life of Mahomet," 7.
91. Prideaux, "Life of Mahomet," 13. Italics in the original.
92. Sarah Hutton, "Platonism and the Trinity: Anne Conway, Henry More and Christoph Sand," in Mulsow and Rohls, *Socinianism and Arminianism*, 209–224.
93. Loop, "Johann Heinrich Hottinger,'" 170.
94. Prideaux, "Life of Mahomet," 16.
95. Prideaux, "Letter to the Deists," 19.
96. Prideaux, "Life of Mahomet," 31, 27.
97. Meggitt, *Early Quakers and Islam*, 30.
98. Derek Hughes, "Dryden's *Don Sebastian* and the Literature of Heroism," *Yearbook of English Studies* 12 (1982): 72.
99. David Bywaters, *Dryden in Revolutionary England* (Berkeley: University of California Press, 1991), 39.
100. John Dryden, Thomas Shadwell, and John Crowne, "Notes and Observations on *The Empress of Morocco*" [1674], in *The Works of John Dryden*, vol. 17, *Prose 1668–1691*, ed. Samuel Holt Monk and A. E. Wallace Maurer (Berkeley: University of California Press, 1971), 83. For a discussion of the extent of Dryden's co-authorship and the scholarly disagreement surrounding it, see vol. 17, 391–393.
101. Dryden, Shadwell, and Crowne, "Notes and Observations," 102.
102. John Dryden, *Aureng-Zebe: A Tragedy*, in *The Works of John Dryden*, vol. 12, *Plays: "Amboyna," "The State of Innocence," "Aureng-Zebe,"* ed. Vinton A. Dearing (Berkeley: University of California Press, 1994), 5.1.239–240. References are to act, scene, and line. According to Dearing, "Although Shah Jahan's [the "old emperor of Dryden's play"] wars nearly bankrupted his empire, his was the great age of Islamic culture in India" (384).

He further notes that Dryden "seems to have depended on" François Bernier's *Histoire de la dernière Révolution des Etats du Grand Mogul* (1670; English translation 1671) and his *Suite des Mémoires* (1671; English translation 1672), though "in theory he could have constructed [the] play from other sources. . . . Also, as Dryden had served in the secretariat of Oliver Cromwell, he presumably had had access to unpublished information transmitted by the ambassadors" to the "court of the Great Mogul" (385).

103. Bywaters, *Dryden*, 33.
104. John Dryden, *Don Sebastian* [1689, published 1690], in *The Works of John Dryden*, vol. 15, *Plays: "Albion and Albanius," "Don Sebastian," "Amphytrion,"* ed. Earl Miner and George R. Guffey (Berkeley: University of California Press, 1976), 1.1.262–263.

2
MINDING THE GAP

THIS CHAPTER CHARTS THE IMPORTANCE of the female soul to several Englishwomen writers in the period 1660–1730. For Katherine Philips, Margaret Cavendish, Mary Astell, Elizabeth Singer Rowe, Penelope Aubin, and Jane Barker, the soul was a crucial way of thinking about the possibilities of female identity outside the bounds of marriage and the reproductive body. For them, the soul, associated with intelligence, was also a site of liberation. Yet while it would make sense for all of these women to reject Islam if they truly believed that misogynistic mortalism was Muslim doctrine, only the later writings of Rowe, Aubin, and Barker are characterized by hostility to Islam. This disjunction further suggests that misogynistic mortalism took an Islamophobic turn in the 1690s and that Rowe, Aubin, and Barker must have been informed by, if not explicitly responding to, the rhetoric that developed around the Trinitarian and related controversies. I first examine how women thought about their status and intelligence in light of the *querelle des femmes*, the philosophies of René Descartes and John Locke, seventeenth-century women's education arguments, and platonic imagery, before I turn to religious polemic and prose fiction.

•

Since the beginning of the *querelle des femmes*—the Renaissance debate on the status of women—women had used a demonized Islam as a benchmark of European domestic tyranny. In the text that marked the first sustained critique of misogyny by a European lay woman, Christine de Pizan's allegorical *The Book of the City of Ladies* (1405), the authorial persona questions Lady Rectitude about whether women really make marriage a hell for men as misogynistic satires maintain. Lady Rectitude responds by noting that Christine herself knows that "there are so many wives who lead a wretched existence bound in marriage to a brutish husband who makes them suffer greater penance than if they were enslaved by Saracens."[1] The military horrors of the Crusades and the growing fear of an Ottoman takeover of Europe are in the background here, as they are in Shakespeare's *Othello* (1604): when Othello condemns his own domestic tyranny in murdering his innocent wife, Desdemona, he likens himself to a Turk.[2] Yet there is no misogynistic mortalism in these texts. Rather, Englishwomen adopted the trope after the Trinitarian Controversy had reached its height in 1695. The alignment of Islam with the oppression of women and the denial of the Trinity enabled Englishwomen to displace their critiques of male authority onto a distant, demonized Islam. One of the main targets of these critiques was the long-held belief that women were less rational than men.

For instance, the philosopher Nicolas Malebranche (1638–1715) argued that "delicacy of the brain fibers is usually found in women, and this is what gives them great understanding of everything that strikes the senses . . . normally they are incapable of penetrating to truths that are slightly difficult to discover. Everything abstract is incomprehensible to them."[3] Women's biology—their delicate fibers, smaller bodies, and attachment to the senses—was their destiny. Biology was tied to one's identity in a social hierarchy that privileged some groups over others on the basis of sex or race. As Londa Schiebinger points out, in the early modern period "women and Africans were seen as sharing similar deficiencies when measured against a constant norm—the elite European man. Women and black males had narrow, childlike skulls; both were innately impulsive, emotional, and imitative."[4] The white male body was the universal ideal, capable of rationality, self-control, and, therefore, government of others. Women were portrayed as lacking the ability to think abstractly, to govern their appetites and emotions, or to exercise political authority.

Women responded by claiming that inadequate education, not nature, was responsible for their alleged irrationality and inferiority and that their souls were equal to those of men. Christine de Pizan, Marie de Gournay (friend and protégé of Montaigne), and Anna Maria van Schurman had argued that women needed greater access to education. Their arguments contributed to the *querelle des femmes* and to the seventeenth-century wave of literature that developed from the rise of *préciosité* and French salon culture. Siep Stuurman, whose scholarship focuses on the proto-feminist literature of François Poullain de La Barre (a Cartesian who claimed that the mind was not sexed), shows that arguments like Poullain's were—if not representative—at least not exceptional in the late seventeenth century. A robust tradition of proto-feminist literature (and an equally robust tradition of misogynist literature), written by both male and female authors in France, began to circulate in England, encouraged by the arrival of Henrietta Maria, queen consort of Charles I. Stuurman even argues that "by the beginning of the seventeenth century the *querelle* represented a well-established and familiar genre."[5] To talk about women's souls was, by 1660, to enter into a wide-ranging intellectual debate with most of western Europe as the stage. Not the least reason the matter of the soul was so fraught was the influence of Descartes's mind-body dualism and, later, Locke's querying of "species" and the ability of mankind to know whether matter could "think."

A "SPIRITUAL SUBSTANCE"?

The mind-body dualism of René Descartes (1595–1650) deeply influenced a number of the women whom Jacqueline Broad has termed the "women philosophers of the seventeenth century."[6] But that influence was not without complications. Broad has argued that for women such as Lady Damaris Masham; Anne, Viscountess Conway; Margaret Cavendish, Duchess of Newcastle; Mary Astell; and Catharine Trotter Cockburn, the limited educational opportunities afforded women meant that they often encountered Cartesian thought only in English translations. Since many of these translations were by men like Cambridge Platonists Ralph Cudworth (Lady Masham's father) and Henry More, who were suspicious of any "radical divide between spirit and matter," the women who read their translations were informed by a complicated reception of Anglicized Cartesianism.[7] Yet there was much that Cartesian mind-body dualism offered to women. Cartesianism centered reason unfettered by the frailties of the body and privileged individual thought free from the tyrannical authority of social custom. As Descartes declared, "My essence consists in this one thing: that I be a cogitating thing. And although I might perhaps . . . have a body . . . it is still certain that I am really and truly distinct from my body, and that I can exist without it.[8] Descartes wished to prove the existence of God and the immortality of the soul by rational means. The attempt called into question both the role of reason in spiritual matters and the nature and function of the soul. Both issues challenged philosophers of seventeenth- and eighteenth-century England, an England beginning to emerge as a modern political state. Central to new political ideas was the question of how the individual conscience ought to relate to religious and political authority. In short, how was human identity to be conceived?

Descartes's thought quickly filtered into English philosophic circles. He and philosophical fiction writer Margaret Cavendish, Duchess of Newcastle (1623–1673), both lived in Paris in the 1640s (Thomas Hobbes, too), and she later tackled some of his arguments in her *Philosophical Letters* (1664).[9] Cavendish's *The Description of a New World, Called the Blazing World* (1666) is in part a fictional response to the materialist arguments of the leading English and continental philosophers of her day. Cavendish figured women's souls as, in some sense, material, but she also identified women's souls with intelligence, companionship, and an escape from the constraints of the female body. Her engagement is representative of a proliferation of published interventions in intellectual debates by women writers of "long" eighteenth-century England. As a young woman, for instance, women's education advocate Mary Astell (1666–1731) initiated a spirited correspondence with John Norris (1657–1711), sometimes grouped with the Cambridge Platonists. Playwright Catharine Trotter Cockburn (1679–1749) ably defended philosopher John Locke (1632–1704) against charges of Socinianism. Lady Damaris Masham (1659–1708) defended Locke against Astell's criticism. The interventions in philosophical discourse of Cavendish, Astell, Cockburn, Lady Masham, and other women of the late seventeenth century refuted the historical conflation of women with appetite, emotion, and the material body while showing that, for women, questions of the soul were implicated in matters of not just intelligence but also intellectual community with men and with each other. Cartesian soul-body dualism enabled them to privilege their immaterial minds rather than the frail, vulnerable female body. A woman's ability to reason made her essentially equal, if not socially or legally equal, to men. An overview of women's uses of Cartesian dualism will explain their complicated understanding of both Locke's thought and Turkey (representing the Ottoman Empire).

"THEY ARE ALSO SHUT IN IN TURKEY"

François Poullain de La Barre's *On the Equality of the Two Sexes* (*De l'egalité des deux sexes*, 1673; the 1676 edition was translated into English as *The Woman as Good as the Man* by Nathaniel Brook in 1677) included several arguments that would circulate in the works of Mary Astell, poet Sarah Fyge Egerton, Eliza Haywood, Mary Wollstonecraft, and others.[10] Most importantly, he argued: there is no sex in souls (or that the mind has no sex; 82); women's and men's differences are physical, not intellectual (56); women's ignorance is a product of custom and bad education, not nature (61, 68, 109–111); and the presumed inferiority of women is an unexamined prejudice that would not withstand scrutiny (50, 55). The influence of Poullain's arguments, though the translated treatise was available in English after 1677, does not seem to have been readily acknowledged. He is not referred to by Astell, and there is no acknowledgment of any debt to him in the proto-feminist

"Sophia" pamphlets of 1739 and 1751 despite significant similarities to his arguments about intellect, custom, and the differences between humans and animals.[11] Poullain also published two subsequent treatises: *On the Education of Ladies* (1674; intended as "a manifesto for the feminine *cogito*"[12]) and *On the Excellence of Men: Against the Equality of Sexes* (1675). Despite the title, this last is a reaffirmation of his argument in *De l'egalité des deux sexes*. It is Poullain's comparison of women's similar experiences of oppression all over the globe with which the present argument is concerned.[13]

Poullain reasoned that women only *seem* to be inferior to men because that is how it has always been everywhere—not how it must be. He explained,

> No one reports ever having seen women in a different situation. We know, too, that this is how things always were, and that there is nowhere on earth where women are not treated as they are right here. There are even some places where women are treated like slaves. In China their feet are bound during childhood to stop them leaving the house, where they see virtually only their husbands and their children. They are also shut in in Turkey. They are not much better off in Italy. Almost all the peoples of Asia, Africa, and America treat their women the way we treat servants. (54–55)

What Poullain describes is the very localizing aspect of sexual identity that Wollstonecraft would later protest. Women all over the world are localized, rendered "much" the same everywhere, whether in China, Turkey, Italy, Africa, or the Americas.

Poullain also used the example of Turkey to argue that anyone, anywhere, could respond to a rational education. He sees that it is having "opportunity and external advantages" (68) that enable individuals to excel. Along those lines, he posits that though many people "imagine that Turks, barbarians, and savages do not have the same capacity as European peoples," if they were to see them having the "aptitude or title of Doctor," they would "admit that these people are men like ourselves, can do the same things, and, if they had the training, would be in no way inferior to us" (69). So, too, of women—if they were given these opportunities and advantages, they could be thought of "neither less favorably nor less rationally" (69). Poullain uses social groups traditionally considered intellectually inferior—barbarians, Turks, women—to make a Cartesian argument about the deleterious effects of cultural bias and the intellectual improvement available to anyone given a proper education. Unfortunately, while many women seem to have been influenced by his arguments about women's responsiveness to education, they did not take up his alignment of Turks and Englishwomen. A comparison of Mary

Astell's writing before the tipping point of 1696 and the work of her friend Lady Mary Chudleigh in the early eighteenth century demonstrates a marked Islamophobic shift in the arguments against misogynistic mortalism in the 1690s.

TAKING UP THE PARADOX

Mary Astell did not rely on Islamophobic misogynistic mortalism, and this is peculiar for two reasons. First, she relied on misogynistic mortalism; second, she used Islam as the "negative ideal" in her attacks on Roman Catholics and Socinians.[14] Why did Astell not resort to Islamophobic misogynistic mortalism in *A Serious Proposal to the Ladies*? The noticeable absence of it in Astell's educational work may have had something to do with her association with Lady Mary Wortley Montagu—Astell praised "Wortley" in her "Ode to Friendship" (ca. 1730) and wrote a preface in 1724 for Montagu's *Turkish Embassy Letters* (published posthumously in 1763). It perhaps indicates that the Islamophobic shift in misogynistic mortalism did indeed occur in or around 1696, after she wrote the first edition of *A Serious Proposal*. Or it might suggest that Astell, unlike other women writers, was actively opposed to a unified "British" identity and advocated a distinctly English one—her hostility to Scottish Presbyterianism would suggest this.[15] In any case, Astell is the exception that proves the rule: after 1696, advocacy of women's education usually included some reference to Islamophobic misogynistic mortalism.

Astell was a vigorous participant in the toleration debates of 1690–1710. But in her rousing defense of women's intellectual abilities, she threw down the gauntlet in perhaps the most succinct formulation of the importance of immortal souls to women of the long eighteenth century: "Let such therefore as deny us the improvement of our Intellectuals, either take up *his* Paradox, who said that Women have no Souls, which at a time when the most contend to have them allow'd to Brutes, wou'd be as unphilosophical as it is unmannerly, or else let them permit us to cultivate and improve them."[16] Astell elided the debate regarding the distinction between animal souls and (rational and immortal) human souls. Few philosophers equated animal souls with human souls. The very distinction between animal and human hinged on the possession of reason, which was the basis for Astell's argument in *A Serious Proposal* that women ought to have access to education. She continued to associate women's immortality with the necessity of educating women in *Some Reflections Upon Marriage* (1700), in which she declared that "the Aspirings of the Soul after true Glory are so much its Nature, that it seems to have forgot it self and to degenerate, if it can forbear; and perhaps the great Secret of Education lies in affecting the Soul with a lively sense of what is truly its Perfection, and exciting the most ardent Desires after it."[17] For Astell, given the dissatisfactions of mortal life, humans *must* be immortal, there *must* be something more to existence. Of course, while a more or less clear line was drawn between animal souls and human souls, the distinction between what an animal is and what a human is was not so clear. Astell was ignoring this distinction: few philosophers would have claimed women did not have souls; more than a few might, however, dispute that women have rational souls (or, at least, souls as rational as men's). The question, then, was whether women had the human faculty of reason, without which they could not be said to have an immortal soul. Astell, despite her elision of the debate on the spectrum of souls, specifically asserted women's possession of an *immortal* soul and therefore their ability to exercise reason. If women could exercise reason, then they should be educated rationally to know how to exercise it properly, since "the Will is blind, and cannot chuse but by the direction of the Understanding; or to speak more properly, since the Soul always Wills according as she Understands, so that if she Understands amiss, she Wills amiss."[18] Education is the cultivation of reason, which is the cultivation of the human soul, and, therefore, is the cultivation of one's immortal identity and eternal happiness.

Astell contrasts women's spiritual and rational dignity with those "things which if obtain'd are as flitting and fickle as that chance which is to dispose of them." She states that her aim is "to fix that beauty, to make it lasting and permanent, which nature with all the helps of art cannot secure, and to place it out of the reach of sickness and old age, by transferring it from a corruptible body to an immortal mind" (4). The concept of the rational, immortal soul opens to all women the passage to happiness based on personal merit rather than arbitrary attributes like attractiveness or wealth. Honoring the soul raises women above the vicissitudes of an uncertain world to an eternal happiness in immortal life. And since all bodies, male and female, are corruptible and vulnerable to the environment, cultivating a glorified and well-formed soul would actually be to cultivate an identity beyond the flux and peculiarities of sensory and gendered experience. All humans are equal before God. Astell believed in an infallible judge (He "who cannot err"; 4) who was merciful, unbiased, and able to see behind the masquerade of propriety to which women were encouraged to adhere. Astell's belief that women will be held morally accountable in eternity assured her that women's current education was woefully inadequate. Education was a moral duty.

For Astell, women are not naturally intellectually inferior but rather capable, if given the chance, of pursuing rigorous inquiry and intellectual discipline. Like Poullain, she rebutted the stereotype of women's lack of intellectual abilities with a trenchant argument for the role of education. Astell asserted that women's "incapacity, if there be any, is acquired not natural. . . . The cause therefore of the defects we labour under is, if not wholly, yet at least in the first place, to be ascribed to the mistakes of our education" (15–17). When Astell admonished women not to "quit the Substance for the Shadow, Reality for Appearance" (24), she explicitly and paradoxically identified the "soul" as "Substance" and the material body as "Shadow": only the soul endures, while the body passes away. To have a soul was the only way of distinguishing women from "ciphers" (15). Alluding to the biblical image of heaven, Astell demanded of women: "Why are you so preposterously humble, as not to contend for one of the highest Mansions in the Court of Heav'n? Believe me, Ladies, this is the only *Place* worth contending for" (8). Rather than focusing on external, physical beauty, women ought, according to Astell, to cultivate their true self, the immortal soul, "that particle of Divinity" that will endure when its "unsuitable and much inferiour Companion is mouldring into Dust" (7). Corporeal beauty and material existence are nothing compared to the "Substance" of the soul. The immaterial pleasures of the next life are the truest and highest pleasures for Astell.

After Poullain and Astell, arguments for women's education began to veer toward Islamophobic misogynistic mortalism. This is evident in the writing of Astell's friend Lady Mary Chudleigh, but some background on the occasion of Lady Chudleigh's writing will contextualize her characterization of Persian women. That background is a sermon on wifely obedience published by Dr. John Sprint in 1699.

"A *MEMENTO* TO HER OF HER ORIGINAL GUILT"

Originally delivered as a sermon on the theme of 1 Corinthians 7:34 ("But she that is Married, careth for the things of the World. And how she may please her Husband"), John Sprint's *The Bride-Woman's Counseller* (1699) caused such an outcry among "some ill-natur'd Females" that the author felt it necessary to "offer it to Publick View" as a print publication ("The Epistle to the Reader").[19] Moreover, Sprint doubled down on the offensive message of the original sermon in dismissing his critics as termagants: not "one Woman among all my Accusers" had a husband who would give her the character of "a dutiful and obedient Wife," he fumed. It is easy to see why women would have been angered by Sprint's conflation of domestic and political authority. He accuses disobedient wives of being "not only as Traitors to their Husbands, whose Authority they usurp, but as Rebels to the Great Monarch of the World, whose Sacred Laws they Impiously Violate" ("The Epistle to the Reader"). A woman might fairly question why, if men were able to displace their kings (as Englishmen had done in the recent past), women should be expected to equate husbandly with divine authority (or why that would work in a husband's favor any better than claiming divine right did for some of the Stuarts).

Sprint was bracingly forthright in the connection he saw between women's intellectual debility, their moral inferiority, and the justness of their subjection to their husbands. Women have "weaker Capacities to learn than Men, and therefore when they have a hard and difficult Lesson, and but weak Abilities to learn it, they had need of more Help and Assistance afforded them; and so it behoves us not only to tell them their Duty in Conjunction with their Husbands, but also to teach them singly and by themselves" (5; *sic*). Further, the "great End" of woman's creation "next the Glory of God" was that she should be "serviceable and helpful unto Man" (6; *sic*), an end Eve violated when she seduced her husband, Adam, to sin. This produced all men's surliness of temper, and if husbands are "hard" (7) on their wives, this is no reason to complain since it is no more than "a *Memento* to her of her Original Guilt . . . it should be a Motive of her greatest deligence" (7; *sic*).

This is all quite conventional misogyny. What distinguished Sprint's argument was his claim that Englishwomen ought to imitate "*Persian* Ladies," who "have the resemblance of a Foot worn on the top of their Coronets, in token that the height of their Glory, *Top-knot* and all, does stoop to their Husbands Feet" (12). This is how married women "in order to please their Husbands, ought to honour them" (12). Sprint is not the first person to link the supposed oppression of women in a Muslim context to the supposed liberties of Englishwomen, but his is an unusual case, at least in the 1690s, of using the increasingly outmoded language of political absolutism to try to legitimize the subjugation of married women. His argument links domestic absolutism in an English context with the subordination of women in a Muslim context. In turn, Lady Mary Chudleigh responded using arguments for women's education and intellectual equality related to the theories of Descartes and Locke.

Lady Chudleigh's *Ladies Defence* (1701) is a poem with four characters: the Parson (clearly a stand-in for Sprint); the despotic, atheistic husband Sir John Brute; the sympathetic libertine Sir William Loveall; and Lady Chudleigh's mouthpiece Melissa. Lady Chudleigh associates the atheist and the misogynistic parson, who want Englishwomen to be "like wise Eastern Slaves."[20] Interestingly, she does not associate the libertine Sir William with them, though the libertine association with the stereotypical despotic Muslim male would become conventional. Lady Chudleigh's exclusion of the libertine from association with the misogynists might be due to the fact that her critique of the pompous clergyman repeatedly echoes the dialogue between Lord Rochester's poetic speaker and the "formal band and beard" of "A Satyr Against Reason and Mankind."

Melissa rejects both the Parson's notion that Englishwomen should follow the example of "*Persian* Ladies" and his advice that they

> . . . Chalk you out the way:
> They humbly on their Heads a Foot do wear,
> . . . .
> Wou'd the good Custom were in fashion here. (11)

Melissa argues instead that it is as ridiculous to expect wives' absolute subjection to husbands as it would be for English husbands to return to the "antiquated Doctrine" of political passive obedience (3). While not Islamophobic, Lady Chudleigh's argument maps the binary of Persian ladies (or, rather, Sprint's characterization of them—she suggests that the account was perhaps fabricated) and English ladies onto a line of temporal progression such that the example of Sprint's Persian ladies is as outmoded as England's political past of divine right absolutism. England's political progress is thus logically associated with Englishwomen's liberation from domestic absolutism. By this line of reasoning, Lady Chudleigh's views on patriarchal authority dovetailed with those of Locke, who saw the ability to reason as crucial to adult participation in civil society.

"THIS STRANGE KIND OF DOMINEERING PHANTOM, CALLED THE FATHERHOOD"

In *Two Treatises of Government* (1690), Locke decimated Sir Robert Filmer's argument that absolute monarchy derives from Adam's paternal power by demonstrating that paternal and political power are not one and the same.[21] Interestingly, Locke makes his case in part by pointing out that if monarchical power is of the same nature as paternal power, it could hardly be absolute: mothers also enjoy power over their children, and that power is also divinely ordained. Locke insists that rationality, not blind obedience to a king, is necessary to be a lawful citizen. But he insists that reason is acquired over time, not present at birth: "We are born Free, as we are born Rational; not that we have actually the Exercise of either: Age that brings one, brings with it the other too. And thus we see how natural Freedom and Subjection to Parents may consist together" (*Second Treatise*, § 61). Subjection is dependent on context and is *temporary* for beings capable of reason. Subjection to parents (distinguished from respect and honor, which ought always to be practiced) lasts only until the acquisition and mature development of reason.

Locke supported his revision of political and paternal power by emphasizing the responsibilities of parents to children; in other words, the *mutual* obligations that ruler and ruled owe to each other. While children owe obedience (when dependent) and honor to their parents, they also have the right "not only to a bare Subsistance but to the conveniences and comforts of Life, as far as the conditions of their Parents can afford it" (*First Treatise*, § 89). In a family there is no essential superiority of parents to children, but rather a human community connected by interlocking rights and duties in which tenderness and gratitude motivate behavior. For Locke, this is so because "Man has a *Natural Freedom* . . . till the manifest appointment of God, who is *Lord over all, Blessed for ever*, can be produced to shew any particular Persons Supremacy, or a Mans own consent subjects him to a Superior" (*First Treatise*, § 67). For Locke, figures of legitimate authority are cognizant of the needs, rights, and natural freedom of the individuals under their aegis. The only power that is absolute is God's, and man, without divine revelation, has limited access to God's intentions. Reason directed by concern for communal welfare must guide man, whether he is in a position to govern or to be governed.

Locke importantly separated political and paternal power, but in his work they remain analogous in a significant respect. Just as a family ought to satisfy the basic needs of all members, Locke argues that, on the state level, "*Salus Populi Suprema Lex* [the welfare of the populace is the supreme law] is certainly so just and fundamental a Rule, that he, who sincerely follows it, cannot dangerously err" (*Second Treatise*, § 158). Locke earlier dismissed Filmer's patriarchal argument as "this strange kind of domineering Phantom, called the Fatherhood" (*First Treatise*, § 6), and it is clear that Locke premises the legitimacy of rule, whether over consenting rational adults or over dependent, imperfectly rational children, not on the ability to dominate but, rather, on effective and benevolent provision for the community. Further, he does *not* include women in the list of people who can never attain reason. As Eve Tavor Bannet points out, women throughout the eighteenth century saw Locke's as a "window of opportunity" to assert women's potential for rational thought against the assumption of their innate inferiority.[22]

Yet the *Essay Concerning Human Understanding* also landed Locke in the middle of the Trinitarian Controversy. In the *Essay*, Locke used several terms to discuss immaterial entities: "self," "consciousness," "spirit," and "soul." He stated, "Our *Idea* of our Soul, as an immaterial Spirit, is of a Substance that thinks, and has a power of exciting Motion in Body, by Will, or Thought."[23] The movement from formal to concrete (material) understandings of terms like "substance" and "person" was crucial to the disagreements among Trinitarian and anti-Trinitarian

Christians in the second half of the seventeenth century.[24] Edward Stillingfleet, the influential Latitudinarian bishop of Worcester and author of *A Discourse in Vindication of the Doctrine of the Trinity* (1697) was central to the Trinitarian Controversy. He took issue with Locke's description of the relationship between immaterial identity and the ability to reason. A brief overview of Locke's epistemological theory will show why Stillingfleet found it so dangerous.

Locke's interest in immaterial identity was primarily an epistemological, not a spiritual, one, though he professes a belief in an immaterial aspect of human identity: "Whilst I know, by seeing or hearing, etc. that there is some Corporeal Being without me, the Object of that sensation, I do more certainly know, that there is some Spiritual Being within me, that sees and hears. This I must be convinced cannot be the action of bare insensible matter; nor ever could be without an immaterial Being" (*Essay*, 2, 23, § 15). In Locke's formulation, this immaterial being capable of self-knowledge is not primarily the soul, but consciousness, "For since consciousness always accompanies thinking, and 'tis that, that makes everyone to be, what he calls *self*; and thereby distinguishes himself from all other thinking things, in this alone consists *personal Identity*" (2, 27, § 9; italics in the original). Moreover, the self must be conscious of itself through time: "Any Substance vitally united to the present thinking Being . . . by a consciousness of former Actions makes also a part of the *same self*, which is the same both then and now" (2, 27, § 25; italics in the original). As A. D Lindsay has pointed out, Locke was delivering one of the most devastating blows to Descartes's *cogito*: thinking entails a recognizable self only if the thinking self always remains the same; to do so the self must have memory, but memory, according to Descartes, gives us probability, not knowledge.[25] Locke argued that sensory information and reflection are our only sources of information and that, while primary qualities exist objectively, secondary qualities like color are a perception in the mind.[26] Human knowledge is unavoidably limited, as is human authority.

Only God knows the nature and fate of the individual human "soul." Neither human bodies as substances nor any immaterial aspect of the human being is enough to guarantee identity, which is the product of consciousness invested with memory. As Locke sees it, "'Tis plain consciousness, as far as ever it can be extended, should it be to Ages past, unites Existences and Actions, very remote in time, into the same Person, as well as it does the Existence and Actions of the immediately preceding moment: So that whatever has the consciousness of present and past Actions, is the same Person to whom they both belong" (*Essay*, 2, 27, § 16). Identity is bound up in consciousness, which is itself informed by memory, sensory experience, and embodiment. Only in a body can we have sensory experiences, but this does not mean we need the *same* body at different times to remain the same person. Rather, we need *a* body and consciousness sustained by memory. Locke did not dismiss the soul, he insisted on the limits of human knowledge about it.

The "defenders of immaterialism" denounced Locke for what they took to be the implications of his position in what came to be known as the "thinking matter" debate.[27] Locke believed that uncertainty about the soul's immateriality need not interfere with spiritual endeavors: "We have the Ideas of *Matter* and *Thinking*, but possibly shall never be able to know, whether any mere material Being thinks, or no. . . . All the great Ends of Morality and Religion, are well enough secured, without philosophical Proofs of the Soul's Immateriality" (*Essay*, 4, 3, § 6). For Locke, spiritual certainty belongs to God, not man. Man is not upholding religion's "great ends" by insisting that he possesses an impossible degree of certainty; he is, rather, falsely claiming to have godlike omniscience. Men can barely agree about the terms they use in philosophical discourse: even "substance" is a term, Locke later points out, that no one can precisely define. It is ideological bias, not pious reflection, to claim a certainty that is beyond any human capacity to acquire.

Stillingfleet, however, feared that if the soul were not immaterial, neither might it be immortal. As Roger G. Walker notes, for Stillingfleet and for many Anglicans, the "immateriality—and hence immortality—of the soul was . . . a major support of the entire Christian moral scheme."[28] Stillingfleet argued that if the concept of "thinking substance" were to be accepted, "then for all that we can know by our Ideas of *Matter* and *Thinking*; Matter may have a Power of Thinking: and if this hold, then it is impossible to prove a Spiritual Substance in us, from *the Idea of Thinking*: For how can we be assured by our *Ideas*, that God hath not given such a Power of Thinking, to Matter so disposed as our Bodies are?"[29] If substance could think, then intellectual functioning could not be used as proof that part of the human person is immaterial and therefore immortal.

But Locke did not deny the possibility of immortality. Rather, he believed that all rational creatures would be held directly responsible to their Maker in eternity. Discussing the fate of changelings, creatures that "may be supposed something between Man and Beast," Locke states, "he [God] hath made known to all those, who are capable of Instruction, Discourse, and Reasoning, that they shall come to an account, and receive according to what they have done in this Body" (*Essay*, 4, 4, § 14). He went further, curtly addressing the notion that physical attributes indicate rationality by wishing to know "what are those precise Lineaments, which according to this Hypothesis, are, or are not capable of a rational Soul to be joined to them"? (*Essay*, 4, 4, § 16).

John W. Yolton points out that, due to the "thinking matter" controversy, Locke was accused of being a "'Socinian,' 'deist,' even atheist.'"[30] Locke's opponents also associated him with Islam and, specifically, with the stereotype of the lustful Muslim despot. One critic, John Edwards, author of *Socinianism Unmasked* and *The Socinian Creed*, accused Locke (in a passage that was removed before publication) of being "governor of the seraglio at Oates," a reference to the estate of Locke's friend Lady Damaris Masham, where Locke lived for the last ten years of his life.[31] Locke's threateningly unorthodox position on thinking matter was maligned by comparing him to a Muslim despot in an English harem. The insult tacitly includes Lady Masham as a sexually available member of a sultan's harem. But the insult to Lady Masham is underpinned by the implication that she has willfully subverted English masculinity by turning her husband's estate into a harem for a supposed materialist.

In this contentious but shared discourse of who should be included and who should be excluded, the concept of a Great Britain united by the shared "other" of Islam gradually emerged. Considered chronologically, the women discussed in this chapter show varying levels of wariness regarding complications of English identity. Katherine Philips grudgingly accepted the geographic unity of England and Wales, civilized by the Roman Empire (and, later, by the return of the Stuarts); Margaret Cavendish displaced Restoration England onto the fantastical world of ESFI (James I styled himself the monarch of England, Scotland, France, and Ireland); Mary Astell envisioned a global Anglicanism that could welcome converts from any nation. But in the work of Elizabeth Singer Rowe, Penelope Aubin, and Jane Barker, who lived during the reigns of two foreign kings (William III and George I), there is a much more explicit current of Islamophobia in articulating a vision of proto-British unity. These last three writers took very different positions on whether it was better to have a foreign or a Catholic monarch on the English throne—this is most obvious in the contrasting depictions of the Battle of the Boyne by Elizabeth Singer (Rowe) and Jane Barker. But all three, as writers of fiction, portrayed Muslim military leaders as a particular threat to women.

DENYING WOMEN THEIR PROPERTIES, SENSE, AND SOULS

Elizabeth Johnson, in her preface to a volume of poems by Elizabeth Singer (Rowe) published in 1696, praised the poet's intellectual activity by distinguishing her from "mere slaves, perfect Turkish wives, without properties, or sense, or souls," women who do not enjoy "the *Liberties of Free-born English Women*."[32] Speaking of Johnson's preface to Rowe's work, Norma Clarke observes that her "references to the constitution and liberties of the freeborn Englishwoman evoked the language of the Whig settlement of 1689."[33] My focus is women's use of the misogynistic mortalism trope, but the trope continued to be used by men even after Dryden's *Don Sebastian*. George Farquhar, for instance, used it to underscore the injustice of England's divorce laws in his popular play *The Beaux' Stratagem* (1707). Trapped in an unhappy marriage, Mrs. Sullen echoes Elizabeth Johnson's preface, commenting on the disparity between English pride and English law: "Were I born an humble Turk, where women have no soul nor property, there I must sit contented. But in England, a country whose women are its glory, must women be abused? where women rule, must women be enslaved? nay, cheated into slavery, mocked by a promise of comfortable society into a wilderness of solitude?"[34] Mrs. Sullen assumes that a Muslim woman would have no recourse within a miserable marriage. She finds herself, without recourse, trapped in a "wilderness of solitude" where she cannot "sit contented" because the "glory" of England really *ought* to have recourse in a case of virtual enslavement. Her domestic experience is radically estranged from the national rhetoric of English liberty.

Also in 1707, Delarivier Manley's *Almyna*—a play that is otherwise fairly sympathetic to Islam—presented misogynistic mortalism as Muslim doctrine.[35] Alhador explains to the Vizier that the Caliph Almanzor has the right

> To explain what in our holy Alcoran,
> Or dark or deep or difficult appears;
> Hence he expounds that frailer womankind
> Have mortal souls in common with the brutes.[36]

He insists that women's bestial souls deny them moral accountability as well as the pleasures of paradise:

> So are they born to die, to perish ever.
> Not to immortal life ordained as we,
> No blissful paradise, nor cursed Tree of Zacon;
> No fears of punishments, nor hopes of blessings;
> But of a piece they die and perish ever.

Like Dryden in *Don Sebastian*, Manley portrays misogynistic mortalism as a tenet of Muslim doctrine.

Yet a counter discourse to feminist orientalism arose almost from the start and extended through the writings of the playwrights of the 1695–96 theater season to those of Lady Mary Wortley Montagu.[37] In *Ibrahim* (1696), Manley's contemporary, Mary Pix, portrayed her heroine Morena as a Muslim woman who clearly believes in her immortal soul. As Cynthia Lowenthal has commented, Morena was "potentially a new kind of heroine: smart, courageous, and bold," and she uses "both rhetoric and action" to try to fend off the violently lascivious sultan of the play's title.[38] After being raped, Morena laments:

> My soul grows weary of its polluted cage
> And longs to wing the upper air where
> Uncorrupted pureness dwells.[39]

She invokes the "Holy prophet," wondering whether it is a sin to "heave these Bleeding hands to thee . . . for justice?" (325). As she dies, she tells her beloved Amurat:

> Let thy kind breath
> Proceed; waft me from one paradise
> To another! (340)

While Morena certainly uses Roman examples to theorize her own model of heroic virtue, there is no misogynistic mortalism here.

In 1696, then, there were non-orientalist versions of Muslim women written by English women. While *Intelligent Souls?* surveys the rise of feminist orientalism from Elizabeth Johnson's preface in 1696 to Mary Wollstonecraft's *A Vindication of the Rights of Woman* in 1792, it is important to keep this counter discourse in mind. Feminist orientalism was not a foregone conclusion in women's writing. Further, the cases of seventeenth-century writers Katherine Philips and Margaret Cavendish demonstrate that cultural difference could be negotiated without recourse to misogynistic mortalism.

In some ways, Philips and Cavendish could not have been more different—where Philips cultivated a reputation for rural retirement and platonic friendship, Cavendish ambitiously claimed creative power for her heroines and herself. Yet both relied on the notion of platonic souls to articulate their belief in women's intelligence. Philips, particularly, was an exemplary influence on prose fiction writers Rowe, Aubin, and Barker. Active between 1690 and 1730, these women wrote poetry and prose fiction that negotiated national identity in a period that saw the death of two queens (Mary II and Anne I, the last of the Stuart monarchs) and the ascent of two non-English kings (William III and George I) to the English throne. These three writers used Christian identities to recast English national identity as extending beyond the geographic boundaries of the nation. I begin with Philips, the "matchless Orinda" who set the bar for how women could enter the grim world of publishing while still maintaining their reputations as women of virtue.

KATHERINE PHILIPS: "I HAD THOUGHT A ROCK AND A MOUNTAIN MIGHT HAVE HIDDEN ME"

Both Katherine Philips and Margaret Cavendish were deeply influenced by the tradition of platonic love imported into England by Charles I's consort Henrietta Maria. The idealization of women in romance and the ameliorative potential of utopian literature were both congenial to the "fashions of *préciosité* and Platonic love"—developed in the salons of France and appealingly fictionalized in Honoré d'Urfé's influential romance *L'Astrée* (1607–27). Henrietta Maria brought these continental influences to the Caroline court upon her marriage to Charles I in 1625.[40]

Even for Englishwomen who did not necessarily share Henrietta Maria's French, Catholic cultural sympathies, the queen consort was important as a woman at the center of English court life who was supportive of a literary genre that celebrated female exemplarity. She was influenced by the teaching of St. François de Sales's *Introduction à la vie dévote* and the valorization of heroic female resistance to a corrupt world as propounded by her confessor, Pierre de Bérulle.[41] Her influence can be seen in the poetry of Katherine Philips. Philips, widely known as the "matchless Orinda," influenced later women writers who sought to establish the legitimacy of their literary voice on the exemplarity of their virtue. Her influence extended to writers as various as Barker, Astell, and Rowe, all of whom in turn influenced the development of the eighteenth-century novel (most noticeably on Samuel Richardson's psychological novels of distressed and virtuous heroines).

Fluent in French and Italian and well-read in European literature, Philips translated French plays (Pierre Corneille's *Pompée* and *Horace*) and wrote neoplatonic poetry. She moved to Wales when her mother remarried, and after marrying James Philips, who was a member of Parliament during the Commonwealth, she settled in Cardigan Priory on the banks of the river Teifi. Upon the restoration of Charles II, Philips developed a reputation as a coterie writer, and she built friendships with royalists in the 1660s. Her professed desire for privacy was flouted when a pirated edition of her *Poems* appeared in 1664, and, as Paula Loscocco points out, her death soon after prevented her from responding to it "on her own professional terms." The posthumous 1667 edition of the *Poems* did Philips a disservice, too, in portraying her as "authorially timid, ideologically conservative, and regressively feminine."[42] But Philips clearly did have public ambitions. Her poems are addressed to, or are praises of, important figures of the 1660s, many of them women with royal or aristocratic connections like the Queen Mother (Henrietta Maria), the Duchess of York, the Queen of Bohemia, and the Countess of Carbury. She also wrote many poems to female friends (or former friends) such as

Lucasia (Anne Owen), Regina Collier (whom she called "the Queen of Inconstancy"), and Mary Awbrey.

Henrietta Maria's aesthetic interests and imagery also influenced Margaret Cavendish, who became her maid of honor in 1643 and went into exile with her during the Civil Wars. But there was a difference between Philips's reception and that of the idiosyncratic Duchess of Newcastle. Sophie Tomlinson has noted that while Philips and Cavendish shared "a charged relationship to theatricality and the idea of performance," it was only Philips who "was hailed by her contemporaries as an exemplary female author."[43] Nevertheless, Henrietta Maria's approval of Amazonian iconography of a powerful but beneficent queen was clearly a source for both Philips and Cavendish.

Philips and Cavendish were also acutely aware of the discursive power of invoking a woman's soul and how this way of conceptualizing identity as essential might help women to resist both bodily vulnerability and the conventional limitations imposed on women's mobility and intelligence. As a coterie writer, Philips wrote to and within a group of friends whose poetic personas evoked the characters and relationships of pastoral romances: Lucasia, Rosania, Poliarchus. This network of neoplatonic friendships, relationships that privileged the soul over the body, was often the pretext and theme of her poems. The soul, like text, gave Philips's poetic speakers the ability to communicate intelligence across distance. In "A Dialogue of Absence 'twixt Lucasia and Orinda," the friends lament that they must endure physical separation, but Lucasia assures Orinda that though their bodies may be divided for a time,

> Our Souls, without the help of Sense,
> By ways more noble and more free
> Can meet, and hold intelligence. (6–8)[44]

The beauties and ardor of female friendship transcend not only the limitations of sense, but even of corporeality itself. Orinda and Lucasia value their friendship because it is soulful—noble and free—and therefore communicative and relational as well as intellectually satisfying.

In an echo of her poem to Lucasia, Orinda again asserts to Mrs. M.A.,

> And thus we can no absence know,
> Nor shall we be confin'd;
> Our active Souls will daily go
> To learn each others mind.
> Nay, should we never meet to Sense,
> Our Souls would hold intelligence. (19–24)

Playing on the dual meanings of "intelligence"—spiritual connection and information—Philips portrays friendship among women not only as a means to transcend their corporeal limitations but also as a celestial experience of the afterlife. In "Friendship," Orinda again rejects the opinion of the "dull brutish World that know not Love," advising her friend that their "noble Flame" is "all the Heaven we have here below" (1–4).

Female friendship could also be a superior alternative to conjugal relationships, and Orinda asserts that the existence of the female soul and of female friendship both serve as rebuttals to denigrations of women's moral capacities. She explains in the poem "A Friend" that friendship is

> Nobler then Kindred or then Marriage-band,
> Because more free; Wedlock-felicity
> It self doth onely by this Union stand,
> And turns to Friendship or to Misery. (13–16; *sic*)

And she continues, sounding very much like Poullain,

> If Souls no Sexes have, for Men to exclude
> Women from Friendship's vast capacity,
> Is a Design injurious or rude,
> Onely maintain'd by partial tyranny. (19–22)

Philips's anxiety about the possibility of patriarchal tyranny in marriage is evident, but she does not rely on misogynistic mortalism to reinforce her point; nor does she demonize Islam. Friendship between husband and wife is possible, but not guaranteed.[45] The disparity of authority in marriage becomes painfully clear when—lacking the shared identity of friendship—marriage becomes not a union of souls but a tyranny of man over wife.

In her letters Philips also characterized urban society as a kind of tyranny. Yet she relied on the country-city trope (mapped onto a Wales-England binary), not the imagined geography of the Ottoman Empire, to criticize life in London. For Philips, the rocks and Cambrian mountain range surrounding Cardigan Priory provided her with what she had imagined to be an intellectual *hortus conclusus* that secluded and protected her from city life. Isolated by the Cambrians, Philips portrayed herself as a woman only reluctantly drawn into the world of London publishing. As she says in a letter excerpted in the anonymous preface of the posthumously published 1667 edition of *Poems*, "I had thought a Rock and a Mountain might have hidden me, and that it had been free for all to spend their Solitude in what Resveries they please, and that our Rivers (thought they are babbling) would not have betray'd the follies of impertinent thoughts upon their Banks; but 'tis only I who am that unfortunate person that cannot so much as think in private, that must have my imaginations rifled and exposed to play the Mountebanks, and dance upon the Ropes to entertain all the rabble."[46] Instead of the virginal fountain of the *hortus conclusus*, symbolic of the personal integrity Philips claims for herself, the "babbling" river Teifi treacherously steals away her intellectual offspring to the cruel waves of St. George's Channel and the coastline that Wales and England share. Like a latter-day infant Moses, her poems have been floated by the currents of the Atlantic and the Thames to London, the urban abode of mountebanks, rabble, wits, and the poetically obtuse. Philips draws on the conventional country-city binary of the pastoral, but her reference to the riverine-oceanic trade route between Cardigan and London, the Teifi and the Thames, suggests that, whether she liked it or not, she saw the two nations as intimately connected. Further, she saw the intellectual freedom enabled by her pristine Welsh seclusion as "betray'd," "rifled and exposed" for the entertainment of the capriciously despotic London "rabble." Philips did not need to displace her anxieties onto an Eastern other. Her example shows that it was entirely possible for a seventeenth-century Englishwoman, one particularly interested in the relationship between women's souls and their intelligence, to critique domestic tyranny—in the home or nation—without demonizing Islam.

The encomiastic textual apparatus of the 1667 edition of Philips's *Poems* emphasized both her example of what a woman's soul could do and her poetic unification of Wales and England. Abraham Cowley and the anonymous "Philo-Philippa" both lauded her intellectually generative soul, substituting her mind for her body as the site of female reproduction. They also situated her work in an explicitly imperial triangulation between Wales, England-Rome, and France.

Cowley's "Upon Mrs. K. Philips her Poem" also extols Philips's ability to unite what was previously at variance, but he first attends to her anomalous appearance as a female exemplar who has canceled "great Apollo's Salick Law." Speaking for men, he mock laments, "We our old Title plead in vain: / Man may be Head, but Woman's now the Brain." He goes further with this inversion of the conventional alignment of men with intelligence and women with reproduction by turning Orinda into an intellectual farmer who has properly husbanded her fruitful intellectual powers:

> Women, as if the Body were the whole,
> Did that, and not the Soul,
> Transmit to their Posterity;
> If in it sometimes they conceiv'd,

> Th'abortive Issue never liv'd.
> 'Twere Shame and Pity, Orinda, if in thee
> A Spirit so rich, so noble, and so high,
> Shou'd unmanur'd or barren lie.
> But thou industriously hast sow'd and till'd
> The fair and fruitful Field:
> And 'tis a strange Increase that it doth yield. (Stanza 2)

Moving from this encomium on Orinda's georgic labor, Cowley turns to nation, empire, and military might, approvingly noting how, through her "Pen," just

> . . . as the Roman Victory
> Taught our rude Land Arts and Civility,
> At once she overcomes, enslaves, and betters Men.

Yet he also displaces military conquest onto the intellectual and gendered conquest he has envisioned throughout the poem: "But Rome with all her arts could ne're inspire / A Female Breast with such a fire." He hopes that Orinda's pen will teach women to prefer "Wit's mild Empire" to the "Arms" of the "Amazonian Train." Similarly, "Boadicia's angry Ghost" will now be able to "boast, / That Rome's o'recome at last by a Woman of her race." Cowley paradoxically aligns an Englishwoman's intellectual production, portrayed as an intimate georgic connection to the native soil of her brain, with the imperial, civilizing conquest of Britain by the Romans.

Philips herself portrays the Stuart family as the bedrock of British identity. But before turning to her own images of national union, it is worth examining another poem of praise in the front matter of the 1667 edition. The poem is written by "Philo-Philippa," who claims to be female and who combines a criticism of the misogynistic mortalism trope with a further assertion of Welsh-English unity. In "To the Excellent Orinda," Philo-Philippa applauds how Orinda has vindicated

> That Sex, which heretofore was not allow'd
> To understand more than a beast, or crowd;
> Of which Problems were made, whether or no
> Women had souls; but to be damn'd, if so.

Philo-Philippa's praise indicates the powerful association of women's souls and their intelligence, particularly as that intelligence was registered in literary excellence. Philips's poems and letters as well as Philo-Philippa's praise demonstrate that, while misogynistic mortalism was a concern of seventeenth-century Englishwomen, protesting it did not require the demonization of Islam. Margaret Cavendish's contemporaneous prose fiction *The Blazing World* (1666) suggests the same. Further, *The Blazing World* shows that cultural differences between the English and Ottomans could be registered without resorting to Islamophobia.

MARGARET CAVENDISH AND THE PLATONIC SERAGLIO

Margaret Cavendish, a royalist from a very different background to that of Philips, also used the capabilities of the soul to explore friendship between women.[47] Cavendish was a prolific writer, but probably her most famous fictional works are *Nature's Pictures* (1656) and her pathbreaking proto-novel *The Blazing World*, a remarkable combination of utopian travel narrative, philosophical inquiry, fantastical romance, heroic adventure, and authorial self-projection.[48] *The Blazing World* is a text that figures imagination in terms of female dominion.[49] In the epilogue, Cavendish instructs, "If any should like the world I have made, and be willing to be my subjects, they may imagine themselves such, and they are such, I mean, in their minds, fancies or imagination; but if they cannot endure to be subjects, they may create worlds of their own, and govern themselves as they please: but yet let them have a care, not to prove unjust usurpers, and to rob me of mine; for concerning the Philosophical World, I am Empress of it myself" (224–225). She addresses controversial issues of her day—political usurpation, female learning and authorship, the relationship between old and new learning—while asserting a woman's right to lead a public discussion of such matters. The novel integrates diegetic levels so that Cavendish becomes a character in her own work and even becomes a friend and scribe of her heroine, the Empress of the Blazing World.

The Empress is originally a young girl of beauty and virtue from the land of "ESFI." She is kidnapped and stranded, finding herself in a strange land in which she must familiarize herself with indigenous creatures and learn their language. When she reaches Paradise, the seat of the Emperor, she is able to address him ("by that time she had pretty well learned their language"; 132), and he, in amazement, makes her his empress and gives her absolute power over his subjects. Having the liberty and leisure to do as she pleases, the Empress commences learning about her new dominion.

She conducts a systematic analysis by examining experts in different fields, from "priests and statesmen" (134) to astronomers, chemists, orators, and logicians (different subjects are studied by different animal-human hybrids, so the chemists are ape-men, the mathematicians are spider-men, and so on). Having examined and refuted the pedantry of most of these intellectual authorities, she decides to take the matter of religious authority into her own hands.

The Empress has "an excellent gift of preaching" and determines to use it to instruct her subjects in "articles of faith" and "to convert them all to her own religion" (162–163). This is the single most important change the Empress makes in Paradise. Significantly, while preaching gives the Empress an opportunity for religious expression, intellectual exercise, spectacular display, and female community—she establishes "a congregation of women" (162)—she later regrets her innovation and returns Paradise to the unity that characterized the Emperor's rule. Under the Emperor there had been "but one sovereign, one religion, one law, and one language, so that all the world might be but as one united family, without divisions; nay, like God, and his blessed saints and angels" (201). Cavendish's is a monarchical, implicitly Christian, but cosmopolitan vision of human community.

Having reorganized her adopted world, the Empress turns her thoughts to her homeland and seeks out immaterial spirits to learn about the mystical means by which she can learn about her home. Her extended discussion with the immaterial spirits is a bit confused (spirits and souls are different, but both can be either material or immaterial, and immaterial entities require material vehicles to move, even though the spirits tell her that "vehicles . . . are but fancies, not real truths"; 174), but it does furnish her with the knowledge to find a spiritual scribe from her homeland with whom to communicate. The spirits recommend the soul of the Duchess of Newcastle, "a plain and rational writer" who will much better serve the Empress than "fine ingenious writers . . . so self-conceited, that they would scorn to be scribes to a woman" (181). The Duchess's soul is such a good match for that of the Empress that the two develop a platonic friendship very similar to that of Orinda and her coterie. At one point, the Empress is able to notice the Duchess's melancholy because "between dear friends there's no concealment, they being like several parts of one united body" (183). The Duchess and the Empress, living in parallel worlds, experience each other only as souls that can travel between the two worlds in vehicles "of the purest and finest sort of air, and of human shape; this purity and fineness was the cause that they could neither be seen nor heard by any human creature" (193). Their airy vehicles enable them to separate from others, or seek them out as they choose. To absent herself from the public duties of a monarch while her soul travels with the Duchess, the Empress instructs the immaterial spirits to find some spirit to animate her body. They are able to supply "such a one as shall so resemble your soul, that neither the Emperor, nor any of his subjects, although the most divine, shall know whether it be your soul or not" (190).

Astonishingly, *The Blazing World* seems to suggest that women's identities—that is, their individual souls apart from their reproductive bodies—are without value in the public realm because what makes them unique is not even registered by others. Neither intimate companions like husbands nor distant subjects nor religious authorities can see the individual, intellectual reality that platonic female friends can discern. The suggestion is consistent with the public misreadings of herself that the Empress encourages by means of her spectacular performances. Her success in the narrative seems to imply that if society judges women merely on appearances, then women should use their appearances instrumentally. Women's rational souls, their true identities, could wield power by using their bodies to manipulate society for its own good.

Significantly, Cavendish most directly considers the space of the seraglio when the women are traveling as disembodied souls. The platonic friendship between the Duchess and the Empress can include other souls, and when they visit the Duke of Newcastle the Duchess is so overcome with longing that her soul "left her aerial vehicle, and entered into her lord. The Empress's soul perceiving this, did the like: and then the Duke had three souls in one body; and had there been but some such souls more, the Duke would have been like the Grand Signior in his seraglio only it would have been a platonic seraglio" (194). Rather than an imagined seraglio of overbearing masculine sensuality and female subordination, the Duke's body becomes a congenial meeting place for three platonic friends whose sociable souls are unhindered by the constraints and capacities of embodiment. Indeed, in what could be seen as a riposte to the platonic tradition of homosocial intellectual pregnancy as the highest expression of love and friendship, it is the man who is intellectually pregnant by women rather than the women who are physically pregnant by a man. Further, there is no overt hostility to Islam in this passage, but it does rely on the contrast of Muslim bodily pleasures and Western intellectual pleasures laid out by Addison and Prideaux and taken up by later writers of the misogynistic mortalism tradition. Still, the pleasure of this platonic seraglio is the very absence of the bodily: souls cannot have sex, so jealousy is unnecessary. The Duchess realizes this upon seeing that the Duke's and Empress's souls "became enamoured of each other" and, becoming jealous, reminds herself that "no adultery could be committed amongst platonic lovers, and that Platonism was divine, as being derived from divine Plato" and so "cast forth of her mind that Idea of jealousy" (194–195). Freed from an embodiment ensconced in a public or institutional setting, women's souls could share delight and intellectual fulfillment with each other and with the souls of men.

Cavendish's ambitious intervention in the homosocial tradition of Western philosophy has a counterpart in her consideration of alternate political systems. When the Duchess and the Empress tour the world to examine different social organizations, they disagree about the relative power of the Grand Signior (the Ottoman sultan) and the monarch of the Duchess's land (Charles II of England). The Empress initially believes that of all the rulers of the world the Grand Signior seems to be "the greatest; for his word was law, and his power absolute . . . he has the command both over church and state, and none dares oppose him." The Duchess concedes this power, but argues that her monarch is "as powerful a monarch as the Grand-Signior; for though his dominions are not of so large extent, yet they are much stronger, his laws are easy and safe, and he governs so justly and wisely, that his subjects are the happiest people of all the nations or parts of that world" (191). Cavendish's characterization points to the distinction between the representations of Ottoman rule (large but unwieldy) and English rule (smaller but more vigorous because harmoniously structured) that was important for English national self-construction. Cavendish participates in the lengthy tradition of associating the Ottoman Empire with military power, absolutism, and sensuality. But she also acknowledges its political power and prestige and does so without relying on misogynistic mortalism. A number of prose fiction writers after Cavendish also struggled to articulate a conflicted proto-British identity vis-à-vis the threat of the Ottoman Empire.

MARY ASTELL: THE POLITICS OF PIETY

Like Philips and Cavendish, Mary Astell was concerned with the intellectual freedom of an all-female space. However, unlike Philips and Cavendish, Astell was an aggressive Anglican polemicist, and it is in her defenses of Anglican orthodoxy that she most directly represented her attitude to the global community. Astell, too, was caught up in the Trinitarian Controversy. While Lady Damaris Masham (daughter of Cambridge Platonist Ralph Cudworth) and playwright Catharine Trotter Cockburn defended John Locke, Astell aligned herself with English theologian-philosopher John Norris and René Descartes. Norris, who was loosely affiliated with the Cambridge Platonists, disagreed not only with Locke, whose work he considered to be atheistic, but also, later, with the nonjuring scholar and controversialist Henry Dodwell regarding the natural immortality of the soul.[50] He was thus part of the politicized tug-of-war between High Church and Latitudinarian Anglicans on the question of the soul's immateriality and, therefore, immortality. Astell's correspondence with Norris was published in 1695 as *Letters Concerning the Love of God*, while Lady Masham took issue with Norris in her *Discourse Concerning the Love of God* (1696). A brief survey of Astell's disagreement with Locke and Lady Masham's disagreement with Norris will show how women adopted and adapted the rhetoric of the Trinitarian Controversy.

In *The Christian Religion, As Profess'd by a Daughter of the Church of England* (1705), Astell defended the mysteries of the "National Church" against a variety of criticisms of Christian mysteries, but primarily that of Locke's *The Reasonableness of Christianity* (1695).[51] Astell argued that a survey of the entire globe—Spain, Italy, Geneva, Amsterdam, and Barbary—would nevertheless lead her directly back to the Church of England. The tenets of the "National Church" would have convinced her of its moral superiority even if she had not been born in England. Astell's round-the-world survey has intriguing implications. Astell is not known for her toleration of other religions; yet she seems to see moral identification with the Church of England as an option for anyone in the world. This means that while her model of patriotic identity leaves no room for religious toleration, it provides great latitude for accepting other differences. Like Cavendish, her vision is Christian (indeed, specifically Anglican) but cosmopolitan. Nevertheless, Astell leaves no latitude to accept Muslim beliefs. As she puts it in *The Christian Religion*, "Indeed, shou'd ever so many People tell me that the Alcoran is a Divine Revelation, and bring what they call evidence, the very reading of it wou'd convince me that they are mistaken. But sensible prejudices are the main hindrances of our obedience to the Gospel, in Countries where it is profess'd, no wonder then that a Religion accommodated even to the lees and dregs of Sense, obtains among too many Sensual Men" (22). Here Astell relies on the conventional alignment of Islam and sensuality: Muslim men are overly "Sensual," they are swayed by "sensible" (sensory) prejudices, and this is why their religion, in her view, privileges the "lees and dregs of Sense" rather than reason or self-governance. But Socinianism is her real target; Islam is collateral damage. She strongly suggests that the author of *The Reasonableness of Christianity* is a Socinian despite his protestation to the contrary (67) and she reinforces her tongue-in-cheek characterization of the weakness of his protest by showing his proximity to Islam: "Tho' he tells us *we must ascribe the* Mahometans *owning and professing of one GOD to that Light the Messiah brought into the World*; whereby we are left to believe if we please, That there is no difference between the Christian and Mahometan Belief of that Fundamental Article: Yet this notwithstanding, who can see into *his Heart*? Who can *charge him with Socinianism*, or say there is any thing in his *Book against the Religion contain'd in the Gospel*?" (69). For Astell, unswerving and absolute adherence to the doctrines of the Church of England is the only acceptable standard for English identity. Socinians should be no more tolerated than their fellow anti-Trinitarians, Muslims.

Yet Astell is an unusual figure in the history of feminist orientalism. For one thing, while she wrote *A Serious Proposal to the Ladies* (1694), one of the most famous defenses of female education, and in it relied heavily on the misogynistic mortalism trope, she did not rely on the Islamophobic version. This is particularly interesting given Astell's status as a vociferous anti-toleration polemicist for the

High Church Tories. Her polemical tracts, such as *A Fair Way with the Dissenters* (1704), show her to be vehemently opposed to Dissenters (whom she likens to the regicides of the Civil War).[52] She admits to wishing their "Total Destruction" (3). She was also hostile to pro-toleration opponents of the bill against Occasional Conformity and to Daniel Defoe as the author of *The Shortest-Way with the Dissenters* (1702). She repeatedly made fun of what she saw as Defoe's peculiar Dissenting vocabulary. Further, she associated Roman Catholicism and the Dissenters—"the Church of Rome, and that dearest Spawn of hers our English Dissenters"—by seeing them as intertwined arch opponents of the Church of England (14). Astell was an aggressive Tory polemicist, and yet she has been most identified with—and was in the eighteenth century most satirized for—her defense of intellectual retreat.

Astell's aggressiveness toward Locke and other advocates of toleration may partly explain why Lady Masham implicated Astell in her criticism of Norris. Astell was, and even today is, known as an advocate of women's intelligence. Yet Lady Masham begins her *Discourse* by juxtaposing adjectives like "Visionary," "Scholastick," and "abstruse" with "Intelligent Persons" and concludes by pointing out that religious retreats are just as well known for "licentiousness" as the world outside the cloister.[53] Lady Masham disagreed with the import of Norris and Astell's published correspondence. Norris, influenced by the French Roman Catholic philosopher Nicolas Malebranche, argued that humans should love God alone and that fellow creatures should not be an object of human love. Lady Masham, believing that sociable life provided the greatest scope for Christian charity, saw Norris's *Practical Discourses* as "built upon the Principles of Pere Malbranche [*sic*]" (A3v), and noted that "one of the Highest order of our Church" criticized its "extravagance" (A3). She dwells repeatedly on Malebranche's influence on Norris—quoting from him extensively in French and repeatedly emphasizing his status as a foreign Roman Catholic priest by referring to him as "Père"—in order to tar Norris with the brush of popery. Indeed, she argues that Norris's argument could encourage both the Romanists and the Dissenters (1).

Lady Masham embroiders this association between Norris, Malebranche, and popery throughout her *Discourse* and eventually portrays the Church of England as the middle way between all "Extreams": Roman Catholicism, Dissent, skepticism, and atheism (71, 126). For Lady Masham, influenced by Locke's sensory epistemology, to espouse "seeing all things in God," as Malebranche proposes, would actually lead to "Scepticism" (71) because it promoted an "Insensibility to Religion" (120). Further, the "wild" "Enthusiasm" this would encourage "can End in nothing but Monasteries, and Hermitages; with all those Sottish and Wicked Superstitions which have accompanied them where-ever they have been in use" (120). Lady Masham also takes aim at Cambridge Platonist Henry More by reading his "Religious Rant" (56) against the grain. In other words, in the fight between Lady Masham and Astell the stakes were those of the Trinitarian Controversy: they defended alternate sides of the controversy. Astell was on the side of High Church Anglicans, while Lady Masham defended Locke and the Latitudinarians with whom he was often associated by the High Church opponents of religious toleration.

I suspect there are two reasons that Astell did not rely on Islamophobic misogynistic mortalism. First, Astell wrote *A Serious Proposal to the Ladies* in 1694, just before the misogynistic mortalism tradition turned predominantly Islamophobic. Second, and most interesting, she had no interest in religious toleration, and, believing that any reasonable person, born anywhere in the world, would convert to Anglicanism if given the chance, she had no need to imagine what tolerating Muslims would look like. She was thus much more hostile to Dissenters—who had been given that chance and refused to convert—than she ever was to Muslims, who would, she believed, convert if given that chance. In this way Astell is, as in many other ways, unique among English women writers. Paradoxically, her utter lack of religious toleration made her more sympathetic to Muslims than those who wished to be more tolerant (to fellow Protestants) but only within reasonable bounds (at minimum a belief in the Christian Trinity). Obviously Astell's sympathy would most certainly have evaporated when confronted with actual Muslims who refused to convert, but the fact that she did *not* rely on Islamophobic misogynistic mortalism speaks to the anxieties of those who *did* rely on it and who *were* trying to theorize the limits of religious toleration among Protestant confessions. The women who wrote after Astell and who wished to establish common ground with men under the umbrella of British Trinitarian orthodoxy were much more explicit in their hostility to, and rejection of, Islam. This was the case even for women who were not themselves Anglican, like Elizabeth Singer (Rowe), who came from a Dissenting background. Islamophobic misogynistic mortalism was a way of establishing community between Christians (and men and women) who might otherwise disagree on important issues.

"THE LIMITS OF THIS HOLY FIRE": ELIZABETH SINGER ROWE'S MARRIAGE OF PLATONISM AND ISLAMOPHOBIA

Elizabeth Singer—for whose *Poems on Several Occasions* (1696) Elizabeth Johnson wrote one of the earliest articulations of Islamophobic misogynistic mortalism—would later marry (taking the surname of Rowe) and become a popular writer of didactic prose fiction. Rowe has met with varied critical fortunes. Most recently,

Paula R. Backscheider has staunchly defended her as a major contributor to the development of the English novel. As Backscheider shows, Rowe not only was "one of the most experimental religious poets of all time," but she also "firmly domesticated novelistic style and produced the ease of expression and appearance of naturalness that came to be so admired after midcentury."[54] Backscheider's intervention was necessary because Rowe's fiction, despite being extremely popular in the eighteenth century, gradually slid into the particular obscurity reserved for pious didactic fiction by women. John J. Richetti has addressed this strange trajectory of Rowe's epistolary *Friendship in Death* (1728) by noting that "one did not in the early eighteenth century speak in the abstract atmosphere of speculative controversy asserting the immortality of the soul." Rather, "it was . . . a highly emotional question, the answer to which put one on either side of a struggle.[55] While finding *Friendship in Death* a "deadening book, written in ecstatic and inflated prose and full of the most explicit and tedious moralizing," one that "reeks of what must be called morbidity about death," Richetti points out that the book's very popularity indicates to the modern reader something important about the values of the contemporary society in which it was written.[56]

Elizabeth Singer Rowe, like Katherine Philips, has been marginalized because of her later conservative literary persona.[57] Jennifer Richards explains that Rowe's "authorial persona is caught up in the complex rejection of Restoration libertine culture" at the turn of the eighteenth century even though "her heavenly effusions did not always quite fit with expectations of orthodox Christian expression."[58] Rowe's contemporary editor feared that her passionate verses could be seen as erotically charged and, therefore, not sufficiently pious. A concerted effort was thus needed to establish Rowe's reputation as a pious, retiring widow to distance her more mature productions from her earlier, passionate poetry, specifically the 1696 *Poems on Several Occasions*. Yet Rowe was also politically attuned, publishing many of her poems in John Dunton's *Athenian Mercury*, a pro-Whig, pro–William III weekly periodical. Rowe's poems include praises of William III's victory at the Battle of the Boyne, paraphrases of biblical passages, poems on mortality, and one titled "Platonick Love" in which Rowe unites passion to spiritual rapture:

> No stragling wish, or symptom of desire,
> Comes near the Limits of this holy fire;
> Yet 'tis intense and active, tho so fine;
> for all my pure immortal part is thine.[59]

Rowe, like Cavendish, associates women's incorporeal identity with platonism. Further, like some of the participants in the Trinitarian Controversy, she identifies platonism with the concept of an immortal soul. She concludes by joining human to divine love, justifying her love of a corporal human individual by situating it within a unified vision of divine goodness as the source of human beauty:

> Nor is the greatness of my Love to thee,
> A sacriledge unto the Deity,
> Can I th'enticing stream almost adore,
> And not respect its lovely fountain more? (2, stanza 4)

In "The Expostulation" she inveighs against the unity of body and soul, echoing Philips in her sense of the weight of the body as it impedes the intellectual liberty of the soul:

> How long shall these *uneasy chains* controul
> The willing flights of my impatient Soul?
> How long shall her *most pure intelligence*
> Be strain'd through an infectious screen of gross, corrupted sense?
> (12, stanza 1)

Rowe's poetic persona, Philomela, is not anti-body, but she does repeatedly evince profound frustration with the body's obscuring of what she feels is a connection between intellectual freedom and the immortal, immaterial soul.[60]

Though Rowe would distance herself from this volume of her youthful poetic productions, several of her themes—the causal connection between behavior in the temporal world and eternal destiny; the importance of self-denial, repentance, and reconciliation with God; the connection between women's intellectual and spiritual identity—resurface in her mature works of didactic prose fiction, including *Friendship in Death* (1728). Backscheider has argued that in *Letters Moral and Entertaining* (published in three volumes and often bound, starting in 1735, with *Friendship in Death*), Rowe's "constructs reinforce agreement and recognition of shared sensibilities far more often than they privilege persuasion. . . . Rowe's texts are . . . monologic and her purposes harmonizing."[61] This notion of a monologic coercion to interpellate a community of readers situates Rowe uneasily between Backscheider's valorization of her "domesticating" of narrative content and Margaret Anne Doody's argument that the English novel gradually became domesticated by excluding the foreign.[62] Rowe contributed both to the development of the novel and its exclusion of those who did not conform to her harmonizing purposes. Like the participants in the Trinitarian Controversy of the 1690s, female prose fiction writers in the 1720s articulated competing visions of national identity, national security, and who ought to be included and excluded. This competition had particular consequences for later generations of women writers. Rowe and Catharine Trotter Cockburn were, as members of what Susan Staves has called "the party of virtue," admired by Bluestockings such as Catherine Talbot and Elizabeth Carter.[63]

For Rowe, her concern with national security began in *Poems on Several Occasions* and continued into her prose fiction of the 1720s. In poems such as "A Pindarick Poem on Habbakuk," "The Athenians to the Compiler of the Pindarick now Recited," "A Poetical Question concerning the Jacobites, sent to the Athenians," "Upon King William's passing the Boyn, &c" and "A Pindarick, to the Athenian Society," the poet and her respondents establish Rowe as the muse of a British territory united under a militant and glorious William III. Rowe adapts the traditional Stuart royalist trope associating the just king with an agriculturally flourishing nation by envisioning William as the "theam" that enables her "Song" to "inchant" her friend and the mermaids in a pastoralized feminocentric river setting ("To Madam S——").[64] Like a latter-day Protestant Saint Patrick, William uses his sword to expel the vipers of Rowe's homeland while mystically entrancing women in a "gentle soft retreat" (*Poems*, 47).

In "A Pindarick Poem on Habbakuk" Rowe compares God's war with the heathens to William's struggle with his enemies: "So now, great God, wrapt in avenging Thunder, / Meet thine and William's Foes, and tread them groveling under" (*Poems*, 21). Over the course of succeeding poems these enemies are identified as the Jacobites. The reply in "The Athenians to the Compiler of the Pindarick now Recited" also politicizes her poems by describing them as sure to make the king's and nation's foes repent:

> How will thy Voice, how will thy Hand,
> Black Rebel-Legions to the Deep Command!
> Black Rebel-Legions murmuring take their flight,
> And sink away to conscious Shades of deverlasting Night:
> While those they left, amazed stand,
> And scarce believe themselves, themselves to find
> Cloath'd, calm, and in a better Mind. (23)

The expulsion of the legions will restore the rest of the subjects of "Great William" to themselves when removed from the satanic witchcraft of the Jacobites. Further, Rowe herself, as the poetess of "Thy God and King," will into a "wide Eternity be born" where "Chast Orinda's Soul shall meet" her (25). Thus, an eternal Anglican, nationalistic, feminine tradition of writing is established that begins with Philips (Orinda) and incorporates Rowe and later writers.

Rowe begins to play with the notion of Muslim otherness in *Poems*. In "A Pindarick, to the Athenian Society" she laments the vices of the age and rejects the "frantick world's imagin'd Joys" that render subjects "Unmanly, sensual and effeminate," using a gendered sensuality to contrast the worldly "Joys" with the "immortal flame" that the Athenians inspire (second part of *Poems*, 17–18). She also registers the gendered imbalance of men's mobility and women's decorum in "To a very Young Gentleman at a Dancing-School" in which the vain "Flammin" behaves like a "Sultan" in "our whole Seraglio's Eyes" (second part of *Poems*, 22). Flammin is not exactly threatening here, but his haughtiness underscores the difference between men's choice and women's enforced passivity. At the dance Flammin "gave his hand as carelessly as Chance," yet the lucky partner is absolutely "transported" and indeed is attended by a "Universal sigh" from the whole jealous "seraglio." Rowe continues this alignment of male sexual privilege and the stereotypical trappings of Ottoman culture in her later prose fiction *Friendship in Death*. It is in *Friendship* that she most explicitly articulates Islamophobic misogynistic mortalism.

A series of fictional letters ostensibly sent by spirits in the next world to friends still alive in the temporal world, *Friendship in Death* was intended, according to Rowe's preface, "to impress the Notion of the Soul's Immortality; without which, all Virtue and Religion, with their Temporal and Eternal good Consequences, must fall to the ground."[65] This statement again shows Rowe to be the bridge between the Trinitarian Controversy (and its concern with the relationship between immortality, Trinitarian Christianity, and the "Temporal" consequences of Anglican authority) and the later fiction of Samuel Johnson and Samuel Richardson. In Rowe's fiction the main concern was clearly to combat domestic religious infidelity, but the slippage between Rowe's criticism of freethinking libertinism and stereotypically Muslim pleasures is implicit. One letter writer in *Letters Moral and Entertaining*, a frivolous beauty named Laura, tells her friend Aurelia, "You have been too often of our party, not to know my brother is a very infidel: he has a sort of vanity in making me a proselyte, and freeing my mind from those prejudices (as he calls them) and superstitious notions, which govern a great part of the world; but as he finds me a little unwilling to resign my immortality he has furnished me with a system of transmigration, and the eternal wandring of the soul from one species of being to another" (226; *sic*). Ultimately, Laura is saved from this libertine education by the example of a "handsome hermit" whose physical attractiveness entices her to pay attention to his reading materials: *A Discourse of the Government of the Passions* and *A Treatise of the Immortality of the Soul* (236).

Friendship in Death explicitly focuses on the importance of moral education and the immortality of the soul, and it is no surprise that it contains a letter pertaining to Islamophobic misogynistic mortalism. In Letter 17, Ibrahim, a Turkish bassa beyond "the State of Mortality," implores Philocles, the man who converted him to Christianity while he was still living, to find the "beautiful *Grecian* Slave" whom he had seduced to Islam before his conversion. Ibrahim asks Philocles to convert her back to Christianity. Ibrahim's memory of the beautiful Grecian's conversion to Islam contributes to the stock seduction scene that will reappear throughout eighteenth-century fiction:

> I only attempted by gentle Methods to gain her Affections, but in vain; her *Christian* Belief still set the View of future Rewards and Punishments before her, and check'd her softest Inclinations. To conquer her Vertue, I was induc'd to pervert her to the Doctrines of the *Alchoran*. As absurdly as I reason'd, she was soon convinced that her Soul was as perishing as her Body, and that there was no Prospect of Immortality for any of her Sex; . . .'Tis this unspeakable Damage that I hope you will find some Method to repair. . . . Your *Charity* will redeem her Person, your *Example* her Mind, from a more deplorable Slavery." (61–62)

Through the figure of Philocles, whose actions even more than his precepts converted Ibrahim, Rowe suggests that living the Christian ideal furnishes others with life, liberty, and enlightenment. Implicitly, the beautiful Greek woman has not received a proper Christian education—her religious belief was not sufficiently intellectually bulwarked to defend her against the supposedly perverted doctrines of the Qur'an or against Ibrahim's absurd reasoning. In this scene—one of many throughout the century—it becomes clear that women's education has become implicated in the Trinitarian Controversy. Philocles's example—his cosmopolitan Christian moral authority—saves the souls of both non-Western men and Western women who do not have the intellectual infrastructure to do so for themselves. Ibrahim's letter—his acknowledgment of Philocles's moral and intellectual superiority—has the full force of intelligence from beyond the grave. This contribution to the popular genre of apparitional literature is also evident in the work of early novelists Penelope Aubin and Jane Barker, women writers committed to the vision of a moral nation.

Like Rowe, Aubin and Barker used the Mediterranean context to characterize exemplary European (Christian) behavior under pressure. Aubin and Barker are critical of Islam and associate it with sensuality and violence, but they do not rely on Islamophobic misogynistic mortalism at narrative junctures where they would be expected to do so. They do, however, repeat the model of converting Muslims through the exemplary behavior of a cosmopolitan European Christian. Their didacticism is a mixture of evangelism and exhortation to fellow Christians to repent their sins and to prefer the pleasures of spiritual nobility to the pleasures of the sensory and sensual. However, since the Trinitarian Controversy identified the former pleasures with Christianity and the latter pleasures with Islam, the fiction of Aubin and Barker contributes to the rise of feminist orientalism.

PENELOPE AUBIN AND GLOBALIZED CHRISTIAN EVANGELISM

Like Elizabeth Singer Rowe, Penelope Aubin has been the victim of the obscurity reserved for women writers with a reputation for pious didactic fiction. Yet even allowing for this trend, of the six authors covered in this chapter Aubin has received the least critical attention. Though Aubin has been included in studies of the development of the novel by leading eighteenth-century scholars such as Paula R. Backscheider, Margaret Anne Doody, John J. Richetti, and Jane Spencer, scholarship devoted to Aubin has been rare. Recent work by a handful of scholars signals a welcome reversal to Aubin's relative neglect.[66] My analysis will be suggestive rather than exhaustive, but it demonstrates the increasing currency Islamophobia had in women's articulation of the proper education for an Englishwoman.

Given her reputation for pious exemplary fiction directed to the youth of the English reading public, it is jarring to realize the scale of Aubin's capaciousness and how thoroughly she situated Great Britain on a global stage. Indeed, though our focuses are somewhat different, Edward J. Kozaczka's conclusion that Aubin writes "narratives of empire" is illuminating. According to Kozaczka, Aubin "narrativizes cosmopolitan and tropicopolitan figures, exploring the ways in which these figures embody and enact . . . queer critiques of nascent British imperialism."[67] While in this chapter I situate Aubin within the early eighteenth-century tradition of English women novelists who used Islam as a negative ideal, Kozaczka's point is a crucial one in that it points to the global dimensions of Aubin's concerns. Aubin was primarily concerned with the integrity of her own nation, but she understood that nation as a player on the global stage.

Aubin's attitude to other women writers was selective: in a prefatory letter included in volume 3 of the 1739 edition of her *Collection of Entertaining Histories and Novels* (the third volume contains her 1723 novel *The Life of Charlotta du Pont*), she explicitly distanced herself from the crowd of "other female Authors."[68] Her strategic isolation mirrors her concern to bulwark a virtuous English identity that threatened to dissipate under the influence of a king (George II) who preferred not to reside in England. Aubin needed to theorize a model of Great Britain that allowed for the willful absence of its king. No wonder that Aubin's novels "share some similarities with the travel narratives popular in the early eighteenth century" as well as providing Samuel Richardson with a "precedent" for his own marrying of the moral and the entertaining.[69] Like Rowe, Aubin was a bridge of pious fiction between the Trinitarian Controversy and the domestic fiction of the 1740s. The author of the preface to volume 1 of her collected works gives "Rules . . . for constituting a good Novel" (*Histories and Novels*, unpaginated) that, in their focus on probability, the need to make morality entertaining for the youth of both sexes, and the pleasures of variety, echo the preface to Richardson's first edition of *Pamela* (1740). Indeed, the author of Aubin's preface may very well have been Richardson.[70]

In any case, the author follows Aubin herself in distinguishing her work from those of contemporary amatory writers. The author approvingly notes her invocation of "Mrs. Rowe" as an instance of "that Affinity and Kindred of Souls, which will always make the Worthy find out one another" (*Histories and Novels*, vol. 1, unpaginated preface). As Chris Mounsey has shown, Aubin's "Mrs. Rowe" is probably the daughter of the Dean of Exeter rather than Elizabeth Singer Rowe.[71] Still, it was logical for the writer of the preface to make the association between Rowe and Aubin. Both women saw their fiction as a defense of immortality and, thus, a defense of Anglican orthodoxy against what they saw as the encroachments of freethinking, deism, Socinianism, and atheism. The appeal of Aubin's novels originated in her pious conclusion that "Religion is no Jest, Death and a future State certain"—her novels will "inspire in us" the "noble Sentiments" that are absent from "loose Writings which debauch the Mind" (*Histories and Novels*, vol. 1, unpaginated preface). Aubin coincided with Rowe in seeing immortality—the promise (or threat?) of moral accountability—as the surest bulwark of national morality.

Aubin explained further in the preface included in the third volume of *Histories and Novels* that she wrote to "encourage Virtue, and excite us to heroic Actions" at a time when the court "being removed to the other side of the Water, and beyond Sea, to take the Pleasures this Town and our dull Island cannot afford; the greater part of our Nobility and members of Parliament retired to Hanover and their Country Seats" (vi). She therefore believed that "something new and diverting would be welcome to the Town." Her critique of the court's behavior seems to address an anxiety about having a non-English king on the throne. She also informs the reader that her booksellers had "advised me to write rather more modishly, that is less like a Christian, and in a Style careless and loose, as the Custom of the present Age is to live. But I leave that to the other female Authors my Contemporaries, whose Lives and Writings have, I fear, too great a resemblance" (vi). In this context, Aubin's tales of a globalized Christian piety could be seen not only as a shaming of the king and of amatory fiction writers but also as a call to establish a morally renovated England. Like Knolles, Aubin used the Turks (often standing in, during the eighteenth century, for all Muslims) to call for greater unity among Christians—and Britons.

While Aubin associated Turks with wealth and lasciviousness, she also implicated Christians who preferred wealth to piety by pursuing the lucrative temptation of trade. She was critical of empire, associating it with avarice and luxury. She saw the Ottoman Empire as a bad moral influence because of its slave trade, but also because it generally dominated all trade in the Mediterranean. Aubin registers this domination by focusing some of her narratives on European men who journey to Ottoman locales in order to make money, imperiling themselves and their virtuous daughters and wives in the process. Aubin includes extended accounts of European entanglements with Ottomans in the Mediterranean throughout her fiction (for instance, in *The Life of Charlotta du Pont* [1723] and *The Adventures of the Count Albertus* [1728]). But one example will suffice to show how she juxtaposes Christian women's education to the sensual pleasures offered by stereotypically envisioned Muslim men.

The narrative drama of *The Strange Adventures of the Count de Vinevil and His Family* (1721) hinges on the convention of a bloodthirsty Turkish bassa (predictably named Mahomet) desiring Ardelisa, a beautiful European Christian. Mahomet's pursuit results in the death of Count de Vinevil (Ardelisa's father), long journeys and shipwrecks, the separation and eventual reunification of Ardelisa and her husband, Count de Longueville, and the threat of sexual force and the possibility of a Christian woman allowing herself to be debauched to Islam.[72] Immediately after their wedding but before their separation, Longueville warns Ardelisa, "If some dreadful chance prevents our meeting, remember both your duty to yourself and me. Permit not a vile infidel to dishonor you, resist to death, and let me not be so completely cursed to hear you live and are debauched" (121). Longueville's is a shocking prioritization of values, but nothing in the story censures his view. Significantly, though, Ardelisa's father premised her virtue on her education rather than on her marital status. When Mahomet demanded that Vinevil sacrifice his daughter's virginity to save his life, Vinevil declares, "No, Villain! Ardelisa never shall be thine. . . . Life is a trifle weighed with infamy; the God I serve shall both preserve her virtue and revenge my death. My daughter is not educated so and will, I know, prefer a noble death to such dishonor" (123). Vinevil ignores her marital status (perhaps because Mahomet is ignorant of it), so his argument implicitly depends on viewing Christian education as the source of female integrity.

The narrative later juxtaposes the sexually untainted Ardelisa and her sexually suspect friend, Violetta. Captured by the "vile infidel" Osmin, Violetta bore him a son, who later died. Comparing her situation to that of Ardelisa, Violetta explains to a priest that she cannot forgive herself for having submitted to Osmin's embraces, a thing Ardelisa would never have done. She remembers miserably, "I confess I even loved him, saw him with a wife's eyes, and thought myself obliged to do so." The priest comforts Violetta, distinguishing her position from that of Ardelisa: "In Ardelisa, who was married to another, it would have been a horrid crime to suffer another man for to possess her, but as you were single, a virgin, and made his by the chance of war, it was no sin in you to yield to him, and it would have been willful murder to have killed him, or but conspired to his death. Nay, a sin not to have been faithful to his bed; whilst he is living you ought not to marry. You might have been a means of his conversion; you ought to pray for him and consider he acted according to his knowledge and education" (139). In Aubin's fiction an awareness of cultural relativism works alongside a belief in the absolute moral superiority of the Christian religion. She drew on the conventions of the early modern "Turk plays" in focusing on the personal influence a woman might have in converting her rapist to Christianity. Strikingly, though Aubin's narrative asserts the power of Christian moral example in a global context, the material hybridity that might entail—the living body of the infant son—cannot survive.

Aubin was explicitly interested in using fiction to stage a moral intervention in contemporary English society. In her "Preface to the Reader" she offered "a story where Divine Providence manifests itself in every transaction, where virtue is tried with misfortunes, and rewarded with blessings. In fine, where men behave themselves like Christians, and women are really virtuous, and such as we ought to imitate" (114). Aubin intended to use fiction as a means of social reform, to represent textually what *could be* and, she felt, *should be* socially and politically realizable. Aubin drew a connection between moral conviction and national welfare. She continues nostalgically: "I heartily wish prosperity to my country and that the English would be again (as they were heretofore) remarkable for virtue and bravery, and our nobility make themselves distinguished from the crowd by shining qualities for which their ancestors became so honored and for reward of which obtained those titles they inherit" (115). For Aubin, Christian conviction was the foundation of national identity and stability. A stout, unified Christian community was her model for the role England could play on the global stage. If Ardelisa represented the talismanic purity of exemplary Christian womanhood, Violetta represented Aubin herself—bound to a ruler she was morally obligated to convert. From the Jacobite perspective, the exilic writing of poet and novelist Jane Barker also modeled a limited Christian cosmopolitanism.

JANE BARKER AND JACOBITE TRANSNATIONALISM

Jane Barker is in many ways an outlier in this chapter. A Roman Catholic and a Jacobite, she modeled her semi-autobiographical prose persona Galesia on

Orinda's example. Similarly, the Roman Catholic persona of her manuscript poems, Fidelia, speaks movingly of an English unity lost with the exiled Stuarts. For Barker, as for Philips, the Stuarts are the repository of English identity. A brief analysis of her Jacobite manuscript poems, collected in Carol Shiner Wilson's modern edited collection along with Barker's Galesia novels, will show her nuanced model of English identity and how it informed her later (Islamophobic) prose fiction.

In "To His Royal Highness" (James Francis Edward Stuart, son of James II and Mary Beatrice of Modena), Barker thinks back through Katherine Philips's royalist understanding of England as banished from itself by the absence of the Stuarts. She addresses James on his birthday, having given him a "Calvary set in a vinyard" (*sic*).[73] The imagery—linking Christ's bloody death with the vineyard's promise of fruitful resurrection—recalls a central trope of Jacobite providentialism: death does not entail defeat; the just king can make a barren land spring back to life. It also recalls the Eucharistic miracle of transubstantiation in which wine becomes Christ's blood, willingly sacrificed for the nourishment of all His followers. She exclaims to the young prince,

> Then let's rejoice, sing, love, and with you smile
> forgetting friends, estates, or native soyle,
> For having you we'r here in full content,
> Tis they in England suffer banishment. (293, 23–26)

In the presence of James Francis Edward Stuart, as in the presence of the Eucharist, his followers are truly home.

In "To My dear cosen Coll——at his return out of Irland into france" she depicts a Great Britain similar to that of Katherine Philips's vision of an anxiously united England and Wales. For Philips, a mountain range had separated her from London, but the river and ocean currents ensure the unity of Wales and England. For Barker, it is the military campaign against William in Ireland that had made her kinsman absent, and she cannot lament that "Irlands loss, has brought you on our coast" since his presence is a comfort to her. She ruefully acknowledges that "I wish, it had long since been lost" despite approving his military prowess in making the "bold Rebells" at "Limerick fall" (300, 1–11). When she imagines him dead she mourns with his "little son," who "rob'd" her of "half my grief" because of his likeness to his father (301, 28–31). The son is an image of his heroic father, but the likeness is precious to her for another reason, for she sees

> . . . in him springing my dear mothers race
> Which carefully I cherish'd as I cou'd,
> As the last little stream of Connocks blood. (301, 33–35)

The Jacobite military campaign in Ireland furnishes Barker's persona with an opportunity to reflect on the sacred and familial blood ties that unite Jacobites scattered across Ireland, Barker's Lincolnshire, and France. Barker's persona explains to her cousin that the news that he was not dead has revivified them: his

> . . . absence caus'd us double banishment.
> For be assur'd, of all your suffrings,
> . . . .
> We bore a part, though seas did us divide. (302, 41–44)

She concludes,

> Nay, I'm ariv'd to such indiffrency,
> That I scarce long my native land to see,
> For my friends safty, all things is to me. (302, 53–55)

Barker privileges the Stuart community, nourished by the presence of the Stuarts, over the geographic territory of her "native land."

Like Aubin, Barker also used a global stage to explore the complexity of achieving unity at home. In this she tellingly reworks the stereotypes of Turkish barbarity and women's oppression. Unfortunately, though Barker's vision of English identity is cosmopolitan—as one would expect from a member of a diaspora—it is, as much as Aubin's and Rowe's, thoroughly Christian. The Muslim woman is welcome in an intellectually free Christian Europe—if she converts. As Nabil Matar and others have pointed out, a profound anxiety regarding the possibility of forced conversion or "turning Turk" from Christianity to Islam troubled Europeans during the early modern era.[74]

Like Rowe and Aubin, Barker can be seen as contributing to the tradition of pious didactic fiction that modeled itself on the authorial example of Katherine Philips. Barker's heroine Galesia explicitly aligns herself with "Orinda" rather than with the amatory tradition of Aphra Behn.[75] In truth, Barker was also influenced by Behn's work, and she was ambivalent about the platonic tradition. Barker's "Galesia trilogy" (a term coined by scholars rather than used by Barker herself) details the adventures of Galesia through jilted young love, alludes to her time in France in the Stuart court in exile, and explores her time in England, both in the countryside and in London. I have examined elsewhere the complicated politicized discourse of national unity that Barker articulated in *A Patch-work Screen for the Ladies* (1723) and its sequel *The Lining of the Patch Work Screen* (1726), but one particular inset narrative in *The Lining* is relevant for a discussion of Islam in women's prose fiction of the 1720s.[76]

The first inset narrative of *The Lining* features a long-lost friend of Galesia's, Captain Manly, who recounts his adventures in evolving from being a rakish ne'er-do-well in England before the Revolution of 1688 to becoming a sincere Christian penitent after being captured and enslaved by pirates in the Mediterranean. By the end of his tale, Captain Manly has collected a cosmopolitan crew of Christians—himself, an ambiguously affiliated and half-hearted Christian; Father Barnard, a pious Roman Catholic priest; and an unnamed Muslim woman who owns them both as slaves and decides to convert to Christianity.

At first Galesia cannot recognize this silent, ghostlike man because of the liminal state of twilight. She admits that she "could not well determine whether he was a Person or a Spectre" (181). The play of light sources—she sees him, obscured but partially illuminated, between "moon-shine" and "fire-light"—foreshadows the complexity of Manly's religious, political, and cultural affiliations in the following tale. Surprisingly, it is only after repeated requests by Galesia to identify himself that Manly finally does so, offering his narrative to account for why his appearance is so much altered. Manly's tale raises the possibility—indeed the likelihood—of mistaking friends for enemies and vice versa in the religiously and politically fractious Mediterranean forum of relations between European and Ottoman powers.

Manly establishes his libertine credentials straight away in narrating his life to Galesia. The Revolution of 1688 maps Manly's amorous intrigues onto the national stage: his wife and mistress, Chloris, pull him in different political directions. Between their mutual manipulations Manly ends up in jail, is eventually released, and, tired of both of them, leaves for St. Germain, the Jacobite court in exile in France. The court at St. Germain proving to be impoverished, and Manly not wishing to take resources for himself that would be better distributed to men who had fought for the king, he sets sail for the Indies to "try" his "fortune" (195). He is promptly captured by pirates, sold as a slave, bought by a Muslim woman in Algiers, part of the Ottoman Empire, and establishes a friendship with a fellow slave, a Roman Catholic priest named Father Barnard.

The two men eventually convert their kindly mistress to Christianity. Manly does not mince words in describing the method by which he and Father Barnard convert the Muslim lady. Indeed, he very much coincides with writers such as Addison and Prideaux who privilege Christianity over Islam by distinguishing Christian fortitude from the stereotypical violence and sensuality of Islam. Though at first unsure of how to "conclude" the Christian history "Authentick, much less sacred" (196), the Lady is eventually brought round by Manly's and Barnard's contrast of the "patient and meek Suffering" of the followers of the "Holy Crucified Jesus" and their description of how the Ottoman Empire "was set up, and how it began with Rebellion, was carry'd on with Injustice, War and Rapine, and established in a compound Religion, of *Jew*, *Heretical Christian* and *Old Heathenism*" (196). Manly's and Barnard's accusations are clearly consistent with, and probably influenced by, the corpus of work published in the 1680s and 1690s characterizing Muhammad as an impostor.

Manly, Barnard, and their mistress-convert decide to depart for Europe. Once in Venice, their former owner decides to enter a convent, and it is here that the Abbess introduces them to a beautiful English woman who turns out to be none other than a penitent Chloris, who is as "surprized" to see Manly as he is to see her (201). Overjoyed, Manly urges her to continue her life of penitence, while he returns to England to live with his wife "justly, and faithfully" (201). Upon returning to England, he finds that his wife has died, leaving him her estate. Thus, two wealthy women (Manley's wife and his owner) and two at least temporarily disenfranchised men (Manly and Father Barnard) mediate a complex network of moral and religious conversions as well as cultural translations and migrations. The ghostly apparition may turn out to be a long-lost friend; the estranged, deceased wife may turn out to be a providential benefactor intent on reconciling an exile to the nation. Within this framework, Barker suggests that the feminine spaces of the convent, home, or tea table are where the religiopolitical hostilities of England can be reconciled in virtuous sociability. Barker constructs a narrative that shows the stranger who appears, unidentifiable, between moonshine and firelight—who can pass as a human or a ghost—as an old friend, someone with hard-earned, private, exilic knowledge, a knowledge that needs to circulate in England's body politic for the public welfare.

Thus, Barker attempted to subvert anti-Catholic stereotypes common in the early eighteenth-century English public sphere by policing England's national boundaries, excluding those unwilling to convert to Christianity. A further complication is the geographic constellation of endpoints of the three main characters in Captain Manly's tale: Manly is free to return to England, to find that his wife has left him a sizable fortune, without which he would be penniless. Indeed, his wife's will is dated the same day as his own conversion to uncompromising Christian virtue in the face of the stereotypical Muslim temptation to have multiple wives (as he tells the Lady, "According to our Christian Law I cannot be Husband to another"; 197). The Catholic Father Barnard remains in Europe. The Lady also decides to remain in Europe, in a convent, suggesting perhaps the lack of sympathy a convert to Christianity would find in Protestant England if that convert chose to confess the Roman Catholic faith. The convent is a site of salvific, female space, for it is here that not only the Muslim convert but also Chloris finds refuge.

Rescuing from a Muslim space a wealthy and beautiful woman who desires to convert to Christianity is a trope of European literature from Zoraida in *Don*

Quixote (1605; 1615) to Safie in *Frankenstein* (1818). It is a trope that merges an argument for the superiority of Christianity over Islam with the knowledge that all is not right in Europe and refracts this complexity through the gender politics of a woman who earnestly seeks for the opportunity to convert—to disagree with her society. In this way, European writers could acknowledge the military dominance of Muslim powers such as the Ottoman Empire, could assert the supposed moral superiority of Christianity over Islam, and could appeal to the potential for a pan-Christian unity. The woman who was once a Muslim has a place in Barker's female space, but Barker does not represent a woman who is still a Muslim permanently coexisting with Christians in a female space. This results in a binary opposition in which Christianity is attractive to women because it encourages charity, mercy, compassion, and courage in rescuing the distressed, while Islam is represented as driving women away because it is brutal, violent, and dehumanizing. This Christianity-Islam binary creates a fictional Christian unity that serves Barker in suggesting that Roman Catholics and English Protestants could work together in a shared endeavor despite their historical hostilities. Further, the binary minimizes cultural differences between "East" and "West" but only at the expense of representing as insurmountable the religious differences between Christianity and Islam. The examples of Aubin and Barker show that, even when Islamophobic misogynistic mortalism is not used—even when Muslim women are clearly depicted as moral agents—Islam itself is excluded from English identity. It continued to be the negative ideal. This is not surprising—pious didactic Christian writers *would* talk about the superiority of Christianity, wouldn't they? What is surprising is that they were ultimately joined—at a significantly later date—by one of the greatest of their amatory contemporaries: Eliza Haywood, the queen of the passions.

NOTES

1. Christine de Pizan, *The Book of the City of Ladies*, trans. Rosalind Brown-Grant (London: Penguin Books, 1999), 109.
2. William Shakespeare, *Othello*, The Alexander Shakespeare, gen. ed. R. B. Kennedy, with additional notes and editing by Mike Gould, Collins Classics, Harper Press paperback edition (London: Harper Press, 2011), act 5, scene 2, lines 365–369.
3. Malebranche adds, though, "There are strong, constant women, and there are feeble, inconstant men. There are learned women, courageous women, women capable of anything. . . . In short, when we attribute certain defects to a sex, to certain ages, to certain stations, we mean only that it is ordinarily true, always assuming there is no general rule without exceptions." Nicolas Malebranche, *The Search after Truth*, trans. and ed. Thomas M. Lennon and Paul J. Olscamp (Columbus: Ohio State University Press, 1980), 130–131. The first edition was published in 1674–75, but Malebranche continued to revise his thought until a final edition of 1712.

4. Londa Schiebinger, *Nature's Body: Gender in the Making of Modern Science* (Boston: Beacon Press, 1993), 158.
5. Siep Stuurman, *François Poulain de la Barre and the Invention of Modern Equality* (Cambridge, Mass.: Harvard University Press, 2004), 55.
6. Jacqueline Broad, *Women Philosophers of the Seventeenth Century* (Cambridge: Cambridge University Press, 2004).
7. Broad, *Women Philosophers*, 11.
8. René Descartes, *Sixth Meditation*, in *Meditations on First Philosophy = Meditationes de prima philosophia*, ed. and trans. George Heffernan, bilingual ed. (Notre Dame, Ind.: University of Notre Dame Press, 1990), 197.
9. Margaret Cavendish, *The Blazing World, and Other Writings*, ed. Kate Lilley (London: Penguin Classics, 1994), 229n22.
10. All quotations are from François Poullain de La Barre, *Three Cartesian Feminist Treatises*, with introductions and annotations by Marcelle Maistre Welch, trans. Vivien Bosley, The Other Voice in Early Modern Europe (Chicago: University of Chicago Press, 2002).
11. See "Note on the Text" in Poullain, *Three Cartesian Feminist Treatises*, 35–36.
12. Marcelle Maistre Welch, "Introduction: Poullain de La Barre's Cartesian Feminism," trans. Vivien Bosley, in Poullain, *Three Cartesian Feminist Treatises*, 12.
13. Poullain, *Three Cartesian Feminist Treatises*, 55, 69.
14. See, for instance, Astell's comment in *Bart'lemy Fair*, her response to Lord Shaftesbury's dismissive attitude to religious gravity, as she saw it: "So long as Principles are fashionable, and there's somewhat to be got by them, whilst Bigottry to a Profession or Party raises Men's Character, and helps them to Preferment, it may be worth their while to be good Church-Men, good Protestants, good any thing, even Papist or Mahometan. And yet since the being ty'd to a Mask, puts too great a force on Native Liberty, it is better, much better, that no countenance be given to such serious Extravagancies, but rather that a universal Freedom prevailing, Men may frankly open themselves, and give the utmost Liberty to Wit!" [Mary Astell], *Bart'lemy Fair: Or, An Enquiry after Wit; In which due Respect is had to a Letter Concerning Enthusiasm, To my Lord ***. By Mr. Wotton* [Mary Astell] (London, Printed for R. Wilkin, at the King's Head in St. Paul's Church-Yard, 1709), 143–144. For an insightful analysis of the gender and class dimensions of Shaftesbury's and Astell's disagreement, see David P. Alvarez, "Reason and Religious Tolerance: Mary Astell's Critique of Shaftesbury," *Eighteenth-Century Studies* 44, no. 4 (Summer 2011): 475–494.
15. Mary Astell, *A Fair Way With The Dissenters And Their Patrons. Not Writ by Mr. L———y, or any other* Furious Jacobite, *whether Clergyman or Layman; but by a very Moderate Person and Dutiful Subject to the QUEEN* (London: Printed by E. P. for R. Wilkin, at the King's-Head, in St. Paul's Church-Yard, 1704), 12.
16. Mary Astell, *A Serious Proposal to the Ladies, For the Advancement of their True and Greatest Interest. In Two Parts. By a Lover of her Sex* (London: Printed for Richard Wilkin at the King's-Head in St. Paul's Church-Yard, 1697), 49–50.
17. Mary Astell, *Some Reflections Upon Marriage*, 2nd ed. (London: Printed for R. Wilkin, at the King's Head in St. Paul's Church-Yard, 1703), 66.
18. Astell, *A Serious Proposal*, 48.
19. John Sprint, *The Bride-Woman's Counseller: Being a Sermon Preach'd at a Wedding, May the Eleventh 1699, at Sherbourn in Dorsetshire* (London: Printed and sold by H. Hills, in Black-Fryars, near the Water-side, for the Benefit of the Poor, 1699).
20. [Lady Mary Chudleigh], *The Ladies Defence: Or, The Bride-Woman's Counsellor Answer'd: A Poem. In a Dialogue Between Sir John Brute, Sir William Loveall, Melissa, and a Parson. Written by a Lady* (London: Printed for John Deeve at Bernard's-Inn-Gate in Holborn, 1701), 6.

21. John Locke, *Two Treatises on Government*, ed. Peter Laslett (Cambridge: Cambridge University Press, 1997). All subsequent references will be parenthetical.
22. Eve Tavor Bannet, *The Domestic Revolution: Enlightenment Feminisms and the Novel* (Baltimore: Johns Hopkins University Press, 2000), 32.
23. John Locke, *An Essay Concerning Human Understanding*, Clarendon Edition, edited and with a foreword by Peter H. Nidditch (Oxford: Oxford University Press, 1975; first paperback edition, reprinted (with corrections) from the Clarendon Edition, 1979), 2, 23, § 22. References are to book, chapter, and section.
24. Philip Dixon, *"Nice and Hot Disputes": The Doctrine of the Trinity in the Seventeenth Century* (London: T & T Clark, 2003), 51–53, 64–65.
25. A. D. Lindsay, introduction to *A Discourse on Method*, by René Descartes, trans. John Veitch (London: J. M. Dent & Sons, 1957), xix.
26. Locke considers "Solidity, Extension, Figure, Motion, or Rest, and Number" to be primary qualities. He describes secondary qualities as being "nothing in the Objects themselves, but Powers to produce various Sensations in us by their *primary Qualities*," bk. 2, chap. 8, "Simple Ideas," § 9–10.
27. John W. Yolton, *Thinking Matter: Materialism in Eighteenth-Century Britain* (Minneapolis: University of Minnesota Press, 1983), xi.
28. Robert G. Walker, *Eighteenth-Century Arguments for Immortality and Johnson's "Rasselas,"* English Literary Studies Monograph Series, 9 (Victoria, B.C.: University of Victoria, 1977), 12.
29. Edward Stillingfleet, *The Doctrine of the Trinity*, in *Three Criticisms of Locke* (Hildesheim: George Olms Verlag, 1987), 241.
30. Yolton, *Thinking Matter*, 3–4.
31. Roger Woolhouse, *Locke: A Biography* (Cambridge: Cambridge University Press, 2007), 399. See also John Marshall, *John Locke, Toleration and Early Enlightenment Culture*, Cambridge Studies in Early Modern British History (Cambridge: Cambridge University Press, 2006; digitally printed version, 2009), 461.
32. Elizabeth Johnson, "Preface to the Reader," in *Poems on Several Occasions. Written by Philomela* [Elizabeth Singer (Rowe)] (London: Printed for John Dunton at the Raven in Jewen-street, 1696).
33. Norma Clarke, *The Rise and Fall of the Woman of Letters* (London: Pimlico, 2004), 164.
34. George Farquhar, *The Beaux' Stratagem*, in *British Dramatists from Dryden to Sheridan*, ed. George H. Nettleton and Arthur E. Case, revised by George Winchester Stone Jr. (Carbondale: Southern Illinois University Press, 1969), act 4, scene 1, lines 1–7.
35. Scholars disagree about whether the play is orientalist. Bernadette Andrea sees it as a "counterorientalist" debut, while Bridget Orr argues that the play "not only recirculates Orientalist political dicta but participates in the construction of feminist Islamophobia." See Bernadette Andrea, *Women and Islam in Early Modern English Literature* (Cambridge: Cambridge University Press, 2007), 91–104; Bridget Orr, *Empire on the English Stage, 1660–1714* (Cambridge: Cambridge University Press, 2001), 134.
36. Delarivier Manley, *Almyna: Or, The Arabian Vow. A Tragedy*, in *Delarivier Manley and Mary Pix: English Women Staging Islam, 1696–1707*, ed. with an introduction by Bernadette Andrea, The Other Voice in Early Modern Europe: The Toronto Series, 17 (Toronto: Iter Inc. and Centre for Reformation and Renaissance Studies, 2012), act 1, scene 1, pages 152–153.
37. Andrea, *Women and Islam*, 104.
38. Cynthia Lowenthal, *Performing Identities on the Restoration Stage* (Carbondale: Southern Illinois University Press, 2003), 171.

39. Mary Pix, *Ibrahim, The Thirteenth Emperor of the Turks: A Tragedy* [1696], in Andrea, *Delarivier Manley and Mary Pix*, act 5, page 337.
40. Erica Veevers, *Images of Love and Religion: Queen Henrietta Maria and Court Entertainments* (Cambridge: Cambridge University Press, 1989), 1. Veevers explains, "Henrietta's version [of *préciosité*] itself was . . . influenced by the salons, but also by the religious enthusiasms of the Counter-Reformation, in particular the Devout Humanism of St. François de Sales. Devout Humanism shared with *L'Astrée* an element of Neoplatonic idealism, and religious writers drew on d'Urfé's popularity to spread the influence of religion, particularly in 'the religious romance'" (2).
41. See Karen Britland, *Drama at the Courts of Queen Henrietta Maria* (Cambridge: Cambridge University Press, 2006), 6–7, 31.
42. Paula Loscocco, introduction to *Katherine Philips (1631/2–1664): Printed Poems 1667*, selected by Paula Loscocco, The Early Modern Englishwoman: A Facsimile Library of Essential Works and Printed Writings, 1641–1700. Series 2, Part 3, vol. 2, ed. Betty S. Travitsky and Anne Lake Prescott (Aldershot: Ashgate, 2007), ix.
43. Sophie Tomlinson, *Women on Stage in Stuart Drama* (Cambridge: Cambridge University Press, 2005), 186.
44. Citations are from Loscocco's edition of Philips's poems. Line numbers are noted in parentheses.
45. Harriette Andreadis points out that Philips's appropriation of the neoplatonic notion of friendship as a unity of souls, of friends being each other's "alter idem or Alter ego," should be seen as a response to Jeremy Taylor's unsatisfactory answer to her query about the nature of women's friendship. Harriette Andreadis, "Re-configuring Early Modern Friendship: Katherine Philips and Homoerotic Desire," *Studies in English Literature, 1500–1900* 46, no. 3 (Summer 2006): 523–524. See also Jeremy Taylor, *A Discourse of the Nature, Offices, and measures, of friendship, with Rules of Conducting it, in a Letter to the Most Ingenious and Excellent Mrs. Katharine Philips* (1657).
46. [Anon.], preface to *Poems By the most deservedly Admired Mrs. Katherine Philips The matchless ORINDA. To which is added Monsieur Corneille's POMPEY & HORACE, Tragedies. With several other Translations out of FRENCH* (London: Printed by J. M for H. Herringman, at the Sign of the Blew Anchor in the Lower Walk of the New Exchange, 1667), unpaginated. The preface is anonymous but was probably written by her friend Sir Charles Cotterell. Instances of the long "s" have been silently modernized. All of the poems of praise in the front matter are unpaginated; I have identified them according to title.
47. Neither Cavendish nor Philips was primarily interested in using religion to justify her decision to write; this was a decisive shift from the tactics of earlier women writers. See Hero Chalmers, *Royalist Women Writers, 1650–1689* (Oxford: Clarendon Press, 2004), 4.
48. Emma L. E. Rees notes that Cavendish, restricted as she was "legislatively, politically, and along gender lines," "manipulated existent literary genres as a way of articulating and negotiating her contrary, triply debarred situation." Emma L. E. Rees, "Triply Bound: Genre and the Exilic Self," in *Authorial Conquests: Essays on Genre in the Writings of Margaret Cavendish*, ed. Line Cottegnies and Nancy Weitz (Cranbury, N.J.: Associated University Presses, 2003), 23, 29.
49. Citations are to the 1994 Penguin Classics edition of Cavendish's *The Blazing World.*
50. On Norris's views on Locke, see the editors' "Introduction: Mary Astell and John Norris: A Correspondence," in Mary Astell and John Norris, *Letters Concerning the Love of God*, ed. E. Derek Taylor and Melvyn New (Aldershot: Ashgate, 2005), 33.
51. Mary Astell, *The Christian Religion, As Profess'd by a Daughter of the Church of England* (London: Printed by S. H. for R. Wilkin, at the King's-Head in St. Paul's-Church-Yeard, 1705), 47.

52. Astell, *A Fair Way With The Dissenters*, 21.
53. Damaris, Lady Masham, *A Discourse Concerning the Love of God* (London: Printed for Awnsham and John Churchil, 1696), A2v–A3, 126.
54. Paula R. Backscheider, *Elizabeth Singer Rowe and the Development of the English Novel* (Baltimore: Johns Hopkins University Press, 2013), 127.
55. John J. Richetti, "Mrs. Elizabeth Rowe: The Novel as Polemic," *PMLA* 82, no. 7 (December 1967): 523.
56. John. J. Richetti, *Popular Fiction before Richardson: Narrative Patterns, 1700–1739* (Oxford: Clarendon Press, 1969), 246.
57. Their poems were gathered together (along with those of Dryden and Norris, in *A Collection of Divine Hymns and Poems on Several Occasions by the E. of Roscommon, John Dryden* Esq*; Mr Dennis, Mr Norris, Mrs. Kath. Phillips, Mrs. Singer, & others. Most of them Never before Printed* (London: Printed for R. Burrough, and J. Baker, at the Sun and Moon, near the Royal-Exchange in Cornhill, 1707).
58. Jennifer Richards, introduction to *Elizabeth Singer [Rowe]*, selected by Jennifer Richards, .The Early Modern Englishwoman: A Facsimile Library of Essential Works and Printed Writings, 1641–1700: Series 2, Part 2, vol. 7, ed., Betty S. Travitsky and Anne Lake Prescott (Aldershot: Ashgate, 2003), xiii.
59. [Elizabeth Singer (Rowe)], *Poems on Several Occasions*, 1–2, stanza 2. Citations give page number followed by stanza number.
60. For an intriguing analysis of how Singer (Rowe) negotiated the platonic relationship she and publisher John Dunton crafted, see Dustin Stewart, "Dunton and Singer after the *Athenian Mercury*: Two Plots of Platonic Love," in *Women's Periodicals and Print Culture in Britain, 1690–1820s*, ed. Jennie Batchelor and Manushag N. Powell (Edinburgh: Edinburgh University Press, 2018), 87–100.
61. Backscheider, *Elizabeth Singer Rowe*, 146–147.
62. Margaret Anne Doody, *The True Story of the Novel* (New Brunswick, N.J.: Rutgers University Press, 1996), 288–294.
63. Susan Staves, *A Literary History of Women's Writing in Britain, 1660–1789* (Cambridge: Cambridge University Press, 2006), 290.
64. [Rowe], *Poems on Several Occasions*, 47.
65. Elizabeth Singer [Rowe], preface to *"Friendship in Death in Twenty Letters from the Dead to the Living" and "Letters Moral and Entertaining,"* ed. Josephine Grieder (New York: Garland Publishing, 1972), unpaginated. This edition is based on the 1733 edition, which includes both texts. Part 1 of *Letters* appeared in 1728 with *Friendship*; parts 2 and 3 appeared in 1731 and 1732.
66. Sarah Prescott, "Penelope Aubin and *The Doctrine of Morality*: A Reassessment of the Pious Woman Novelist," *Women's Writing* 1, no. 1 (1994): 99–112; Aparna Gollapudi, "Virtuous Voyages in Penelope Aubin's Fiction," *Studies in English Literature, 1500–1900* 45, no. 3 (Summer 2005): 669–690; Chris Mounsey, "Conversion Panic, Circumcision, and Sexual Anxiety: Penelope Aubin's Queer Writing," in *Queer People: Negotiations and Expressions of Homosexuality, 1700–1800*, ed. Chris Mounsey and Caroline Gonda (Lewisburg, Pa.: Bucknell University Press, 2007), 246–260; Debbie Welham, "The Particular Case of Penelope Aubin," *Journal for Eighteenth-Century Studies* 31, no. 1 (2008): 63–76; Edward J. Kozaczka, "Penelope Aubin and Narratives of Empire," *Eighteenth-Century Fiction* 25, no. 1 (Fall 2012): 199–225; Debbie Welham, "The Political Afterlife of Resentment in Penelope Aubin's *The Life and Amorous Adventures of Lucinda* (1721)," *Women's Writing* 20, no. 1 (February 2013): 49–63; Adam R. Beach, "Aubin's *The Noble Slaves*, Montagu's Spanish Lady, and English Feminist Writing about Sexual Slavery in the Ottoman World," *Eighteenth-Century Fiction* 29, no. 4 (Summer 2017): 583–606. See also chap. 2 in Eve Tavor Bannet,

Transatlantic Stories and the History of Reading, 1720–1810: Migrant Fictions (Cambridge: Cambridge University Press, 2011).

67. Kozaczka, "Penelope Aubin," 200.
68. Penelope Aubin, *A Collection of Entertaining Histories and Novels, Designed to Promote the Cause of Virtue and Honour*, 3 vols. (London: Printed for D. Midwinter, A. Bettesworth and C. Hitch, J. and J. Pemberton, R. Ware, C. Rivington, A. Ward, J. and P. Knapton, T. Longman, R. Hett, S. Austen, and J. Wood, 1739), 3:iii, vi.
69. Jane Spencer, *The Rise of the Woman Novelist: From Aphra Behn to Jane Austen* (Oxford: Blackwell, 1986), 87, 88.
70. Spencer, *Rise of the Woman Novelist*, 88n39.
71. Chris Mounsey, "'. . . bring her naked from her Bed, that I may ravish her before the Dotard's face, and then send his Soul to Hell': Penelope Aubin, Impious Pietist, Humourist or Purveyor of Juvenile Fantasy?," *British Journal for Eighteenth-Century Studies* 26 (2003): 61–62.
72. Paula R. Backscheider and John J. Richetti, eds., *Popular Fiction by Women, 1660–1730: An Anthology* (Oxford: Clarendon Press, 1996), 120. All quotations from *Vinevil* are taken from this volume.
73. Jane Barker, *The Galesia Trilogy and Selected Manuscript Poems of Jane Barker*, ed. Carol Shiner Wilson (Oxford: Oxford University Press, 1997), "To His Royal Highness the Prince of Wales, on His birth day 1689: or 99: The author having presented him a Calvary set in a vinyard," 292. References are to page number and line (where available).
74. Nabil Matar, "'Turning Turke': Conversion to Islam in English Writings," chap. 1 in *Islam in Britain, 1558–1685* (Cambridge: Cambridge University Press, 1998), 21–49. See also Daniel Vitkus, *Turning Turk: English Theater and the Multicultural Mediterranean, 1570–1630* (New York: Palgrave Macmillan, 2003).
75. Galesia at one point envisions the Muses promising to assist her poetic flights till they "reach fair Orinda's Height" if she forsakes her "faithless Swain" and vows "a Virgin to remain." Barker, *Galesia Trilogy and Selected Manuscript Poems*, 13.
76. See Samara Anne Cahill, "Realist Latitudes: Textilic Nationalism and the Global Fiction of the 1720s," *Digital Defoe: Studies in Defoe & His Contemporaries* 7, no. 1 (2015): 66–91; and Samara Anne Cahill, "Novel 'Modes' and 'Indian Goods': Textilic Nationalism in *A Patch-Work Screen for the Ladies* and *The Lining of the Patch Work Screen*," *Studies in Eighteenth-Century Culture* 44 (2015): 163–184.

3
THE CANAL OF PLEASURE

THE FOLLOWING CHAPTER EXAMINES HOW the hierarchy of pleasures mapped onto the perceived distance between Christianity and Islam in the 1690s was leveraged by Englishwomen to represent themselves as subjects of intellectual rather than merely physical pleasure. Roy Porter has pointed out that "pleasure came into its own in the eighteenth century."[1] This is so specifically because, against the backdrop of Christianity's hostility to hedonism, the eighteenth century saw a "new accent upon the legitimacy of pleasure," a revitalized belief that "a rational and benevolent God had created a universe in which earthly ends were desirable as well as Heavenly bliss."[2] Yet this democratization left in place the platonic hierarchy of pleasures in which intellectual pleasures are superior to those of the flesh. For sensual or sensory pleasure to be part of that democratization it would need to be aligned with the higher pleasures of the mind.

This was a problem for women because, as Marie Mulvey Roberts observes, women, "even when they were not blatantly regarded as *machines de plaisir*, were generally perceived as more of a source than a subject of pleasure."[3] Women's pleasure in the privacy of novel reading served both to highlight and to theorize women's place in the economy of pleasure. Not all pleasures result in shared sociability between social agents. Novel heroines thus had to be accommodated to this newly democratized hierarchy of pleasures, and no author more effectively adapted the pleasures of amatory fiction to the pleasures of moral didacticism *and* of the new realist fiction than Samuel Richardson. Richardson's heroines claim superiority of soul as a means to counteract the libertine view of them as *machines de plaisir*. It is no coincidence that Richardson's tragic heroine Clarissa is pursued by a villain who identifies himself with religious alterity (Judaism and Islam in different editions, as I discuss below), while Richardson's comic heroine Pamela recuperates her husband from behaviors like polygamy associated with religious alterity. But in order to better understand the role that women's spiritual pleasures played in Richardson's fiction, let us turn to a surprising example of continuity between the pious didactic writers of the 1720s and Richardson's heroines: the strange case of Eliza Haywood.

Primarily known, alongside Aphra Behn and Delarivier Manley, as one of the "amatory triumvirate" of women writing between 1670 and 1730, Haywood was a prodigious writer across multiple genres and modes. She also transitioned from an early focus on amatory fiction, political critique, and theater to periodical writing and morally didactic fiction. Like her theatrical collaborator Henry Fielding, she was pushed by the repressive 1737 Licensing Act to channel her social critiques in the direction of the new domestic fiction epitomized by Richardson's *Pamela* (1740). Haywood embodied a sinuous creative responsiveness to changing literary contexts. Her *Anti-Pamela; or Feign'd Innocence Detected* (1741) dovetailed with Fielding's *Shamela* (1741) and *Joseph Andrews* (1742), skeptical spoofs of Richardson's portrayal of the lucrative marriage of a lowly servant girl to her master. Haywood's novel *The History of Miss Betsy Thoughtless* (1751) adopted the Richardsonian vein of didactic fiction while adapting it to show how a woman could be both flawed and the heroine of a novel.

But, throughout a career characterized by innovation, adaptation, and reinvention, Haywood demonstrated an abiding concern with the consequences of women giving way to certain pleasures rather than others. Haywood—like Mary Astell and, later, Samuel Johnson and Mary Wollstonecraft—sought to adapt women's education to a more modern, presumably more enlightened, context in which women could regulate their pleasures and direct themselves to intellectual ones. Her periodical the *Female Spectator* (1744–46), particularly, was a bridge between the older Cartesian-influenced defenses of women's intelligent souls and the increasingly calcified belief that intelligence was aligned with Christian rather than Muslim pleasures.

THE "STOREHOUSE OF THE MIND"

The *Female Spectator* was a periodical established on the premise that a group of women, led by the eponymous Female Spectator, receives letters from readers who wish to discuss pressing matters of the day. But despite covering a range of topics—from war and trade imbalance to censorship and the facticity of travel writing—the periodical primarily concerns itself with the deleterious effects of bad customs and how best to cultivate good ones. Intellectual pleasures such as reading, attending tragic drama, and contemplating gardens are presented as the best ways of cultivating good customs. Haywood's Female Spectator models the intellectual movement of education in her own brief autobiography in which she describes herself as having never been "a Beauty" and being now "very far" from young.[4] From this position she looks back on a youth during which she was "the greatest Coquet of them all" and in which her life was "a continued Round of what I then called Pleasure." Now older, she has learned that it is "very much, by the Choice we make of Subjects for our Entertainment, that the refin'd Taste distinguishes itself from the vulgar and more gross" (1:1). In identifying "reading" as one of the most "universally improving, as well as agreeable Amusements," however, she also takes care to re-emphasize the importance of judiciousness of choice, for, given the "Number of Books which are perpetually issuing from the Press," not all will be equally "conducive" to "those Ends" of improvement as well as pleasure. The Female Spectator reasons that as her early acquaintance with a general rather than judiciously selected crowd of people has given her a stock of ideas with which to assist the public, so, too, her own curiosity will likely interest others, for curiosity has "a Share in every Breast" (1:4).

Nevertheless, there are differences as well as similarities among individuals, and the Female Spectator realizes that she needs a diversity of voices. She enlists "Mira," a young woman of wit, happily married, and of a good family; a "Widow of Quality," urban, fashionable, but honorable; and, finally, Euphrosine, a cheerful, virtuous merchant's daughter. The Female Spectator explains that these women present their views "as several Members of one Body, of which I am the Mouth" (1:5–6). The Female Spectator thus explicitly frames herself as a channel of information—she is the mouthpiece for a variety of points of view.

Much of the periodical's perspective on women's intelligence was invested in a natural theology model of the universe as ordered, hierarchical, and comprehensible. Haywood's investment in natural theology, with its attention to reason and observation, very much anticipated what Karen O'Brien has argued of the investment of the Bluestockings in Joseph Butler's common-sense focus on the probable truths of an orderly but ultimately unknowable universe over the abstractions of debates like the Trinitarian Controversy.[5] Yet the Trinitarian Controversy was still very much alive when Haywood was writing the *Female Spectator.* The threat of deism, or freethinking more generally, in the eighteenth century was both a continuation and a mutation of the Trinitarian Controversy. Haywood aligned herself with orthodox Anglicanism: the sympathies of the *Female Spectator* are explicitly anti-mortalist (more specifically, anti-annihilationist) and anti-materialist.

Throughout the *Female Spectator* Haywood's eponymous narrator explicitly sets herself up to channel the right kind of pleasure to women. She says at one point that a "Variety of Opinions . . . affords a good deal of Pleasure to a contemplative Mind" while emphasizing that humans have "Souls very different from what are to be found in any other Specie of created Beings we have any Acquaintance with" (2:257). Significantly, she resorts to Islamophobic misogynistic mortalism to reinforce her point about the unique qualities of human souls. The nature of women's souls is important, for immortality is the ground of morality (2:321) even though the "*Turks* maintain that Women have no Souls, and there are not wanting some among *Christians* who lean to that Opinion," despite "Thought and Reflection" being "the Essence of the Soul" (3:12). But for the Female Spectator, it is clear that the soul "must endlessly abide an active perceptive Substance, with either Fears or Hopes of dying thro' all Eternity" (3:50). Further, since women have "reasonable Souls" (3:165), they ought to study history, particularly the rise and fall of empires. Throughout, the emphasis is on educating women to accumulate in their minds a stock of ideas and observations upon which they can reflect fruitfully. She even connects this stocking of the mind to a natural theology understanding of women's place in the world, for "the Study of *Nature* is the Study of *Divinity*" (3:156). Contemplating the natural world is rewarding because that world is "full of an exact Order and Harmony," not filled with "jostling Atoms" as the materialists maintain (3:187). Thus Haywood's engagement with natural philosophy and the doctrinal provocation of the Trinitarian Controversy (continued into the eighteenth century by Matthew Tindal and John Toland) were central to her characterization of women's education.

"THOSE REFINED PLEASURES WHICH LAST TO IMMORTALITY"

The *Female Spectator* includes perspectives from a variety of women and also some male correspondents. As the Female Spectator explains, they "were beginning to lament the Misfortunes our Sex frequently fall into through the Want of those Improvements we are, doubtless, capable of, when a Letter . . . was brought in" (2:229). The letter is ostensibly from Cleora, a lady supportive of the intervention of the writer(s) of the *Female Spectator*, an intervention that she sees as "the noblest Act of Charity you could exercise in an Age like ours, where the Sense of Good and Evil is almost extinguish'd, and People desire to appear more vicious than they really are, that so they may be less unfashionable" (2:230). Lamenting that this "Humour" is "too prevalent in the Female Sex" due to "a wrong Education" (2:230), she concludes that "it is therefore only the Men, and the Men of Understanding too, who, I effect, merit the Blame of this, and are answerable for all the Misconduct we are guilty of:—Why do they call us *silly Women*, and not endeavor to make us otherwise?" (2:230). Cleora's argument very much coincides with Cartesian arguments for women's education that blamed patriarchal custom rather than women's nature for women's intellectual inferiority: if women are stupid, it is because men have kept them so. Asserting the historical injustices of women's education thus enabled a regulation of acceptable and unacceptable contemporary masculinities, too: enlightened men of progress support improvements in women's education; men who do not are tied to a benighted, illiberal past of domestic tyranny.

The *Female Spectator* stages this regulation in a subsequent letter, from "a Man" but "none of those lordly or tenacious Tyrants who would deny them [women] any Privileges they are capable of making a good Use of" (2:256). The correspondent praises the Female Spectator's recommendation of "the Study of Philosophy to the Ladies" (2:256). Significantly, he uses this praise as a soapbox from which to denounce mortalism and materialism. He begins, "THAT we have Souls very different from what are to be found in any other Species of created Beings we have any Acquaintance with, neither Lucretius nor any of his Followers ever pretended to deny; but then they bring Instinct in the Brute World so near to Reason in the Human, that the Preference given to the latter is very small, if any" (2:257). He later links this Lucretian materialism to the ongoing mortalist debate: "IN an Age such as this, when the Belief of Annihilation is the Creed in vogue, all Attempts to prevent a Doctrine so absurd, and of so manifestly wicked a Tendency, from taking too deep a Root ought to be encourag'd" (2:261). He signs himself "Platonides," situating himself in a long line of male platonic correspondents with intellectual women. The tradition extends back from John Dunton and Elizabeth Singer Rowe through Mary Astell and John Norris to Katherine Philips and Jeremy Taylor.

The ladies of the *Female Spectator* declare that Platonides's letter "very much charm'd us all" (2:261), and, in turn, they use the letter as a jumping off point for their own rejection of annihilationism. The Female Spectator herself concludes, "I hope, and am perswaded [*sic*], that this Doctrine of Annihilation is but from the *Lip*;—that the Heart, at least in most People, disavows so low and groveling a Principle" (2:263). Yet she doubles down on her rejection of mortalism by associating it with the stereotype of the "Mahometan" paradise (if not, strictly speaking, with Islamophobic misogynistic mortalism). She says that if "there be any weak enough to adopt in reality so absurd a Principle, it can be only those who, indulging themselves in a continual Series of Voluptuousness, assign no other Employment for the Mind than the Study of new Pleasures . . . and they would not deny themselves the least Enjoyment of the *present now*, even for the assurance of a Mahometan Paradise *in futuro* (2:263). This indictment of mortalism is succeeded by a lengthy criticism of the experiments of the "Virtuosos of the Royal Society" (2:264)—"those who may unhappily have suffered the *Animal* Soul to get the better of the *Rational*" (2:266)—and "our modish Sceptics" (2:268). The letter concludes with a rousing defense of "the Doctrine of the Soul's Immortality" in which the Female Spectator argues that not only "the Divines and Poets of all Ages, but the best and wisest of the ancient Philosophers, have vindicated" it (2:268). This extended discussion of mortalism shows that even in the 1740s the Trinitarian Controversy of the 1690s lingered on and, with it, the usefulness of the "negative ideal" of Islam to police the boundaries of Englishness. This was because the works of Tindal and Toland had aroused fears of deism or even atheism, which challenged the stability of a society whose civil authority was tied to Trinitarian orthodoxy. Indeed, the *Female Spectator* even brings in the old charge that Latitudinarians are too tolerant and trusting of the "Honour" of others not to commit "any Action to the Prejudice of Society" (2:285). Yet Haywood also coincided with the Lockean emphasis on observation and reflection in cultivating the understanding. For her, a fashionable education—teaching a girl "to sing, dance, play on the Spinet, and work at her Needle"—is only "sufficient for a Woman" according to the "common Opinion." Such an education does nothing for "improving her Understanding" or teaching her that "Reflection was necessary to ripen [her] *Wit* into *Wisdom*" (2:229). Haywood very much saw the assurance of immortality as a necessary but not a sufficient condition of a girl's proper education.

Describing the fashionably educated Sabina, the narrator states that, despite the fact that "those who had the Care of her Education told her what she must do in order to acquire the Love and Esteem of this World, and the Happiness promised to the Virtuous in the other" she never learned the value of reflection because "they indulg'd her in all the modish Amusements of the present Age" (2:229). The description of Sabina's inadequate education begins a series of reflections on what constitutes a solid education for women. Cleora contributes a letter reminiscent of Cartesians like François Poullain de La Barre, Mary Astell, and Lady Mary Chudleigh when she inveighs against "*Custom*" and "the Men of Understanding" who conspire to keep women ignorant (2:230). Cleora soon resorts to Islamophobic misogynistic mortalism to reinforce her point: "The Mahometans, indeed, enslave their Women, but then they teach them to believe their Inferiority will extend to Eternity; but our Case is even worse than this, for while we live in a free Country, and are assured from our excellent Christian Principles that we are capable of those refined Pleasures which last to Immortality, our Minds, our better Parts, are wholly left uncultivated, and, like a rich Soil neglected, bring forth nothing but noxious Weeds" (2:231). Just as Lancelot Addison, Humphrey Prideaux, and others had done before, and Samuel Johnson would do in *Rasselas*, Cleora aligns the superior, intellectual pleasures of the soul with Christianity while associating tyranny and the pleasures of the body with Islam. Cleora believes that in a "free Country" women should be able to cultivate the "rich Soil" of their minds. The imagery of women's intellectual fertility foreshadows Wollstonecraft's later denigration of the unfruitfulness of Turkey. A nation truly working according to "Christian Principles" would maximize the intellectual yield of its women through the cultivation of education. For Cleora, only "Mahometans," and the outdated, illiberal tyrants who agree with them, treat women like "Clay" (2:231). Cleora thus sees Christian women and Muslim women as equally oppressed, but not in the same way. Indeed, because of their education, Muslim women (the author assumes) cannot be aware of their oppression. British women, on the other hand, are constantly confronted with the disparity between the "Christian Principles" of their society and the failure of men to live up to those principles. Not only oppressed, Christian women are also confronted with obvious religious hypocrisy. Cleora's misappropriation of Muslim doctrine enables her to draw a striking parallel between what she takes to be Muslim doctrine and Christian hypocrisy while aligning British identity with Christianity and with the right sort of enlightened man.

There is, then, a critique of British society here. For the "Mahometans," it is part of their doctrine, Cleora believes, to assert women's eternal inferiority; for Christians, there is an indisputable inconsistency between what they profess (moral accountability in eternity) and how they treat women (educating them to focus on "Dress" rather than "the true Beauty . . . seated in the Mind"; 2:231). If Christian "Men of Understanding" insist on being hypocrites, they cannot but expect that their women will produce only "noxious Weeds" of the intellect. Cleora touches upon several of the combined pulse points of Cartesian-influenced soul-body arguments such as those of Poullain ("There is, undoubtedly, no Sexes in Souls"; 2:231) and Astell ("Surely our Bodies were not form'd by the great Creator out of the finest Mould, that our Souls might be neglected like the coarsest of the Clay"; 2:231). In agreeing with Cleora, the Female Spectator also echoes Chudleigh's argument that "the Management of her Family" should not be the sole fixation of a woman's learning (2:233); rather, a well-educated woman would execute her domestic duties "more through Principle than Custom" (2:233).

The emphasis on "Christian Principles" is thus key to Haywood's thoughts on women's education and Englishwomen's distance from the global community of women. Seguing from women's education to the need for moral reformation, the Female Spectator insists on the need to save England from "the Calamities under which this Nation at present groans . . . owing to the general Corruption and Depravity" (2:253). The letter from Platonides is useful here. Platonides encouraged improvements in women's education as a means of uprooting the "Belief of

Annihilation," which is not only a "Doctrine so absurd" and "manifestly wicked" in "Tendency" but is also "the Creed in vogue" (2:261). Platonides's letter returns readers of the *Female Spectator* to the mortalist and Trinitarian debates of the 1690s, demonstrating that the issues still had rhetorical force. For Platonides, the best way to combat annihilationism is to recognize the spark of divinity—the "intellectual Warnings" (2:261), this "*something* in us which neither *Nurse* nor *Priest* could be able to inspire us with;—a *something* which we have not at Command . . . a Ray of this Divine Attribute" which "shall shoot upon us, and tell us that such or such a thing will happen" (2:259). The members of the *Female Spectator* coterie agree that this "Flash of Prescience" (2:261) "must proceed from something more than Chance, that such a Ray of Knowledge, or of Inspiration rather, should all at once, and without any Endeavour or even Desire of it, strike upon the Mind; and that it is one of those many Marks we carry about us, of being form'd according to the Image of our all-wise Creator" (2:262). It is at this juncture—the women's combined assertion that divine intelligence can "strike upon the Mind"—that Haywood begins to contrast Englishwomen's intelligence with Indian (presumably Mogul and therefore Muslim) space.

The Female Spectator coincides with Platonides regarding the danger of annihilationism, but professes herself skeptical that most people truly believe in it. Rather, the only true annihilationists are those whose "Voluptuousness" aligns them with the "Mahometan Paradise" of sensual delights (2:263). The Female Spectator thus invests in Englishwomen's binary of Christian moral pleasures and Muslim sensual pleasures that was already coalescing in the fiction of Rowe, Aubin, and Barker.[6] She comments that "People so far gone in this wretched Lethargy" may actually "repine at Nature for making them of human Kind, and giving the Preference to the Brute Creation, merely because many of them are endued with higher and more poignant Sensations" (2:264). Yet such people "being by their Debaucheries rendered incapable of any Ideas of spiritual Felicities, take a Pleasure in believing they shall be no more, when they can no more act as at present" (2:264). Thus, the appeal of annihilationism, the termination of human identity, is directed only toward those who forsake Christian, human, intellectual pleasures.

For the Female Spectator, the belief in immortality is central to national morality, for "even those who neither fear'd nor hop'd a *future* World, [would] become honest, when they found it was for their Interest in *this* to be so" (2:266). Having asserted that not only "the Divines and Poets of all Ages, but the best and wisest of the ancient Philosophers, have vindicated the Doctrine of the Soul's Immortality, and existing in some future State, tho' they agree not as to what Kind" (2:268), the Female Spectator introduces a contribution by the reader "A.B." that describes an episode of apparitional intelligence set during the height of the Trinitarian Controversy. A.B. declares himself or herself aware that to entertain "such an Opinion" about the "intellectual World" as to believe in "the possibility of Spirits appearing after their Bodies are laid in the Earth" is "now laugh'd out of Doors" (2:269–270). Yet the contributor establishes credibility by acknowledging that "there are many ridiculous Reports of Apparitions; but what of that? Must we discredit all History because some Romances have born that Title?" (2:270). A.B. sees "renouncing a Belief of the Immortality of the Soul" as "the greatest and severest Blow that can be given to all Virtue and Religion in general" and suspects that the Female Spectator coincides since she is not "of the Number of those modern Infidels" so assured of their own "Penetration" that they "reject as fabulous whatever is not to be accounted for by Human Understanding" (2:270). Thus A.B. begins the story of the "celebrated Dutchess of Mazarine, Mistress to King Charles II" and her friend "Madam de Beauclair, who was no less admired and loved by his Royal Brother and Successor, James II" (2:271).

The initial period of this episode is set after "the Burning of Whitehall" at about the time "that *Reason* first began to oppose itself to *Faith*" (2:272). The fire that destroyed Whitehall occurred in 1698 and thus situates Mazarine's and Beauclair's subsequent conversation about immortality during the period of the Trinitarian Controversy. A.B. cannot be certain that "either of them were thoroughly convinced" of annihilationism, yet "the specious Arguments made use of by Persons of high Reputation for their Learning had such an Effect on both, as to raise great Doubts in them concerning the Immateriality of the Soul, and the Certainty of its Existence after Death" (2:272). Uncertain what to believe, the two friends make a pact that whoever dies first will visit her friend to confirm her existence after death.

Mazarine dies, and Beauclair subsequently despairs of the afterlife when she never hears from her friend. A.B. himself or herself, upon becoming acquainted with Beauclair, tries to persuade her of the "strong Probability" (2:274) that souls in the next world are not allowed to communicate with living mortals and that Mazarine's nonappearance is no evidence that she does not continue to exist. Beauclair is not convinced, insisting that since Mazarine has not performed her promise there must be no afterlife. Yet a few months later A.B. is just sitting down to cards with an unnamed friend of Beauclair's when Beauclair's servant enters with the request that the friend "would come that Moment to her, adding, that if she desir'd ever to see her more in this World, she must not delay her Visit" (2:275). An apparition had appeared to Beauclair soon before she was to die. She has time to summon a priest for confession and to receive a final visit from her friend and A.B. As she describes the apparition to them, Mazarine had appeared to her in her usual form, took a "little Circuit" around the room, "seeming rather to swim than walk," and eventually "*stopp'd by the Side of that* Indian Chest, *and looking on me with her usual Sweetness,* Beauclair, said she, *between the Hours of Twelve and One this Night you will be with me* (2:278; italics in original). I will say more about the Indian chest below, but this passage both anchors the reader in the material context of Beauclair's room, where she speaks to her friend and A.B. (and they are able to verify the presence of the chest), and sets up a rubric and a timeline for evaluating spiritual intelligence. Mazarine's prediction, her spiritual intelligence, will be verified or not by one o'clock.

Probability is on the side of the senses, for A.B. and Beauclair's friend think she seems in perfect health and protest that she should not entertain such gloomy thoughts. Yet as they continue talking and the time passes beyond midnight, Beauclair suddenly cries "I am sick at Heart!" and expires within the half hour (2:279). Thus Mazarine's intelligence is vindicated and the annihilationism of the deists and modern infidels is debunked. Of particular significance for the consideration of feminist orientalism is the fact that the "Indian Chest" serves as a material grounding of Mazarine's intelligence. As an object circulated through globalized trade, it marks Beauclair as a woman of status, but also metonymically registers Mazarine as someone who has taken a "circuit" of the sublunary world and can communicate intelligence authoritatively.

The "Indian" coding was obviously significant for Haywood since she also contrasted "Indian" tea with English herbal tonics as having pernicious effects on the English body politic.[7] The *Female Spectator* includes a letter from Mr. Careful, a correspondent who writes at length on the "immoderate Use of Tea" as a "kind of Debauchery" (2:95). After berating its effect on the domestic economy, the writer continues that "too much of this *Indian* Herb" causes a "Dejection of Spirits" which obliges English wives to seek "more animating Liquors" so that they "drink Wine pretty freely" (2:99). The Female Spectator partly agrees, despite acknowledging that the tea table is a particular site of feminine sociability. But she, too, uses "*Indian*" tea to make an argument about domestic economy. While observing that tea is "in itself a very harmless Herb . . . when taken moderately," the Female Spectator notes that England has "Plants of our own Growth" that would do just as well (2:101). Yet women's consumption of tea is like men's consumption of women. The "*Indian*" variety is preferred to the English: because of "the Passion we have for Exotics . . . we neglect the Use of what we have within ourselves for the same Reason as some Men do their Wives, only because they are their own" (2:101). Infidelity to English wives is linked to the eighteenth-century luxury debate and worries about globalized consumption

Taken together, Haywood's "*Indian*" commodities suggest the displacing mechanism at the heart of feminist orientalism. The consumption of "*Indian*" tea befuddles the mind and vitiates the body (2:102), so Englishwomen's physical pleasure in exotic commodities must be regulated and controlled by women's reason. Similarly, Indian spaces are necessary within the English home because they signal status, the control of globalized commodities, and Englishwoman's intelligence. While such a chest as Beauclair's historically might have originated from a Hindu-majority region, it is more likely, given Haywood's use of misogynistic mortalism, that these would have been artisanal products of Mogul India. It is also likely, historically, that her "*Indian*" tea would have originated in China. In any case, the proto-colonial commodification of India-as-portable-space is integral to Haywood's characterization of Englishwomen's spiritual intelligence.

PRINCESSES OF THE SOUL

Haywood's *Female Spectator* was an important link between her amatory novels of the early eighteenth century, the pious didactic fiction of the 1720s, and Samuel Richardson's novels of exemplary women in the 1740s. A brief overview of Richardson's earlier exemplary heroines, Pamela Andrews and Clarissa Harlowe, and their tactical use of immortality, will help to contextualize why the Bluestockings should have been so invested in Richardson's heroines and so conflicted in their responses to *Sir Charles Grandison*. But before addressing the Bluestocking reactions to Richardson's fiction in chapters 4 and 5, it is necessary to look at the mechanism by which a crucial stereotype—the "Platonic Lady"—shifted seventeenth-century platonic discourse from the region of feminocentric respectability identified with Katherine Philips to extreme cultural (sexual, religious, political) alterity. Paradoxically, Pamela and Clarissa represent a continuation of feminocentric platonic discourse even while *Pamela* and *Clarissa* contributed to its increasing marginalization. Pamela and Clarissa, like the poetic speakers or heroines of Philips, Cavendish, Rowe, Barker, and Haywood's *Female Spectator*, privilege intellectual and spiritual pleasure over bodily pleasures. The Platonic Lady stereotype, however, suggests that all these platonic professions may be simple hypocrisy, a denial of the pleasures Platonic Ladies really want.

In *Pamela* (1740–41), a lowly servant girl justifies her refusal to prostitute herself by staking her integrity on the immortality of her soul. Her example of pious integrity persuades her would-be seducer, Mr. B., to defy the class hierarchy and to marry her. *Clarissa* (1747–48), Richardson's tragic masterpiece, details how an individual's belief in the existence of an immortal soul, which can be known and judged only by God, enables her to resist abusive authorities, whether those are parents or aristocratic libertines. *Sir Charles Grandison* (1753–54) sets forth the character of a "good" man who understands his exercise of authority as a divine duty that opposes domestic, religious, and political tyranny. There is, then, a crucial role that the immortal soul performs in the lives of Richardson's protagonists: it makes them independent moral agents who can judge, and if necessary reject, the temporal world.

Pamela's ultimate success in proving her worthiness to be Mr. B.'s wife hinges on her demonstration of intrinsic merit. She asserts it in pleading that her "Honesty" means more to her than her "Life," because, as she states, "my Soul is of equal Importance with the Soul of a Princess, though my Quality is inferior to that of the meanest Slave."[8] After Pamela's fortitude persuades Mr. B. to propose honorable marriage, Pamela envisions her elevation as a chance to do good on earth, an opportunity for her to be more than "a mere Cypher on the wrong Side of a Figure" (363). She thanks God that through her wealth she, "tho' nothing worth," will give "Signification by my Place, and multiply the Blessings I owe to God's Goodness, who has distinguish'd me by so fair a Lot!" (363). She considers "how great must be the Condemnation of poor Creatures, at the great Day of Account, when they shall be asked, What Uses they have made of the Opportunity put into their Hands? and are able only to say, We have lived but to ourselves" (363). For Pamela, the eternal perspective, in which a perfect arbiter judges individual immortal souls, determines earthly life's meaning and reprioritizes temporal values. Pamela prioritizes moral productivity, having something to show for one's cultivation of the self. She is not an empty "Cypher" but a moral agent who will be able to answer for herself on the "Day of Account."

After Pamela and Mr. B. are married, his proud sister, Lady Davers, confronts him about his shaming of his family through the unequal match. She uses the vocabulary and imagery of the struggle between pagan and Judeo-Christian figures of religious authority to make her point, but her interpretation is weak, for she has privileged worldly values over eternal ones. Lady Davers accuses Mr. B. of being "worse than an Idolater," of having "made a graven Image" of his lowborn wife, while he, "*Jeroboam* like, would have every body else bow down before thy Calf! (423). Shifting religious registers, she imagines her brother as already dead, as having allied his aristocratic breeding to the dirt from which all mortal life arises and to which it ultimately returns. But Lady Davers unconsciously undermines her own argument: thinking that she has injured her brother's snobbery by implying that in marrying a servant girl he has found his natural level, she ignores the leveling effect of death. For her, "*Ashes to Ashes, and Dirt to Dirt!*" (424) is an accurate description of the social suicide of marrying down, of classing oneself with the dirt of the street. But Mr. B., instructed by the arguments Pamela had used to resist his ignoble advances, reminds his sister that she is deploying the language of an eternal, not a temporal, perspective: "Ay . . . Lady Davers, and there we must all end at last; you with all your Pride, and I with my plentiful Fortune, must come to it; and then where will be your Distinction? Let me tell you, except you and I both mend our Manners . . . this amiable Girl, whom your Vanity and Folly so much despises, will out-soar us both, infinitely out-soar us; and He that judges best, will give the Preference where due, without Regard to Birth or Fortune" (424). Mr. B. thus inverts his sister's hierarchy of social values by privileging an afterlife of spiritual meritocracy. Tacitly, he also suggests that Lady Davers is not particularly familiar with the Book of Common Prayer, thus calling into question her Anglican integrity and identity. All women have bodies that will eventually decay and die; but a woman like Pamela will have pleasures in the next life, regardless of her "Birth or Fortune" in the temporal realm. Richardson's novels, like his heroines, can best be understood if the heroines' insistence on legitimating their identities through their relation to eternal, divine authority is taken seriously. Pamela compares her experience to that of the Virgin Mary, alluding to the Magnificat in telling Mr. B., "*My Soul doth magnify the Lord*; for *he hath regarded the low Estate of his Handmaiden,—and exalted one of low Degree*" (311). God, not temporal authority, ultimately confers glory. Pamela is also ambitious. She may claim her social status as a "Handmaiden," but the implication is that she is emulating the mother of God. She sees her social elevation as evidence of the triumph of her spiritual reality. Terry Eagleton figures this critique of temporal authority in terms of class, seeing *Pamela* as a "fierce polemic against the prejudice that the most inconspicuous serving maid cannot be as humanly valuable as her social superiors."[9] More recently, Paul Kelleher has pointed out that Pamela is also challenging the gender hierarchy as well as the "narrative conventions of heterosexual desire" by appropriating "what traditionally have been considered *male* forms of virtue."[10] While coinciding with Kelleher, I wish to argue that Pamela's challenge to the gender hierarchy could be seen as even *more* radical. Not only does she use the soul to collapse the difference between herself and a princess, but the soul in Western literature is often described as feminine. Indeed, Gilbert Burnet in his *Exposition of the Thirty-nine Articles* refers to the soul as "she" and—astonishingly—does so when discussing the power of reason to evaluate both sensory information and revelation. Thus, Pamela's belief in her immortal soul is at once an assertion of her identity as a moral agent on an eternal timescale, a deeply social tactical rebellion by a subaltern, and a way of suggesting that, perhaps, the only superiority men have over women is in this present, temporary world.

Clarissa Harlowe is not a subaltern like Pamela, but she, too, uses the moral agency that immortality gives her to reject social coercion. Toni Bowers sees the evolution of Richardson's resistant heroines as being informed by the Jacobite rebellion of 1745–46. While in *Pamela* the problem of resistance is the negotiation of an "excessive exercise of rightful authority," in *Clarissa* the heroine must confront the power that ascends when "legitimate authority abdicates."[11] Clarissa encounters many obstacles over the course of a lengthy novel, but the first major hurdle is resisting her family's psychological abuse as they try to coerce her into marrying Mr. Solmes, someone for whom she feels an utter aversion. The second hurdle is resisting Robert Lovelace, the aristocratic libertine who helps her escape from her family but only in order to make her more vulnerable to his attempts to debauch her. The final hurdle is resisting those who encourage her to marry Lovelace to paper over the shame of having been drugged and raped. Ultimately, Clarissa chooses the afterlife over a world in which authority is abused and in which everyone prefers something to justice. Clarissa's is a dramatic deathbed scene, but her investment in the afterlife is a consistent aspect of her character from the earliest pages.

Before she flees home, for instance, Clarissa insists to her friend Anna Howe that if her parents will refrain from insisting on her forced marriage to Mr. Solmes, they need not worry about her marrying Lovelace, for "if they will signify as much to me, they shall see that I never will be *his*: For I have the vanity to think my soul his soul's superior."[12] *Clarissa* is, at its foundation, an exploration of competing systems of authority, its drama driven by the exertion of the human will against abusive materialist power. Accordingly, Clarissa consistently justifies her rejection of Solmes on the grounds of her eternal welfare: "What are Riches, what are Settlements, to Happiness? Let me not thus cruelly be given up to a man my very Soul is averse to. Permit me to repeat, that I cannot *honestly* be his. Had I a slighter notion of the matrimonial duty than I have, perhaps I might. But when I am to bear all the misery, and That for *life*; when my *heart* is less concerned in this matter than my *soul*; my *temporary*, perhaps, than my *future* good; why should I be denied the liberty of *refusing*? That liberty is all I ask" (2:32). Her family does not believe her protestation that her soul, not her heart, is at stake in her refusal of Solmes. They can only see her in terms of the errant heroines who become the ruined beauties of amatory fiction, used and abandoned by dashing rakes. This misreading of Clarissa—locating her motivations in the heart rather than in the soul—explains why they are surprised at her resistance. They have ignored the religious framework within which Clarissa chooses to function and to which the narrative continually gestures. They think that her pleasures are located in the body; she insists that her happiness comes from the spiritual pleasures that endure.

Like Pamela, Clarissa values her spiritual over her social identity. Lovelace is superior to her in social distinction. Yet it is Lovelace, with all his charm, status, and wealth, who is exiled from English identity by associating himself with the stereotypical Muslim despot. As he reminds Belford, a fellow member of a band of rakes, "We have held, that women have no Souls: I am a very Turk in this point, and willing to believe they have not. And if so, to whom shall I be accountable for what I do to them? Nay, if Souls they have, as there is no Sex in Ethereals, nor *need* of any, what plea can a Lady hold of injuries done her in her Lady-*State*, when there is an end of her Lady-*ship*?" (4:330). Lovelace grandly covers both possibilities of women's future state and speciously dismisses their relevance to his own case. His latter point relies on a stringent and sexist soul-body dualism, in which a sexual injury done to a woman ceases to exist as soon as her female body does. Significantly, as Angus Ross points out, this third, heavily revised, edition of *Clarissa* substitutes "Turk" where the first edition had "Jew." The revision was possibly in response to the Jew Bill of 1753.[13] The revision thus reassigns the belief in women's mortality from the Jewish to the Muslim faith. In either case, Lovelace aligns himself with an inaccurate construction of a non-Christian identity as a means of establishing his right to objectify women by denying them an immortal soul. His symbolic religious alterity exiles him from English identity and from Clarissa's heart. They do not share the same pleasures.

Lovelace's rhetorical and behavioral investment in women's mortality is primarily directed toward sexual conquest—his empire of accumulated sexualized bodies. He sees unlimited sexual access to women as part of his prerogatives as a man and claims, "The most charming woman on earth, were she an Empress, can excel the meanest, in the customary visibles only—Such is the equality of the dispensation, to the Prince and the Peasant, in this prime gift, WOMAN" (3:221). Lovelace, as a privileged and arrogant aristocrat, has no real interest in democratizing men's sexual access to women. He means that women are infinitely replaceable when the lights go out. And yet the "customary visibles" of clothing, grooming, and jewels only pertain to women's bodies. A well-stocked mind cannot be seen, but can only be encountered. Further, it is the mind, not the "customary visibles," that has an eternal identity, a memory of a consciousness across time. Locke would have been the first to point out that sinning against a lady's "*ship*" (her physical body)—whether through drugging her or raping her, or both—would of course also be to wrong her consciousness and memory, too.

Clarissa privileges spiritual identity and sees the rape as Lovelace's attempt to put them on an equal footing emotionally, since he cannot bear Clarissa's moral superiority. Even Lovelace ultimately gives some credence to Clarissa's formulation of their relative "value" as human beings: "*Marry and repair, at any time*; This, wretch that I was! was my plea to myself. To give her a lowering sensibility; to bring her down from among the stars which her beamy head was surrounded by, that my Wife, so greatly above me, might not despise me; this was one of my reptile motives, owing to my *more* reptile envy, and to my consciousness of inferiority to her!" (7:399). By using the image of the serpent, Lovelace emphasizes his proximity to the earth rather than to heaven and his affinity to Milton's Satan. Unlike Mr. B., Lovelace does not realize in time that, in the eternal perspective, the social benefits of wealth, attractiveness, status, and eloquence carry very little weight. It would seem that it is he who is characterized by the "customary visibles."

Pamela and Clarissa, despite the difference in their social status, both share an eternal perspective that the Harlowes and Lovelace do not. Their vision encompasses the detritus of material reality—social status is as temporary as ashes and dung—and like pilgrims, rather than "sensual Travellers" (*Pamela*, 377), they journey on toward something better. Pamela remarks of the transience of earthly plenty: "How do these Gentry know, that . . . one hundred Years hence or two, some of those now despised upstart Families, may not revel in their Estates, while their Descendants may be reduced to the other's Dunghils?" (258; *sic*). The Harlowes fit the description of an upstart family, and Lovelace dismisses their pretensions by noting of Harlowe Place, "like Versailles, it is sprung up from a dunghil within every elderly person's remembrance" (*Clarissa*, 1:231). It is typical of Lovelace that he can dismiss Versailles by associating it with dung while being utterly invested in the spectacular politics and privilege that it represents.

Neither the wealthy aristocrat nor the grasping bourgeois family realizes the richness and depth of Clarissa's religious education. As Margaret Anne Doody recognizes, Clarissa is "without knowing it, a martyr for her faith. . . . To live and die in faith—the substance of things hoped for, the evidence of things not seen—seems crazed to the respectable."[14] This is precisely the power of Pamela and Clarissa as moral agents. They believe in accountability in the afterlife. That perspective, that witnessing at the heart of martyrdom, neutralizes the power of "respectable" members of society who see the abduction of a servant girl or the rape of a teenager as acceptable costs in preserving the status quo. Mortalism of any kind is thus antithetical to Richardson's heroines' revolutionary potential.

Richardson's long-suffering heroines modeled heroic femininity as a rejection of a social hierarchy in which worldly rather than spiritual and intellectual pleasures were promoted. But in crafting his heroines, Richardson implicitly contradistinguished them from the stereotype of the "Platonic Lady," a ridiculous figure of distorted female sexuality and intellectual inadequacy. The "Platonic Lady" claims to be virtuous, perhaps even believes that it is true. But she is softheaded and misunderstands her own "natural" needs and duties. Her canal of pleasure is definitely of the kind Lovelace prefers.

PLATONIC LADIES AND THE MAHOMETAN PARADISE

The previous chapter examined the potential for seventeenth-century feminocentric platonism to leverage creative and professional possibilities for women writers. This feminocentric platonic tradition influenced eighteenth-century writers like Elizabeth Singer Rowe, Penelope Aubin, Jane Barker, and even Eliza Haywood and Samuel Richardson. But that tradition, so strongly identified with the defense of immaterial identity at the heart of the Trinitarian Controversy, was gradually shut down. Theologian Jeremy Taylor, in reply to Philips's request for a clarification about the nature of friendship, replied partly by describing platonic love and platonic friendship as "tinsel dressings," associating them with romances and castles in the air, and dismissing them as "good for nothing" in his *A Discourse on Friendship* (1657).[15] Walter Charleton took a "naturalistic" approach to criticizing platonic love, representing his version of the legendary Ephesian Matron as rejecting platonic love for the very reason that immaterial love cannot give as much pleasure as can the "flames" that "arise from the difference of Sex."[16] Philip Souers notes that platonic love "was so much a part of the Cavalier poetry that to neglect it is to fail to understand the poetry itself; it is an index to the Cavalier mind, a key to Cavalier gallantry." But though it persisted as a "tradition of courtliness" throughout the "uncongenial days of the Commonwealth," he also notes that all the Cavalier poets "turned round, at least those who were not without a sense of humor, and made sport of the very absurdities that they had before exalted."[17] The "Platonic Lady" embodied this Caroline tension. Essentially the Platonic Lady was a "negative ideal" of feminine identity in an Anglican context.

This section surveys the satire of the Platonic Lady (with particular focus on Madonella in the *Tatler* [1709] and on Honoria in *Letters from a Persian* [1735] by George, Lord Lyttelton); the fulcrum point of Samuel Richardson's sublimation of the trope in his fiction; and the politically informed deployment of the revised trope to criticize the fashionable, elite "Ladies' Coterie" in the newspapers of the 1770s. The satire depicted the withdrawal of women from normative patriarchal heterosexuality into a feminocentric site (or discourse) as a symbol of potential foreign contagion that needed to be disciplined and regulated. Given the association of the libidinous and public ladies of the "Coterie" and the public example of the more intellectual Bluestockings, the Platonic Lady stereotype was a negative ideal against which the Bluestockings had to distinguish themselves. That effort to distinguish themselves—clear in the fiction of Charlotte Lennox, the polemical nonfiction of Mary Wollstonecraft, and the letters of Catherine Talbot and Elizabeth Carter—further contributed to feminist orientalism because the Platonic Lady was a stereotype that encompassed critiques of stereotypical Roman

Catholic and Muslim masculinities. The Platonic Lady performed an important regulatory function in the rhetorical construction of national unity, a unity fabricated, as Dana Rabin, Stephen H. Gregg, Gillian Russell, and other scholars have shown, through the identification of national security with the integrity of British (Anglican) masculinity.[18]

Sarah Chapone made the importance of the state church clear in her 1735 defense of married women's rights. Speaking for all "his Majesty's faithful *Female* Subjects," she declares that being a wife in England is "a worse Condition than *Slavery*" and that "we are now apprehensive of more frequent Oppression from these Laws [governing marriage], as this is an Age in which the Foundation of all the noble Principles of Christianity (which are our only Protection) are broken up, and *Deism*, that Underminer of all that is truly laudable, with its Legions of Immorality, Prophaneness, and consummate Impudence are let in upon us."[19] Chapone then proceeds to make the (by 1735) standard argument that to treat women as the English legal system currently does is an abdication on the part of Englishmen from their Christian duty in favor of (indeed, going further than) stereotypical Muslim despotism. She points out that under the current legal system, "supposing a Man no Christian, he may be as *Despotick* . . . as the Grand Seignior in his Seraglio, with this Difference only, that the *English* Husband has but *one Vassal* to treat according to his variable Humour, whereas the Grand Seignior having *many*, it may be supposed, that some of them, at some Times may be suffered to be at quiet" (5). In other words, England's treatment of its women did not conform to the doctrine of the Church of England. Englishmen were able to treat their wives worse than the Ottoman despot *could* treat the women of his seraglio. Noticeably, this Eurocentric argument used the Ottoman Empire to castigate deism: Chapone clearly positions herself on the side of Anglican orthodoxy. Chapone, and many other Englishwomen, used the example of the Muslim despot as a shaming tactic to point out the failures of Englishmen to conform to their professed beliefs. However, while Chapone's indictment of the English legal system is an instance of feminist orientalism, she was not simply displacing patriarchal oppression onto a Muslim other. Rather, like anti-Socinians in the Trinitarian Controversy, she was playing off against each other "ideal" (Anglican) masculine behavior, Muslim despotism, and the national threat posed by deism. Islam here functions as the negative ideal; yet in Chapone's view it is Anglican men who are behaving the worst toward women. Chapone's argument, and its connection to Anglican orthodoxy, was echoed by Elizabeth Robinson (later Elizabeth Montagu, "Queen" of the Bluestockings). She wrote to her acquaintance William Freind that "there is a Mahometan Error crept even into the Christian Church that Women have no Souls, & it is thought very absurd for us to pretend to read or think like Reasonable

Creatures."[20] To deny women an education was to dispense with Anglican orthodoxy, but conformity to that orthodoxy determined men's political and educational access. The "Mahometan" argument thus created a toxic perfect storm in which it was the interest of both British men and women to demonize Muslim men as sexually threatening and to cast Muslim women as passive victims cruelly denied, and in need of, the dignifying liberty of Christian education.

In eighteenth-century England, the "Platonic Lady" was overdetermined as a figure—variously a stand-in for the nun, the *précieuse*, the female preacher, or the inhabitant of a seraglio—of deviant feminine literacy and sexuality.[21] In *Shamela*, Fielding aligns the eponymous protagonist's bawd mother with the feminocentric cult of platonic love of Charles I's consort by naming her Henrietta Maria Honora Andrews.[22] Further, in *Tom Jones* (in which Sophia's servant woman "Honour" is also characterized as mercenary, sexually suspect, and lacking in personal integrity) the narrator satirically and backhandedly implies that platonic love is both unnatural and fabricated to satisfy women's vanity.[23] Fielding dedicated *Tom Jones* (1749) to Lord Lyttelton, who had written one of the most scathing Platonic Lady satires and who would go on to become a good friend of the "Queen" of the Bluestockings, Elizabeth Montagu.[24] Lyttelton is, then, an important historical link between Augustan satires of the Platonic Lady and the possible reception of that satire among the Bluestocking circle of women intellectuals in the second half of the eighteenth century.

Lyttelton's inset narrative "Ludovico and Honoria" in *Letters from a Persian in England, to his Friend in Ispahan* (1735) launched an extensive attack on the Platonic Lady. Published in the same month as Lyttelton's entrance to the House of Commons and going through four editions in the same year, *Letters from a Persian* was written, according to one view, "to bring over public opinion to [opposition leader Lord] Bolingbroke's ideas."[25] This would situate *Letters* directly in the tug-of-war between Prime Minister Robert Walpole and the political opposition headed by Lord Bolingbroke in the 1730s. Explicitly modeled on Charles Montesquieu's *Persian Letters* (1721), Lyttelton's *Letters from a Persian* records an ostensibly disinterested foreigner's assessment of contemporary England. The Persian observer Selim writes to his friend Mirza in Ispahan, detailing all the strange activities and relationships that characterize 1730s London. Opera, gaming, cards, marriage, conspicuous consumption, party politics, bearbaiting, war, and education all come under Selim's observation. English masculinity is linked to national character (and national security) early on. Selim's assessments of English masculinity use female sexuality and cross-cultural (and trans-historical) comparisons effectively function to warn Englishmen that they appear weak and ineffectual to outsiders. Selim at one point exclaims, "Bless me . . . why should the Women in this Country be so fond of Eunuchs? Methinks they have Men enough about them."[26] And one of the John Bull-ish spectators at the bearbaiting censures Selim's friend and his French interlocutor's criticism of the activity, declaring that this "Gentleness and Effeminacy in our Manners will soften us by Degrees into Slaves, and we shall grow to hate fighting in earnest when we don't love to see it in Jest. You fine Gentlemen are for the Taste of modern *Rome*, squeaking Eunuchs and a Pension, but I am for that of ancient *Rome*, Gladiators and Liberty" (Letter 4, 8–9). This irascible advocate of a manly England clearly sees all contemporary Italian men as mercenary Roman Catholic castrati.

In Letter 8, Selim informs Mirza that he is astonished by how "some Women in this Country talk of Love. Their Discourses about it are as refin'd as their Notions of Paradise, and they exclude the Pleasure of the Senses out of both" (18). Selim expresses his incredulity that these women, or "Platonics" as they call themselves, really mean what they say. As he tells Mirza, "It is my Opinion, that the nicest of them all, if she were to enjoy her Paradise here woul'd make it a Mahometan one." The implication is that women who profess their lack of interest in sensual pleasure would actually like nothing better than a "Mahometan" paradise. Here we have, again, the alignment of Islam with physical pleasure over and against Christian intellectual pleasures. Selim then proceeds to narrate the story he told a "Platonic" acquaintance of his in response to "all her pretty Reasonings" (18).

The narrative, titled "*The Loves of* Ludovico *and* Honoria," is set in Genoa, "famed above any Town in *Europe* for the Refinement of its Gallantry," and revolves around the courtship and misadventures of Honoria Grimaldi, a senator's daughter and a "fair Lady who was a Platonic," and Ludovico, who, of all the "sighing Tribe" of gallants, was "the most enamour'd, the most constant, and the most respectful" (19). The setting of the tale—the Mediterranean, especially Genoa, Corsica, and Tunis—not only allows for a cross-cultural comparison of gender relations but also invokes the power of Ottoman military, naval, and economic might.

Ludovico and Honoria declare the violence of their mutual passion to each other. But Honoria believes that the freedoms of a husband are "entirely inconsistent with the Respect that Character requires" (19). She insists that "it was his Mind she loved, and cou'd enjoy that without going to Bed to him" (19). But in his bed is precisely where Ludovico wants them to be, and he offers to marry her without any dowry. This enticing financial offer is accepted by her father, who then "roundly" informs Honoria that "she must be married the next Day or go to a Nunnery" (20). In "spite of all her Repugnance to the Marriage Bed," Honoria then discovers that "she found something about her still more averse to the Idea of a Cloister." Not knowing which way to turn, Honoria appeals to those staples of the Platonic Lady's reading material—she "turn'd over above a hundred Romances to search for Precedents" and eventually decides to marry Ludovico if he will "not pretend at once to all the Rights and Privileges of a Husband." They are married and then depart for Corsica, where Ludovico has just inherited a large estate. After about a month on the seas, Ludovico has managed to arrive "at the full Enjoyment of her Lips" and is proceeding on to further liberties, "sailing on with a fair Wind, and almost in the Port," when they are attacked and taken prisoner by an African corsair (21). Honoria is sent as a prize to the "Seraglio of the Dey" at Tunis, while Ludovico, "unfit for any Labour," is employed by the corsair as a music teacher to his children (22).

The narrator steps out of the narrative description to exclaim of Honoria's predicament, "O unfortunate End of all her pure and heroical Sentiments! Was it for this that her Favours were so long and so obstinately denied to the tender Ludovico, to have them ravish'd in a Moment by a rude Barbarian, who did not so much as thank her for them?" (22). Several points are suggested by this outburst: first, a woman who insists that she has erotic preferences is "obstinate"; second, if she does not cooperate with a "tender" lover, she will be sexually punished by a "rude Barbarian" who has *no* regard for her desires; and, third, tender lovers are ineffectual defenders of themselves and their property—they are not fit for manly labor of any kind.

Imagining that Honoria must by now have killed herself "rather than submit to so gross a Violation" (22) as he imagines she must be threatened with by the Dey, Ludovico is doubly afflicted to find himself desired by the corsair's wife. However, since he is assured she will kill him if he does not comply, he resolves to submit and in her finds a "Mistress infinitely more complying than his fantastical *Italian*" (23). However, the couple's pleasure is short-lived—the corsair discovers the affair and has Ludovico castrated "with a *Turkish* Rigour far more desperate and compleat than any such thing had been ever practis'd in *Italy*" (24). Muslim Turkey and Roman Catholic Italy are conflated in the act of castration—one culture uses the act to render servants docile and tractable (turning men into eunuchs); the other uses it to render singers as moving and as entertaining as possible (turning boys into castrati). In another infantilization of Ludovico, he is portrayed as being so boyish that castration can still alter his voice.

Indeed, Ludovico's voice improves so much that he is sent to perform in the seraglio of the Dey, where he finds his beloved Honoria very much alive. He tells her, "in a softer Tone of Voice than she had been us'd to," that he has lost that which caused her so much offense and has prepared an escape for them. "You may now be happier with me than you was before," he tells her, "as I shall not trouble you with *those coarse Sollicitations* which gave you so much uneasiness. We will love with the Purity of Angels, and leave sensual Enjoyments to the Vulgar, who have not a Relish for higher Pleasures. . . . I have often heard you say, that your Love was only to My Mind, and that, I do assure you, is still the same" (25). Honoria, however, finds something about her less averse to coarse solicitations than to escaping from apparent sexual bondage; she responds in about the way we would expect William Wycherley's Lady Fidget of *The Country Wife* to do in her place: "How . . . are you really no Man?" she demands in astonishment. Assured by Ludovico that this is so, she responds in a way that is decidedly not platonic: "Since my being here, I am turn'd *Mahometan*, and my Religion will not suffer me to run away with an Unbeliever. My New Husband has taught me certain Doctrines unknown to me before, in the Practise of which I am resolved to live and die. Return to your own Country, good Signor Eunuch . . . my Conscience won't permit me to have a longer Conversation with such an Infidel." Honoria denies her sexual hypocrisy by resorting to an intellectual (that is, immaterial) lexicon—"Conscience," "Doctrines," "Religion"—to describe her sex drive. For it is really the sensual "Paradise" of stereotypically represented "Mahometan" sexuality that she desires, not the "Visionary Joys" (18) that this "fantastical *Italian*" (23) has been taught to prefer by her romances.

None of the characters in this narrative is particularly sympathetic because the narrative is a satire of Italian Catholic masculinity and the femininity of the "Platonic lady," with the "Barbaric" but potent sexuality of the stereotypical Muslim despot functioning as the satire's vehicle. Lyttelton depicts the Dey of Tunis, for all his barbarity, as knowing what women really want. Honoria is woefully ignorant of her own desires at best and ultimately cruelly hypocritical. Ludovico is silly and "unmanly"—he takes Honoria at her word, is unfit for conventional masculine labor, and ends up as a castrato, the embodiment of stereotypically effeminate Italian masculinity. The anxiety about the dwindling masculinity of Englishmen expressed in Selim's earlier letters is here displaced onto the effeminate Italian who cannot even keep his own woman in line but rather lets her "fantastical" "Caprices" dictate the expression of his sexuality and limit the "Rights and Privileges of a Husband" (Lyttelton, 20). Muslims and libertines do not have this problem with women, of course. As we shall see in the satire on Mary Astell as Madonella in the *Tatler*, even as models of masculinity became more domesticated and bourgeois from the Restoration to the mid-eighteenth century, libertines still performed a useful satiric function: they turned "women of honor," who threatened to remove themselves from the heterosexual economy, into figures of ridicule. The libertine shows the Platonic Lady to be, despite her protestations, a non-threatening rebel who can easily be brought into line with a little tickling of the feminine text. The responsiveness of the unacknowledged sexual appetite of the ignorant, unnatural, and usually Roman Catholic Platonic Lady serves as an index of a man's sexual potency, keenness of perception, and ability to defend himself and his nation. Who she enjoys having sex with—whether Muslim despot, libertine, or Anglican gentleman—says more about the model of masculinity that the author is negotiating than anything about the Platonic Lady herself.

Lyttelton thus shows a barbaric Muslim masculinity, in the figure of the Dey of Tunis, as capable of a sexual and territorial conquest to which Roman Catholic European masculinity cannot stand up, literally or figuratively. The sexually permeable body of the Platonic Lady, the marker of her sexual hypocrisy, thus also suggests the inability of men who take platonic discourse seriously to defend themselves either physically or intellectually. This representational framework—the use of foreign (or libertine) masculinity to triumph over the self-exile of women from the domestic heterosexual economy, naturalizing femininity that was English, Anglican, domestic, and naturally responsive to Anglican men—was current throughout the eighteenth century. The Platonic Lady was satirized in roughly similar fashion by Susannah Centlivre (*The Basset Table*, *The Platonic Lady*); Alexander Pope, John Gay, and John Arbuthnot (*Three Hours after Marriage*); and Richard Steele and Joseph Addison in the *Tatler*.

Interestingly, Samuel Richardson also relies on this conflation of stereotypical Muslim and libertine masculinities in *Clarissa*. We have already seen that Lovelace called himself a "Turk" and reminded Belford that they had both professed "that women have no Souls" (4:330). Moreover, Lovelace's comments indicated the bifurcated view of platonic love at mid-century. In the context of discussing tragedy (a crucial theme given Richardson's "religious plan" for *Clarissa*), Lovelace entertains the prostitute at Mrs. Sinclair's by describing his love for Clarissa as "platonic." Lovelace emphasizes to Belford that this is a performance; he knows that Clarissa is listening (the scene occurs before the rape and before Clarissa realizes who the prostitutes are). Accordingly, he describes the scene to Belford as if it were a stage performance with an aside to the audience (Belford): "My passion for my Beloved (which as I told them in a high and fervent accent, was the truest that man could have for woman) I boasted of. It was, in short, I said, of the *true Platonic kind*; or I had no notion of what Platonic Love was. . . . So it is, Jack; and must end as Platonic Love generally does end" (4:142). Lovelace describes his "*Platonic*" love in such a way that he believes Clarissa will recognize it as a requisite element in a flattering and reassuring feminocentric romance. He delivers this description in a high, fervent voice so that she will be sure to hear him. He delightedly notes, in his *androcentric* correspondence with Belford, that this is in fact a cynical performance of romantic conventions. Lovelace is invested in the libertine understanding of platonic love—professing it is an easy way of getting softheaded women into bed, of taking advantage of their inadequate literacy to make them perform the only function for which they are fit—that of the sexually pleasurable (but not necessarily pleasured) and reproducing body.

Lovelace's view of women contrasts starkly with that of Richardson's ideal English gentleman, Sir Charles Grandison, who explicitly asserts women's immortality and intellect. (As he assures a mixed party of men and women, "When Sex ceases, inequality of Souls will cease; and women will certainly be on a foot with men, as to intellectuals, in Heaven."[27]) Significantly, Bonnie Latimer has criticized Sir Charles for a manipulative sadism that regulates both women and non-Christians. She also portrays him as modeling the very "tactical performances" of virtue promulgated by leading Latitudinarians like Archbishop John Tillotson. Further, Samuel Clarke's sermons were among Richardson's reading materials as he set about creating his "good man."[28] An exemplary Latitudinarian gentleman, Sir Charles pointedly marries the modest, Protestant, English girl Harriet Byron rather than the flighty, Roman Catholic, Italian Clementina della Porretta. No nice English girl who was fit to marry a nice English gentleman could be a Platonic Lady, in other words. If national identity is mapped onto Anglican masculinity, then the Platonic Lady—susceptible to seduction *and* conversion by non-English "others"—represented a symbolic and, perhaps, actual breach of national security.

By far the most contentious woman writer associated with feminocentric platonic discourse was the Tory polemicist and women's education advocate Mary Astell. Author of the combative *Some Reflections Upon Marriage* (1700), Astell is perhaps best known for her prose tract *A Serious Proposal to the Ladies* (1694), in which she famously and controversially proposed the creation of an academy to which women could retreat to cultivate their piety and learning. Astell's plan was controversial because a female academy seemed tantamount to a Roman Catholic convent or "nunnery." The idea of a "Protestant nunnery" was a matter of serious concern, but also a target of satire, throughout the eighteenth century. As Frances Dolan has argued, female communities in post-Reformation England smacked of continental Roman Catholicism, and it was a short leap to equate convents and brothels in order to discredit Roman Catholic practice.[29] Yet the idea was also entertained in mid-century fiction such as *Sir Charles Grandison* and Charlotte Lennox's *The Female Quixote* (1752)—and even beyond, as Bridget Hill has shown.[30] In the satire of the Platonic Lady in the *Tatler* we see that while the model of masculinity at work is that of a British libertine rather than a Muslim despot, the mechanism of regulating recalcitrant women is much the same; further, the threat of a "foreign" presence being established in a domestic space through women's weak judgment is as present as ever.

Richard Steele's the *Tatler* (1709–11) attacked Astell by satirizing her as the pedantic author "Madonella" in issue no. 32 (June 18, 1709). Presented as a forum for the observations of the persona "Isaac Bickerstaff," the *Tatler* included letters from the periodical's readers, real or fictional, seeking advice. In issue no. 32 of the *Tatler*, "Charles Sturdy" writes to Bickerstaff seeking his advice about how to woo a "professed Platonne, the most unaccountable Creature of her Sex."[31] She reads "*Norris*, and *Moor*, and *Milton*" and insists on understanding metaphors "literally." Sturdy complains, "Why should she wish to be a Cherubim, when 'tis Flesh and Blood that makes her adorable?" She is a "dear Declaimer" who contemplates "Ideas" and extols "Intuition." Sturdy has "very fine Views of Pleasure" and yearns for the shared sensory experiences of speaking and kissing. She desires, or claims to desire, a life of the mind; he desires to take pleasure from the "Flesh and Blood" and is frustrated at her unresponsiveness. Her "Aversion" to his robust physical presence leaves him at a loss. She "shrinks from the Touch like a sensitive Plant, and would contract herself into mere Spirit," he complains. In response to her Christianized Platonism, Sturdy fabricates a religiously inflected fantasy of violence aimed at forcing her to recognize their shared physicality: "I had hopes in the Hypocrisy of her Sex," he explains, "but Perseverance makes it as bad as fixed Aversion. I desire your Opinion, whether I may not lawfully play the Inquisition upon her, make Use of a little Force, and put her to the Rack and Torture, only to convince her she has really fine Limbs, without spoiling or distorting them" (1:231).

Bickerstaff's response is cynical and expedient: force is not necessary when lovers learn how to manipulate women for their own good. Flattery works well on women, Bickerstaff opines, but this "Order of Platonic Ladies are to be dealt with in a peculiar Manner from all the rest of the Sex" (1:231). With them, flattery "is not to be done grossly." He goes on to relate the tale of Madonella (clearly modeled on Anglican Mary Astell, but with a glance at the Roman Catholic attachment to the Virgin Mary or Madonna). Madonella was the leader of a group of seven women who had retired from public life to devote themselves to the development of the mind and soul. These women "gave out, That Virginity was to be their State of Life during this mortal Condition, and therefore resolved to join their Fortunes, and erect a Nunnery" (1:231–232). In the legal context of eighteenth-century England this move would, of course, remove their bodies and money from the control of potential husbands. As William Blackstone explained, "By marriage, the husband and wife are one person in law: that is, the very being or legal existence of the woman is suspended during marriage. . . . For this reason, a man cannot grant any thing to his wife, or enter into covenant with her: for the grant would be to suppose her separate existence."[32] While Sturdy had alienated himself from his Englishness by entertaining the idea of playing a Roman Catholic inquisitor, Bickerstaff alienates the "Platonic Ladies" by styling Astell's female academy a "Nunnery" and Astell herself as a would-be Virgin Mary selfishly denying her reproductive and financial services to a potential English husband.

Further, Bickerstaff retains and embellishes Sturdy's plant metaphor. While Sturdy's mistress "shrinks" from his touch like a "sensitive" plant, a "famous *Rake*" and seven of his fellow rakes infiltrate the Platonic projectors' sylvan asylum of "shady Coverts, and flowry Arbours," the "Mansions of intended Severity" as Bickerstaff calls them (1:232). Hidden behind a grate, the "Platonics" observe the men gain entrance by stymieing the befuddled maid, Susan. They react physiologically, like Sturdy's Platonne, to the invasion of personal space and the flouting of their professed desire for privacy. In Bickerstaff's narration, it is manipulating women into physical proximity and unconventional intimacy that gives the lovers the upper hand. Rake effectively neutralizes Susan's intended refusal of entrance by persuading her that having a crowd of gentlemen kiss her in series is "the Favour of a civil Salute" (1:232). Bickerstaff signals his chummy identification with Rake by referring to Susan with the patronizing "Suky." Using the advantages of class and gender, Rake puts Susan and, by extension, the foundresses, at an immediate disadvantage: "The poor Girl was in the middle of the Crowd of these Fellows at a Loss what to do, without Courage to pass through them; and the *Platonics*, at several Peep-holes, pale, trembling and fretting" (1:232). This physiological reaction of the Platonics is significant. They are distressed, incapacitated, disarmed, vulnerable, and afflicted—Rake is fulfilling Sturdy's fantasy of putting the Platonics on the rack; their physiological reactions prove that they have a body and that it responds to a man's presence. Stripped of the vocabulary and personal space that structure their identity, they are, really, just like other women and will sooner or later fall in line with nature.

Madonella, "a Lady who had writ a fine Book concerning the recluse Life, and was the Projectrix of the Foundation," is the only woman other than Susan who finds the courage to approach the group of men (1:233). Upon meeting Rake, she points out to him the breach of social hierarchy and etiquette that his officiousness has occasioned: "Sir, I am obliged to follow the Servant, who was sent to know, What Affair could make Strangers press upon a Solitude which we, who are to inhabit this Place, have devoted to Heaven and our own Thoughts?" Rake refuses to take Madonella's (albeit pedantic) insistence on her own desires seriously, and adopting an appearance of "great Distance, mixed with a certain Indifference," he proceeds to play upon her vanity and credulity. He claims that the men are "Travellers, who have seen many foreign Institutions of this Kind, [and] have a

Curiosity to see, in its first Rudiments, the Seat of primitive Piety." He represents the band of rakes as having a purely intellectual interest in investigating the nunnery and empirically comparing it to institutions on the Continent. This coincides with what he had told "Suky," namely, that the rakes are "Gentlemen that are travelling England; after which we shall go into Foreign Parts, where some of us have already been. . . . Now you must know we have an Ambition to have it to say, That we have a Protestant Nunnery in England" (1:232). He thus represents an invasion of personal space as motivated by a gentlemanly spirit of scientific inquiry, but also by the enlightened project of cross-cultural comparison and national glory. The "nunnery" is represented as *both* a foreign, continental, Roman Catholic element on British soul *and* a potentially domesticated version of that foreignness: the women's responsiveness will indicate whether they are nice, natural English girls, after all, or whether they are truly different: figures of curiosity, inquiry, and, possibly, contagion.

Rake, the consummate actor, pretends not to know to whom he is speaking, but professes himself to be impressed by Madonella's authorship of a "seraphick Discourse" on the subject of the single life and to be interested in exploring the "Seat of primitive Piety" that the Platonics have established. This appeal to Madonella's vanity results in her identifying herself as the author of the discourse, and Rake effects to fall back "with the profoundest Veneration" and to humbly request to "approach Lips which have uttered Things so sacred" (1:233). He and his fellows proceed to repeat the same "civil Salute" to which they had subjected "Suky." Once this hurdle is gotten over, no further obstacles present themselves for the rakes. Madonella introduces them to the other "Platonic ladies," they pair up, and then all the pairs visit the garden together like Adams and Eves in a prelapsarian Eden.

The conversation turns to flowers and reproduction. Rake, with "solemn Impudence," declares that "he sincerely wished Men might rise out of the Earth like Plants; and that our Minds were not of Necessity to be sullied with carnivorous Appetites for the Generation, as well as Support of our Species" (1:234). Rake's self-confidence as a performer serves him well: Madonella immediately responds, "Sir, under the Notion of a pious Thought, you deceive yourself in wishing an Institution foreign to that of Providence. These Desires were implanted in us for reverend Purposes, in preserving the Race of Men, and giving Opportunities for making our Chastity more heroic." Rake's flattery has undermined Madonella's reserve at its weakest point, her vanity, and has led her into admitting indirectly that she has sexual thoughts and desires. The actual merit of the intellectual system of the "Platonic ladies" and their personal conviction of its desirability are dismissed in Bickerstaff's observation that there was "hardly one of them but was a Mother or Father that Day Twelvemonth." The entire conceptual structure of a Protestant "nunnery" is undermined by the reproductive appeal of the lilies and roses in the garden of the "Platonic ladies." For, as Bickerstaff opines, any "unnatural Part is long taking up, and as long laying aside" (1:234). If Sturdy will pursue Rake's method of courtship, his "Platonica" will "fall in with the Necessities of mortal Life, and condescend to look with Pity upon an unhappy Man, imprisoned in so much Body, and urged by such violent Desires" (1:234–235).

Relying on the common processes of nature as his authority, Bickerstaff denies women's individual identities and desires. For reproduction is not one of "the Necessities of mortal Life" for individuals, but only for the species. Yet all the "Platonic ladies" pair up with the members of Rake's cohort, and, a few botany lessons later, they have all given up their "heroick" chastity, contemplating heaven, and caring about their own thoughts. They have decided they want a bit of heaven right here on earth. In spite of Madonella's vanity and pedantry, there is something insidious beneath all this breezy gentlemanly assurance that women will fall in with the natural needs of "mortal life." On the one hand, confronted with their attraction to the men's physical presence (the women's heterosexuality is assumed), the trembling "Platonic ladies" clearly did not have a chance. They had committed to a life of virginity without fully examining the consequences or the alternatives. On the other hand, given—we are to infer—an attractive alternative in the persons of Rake's cohort, the "Platonic ladies" put up little or no resistance. They make no intellectual effort to evaluate themselves, their desires, or their beliefs upon being confronted with the disruption of their isolation. The women's easy assent to the dictates of biology suggests that their professed interest in God, the mind, the soul, and their own thoughts was at best ignorant and misguided and at worst a deceitful sham of vain, pedantic prudes. Women's biology, this satire soothingly assures its audience, is indeed destiny.

Intellectual women were not only figures of ridicule, however. As Maria Dzielska observes, John Toland, Voltaire, and Edward Gibbon all praised Hypatia of Alexandria, ostensibly persecuted by Saint Cyril for her devotion to learning, reason, and science.[33] For these Enlightenment thinkers, Hypatia represented the free flight of the human mind unshackled by dogma, superstition, or enthusiasm, and they "used her as an instrument in religious and philosophical polemic" (4). Dzielska notes that Hypatia even makes an appearance in Henry Fielding's *A Journey from This World to the Next* (1743). What is clear about the intellectual woman of eighteenth-century England is that the degree of sympathy toward her use of that intellect was indicated by the degree to which her intellectualism was represented as *not* influenced by the French salon cultures of the *précieuses*, by Roman Catholicism, or by Islam.

DOMESTICATING THE PLATONIC LADY

After the satire of Madonella and Lord Lyttelton's *Letters from a Persian*, the extinction of feminocentric platonism as a serious life choice for women proceeded apace. The final stage can be traced from the continuation of Samuel Richardson's *Pamela* to the early 1750s novels of Tobias Smollett and Henry Fielding. This period coincides with what Margaret Anne Doody and Jane Spencer have identified as both a stifling domestication of the British novel and an increasingly conservative array of narrative possibilities and self-constructions for women novelists. In short, the ridicule of the intellectual woman who is coded as a "Platonic Lady" when she shows any susceptibility to foreign influence (whether intellectual, religious, or sexual) is complete by the mid-1750s. The Lady vanishes.

The stereotype of the Platonic Lady had very effectively done its cultural work by 1755. From about the mid-century mark platonic love was satirized while the direct, blunt-force satire of the Platonic Lady dwindled. There is, for instance, a distinct difference in Smollett's portrayal of the Platonic Lady in two of his works on either side of the mid-century mark. In *Roderick Random* (1748), he includes a lengthy description of Narcissa's pedantic, harebrained maiden aunt, clearly drawn from the Platonic Lady tradition since she is a "visionary" and a "perfect female virtuosi" who "professes the principles of Rosicrucius" and has "contempt for the male part of the creation."[34]

Narcissa's aunt seems also to be partly descended from the poetic, slovenly pseudo-intellectuals epitomized by Pope's Sappho. The maiden aunt's misandry is clearly relished and encouraged by her nephew, who hopes to "keep her fortune, which is considerable, in the family."[35] Narcissa, of course, indicates her self-awareness by her modest lack of vanity. This is signaled, naturally, by her sense of the limits of her judgment, but also by her tact—she professes herself unable to judge poetry, yet she quietly requests a copy of Roderick's "Ode" that her aunt had scornfully dismissed as inferior to the aunt's own production.

Yet only a few years later, in *The Adventures of Peregrine Pickle* (1751), Smollett dissociates the "Lady of Quality" whose "Memoirs" (possibly based on the life of Frances Anne Hawes, later Lady Vane) take up a substantial portion of the book from platonic love, by showing that she is, ultimately, aware that the discourse of platonic love is merely a seduction technique. This coincides with a gradual shift of satirical emphasis from the Platonic Lady to "platonic love." While the Platonic Lady was a figure of ridicule from 1700 (and earlier) to 1740, the notion of platonic love, from which ostensibly normal young women could easily be weaned, became the object of ridicule from roughly 1740 onward. Of course, this is not a strict demarcation—residual positive references persisted (Elizabeth Montagu claimed to be "in Platonic Love" with the "Dread Satirist" of women, Edward Young, in her October 17, 1740, letter to Anne Donnellan), while some references by women writers to platonic love as a sham to seduce women occur earlier.[36] For instance, Belinda, a spoiled, vain character in Jane Barker's *A Patch-work Screen for the Ladies* (1723) is seduced by professions of "*Platonick Love*, and the happy State any *Two* might injoy, that lived together in such a chaste Affection," but "at last, the Mask of *Platonick Love* was pull'd off, and a personal Injoyment concluded the Farce."[37] Belinda ends up pregnant by a married man. Ashamed of herself and abandoned by her lover, she runs off, eventually meeting Galesia while trying to escape arrest.

Further, in Smollett's *The Adventures of Peregrine Pickle* (1751) the lusty and imprudent but otherwise sympathetic "Lady of Quality" describes how she was seduced into her first affair despite her best intentions, by the canny Mr. S——. Though she insists that she wants only an "unreserved intercourse of souls, abstracted from any sensual consideration," Mr. S. is clever enough to realize that a strategic submission to this "Platonic proposal" will get him what he wants.[38] This kind of manipulation of overindulged female visionaries echoes the *Tatler*'s characterization of Madonella and Lovelace's attempt to manipulate Clarissa. The subtext is that the potential Platonic Lady is too vain to see that she is being seduced. The feminocentric possibilities of neoplatonic discourse were increasingly forgotten. The disciplinary ridicule of the Platonic Lady trope triumphed by articulating a fundamentally heterosexual model of acceptable femininity: women who are *not* Platonic Ladies are chaste but not prudish; discerning, but not learned; conventionally attractive, but notably modest; demure, but definitely interested in heterosexual union—in stark contrast to the militantly misandrist and (or) sexually hypocritical Platonic Lady. In a fictional analogue of conversion therapy, the Platonic Lady is successfully subsumed into normative heterosexuality: ridicule converts her from her unnatural distaste for heterosexual union.

PLATONIC LOVE AMONG THE GENTLEMEN

In 1731, the *Gentleman's Magazine* considered platonic love as an expression of male heterosexual desire. It places the "Platonic Lover" within "the numerous Tribes of Lovers" thus: above the "sensual" and "general" lovers (both are "below the Standard of real Passion") but alongside the "Romantick" lover (a "species of Lovers as far beyond it") in going beyond the golden mean. The author sees this male lover as one who "fixes his *Affections* on the Mind, rather than the Form of her he *loves*; this sort of Affection he calls an *Intercourse of Souls*."[39] Negotiating history and contemporary life, heterosexual relations, class difference, literary genre, and even different models of masculinity, the author identifies platonic love as a recognizable, though unnatural, form of *male* heterosexual affection. A few years later, in 1735, the *Gentleman's Magazine* briefly mentioned platonic love in an entry "devoted to the fair Readers" in a series of contrasts meant to help them to distinguish between different male lovers: "As plants take a Tincture from the Soil they grow in, Love receives a Colouring from the Lover's Temper; hence the Platonic, and Sensual; Jealous, and Indifferent; the Constant, and Roving; the Over-warm, and Too-cool; the Disinterested, that has the Happiness of the Object beloved in view, and the Interested, that only consults his own."[40] Platonic love is portrayed as an idealized, non-sensual option for heterosexual male lovers. This description contrasts starkly with the misogynistic satirical stereotype, which developed in tandem and eventually overtook this characterization of platonic love. As is evident in an entry published in the same journal twenty years later, by mid-century "platonic love" was a joke used against pretentious female intellectuals. Love may mean many things, but platonism has no part in it. Rather, as an entry from 1751 explains, platonic love is "a system of art, formed out of a whimsical imagination, than springing from the foundation of nature." Women laugh at men who take it seriously because "as the ladies judge very rightly . . . they were not intended as the mere objects of imagination." Thus, "if a man once courts them under the character of friendship, they are sensible that a very little more will make him a husband.[41] Platonic love is idealistic, whimsical, unnatural and therefore dangerous; it appeals to women, but if they are not vain idiots themselves, they secretly laugh at men who take it seriously. Women duplicitously call it "friendship" while intending (or not realizing) that it will necessarily result in marriage or sex. "Natural," reasonable, observant men ought to manipulate its conventions in courtship (or, as Lovelace intends, seduction). The stereotype assumes that women do not want to inhabit men's imaginations; they want to be acted upon. Strikingly, this assessment of platonic love was shared by both Henry Fielding *and* Samuel Richardson.

Fielding ridiculed platonic love as unrealistic in both *Joseph Andrews* and *Tom Jones*. In *Joseph Andrews*, when Pamela's brother Joseph learns that he and his beloved Fanny might be related, Pamela chides him that "if he loved Fanny as he ought, with a pure affection, he had no reason to lament being related to her.—Upon which [Parson] Adams began to discourse on Platonic love; whence he made a quick transition to the joys in the next world; and concluded with strongly asserting, that there was no such thing as pleasure in this. At which Pamela and her husband smiled on one another."[42] Parson Adams is Joseph's friend and mentor and a sympathetic character, but the smiling of Pamela and her husband suggests that they know better than he does how little Joseph wishes to make quite so quick a transition to the "joys of the next world." In *Tom Jones* platonic love is associated with women, duplicity, and improbability. The narrator informs the reader that the "refined Degree of *Platonic* Affection which is absolutely detached from the Flesh, and is indeed entirely and purely spiritual, is a Gift confined to the female Part of the Creation: many of whom I have heard declare, (and doubtless with great Truth) that they would, with the utmost Readiness, resign a Lover to a Rival, when such Resignation was proved to be necessary for the temporal Interest of such Lover. Hence, therefore I conclude, that this Affection is in Nature, though I cannot pretend to say, I have ever seen an Instance of it."[43] At its foundation, the stereotype policed what is "natural" to women's sexuality. The narrator's gentlemanly deference to the ladies' declaration is a polite performance: he knows what they really want.

Richardson also used platonic love to regulate women's "natural" sexuality. Lovelace characterized platonic love as a set of rules used in the game of seduction in *Clarissa*. But Richardson had taken the critique even further in *Pamela in Her Exalted Condition* (1741). The critique arrives at a pivotal moment of reconciliation after Pamela and Mr. B. have discussed whether they should separate. Pamela has been heartbroken but resolute: believing that Mr. B. is having an affair with a beautiful dowager countess, she refuses to share his affections and volunteers to separate from him if he insists on a triangulated relationship that, to her, resembles polygamy. The couple had first encountered the Countess at a masquerade soon after Mr. B. had brought the heavily pregnant Pamela to London for the first time. The masquerade, as Terry Castle has argued, was a controversial social practice in eighteenth-century London, one associated with the carnivalesque upturning of social hierarchies and proper decorum.[44] It was a site of sexual temptation and risk. Pamela dresses as a "prim" Quaker, Mr. B. as a "stately" Spaniard; the Countess signifies her doubly threatening exotic appeal by appearing as a "fair Nun" and speaking in fluent Italian. The masquerade threatens Pamela by surrounding her with a simulacrum of globalization (among the attendees are "One *Indian* Prince, One *Chinese* Mandarin, several Domine's, of both Sexes, a *Dutch* Skipper, a *Jewish* Rabbi, a *Greek* Monk, an Harlequin, a *Turkish* Bashaw, and a *Capuchin* Frier") that masks a fashionable society whose currency of wit is double *entendres* and religious conflations. A "Quaker and a Jesuit is the same Thing," one man in a cardinal's costume informs her.[45] Mr. B. is the object of universal female attention, but it is the "fair Nun" who gives Pamela the most concern. Indeed, as Mr. B. later confesses, that night was the beginning of what became a "platonic" affair with the Countess.

After she gives birth to her first son, Billy, Pamela becomes increasingly worried that the Countess has alienated her from Mr. B.'s affections. Gossip stirs up her worst suspicions, and Mr. B.'s musings on polygamy, which the Countess seems to share, convince Pamela that she must break with her husband if he intends to share his affections with both women (313, 405).[46] But when she confronts him, Mr. B. assures her that he and the Countess are "innocent as to Deed," that the Countess fled from him when she realized he was married, and that their flirtation and continued friendship has been platonic (433). Indeed, he has begun a "Family Intimacy" with the Countess and her sister, and, together, they "accounted to one another's Honour, by entering upon a kind of *Platonick* System, in which Sex was to have no manner of Concern" (448). Immediately, however, Mr. B. shows that he is aware that platonic friendship is a pretense. He admits, "I must own myself extremely blameable, because I knew the World, and human Nature, I will say, better than the Lady, who never before had been trusted into it upon her own Feet; and who, nothwithstanding that Wit and Vivacity which every one admires in her, gave herself little Time for Consideration" (448). Once again, platonic love is depicted as counter to human "Nature" and particularly to women's "natural" sexuality. Mr. B. manages both to indict platonic love and redeem the Countess from being the "vile" woman Pamela had believed her to be. Yet Pamela knows better than to believe platonic friendship can remain "innocent as to Deed" forever.

As Pamela notes in her observations on Mr. B.'s account of the platonic affair, neither partner seemed to be in earnest about the purely spiritual character of their relationship. When, on a rainy afternoon, Mr. B. had entertained the Countess with a conventional blazon of her various beauties, including the "Whiteness of her Skin, and the clear Blueness of her Veins," the Countess had warned him to keep his distance, teasing him that his eye "pierces not deep enough for a *Platonic*, if you cannot look farther than the White and the Blue, and discover the Circulation of the Spirit; for our Friendship is all Mind, you know." After more of the same, Mr. B. finally provokes the Countess, she slaps him, and he kisses her "in Revenge," prompting Pamela's acerbic aside "Fine Doings between two *Platonics*!" (450–452).

When Mr. B. has finished his account of the platonic affair, Pamela laments to him "how dangerously you might have gone on, both you and my Lady, under the Notion of this *Platonic* Love, till two precious Souls might have been lost: And this shews one, as well in Spirituals as Temporals, from what slight Beginnings the greatest Mischiefs sometimes spring" (456–457). Mr. B. affirms Pamela's caution, telling her: "I am confident the Lady was more in Earnest than myself in the Notion of *Platonic* Love, yet am I convinc'd, and always was, That *Platonic* Love is *Platonic* Nonsense" (457). While exculpating the Countess from serious wrongdoing, both Mr. B. and Pamela ultimately censure platonic love as a dangerous temptation to the young.

The stereotype of platonic love, in other words, was a rare point of agreement between the satirical and sentimental traditions of the mid-eighteenth-century British novel. No wonder that women authors failed to continue the otherwise richly productive feminocentric platonic literary tradition centered on the possibilities afforded by the intelligent soul. That tradition had, by 1750, been associated with women whose Christian convictions, as well as their chastity, were vulnerable not only to stereotypical Muslims but also to libertines. After mid-century, the stereotype took an even darker turn, being used in the press, not just in fiction, to marginalize a variety of high-ranking women who were associated with both sexual crimes and imperial politics. Platonic love came to be linked with the members of the "Female Coterie," a fictionalized version of a loosely associated group of women of high rank and dubious reputation. The Coterie's platonic love continued the theme of the Platonic Lady's professed virtue masking sexual hypocrisy while transitioning it into the secularized world of fashionable polite society. The connection to Muslim men also diversified: not only Ottoman or Barbary despots, as in Lyttelton, but also men from the Indian subcontinent and African slaves.

PLATONIC LADIES AND CRIMINAL CONVERSATION

In the 1770s, a number of high-profile "criminal conversation," or *crim. con.* (adultery), cases delighted the London scandal magazines and gave authors an opportunity to use the trope of platonic love to ridicule aristocratic and even royal offenders like Lady Grosvenor and the Duke of Cumberland (younger brother of George III). Grosvenor and Cumberland's affair was particularly piquant because their quasi-literate love letters were entered as evidence in the court proceedings and could therefore be published. The press had a field day. As Paul Tankard has argued, eighteenth-century newspapers encouraged anonymous and "allusive" writing that sought "not to inform but to entertain, and particularly to entertain by looking *as if* it is meant to inform."[47] The newspapers catered to the needs of "an expanding literate public of hurried, curious browsers" looking for "not so much *the* truth as some purported 'intelligence' that was new or telling" (xxxiii). The Duke of Cumberland's saccharine, badly spelled letters to Lady Grosvenor were the objects of particular ridicule.

The *Town and Country Magazine*, for instance, managed a swipe at both his excessive sentimentalism and his softheadedness in situating his correspondence within the epistolary tradition of platonic lovers, opining, that "in common life, far distant from the plains of Arcadia, when we hear of a man's being enamoured with a woman, we must take the declaration in its simple latitude, and allow a very small portion of Platonic love to make part of the composition. The D. of C. was . . . so struck with lady G_____r, as to deprive him of his senses, and make him write nonsense."[48] Lord Grosvenor was awarded £10,000 in damages.

The platonic riff was used not only to condemn Lady Grosvenor and the privileged members of the Female Coterie, notorious for undermining their husbands in high-profile *crim. con.* cases, but also to discipline an infringement on the marital rights of a middle-class husband. In an earlier volume of *Town and Country Magazine*, "Maria Frankly" complains to the printer "Mr. Hamilton" that her husband "violated my bed in despite of all the opposition and outcries I made, and not one of the barbarous servants, though there were several females in the house, came to my assistance or relief."[49] But when Maria inquires whether she should "swear the peace or a rape against him," the printer smugly dismisses her complaint as the frivolous misunderstanding of a misandrist Platonic Lady. Rape is portrayed as the just punishment for a woman brought up on a lifelong diet of hatred of men and of heterosexuality.

Maria's "maiden aunt," under whose "tuition" Maria was brought up, is the sort of man-hating spinster familiar to readers of Fielding and Smollett. As Maria recalls, her aunt "inculcated into me the strictest precepts of virtue and morality; and among many other just notions, I imbibed from her a proper aversion for the male part of the creation." Maria's spinster aunt has trained her to associate virtue with misandry and to feel only disgust toward heterosexuality. When her father ("a very good sort of a being for a *man*") proposes several potential marriage partners for her, she puts him off because of "the dread I had always entertained at being so closely united with that *sex*." She is ultimately won over by Mr. Frankly, however, because "my aunt was gone out of town, and I had not for some days repeated her *anti-masculine Catechism*"—and because Frankly agrees to her condition that they "*should always have separate beds*." Maria is characterized as a badly instructed Platonic Lady who must be reeducated by her husband: she professes virtue, but her principles last no longer than her short-term memory; her deviant literacy is linked to her softheaded religious alterity (her aunt's man-hating "Catechism"); like Lyttelton's Honoria, she consents to marriage if her husband does not insist on consummation. With this condition, Maria considers that "there could be no great difference between marriage and celibacy" and daydreams about the "many advantages a married woman had over a single one."

After they are married, however, and Maria insists on the performance of the promise, Mr. Frankly informs her that such an expectation is "extremely ridiculous" and hopes that she will not "persevere in so whimsical a resolution." He warns her that though he had initially acquiesced when she bolted her bedroom door against him, she may expect a "very different kind of behavior" in the future. Maria reveals herself to be a true Platonic Lady in dismissing this threat as "the mere jargon of disappointed husbands, a race of vicious animals, who are utterly unacquainted with the pure, immaculate system of Platonic love." Mr. Frankly has another system in mind: his wife may have been taught by a Platonic Lady, but platonic love will not be part of their marriage.

The next night he breaks the door open, "though it had been locked and bolted," and Maria learns the lesson that all society colludes in upholding the patriarchal household. Female servants do not help her; upon hearing of the rape, her father laughs at her; and her aunt says she "deserved it" for marrying at all. The entire episode reads like an episode of conversion therapy for misandrists. Maria imagines that she will "endure such brutal treatment till the end of the month," at which time she hopes to receive "proper instructions" from the printer for her "future conduct." The response is needless—a month of forced sex will likely result in pregnancy and the consolidation of Mr. Frankly's status as a husband, father, and property owner. But the printer replies anyway: "This Lady's case, though it may appear at present very lamentable to her, will, we imagine, in a short time wear a more favourable aspect; and the only instruction we shall pretend to give her is, *never to bolt the chamber door against her husband, as she will thereby prevent his forcing it open: she is, however, advised to use this necessary caution against all the rest of the sex.*" Marital rape is a joke and the blame is the victim's, in other words. Maria deserved this treatment because she refused to recognize her husband's sexual rights over her body. But the image of the bolted door is a significant one. The body of the Platonic Lady represents the threat of invaded national security, but it also represents the nation's potential to reproduce itself in the next generation. Maria must only bolt the door against every man except her husband. Giving him sexual access is obligatory—whatever catechism her maiden aunt has taught her and whatever promises he made before marriage.

Platonic love, associated with the sexual excess of the privileged women of the Coterie, was also interconnected with representations of England's global fortunes. The Coterie was satirized as hypocritically pawning itself off as a "respectable Amazonian society" while blackballing a man "turned of fifty" but admitting one who was "young, graceful, generous, well-built."[50] The prerequisites for male admission to the Female Coterie are clearly found below the belt. The satire did not stop at generational privilege but extended to those of politics and race by associating the Coterie with the reproducing bodies of various figures of domestic or imperial politics. William Beckford (Lord Mayor of London and father of the author of *Vathek*), famous for both his spectacular wealth (derived from slave labor on his West Indies sugar plantation) and his controversial address to King George III, was satirically reduced to a reproductive body of illegitimate offspring and illegitimate politics. The same was true of the Earl of Sandwich and John Wilkes. Beckford and the Earl of Sandwich were notorious for fathering multiple illegitimate children, and their sexual escapades enabled the popular press to link their private lives to their politics (and political entanglements) via the representational conventions already formulated for the Coterie. The Coterie was used to cast aspersions on powerful men who had produced more illegitimate children than legitimate heirs, thereby endangering the stability of property transmission.

According to a 1770 issue of the *Public Advertiser*, the members of the Coterie were planning a somewhat incongruous dual commemoration of Lord Mayor Beckford's death and virility "in Imitation of the spirited Example of the Livery of London."[51] Like the Common Council members' real erection of a statue of Beckford at London's Guildhall in honor of his "inimitable Oration to the King" in defense of the British constitution, the Coterie plans an erection of its own to celebrate the "*manly Virtues* of the late truly amiable Lord Mayor." The members of the Coterie have

> unanimously decreed a Statue to his Memory of the purest and most unspotted white Marble, as an Emblem not only of the Purity of his Lordship's Morals, but of their own likewise. It is to be placed in the most honourable Part of the Club Room, among the other Gods of their Idolatry, in the Character of *Adonis*. The Pedestal is to be ornamented with an elegant Bas-relief, representing, under the Figures of little Cupids, as many of his Lordships *natural Children* as have come to the Knowledge of the World, or can be grouped together without Confusion. This, it is imagined, will be a great Encouragement to the *rising* Generation to pursue *with Vigour* the important and patriotic Work of Population.

The "Coterie" is represented as an association of religious alterity, sexual hypocrisy, fashionable consumption, and illegitimate reproduction. Its members' patriotic concern for England's rising generation sounds strikingly similar to the emotions felt by Fielding's unwittingly pornographic reader Parson Tickletext while contemplating Shamela's little "&c." But the author expands on the contrast between their sullied desires and the "unspotted white Marble" of their aesthetics by aligning the Coterie with the wrong kind of posterity and the wrong kind of liberty. The author claims that a second monument was erected by those who, fearing that a "misjudging Posterity" might judge Beckford's "oration to the King" (advising him to dissolve Parliament) as "Sedition or Impudence," have "altered" their "original Design" and "propose to have the Figure supported by *four Negroes in Chains*, in black Marble; a clear and explicit Testimony of his Lordship's universal Philanthropy, of his tender Regard and unbounded Zeal, for the *natural Rights and Liberties* of his Fellow Creatures in general." It is not clear that the author of this satire was particularly interested in the cause of abolition; what is clear is the author's recognition of Beckford's hypocrisy. In the author's view, Beckford benefited from the performance of political virtue by invoking natural rights and liberties while also financially benefiting from denying those rights and liberties to others. Members of the Common Council of London, meanwhile, never changed their plan to include the inscription of Beckford's controversial address to the king—it can still be viewed in London's Guildhall today.

But the fantasy of the revised statue allowed the author to contrast Beckford's liberal politics with his vast wealth derived from slave labor. The association with the Coterie further enabled the author to contrast the hypocritical "white Marble" of the Coterie's Adonis with the real suffering of the "black Marble" slaves. So, too, the "*natural Children*" of the Lord Mayor are contrasted with the "*natural Rights*" he denies to those who produce his wealth. It is a swift, devastating caricature of the Lord Mayor, his politics, and the fashionable women likely to support both. It portrays Beckford as "manly" in the superficial way that would appeal to the stereotypical women of the Coterie while underscoring his penchant for expressing his masculine "Vigour" through illegitimate channels. Warning readers about the "Instability and Precariousness of human Opinion," the author positions "Posterity" (including Beckford's own) as the final judge of Beckford's principles and behavior.

But association with famous politicians was not necessary for the Coterie to be inter-implicated in contemporary controversies. The *Public Advertiser* undermined the abolition movement by aligning it with the Coterie: "The Female Coterie are very anxious for the Determination of the Negro Cause, and fear, if it should go against the Black, it will discourage all of his Complexion from coming to England, to the great Disappointment of those Lovers of Variety, who, thinking White Men so like the Fair Sex, wish to introduce the manly Breed of Negroes or Morattoes."[52] In a throwback to the Ludovico-Honoria narrative, but with the "manly Breed of Negroes" replacing the barbaric Ottoman despot, the *Public Advertiser* warns Englishmen that their property (slaves) may be taken away from them with the help and support of their own women. If Englishmen want to protect their property, they must stop acting like "the Fair Sex" and adopt the virile sexuality of the "manly" Negroes, Muslim despots, and the "Morattoes" (Marathas, the rivals of the Moguls in northern India). In this passage, abolition is reduced to the concern of nymphomaniacs and racial others in need of discipline by a firm, masculine Anglican hand; otherwise, the next generation of the body politic will be a new "Breed" of mixed-race bastards. Women's sexuality is here figured as the greatest point of weakness in preserving national integrity.

Between 1770 and 1790, the anti-platonic riff could be used against any high-profile woman who publicly challenged the status quo of male privilege. As Gillian Russell notes, publications like the *Town and Country Magazine* were "not merely reporting adultery as a sign of the degeneracy associated with the Coterie." They were "involved in producing adultery as a discursive phenomenon" that could be used to uphold Christian morality, to channel misogyny, or to engage in political critique.[53] Given that the press sometimes conflated the Female Coterie and the Bluestockings and given that the politically minded historian and Bluestocking Catharine Macaulay was vilified as the "Platonic Lover" in the press, it is no wonder that the Bluestockings wished to distance themselves from the Platonic Lady and all her attendant characteristics: her vanity, Roman Catholic leanings, pedantic language, excessive idealism and sentimentalism, and her sexual predilection for non-Anglican men, particularly those who denied that women had souls—libertines and Muslims.[54] In the next two chapters, we will see how that distancing manifested in literature written by women influenced by Samuel Richardson and Samuel Johnson, including Charlotte Lennox, members of the Bluestocking circle, and Mary Wollstonecraft.

NOTES

Parts of this chapter previously appeared in Samara Anne Cahill, "Madonella's Other Convent: 'Platonic Ladies,' Randy Rakes, and the 'Mahometan' Paradise," *Religion in the Age of Enlightenment* 4 (2013): 55–79.

1. Roy Porter, "Enlightenment and Pleasure," in *Pleasure in the Eighteenth Century*, ed. Roy Porter and Marie Mulvey Roberts (Houndmills, MacMillan Press, 1996), 3.
2. Porter, "Enlightenment and Pleasure," 3.
3. Marie Mulvey Roberts, preface to Porter and Roberts, *Pleasure in the Eighteenth Century*, xiii.
4. Eliza Fowler Haywood, *Female Spectator*, 4 vols. (London, 1744–46), 2:2.
5. Karen O'Brien, *Women and Enlightenment in Eighteenth-Century Britain* (Cambridge: Cambridge University Press, 2009), 57.
6. Significantly, the three earlier writers also include episodes of apparitional intelligence in their novels. All four women treated with utter seriousness the possibility of intelligence being communicated by apparitions.
7. Since the British East India Company did not begin large-scale exportation of tea from India until the 1820s, this tea would most likely have come from China.
8. Samuel Richardson, *Pamela; or, Virtue Rewarded* [1740–41], ed. Thomas Keymer and Alice Wakely (Oxford: Oxford University Press, 2001), 158.
9. Terry Eagleton, *The Rape of Clarissa: Writing, Sexuality and Class Struggle in Samuel Richardson* (Minneapolis: University of Minnesota Press, 1986), 34, 37.
10. Paul Kelleher, *Making Love: Sentiment and Sexuality in Eighteenth-Century British Literature* (Lewisburg, Pa.: Bucknell University Press, 2015), 133, 149.
11. Toni Bowers, *Force or Fraud: British Seduction Stories and the Problem of Resistance, 1660–1760* (Oxford: Oxford University Press, 2011), 263.
12. Samuel Richardson, *Clarissa. Or, the history of a young lady* [1747–48], 3rd ed., 8 vols. (London: Printed for S. Richardson, 1750–51), 3:255.

13. This point is informed by Bonnie Latimer's paper "Samuel Richardson and the 'Jew Bill' of 1753" presented at the annual conference of the British Society for Eighteenth-Century Studies (BSECS) in Oxford (United Kingdom), January 6, 2010. As for Lovelace's mischaracterization of Judaic theology, see Adin Steinsaltz, *The Essential Talmud*, 30th anniversary ed. (New York: Basic Books, 2006), 182–183.
14. Margaret Anne Doody, *A Natural Passion: A Study of the Novels of Samuel Richardson* (Oxford: Clarendon Press, 1974), 105.
15. Philip Souers, *The Matchless Orinda* (Cambridge, Mass.: Harvard University Press, 1931), 74.
16. George Williamson, "*The Ephesian Matron* versus the Platonic Lady," *Review of English Studies* 12, no. 48 (October 1936): 447.
17. Souers, *Matchless Orinda*, 259.
18. See Dana Rabin, "The Jew Bill of 1753: Masculinity, Virility, and the Nation," *Eighteenth-Century Studies* 39, no. 2 (2006): 157–171; Stephen H. Gregg, "'A Truly Christian Hero': Religion, Effeminacy, and Nation in the Writings of the Societies for Reformation of Manners," *Eighteenth-Century Life* 25 (Winter 2001): 17–28; and Gillian Russell, *Women, Sociability and Theatre in Georgian London* Cambridge: Cambridge University Press, 2010).
19. Sarah Chapone, *The hardships of the English laws. In relation to wives. With an explanation of the original curse of subjection passed upon the woman. In an humble address to the legislature* (London: Printed; Dublin: Reprinted by and for George Faulkner, 1735), 4, Eighteenth-Century Collections Online. I have modernized all instances of the long "s." All italics are in the original. I have used the 1735 Dublin edition because the Eighteenth-Century Collections Online copy of the 1735 London edition is not perfectly legible on this page.
20. Robinson (later Montagu), ca. 1737, quoted in Sylvia Harcstark Myers, *The Bluestocking Circle: Women, Friendship, and the Life of the Mind in Eighteenth-Century England* (Oxford: Clarendon Press, 1990), 41.
21. See Nicholas McDowell on the perceived connection between heresies and women's literacy, preaching, and deviant sexuality. His article, which examines Swift's anti-heretical satire, is particularly germane to the discussion of Augustan hostility to the "Platonics." Nicholas McDowell, "Tales of Tub Preachers: Swift and Heresiography," *Review of English Studies* 61, no. 248 (August 4, 2009): 72–92.
22. See Henry Fielding, *An Apology for the Life of Mrs. Shamela Andrews*, in *"Anti-Pamela" and "Shamela,"* ed. Catherine Ingrassia (Peterborough, Ont.: Broadview Literary Texts, 2004), 229–276.
23. Henry Fielding, *Tom Jones*, ed. Sheridan Baker, Norton Critical Editions, 2nd ed. (New York: W. W. Norton, 1995), 554 (bk. 16, chap. 5).
24. Interestingly, given the association between "Platonic ladies" and Roman Catholicism, Lyttelton addressed Montagu as "Madonna" in his correspondence with her. See Myers, *Bluestocking Circle*, 182.
25. Albert Von Ruville, biographer of William Pitt the Elder, quoted in Rose Mary Davis, *The Good Lord Lyttelton: A Study in Eighteenth Century Politics and Culture* (Bethlehem, Pa.: Times Publishing Company, 1939), 36. Davis, however, thinks that Von Ruville's assessment is "simplifying matters too much" (36). The historical context of the publication of the first and subsequent editions is also from Davis. Davis further points out that the "early editions of the *Letters from a Persian* were treated by current periodicals as a manifesto of the Opposition to the ministry" and that the "most important fact about the *Letters from a Persian* for the student of English Literature is their influence on Goldsmith's *Citizen of the World*, which first appeared in 1760" (43).
26. Lyttelton, George Lyttelton, Baron, Letter 2, in *Letters from a Persian in England, to his Friend at Ispahan*, 2nd ed. (London: Printed for J. Millan, Buckingham-Court, near the Admiralty-Office, 1735), 4, Eighteenth-Century Collections Online.

27. Samuel Richardson, *The History of Sir Charles Grandison*, ed. with an introduction by Jocelyn Harris, 3 vols. (London: Oxford University Press, 1972), 3:250.
28. Bonnie Latimer, *Making Gender, Culture, and the Self in the Fiction of Samuel Richardson: The Novel Individual* (Farnham: Ashgate, 2013), 118–129.
29. Frances Dolan, "Why Are Nuns Funny?," *Huntington Library Quarterly* 70, no. 4 (2007): 509–534.
30. For an excellent overview of the long-term appeal of Protestant nunneries in England, in terms of women's education, see Bridget Hill, "A Refuge from Men: The Idea of a Protestant Nunnery," *Past and Present* 117 (November 1987): 107–130.
31. *The Lucubrations of Isaac Bickerstaff Esq; Revised and corrected by the author* (London: Printed and sold by Charles Lillie, at the Corner of Beauford Buildings in the Strand; and John Morphew, near Stationers-Hall, 1710), 1:230, Eighteenth-Century Collections Online.
32. Sir William Blackstone, *Commentaries on the laws of England* [. . .] *By William Blackstone, Esq. Vinerian Professor of Law, and solicitor general to her Majesty*, 4 vols. (Oxford: Printed at the Clarendon Press, 1765–69), 1:430.
33. Maria Dzielska, *Hypatia of Alexandria*, trans. F. Lyra, Revealing Antiquity 8 (Cambridge, Mass.: Harvard University Press, 1995), 2–3.
34. Tobias Smollett, *The Adventures of Roderick Random*, edited with an introduction and notes by Paul-Gabriel Boucé, Oxford World's Classics (Oxford: Oxford University Press, 1999; reissued 2008), 216–217.
35. Smollett, *Roderick Random*, 216.
36. Elizabeth Montague, quoted in Myers, *Bluestocking Circle*, 36.
37. Jane Barker, *The Galesia Trilogy and Selected Manuscript Poems of Jane Barker*, ed. Carol Shiner Wilson (Oxford: Oxford University Press, 1997), 130–131.
38. Tobias Smollett, *The Miscellaneous Works of Tobias Smollett, M.D. with a Life of the Author. In Twelve Volumes* (London, 1824), 4:309.
39. [Anon.], *Gentleman's Magazine: Or, Monthly Intelligencer*, by Sylvanus Urban, no. 1 (January 1731): 331–332, 4th ed. (printed and sold at St. John's Gate; by F. Jefferies in Ludgate-street, and most booksellers in Town and Country, London, 1732), Noel Collection, Noel Memorial Library, Louisiana State University, Shreveport. My thanks to the Noel Foundation for the fellowship that enabled me to conduct research at the Noel Memorial Library. Special thanks to Kevin Cope, Martha Lawler, and Bob Leitz for their hospitality, kindness, and assistance. *Pylades and Corinna* was a series of letters written by poet Elizabeth Thomas and her betrothed, Richard Gwinnett (1731–32; later republished as "The Honourable Lovers" in 1732 and reprinted in 1736). Thomas was praised by John Dryden and later became part of a literary circle that included Mary Astell and John Norris. Pope castigated her as "[Edmund] Curll's Corinna" in *The Dunciad*. See Norma Clarke, *The Rise and Fall of the Woman of Letters* (London: Pimlico, 2004), 277–293.
40. [Anon.], *Gentleman's Magazine, or, Monthly Intelligencer*, by Sylvanus Urban, vol. 5 (1935) (printed by Edward Cave, at St. John's Gate, London, 1735). Extract taken from the *Prompter*, no. 5 (January 1735), Noel Collection.
41. [Anon.], *Gentleman's Magazine, and Historical Chronicle*, by Sylvanus Urban, 21 (1751): 407–408 (printed for Edw. Cave, at St. John's Gate, London, 1751). Noel Collection.
42. Henry Fielding, *Joseph Andrews with Shamela and Related Writings*, edited by Homer Goldberg, Norton Critical Edition, 1st ed. (New York: W. W. Norton & Company, 1987), 258 (bk. 4, chap. 13).
43. Fielding, *Tom Jones*, 554 (bk. 16, chap. 5).
44. Terry Castle, *Masquerade and Civilization: The Carnivalesque in Eighteenth-Century English Culture and Fiction* (Stanford, Calif.: Stanford University Press, 1986).

45. Samuel Richardson, *Pamela in Her Exalted Condition*, ed. Albert J. Rivero, The Cambridge Edition of the Works of Samuel Richardson (Cambridge: Cambridge University Press, 2012), 365–366.
46. For an analysis of the historical and political context of the consideration of polygamy in *Pamela in Her Exalted Condition*, see Howard D. Weinbrot, "Johnson's *Irene* and *Rasselas*, Richardson's *Pamela Exalted*: Contexts, Polygamy, and the Seraglio," *Age of Johnson* 23 (2015): 89–140. My thanks to Professor Weinbrot for allowing me to read a draft of this article before publication.
47. Paul Tankard, introduction to *Facts and Inventions: Selections from the Journalism of James Boswell*, ed. Paul Tankard (New Haven, Conn.: Yale University Press, 2014), xxiii–xlviii.
48. [Anon.], *Town and Country Magazine* 5 (1773): 121–123, Google Books . The duke's later indiscretion in marrying a commoner, Anne Horton, prompted the Royal Marriages Act (1772).
49. "Singular Resolution of a married Lady," *Town and Country Magazine; Or, Universal Repository of Knowledge, Instruction, and Entertainment*, vol. 2 (London: Printed for A. Hamilton, Junr. Near St. John's Gate, 1770): 360–361, Google Books. All quotes from this source occur on these pages.
50. [Anon.], *Gazetteer and New Daily Advertiser* (London), no. 12 (Thursday, May 24, 1770): 864.
51. [Anon.], *Public Advertiser* (London), no. 11097 (Friday, July 3, 1770), n.p., 17th and 18th Century Burney Newspapers Collection.
52. [Anon.], *Public Advertiser* (London), Friday, May 29, 1772, n.p., 17th and 18th Century Burney Newspapers Collection.
53. Russell, *Women, Sociability and Theatre*, 86.
54. One entry in the *London Chronicle* states: "The Ladies Subscription Purse for a Sunday concert is already filled. The Duke of Queensberry is the Treasurer, as being a member of the Female Coterie, known by the name of the Blue Stocking Club." *London Chronicle*, no. 5006 (November 25–27, 1788), 17th and 18th Century Burney Newspapers Collection. For the characterization of Catharine Macaulay as the "Platonic Lover," see Devoney Looser, *British Women Writers and the Writing of History, 1670–1820* (Baltimore: Johns Hopkins University Press, 2005).

4
A "FOREIGN AND UNINTERESTING" SUBJECT

IN THE PREVIOUS CHAPTER, I ARGUED that intellectual pleasures were identified with Christianity, while sensual pleasures became increasingly identified with Islam (and with the overdetermined trope of the Platonic Lady). The assumption that Muslim women could have no intelligence to communicate because their experience and observation had been limited by the constraints of the seraglio was also reinforced by the fiction of Samuel Johnson and members of his literary circle. The circle included writers such as Charlotte Lennox and the Bluestockings—women who theorized a moral and domesticated England and who had to negotiate the satire on the Platonic Lady, a stereotype of the learned lady with which they could easily be linked given their investment in a discourse centering on women's intelligent souls. These writers exemplify the use of Islamophobic misogynistic mortalism in the second half of the eighteenth century and show how it was implicated in questions of women's education and national identity. This chapter begins with the problem of historiography, curiosity, and epistemological distance in Samuel Johnson's periodical the *Rambler* (1750–52) before turning to the representation of Islam in Johnson's fiction and in Samuel Richardson's fiction and, finally, attending to the crucial turning point represented by Johnson's and Richardson's protégée—Charlotte Lennox, author of *The Female Quixote* (1752).

"SOME COUNTRY TOTALLY DIFFERENT FROM WHAT I HAVE BEEN USED TO"

In the *Rambler*, no. 122 (May 18, 1751), Johnson explored the art of historical narrative, beginning with the distance between the apparent ease of performing certain actions and the actual difficulty of executing them well.[1] Narrative would appear to be the easiest of literary tasks, for of "the various kinds of speaking or writing, which serve necessity, or promote pleasure, none appears so artless or easy as simple narration; for what should make him that knows the whole order and progress of an affair, unable to relate it?" (5:138). But apparent ease conceals the real difficulty of imagining oneself in the position of the audience and avoiding filling "the ear with empty sounds" that deter the pleasurable experience that alone leads to learning (5:138–139). In other words, narration is a performing art and the performer has a responsibility to be pithy, memorable, and pleasurable.

Johnson turns to historical narratives, positing that it "is natural to imagine . . . that no writer has a more easy task than the historian" (5.139), since "the happy historian has no other labour than of gathering what tradition pours down before him, or records treasure for his use. He has only the actions and designs of men like himself to conceive and to relate" (5:139). But if history writing is so easy, what accounts for the dearth of distinguished historians? In fact, Johnson saw history writing as a difficult genre in which to perform well—difficult because once "fashion and novelty have ceased to recommend," particular histories become mere "chronological memorials" (5:140). A reader would turn to them out of "necessity," not "curiosity" (5:140). But, in Johnson's view, the case was peculiarly difficult in England: so "barren of historical genius" was his own country, that Johnson echoed those who "have doubted whether an *Englishman* can stop at that mediocrity of style, or confine his mind to that even tenour of sentiment which narrative requires" (5:140; emphasis in original). Englishmen seemed to be peculiarly unfit to write histories, despite English authors achieving eminence in "almost every other species of literary excellence" (5:140).

Johnson endeavored to defend his countrymen, arguing that those "who imagine that nature has so capriciously distributed understanding, have surely no claim to the honour of serious confutation"; if his countrymen have "failed in history," they have failed "only because history has not hitherto been diligently cultivated" (5:140–141). After surveying the historical work of Raleigh (whom he describes as having more judgment than genius) and Clarendon (possessed of "a rude inartificial majesty" but stylistically clunky), Johnson concluded his survey with Richard Knolles, author of *The Generall Historie of the Turkes* (1603). Of Knolles, Johnson declared that "none of our writers can . . . justly contest" his superiority. His style "has displayed all the excellencies that narration can admit" (5:142). This seems to be the highest praise possible, a counterexample to the charge that Englishmen cannot write history. Indeed, so clearly organized and logically contextualized was Knolles's narration that "a great part of the world is brought into view" (5:142). And, yet, even Knolles had a weakness as a narrator: his subject material was boring. In Johnson's view, English readers could not care less about the Turks, and this threatened to render England's greatest historian a chronological memorial himself. The passage is worth quoting in full: "Nothing could have sunk this author in obscurity, but the remoteness and barbarity of the people whose story he relates. It seldom happens, that all circumstances concur to happiness or fame. The nation which produced this great historian, has the grief of seeing his genius employed upon a foreign and uninteresting subject; and that writer, who might have secured perpetuity to his name by a history of his own country, has exposed himself to the danger of oblivion by recounting enterprises and revolutions of which none desire to be informed" (5:202). This remarkable passage invites extensive commentary, but, for the purpose of discussing Johnson's influence on the Bluestockings, the most important point is that he is surely not expressing the full range of his own sentiments. Throughout his career, Johnson praised curiosity and returned to Muslim contexts in his own fiction. What accounts for this seeming about-face? A brief survey of Johnson's thoughts on the value of curiosity and attention to the foreign sheds some light.

In the *Rambler*, no. 103 (Tuesday, March 12, 1751), Johnson observed: "Curiosity is one of the permanent and certain characteristics of a vigorous intellect, to which every advance in knowledge opens new prospects, and produces new incitements to farther progress. All the attainments possible in our present state are evidently inadequate to our capacities of enjoyment" (4:191). Sounding very much like Haywood, he considered that the "passion" of curiosity "is, perhaps, regularly heightened in proportion as the powers of the mind are elevated and enlarged" (4:192). Johnson saw curiosity as a foundational, but not a simple, pleasure: "The gratification of curiosity rather frees us from uneasiness, than confers pleasure; we are more pained by ignorance, than delighted by instruction. Curiosity is the thirst of the soul; it enflames and torments us, and makes us taste everything with joy, however otherwise insipid, by which it may be quenched" (4:193). But if ignorance is painful and the satisfaction of curiosity a freedom from such uneasiness, then the curious run a real risk of being satisfied with "the delusive opiate of hasty persuasion" as the Scots had been, at least in Johnson's view, in taking the *Poems of Ossian* to be authentic.[2] Johnson was thus well aware that national pride was tied to the pleasure of certainty. Distant, foreign locales could evoke curiosity, but most English readers—like Johnson himself—could hardly undertake the travel necessary to satisfy that curiosity. Generalizing knowledge, appealing to universals, and projecting the domestic onto a foreign backdrop were ways of negotiating the tension between distance and curiosity.

Johnson's attitudes to pleasure and generalization were complex, and he displayed these complexities in his philosophical tale *Rasselas* (1759). Howard D.

Weinbrot has argued that for Johnson "normative generality is based upon careful, detailed, and laudable close observation; and it is intended to evoke not an 'ideal' image, but the original, with all its sublunary particularity."[3] Thomas Keymer focuses on the emotional difficulties—constitutional melancholy, physical pain, grief over the loss of loved ones—that Johnson channeled into *Rasselas*, noting that "the acts of repression involved for Johnson in transforming private agonies of guilt and loss into generalizing exploration of large abstractions . . . left traces of specific trauma in the text."[4] Foreign locales seem to have been an important emotional terrain for Johnson in thinking through personal difficulties. Mental travel was a way of gaining a more objective perspective on the self.

For Johnson, the wrong kind of pleasure, the sensual kind that Haywood also rejected in the *Female Spectator*, was the greatest obstacle to curiosity and to the acquisition of intelligence. Lack of curiosity is "frequently the consequence of a total immersion in sensuality. Corporeal pleasures may be indulged, till the memory of every other kind of happiness is obliterated" (4:194). Johnson was describing the human mind preyed upon by the habit of overindulgence in bodily pleasures, but this passage sounds very like the experience of the women of the harem in *Rasselas* (discussed below). In Haywood's and Johnson's periodical writings of the 1740s and 1750s, it is clear that pleasure must be both accepted as a natural inclination of human life and carefully channeled and calibrated. Cultivating pleasures of the mind renders one a thinking human individual; submitting to, or stopping at, the ostensibly lower pleasures of the body deprives one of human intelligence and, therefore, of human identity. Accordingly, the harem figures centrally in Johnson's modeling of bad education for women. In the stereotypical, textually represented harem—the only one Johnson ever encountered—there could be nothing but bodily pleasure. There could be no curiosity in a space dedicated to physical pleasure, thus there could be no opportunity for education or the cultivation of intelligence. Johnson's representation of the harem in *Rasselas* embodies his belief in the centrality of curiosity to excite a reader's pleasure in historical narrative.

Despite his dismissive characterization of the harem, Johnson seems to have been aware of the importance of attending to alternate historical traditions. He declared to James Boswell that "there are two objects of curiosity,—the Christian world, and the Mahometan world. All the rest may be considered barbarous."[5] This astonishing comment directly contradicts Johnson's castigation of the "barbarity" of the Ottoman Empire as a "foreign and uninteresting" subject. Convictions can change over time, of course, but since Johnson exhibited a career-long interest in Ottoman history and the "Mahometan world"—from his early drafts of *Irene* in the 1730s to this 1783 conversation with Boswell—his comments on English historiography in the *Rambler* seem motivated by something other than personal conviction. They seem to have sprung more from a disappointed assessment of how to give pleasure to an English audience. The context of Johnson's praise of the "Mahometan world" is significant here, and it may also shed light on the conclusion of *The Female Quixote*, which, like Johnson's *Rambler* essay on historiography, concludes that an English audience (though perhaps not the author?) does not care about the "Mahometan" world.

In 1773, Johnson and James Boswell had undertaken their famous tour of the Hebrides. Boswell brought up this trip to his homeland when introducing Johnson to his friend William Stuart, the son of the Scottish Earl of Bute. Perhaps to give the two Scotsmen and the renowned English author a conversation topic, Boswell asked whether Johnson would ever wish to "make the same journey again."[6] Johnson replied that, in fact, one view had satisfied his curiosity. Did Boswell take it as an affront that it was possible for Johnson to believe that one tour could exhaust all that his homeland had to offer? Possibly. But his response focused on Johnson's attention to curiosity about the foreign. He rejoined, "I should wish to go and see some country totally different from what I have been used to; such as Turkey, where religion and everything else are different."[7] Boswell was certainly better traveled than Johnson and, in some ways, more cosmopolitan in his outlook. But there was a connection between Scotland and Turkey in this conversation: Stuart's mother was the daughter of Lady Mary Wortley Montagu, who gave birth to her in Turkey. Thus, Boswell's enthusiastic endorsement of Turkey may have been intended to praise the birthplace of one of Stuart's parents since Johnson had dismissed the birthplace of the other.

Whatever his views on Scotland, and whatever his declaration in the *Rambler* may have been motivated by, Johnson had an abiding interest in Turkey. He used Turkish material in both his tragedy *Irene* (1749) and in *Rasselas* (published in 1759, *after* his *Rambler* commentary on Knolles). I will discuss the harem scene in *Rasselas* below, but it is significant that Johnson felt that *Irene*—his one dramatic production—was one of his greatest disappointments. Of *Irene*, Boswell said: "Johnson was wise enough to be convinced that he had not the talents necessary to write successfully for the stage, and never made another attempt in that species of composition."[8] Were Johnson's *Rambler* comments about the lack of interest afforded to English readers by narratives of Turkish events prompted in part by his recent disappointment with *Irene*? Had he been compelled to learn the hard lesson himself that an Englishman who labored to excel in every species of literature could not excel in all of them—that he himself could not please an English audience with a Turkish subject? There is no way to know, although Boswell observed bluntly that "the tragedy of *Irene* did not please the public."[9] What is clear is that Johnson used a Muslim context in both *Irene* and, ten years later, *Rasselas* to explore issues of female education. Further, in line with the Platonic Lady stereotype, in both texts he juxtaposed a solid Christian education with the weakheadedness of women who choose to live in a Muslim context.

IRENE IN THE SPIRITUAL COURT

According to Boswell, Johnson borrowed a copy of Knolles's "*Turkish History*" from David Garrick's brother Peter "in order to form his play from it." He showed an unfinished draft of the play to Mr. Walmsley, an acquaintance during his brief days at the Lichfield academy, and when Walmsley exclaimed against the "great distress" of the heroine, asking how Johnson could possibly imagine how to make her suffer more than she already had in the unfinished draft, Johnson, according to Boswell, "in sly allusion to the supposed oppressive proceedings of the court of which Mr. Walmsley was register, replied, 'Sir, I can put her into the Spiritual Court!'"[10] Indeed, *Irene*—with its contest between Christian and Muslim doctrine (as it was conventionally represented), its discussion of good and bad judgment, and its heroine's death by despotic (and erroneous) decree—does suggest a certain juridical concern.

An ideal of lived integrity through proper education is at the center of Samuel Johnson's fiction. Johnson also explored the connection between moral and intellectual rigor in the relationship between Irene and Aspasia in *Irene*. Set against the religiopolitical backdrop of the conquest of Constantinople by Mahomet II in 1453, *Irene* juxtaposes the fates of Aspasia, a stalwart Christian heroine fortified by a male-identified Western education, with Irene, a more submissive, traditionally educated Western woman who converts to Islam. It is no surprise that the man who praised Richardson's fiction and wrote the poem "The Vanity of Human Wishes" would be preoccupied with immortal spiritual identities and eternal rewards and punishments. What is remarkable is that Johnson's fiction repeatedly attends to the moral failures of badly educated women. In line with women's didactic fiction of the 1720s, Johnson presented women's intelligence and their immortal fate as deeply dependent on an adequate education. Women were morally accountable; to deny them an education was effectively to damn them.

The basic plot of *Irene*, as David Nichol Smith shows, had been extant since the mid-sixteenth century, if not much earlier, although Johnson departed from his sources considerably. As Smith puts it, Johnson "converted a record of senseless cruelty into a study of temptation."[11] The tale underscores the irrational sexual violence associated with the stereotype of the Muslim despot. According to the tale, Mahomet II fell in love with a beautiful Greek slave after she was captured at the siege of Constantinople in 1453. He became so enamored of her that his army commanders began to doubt his ability to achieve further military glory. Incensed, Mahomet staged a spectacle in which he had Irene, arrayed in her loveliest garments, displayed before his men. When they had all admitted that they could not have resisted her had they been in his position, he promptly killed her as a proof of his willpower.

Italian bishop and writer Matteo Bandello first fictionalized the account in 1554. Writers in French (Pierre Boaistuau, 1559), English (William Painter, 1566), and Latin (Martinus Crusius, 1584) quickly took up the tale. Richard Knolles drew on previous authors in writing his 1603 *The Generall Historie of the Turkes*. A handful of English plays were also based on the tale. Familiar with the tale through his reading of Knolles, Johnson altered the story to analyze how a tense political scenario brings two different modes of female learning to fruition. As a band of Greek soldiers following the sack of Constantinople struggle to overthrow Mahomet (or, failing that, to escape), two captured women—Aspasia and Irene—must resist the advances of the enamored tyrant. Both women are intelligent, pious Christians, yet Aspasia's education has been more rigorous than Irene's. Mahomet at first falls in love with Aspasia, but she is so stalwart in her rejection of him that he soon turns to the more accommodating Irene, who is of "equal Beauty, but of softer Mien, / Fear in her Eye, Submission on her Tongue."[12] Kathleen Nulton Kemmerer notes that Irene "dramatizes Johnson's assumptions about women's rationality and the relationship of their education to virtue. . . . By naming the play *Irene* . . . Johnson focuses attention on her conflict, on what he feels to be her real tragedy."[13] Irene's moral struggle—Aspasia experiences no real temptation from Mahomet—provides the drama.

Despite *Irene*'s lack of popularity as a tragedy, one scene became sufficiently well known to be invoked by Hannah More in her own argument for women's education (as I discuss in chapter 5). In this key scene, the stereotypically lascivious Mahomet cavalierly assures Irene that her soul is mortal. He tells her that her worries about the eternal consequences of apostasy are

> Vain Raptures all—For your inferior Natures
> Form'd to delight, and happy by delighting;
> Heav'n has reserv'd no future Paradise,
> But bids you rove the Paths of Bliss, secure
> Of total Death and careless of Hereafter;
> While Heav'n's high Minister, whose awful Volume
> Records each Act, each Thought of sov'reign Man,
> Surveys your Plays with inattentive Glance,
> And leaves the lovely Trifler unregarded. (2.7.28)

The speech both epitomizes Islamophobic misogynistic mortalism and sets the stage for a (problematic) refutation by Irene. It represents, in other words, the moral hierarchy of the Ottoman sultan, a badly educated Western woman (Irene), and a well-educated woman (Aspasia). Aspasia, trained in the Greco-Roman tradition, rejects all Mahomet's arguments and enticements, unlike Johnson's Irene and Rowe's "beautiful *Grecian* Slave."[14] Proper English (or, more broadly, Western) women do not fall for alluring "Mahometan" arguments such as misogynistic mortalism or the pleasures of worldly glory.

Irene's choices are the dramatic center of the play, while Aspasia provides intellectual and moral authority. Aspasia is insistent that eternal welfare, not worldly power, is where women's interest truly resides. She warns Irene not to let cowardice obscure her sense of the eternal perspective. As she tells Irene,

> Reflect that Life and Death, affecting sounds,
> Are only varied Modes of endless Being;
> Reflect that Life, like ev'ry other Blessing,
> Derives its Value from its Use alone;
> . . . .
> Thus Life, with loss of Wealth, is well preserv'd,
> And Virtue cheaply sav'd with loss of Life. (3.8.41)

But Irene is not convinced, and this rational failure signals—to readers familiar with the didactic fiction of the 1720s—that she is not a properly Western heroine. Like the Platonic Lady, Irene is sufficiently softheaded, vain, and worldly to be persuaded by stereotypically "Mahometan" allurements.

Irene herself admits her intellectual and emotional frailties and identifies the main difference between the two women as one of education: "Not all like thee can brave the Shocks of Fate," she tells Aspasia, since

> Thy Soul by Nature great, enlarg'd by Knowledge,
> Soars unencumber'd with our idle Cares,
> And all Aspasia but her Beauty's Man. (2.1.18)

Irene locates Aspasia's strength of mind and character in her masculine education. Aspasia, for her part, warns Irene that women's stereotypical feminine frailty is also a matter of nurture rather than nature, for women "*learn* to shudder at the rustling Breeze" until "*Habitual* Cowardice usurps the Soul (2.1.18; my emphasis). Aspasia refutes the conventional misogynistic claim that women are naturally cowardly, attributing women's cowardice to their faulty education in feminine performance. Courage is a choice for her, not a gendered virtue.

But Irene is no martyr, and she lacks the intellectual foundation to defend herself against Mahomet's enticing suggestion to turn her thoughts "henceforth to Love and Empire" (2.7.27). Again, like the Platonic Lady, she at first makes a feeble objection to worldly "Mahometan" temptations by asserting her immortality: "Must I for these renounce the Hope of Heaven, / Immortal Crowns and fullness of Enjoyment?" (2.7.27), she asks Mahomet. Although initially amused by, and dismissive of, the notion that women could be immortal, Mahomet begins to gain ground when he changes his approach. He begins to realize, as Rake did with Madonella, that promises of glory will tempt her vanity. Thus, when Irene claims that women's rationality and love of glory are equal to those of men, she seems not to realize that in restructuring her argument to base women's value on both intangible *and* temporal assets (which are within Mahomet's power to bestow), she has weakened her position:

> Then let me once, in honour of our Sex,
> Assume the boastful Arrogance of Man.
> . . . .
> Do not we share the comprehensive Thought,
> Th'enlivening Wit, the penetrating Reason?
> Beats not the female Breast with gen'rous Passions,
> The thirst of Empire, and the Love of Glory? (2.7.29)

In fact, it is not clear that "Arrogance" or the "thirst of Empire" (which Johnson himself scorned) honor women or put them on an equal footing with men in regard to comprehensive thought, wit, or reason. Rather, Irene's wrongheadedness in locating women's "honour" in the temporal world—a world in which Mahomet has a great deal of power—gives Mahomet the leverage that will be Irene's undoing. He immediately grants her the recognition her rhetorical stance demanded and identifies it with his own desires:

> Illustrious Maid, new Wonders fix me thine,
> Thy Soul compleats the Triumphs of thy Face.
> . . . .
> Will it not charm a Mind like thine exalted,
> To shine the Goddess of applauding Nations,
> To scatter Happiness and Plenty round thee,
> To bid the prostrate Captive rise and live,
> To see new Cities tow'r at thy Command,
> And blasted Kingdoms flourish at thy smile? (2.7.29)

Irene seems not to realize that in order for captives to rise, cities to tower, or kingdoms to flourish under her wondrous influence, they must first be prostrated, destroyed, and blasted by a military invasion. Like the Platonic Lady, her vanity obscures the real costs of her ultimate complicity in an imperial, patriarchal system. Mahomet's argument appeals to Irene's piety, warped by a misguided and shortsighted vanity, and she agrees to marry him in the hopes that she will be the means of saving her persecuted fellow Christians. Irene's is a moral as well as an intellectual error from Aspasia's point of view. Irene seeks refuge in the power she thinks she will have over her lover, not realizing that temporal power is unreliable even for rulers and that the only power a woman has over her husband is what he chooses to give her. When Irene feels certain of her triumph, she abandons Aspasia's precepts and scoffs that her former friend is afraid of greatness. Significantly, Irene's choice of Mahomet aligns her with a masculinity characterized by violence, ambition, and empire, while Aspasia's final escape with the Greeks aligns her with men who are rational, affectively sophisticated, vulnerable exiles. A woman's education says as much about her moral agency as about the man she ultimately approves of in Johnson's moral schema. With this in mind, Aspasia's rebuttal of Irene's preference for ambition and empire (a "glitt'ring Fallacy") is directed not just at Irene but also at Mahomet and Milton's Satan. As she tells Irene,

> Angelic Greatness is Angelic Virtue.
> Amidst the Glare of Courts, the Shout of Armies,
> Will not th'Apostate feel the Pangs of Guilt,
> And wish too late for Innocence and Peace?
> Curst as the Tyrant of th'infernal Realms,
> With gloomy State and agonizing Pomp. (3.3.44)

The language of moral and intellectual grandeur that Aspasia utilizes shows the flaws of Irene's thinking, just as Irene's death proves Aspasia right about women's relative power. Mahomet, wrongly believing that Irene has betrayed him, has her strangled without even giving her an opportunity to defend herself. Kemmerer concludes of Irene's execution by Mahomet's mute slaves, "Their silence is physically enforced; hers, culturally mandated. She is executed without trial, without opportunity of making a defense. She dies innocent and ignorant of the cause of Mahomet's change of heart."[15] Lacking Aspasia's rigorously rational "masculine" education, Irene suffers in the temporal world, knowing that she dies innocent of betraying her husband, but also knowing that she has freely chosen to imperil her immortal soul. Johnson makes it clear that giving women a "female" education is a moral as much as an intellectual disservice; it stunts their temporal relationships and endangers their immortal identities. For him, inadequate female education is identified with the Muslim harem, while the proper education for women is identified with Christianity. This is most starkly shown in *Rasselas*.

PEKUAH IN THE HAREM

In the philosophical novel *Rasselas* (1759), Johnson presents a group of privileged travelers on a quest to discover what constitutes the happy life. Bored with living in the isolated comfort of the Happy Valley, the eponymous prince sets out to see the world with his sister, the Princess Nekayah; her faithful servant Pekuah; and their guide, the philosopher-poet Imlac. The travelers observe all different levels of society in many different countries, but their quest remains famously unconcluded.

Rasselas owed a debt to the increasingly popular genre of the "oriental tale," which tended to involve elements of fantasy, magic, and exotic travel. Johnson, ever the moral instructor, used the oriental tale to address several central philosophical questions, such as the nature of the soul, the proper training needed to produce poetry, and how women should be educated. The travelers learn about the world, various philosophies, and themselves as they encounter strange lands and foreign customs. When the group explores the pyramids, however, Arabs abduct Pekuah. Readers might expect the abduction to initiate an episode of sexual trauma. But, as Thomas Keymer observes, "wherever Johnson looks to be on the cusp of a cliché of oriental fiction, his next move is to overturn generic expectations or frustrate readerly desires."[16] In fact, the Arab chief "turns out to be a world-weary Johnsonian melancholic" (xxiv). Further, given Johnson's antipathy to empire, it is telling that Johnson's Johnsonian Arab chief sees "banditry as a just mode of resistance to Turkish imperialism" (xxiv). Johnson's internal critique of his own nation's imperial expansion suggests the complexity of his feelings about Turkey.

Unambiguously, Johnson presents the space of the seraglio as intellectually stultifying for women. Pekuah resists it, but she comes from the Christian (Monophysite) land of Abyssinia. In fact, Pekuah's experience in the Arab seraglio reinforces the alignment of Muslim spaces and bodily, rather than intellectual, pleasures that we have seen in writers from Lancelot Addison to Eliza Haywood. It is only when the Johnsonian bandit talks to Pekuah outside of the harem that she has any intellectual stimulation. He, too, is bored of the bodily pleasures of the harem.

In the harem, unable to depend on the example of Nekayah, Pekuah begins to take charge of her servants herself and to set them an example of courage. The separation also enables Nekayah to learn how to deal with grief. After Pekuah's abduction, Imlac comforts Nekayah, who is contemplating a recluse life.[17] He tells her not to feel responsible since "man cannot so far know the connexion of causes and events, as that he may venture to do wrong in order to do right" (74). Choosing wrong in order to do right is precisely the mistake that Irene had made. Further, while Imlac persuades Nekayah to turn away from the space of female seclusion identified with Roman Catholicism, Pekuah turns away from a space of female seclusion identified with Islam.

After she is ransomed, Pekuah recounts to Nekayah her experience in the harem in terms that would echo in the descriptions of harem women in Wollstonecraft's work. The descriptions are worth quoting at length because they show the alignment of Monophysite (Eastern) Christianity with intellect and Islam with physical pleasure. In Pekuah's view, the diversions favored by the women of the bandit's harem were

> *only childish play*, by which the mind, accustomed to stronger operations, could not be kept busy. I could do all which they delighted in doing by *powers merely sensitive*, while *my intellectual faculties were flown* to Cairo. They ran, from room to room as a *bird* hops from wire to wire in his cage. They danced for the sake of motion, as *lambs* frisk in a meadow. . . . Their business was only needlework, in which I and my maids sometimes helped them; but you know that *the mind will easily straggle from the fingers*, nor will you suspect that captivity and absence from Nekayah could receive *solace from silken flowers*. (85–86; my italics)

Pekuah aligns a Christian woman (herself) with intellectual depth and mobility, while she aligns the women of the harem with the "merely" sensory responsiveness shared with animals, children, and flowers. Because their pleasures stop at the body, these women have not cultivated intelligence. Within this scene, it is not worth a Christian woman's effort to try to communicate with beings so static and limited in perspective. By implication, their perspective is a product of the cramped Muslim context, a context that has prevented them from developing the intellectual skills necessary to hold satisfying conversation, for "*of what could they be expected to talk*? They had *seen nothing*; for they had lived, from early youth, in that *narrow spot*: *of what they had not seen they could have no knowledge*, for *they could not read*. They had *no ideas* but of the few things that were within their view, and had hardly names for any thing but their clothes and their food" (86; my italics). Ironically, a man who never left the British Isles portrayed the intellectual stultification of Muslim women as stemming from having only ever known one "narrow spot." Further, Johnson could not have known about the real experiences within this "spot," both because of his limited international travel and because he would not have been given access to an imperial harem. The "spot" of the harem is a fantasy projection informed by the same spatial limitations Johnson identified as inhibiting the intellectual development of the fictional women of the harem.

Nevertheless, Pekuah understands the women's ignorance in terms not of innate inferiority but, like Aspasia, of learned femininity. They have no intelligence because they have been confined to a "narrow spot" that provides them with no knowledge beyond what their bodies can encounter. Their language and ideas are limited to the material rather than the intellectual world. However, Johnson also shows that women of the affluent private homes Princess Nekayah visits are not very different from the women Pekuah meets in the harem. Again, the description maps subhuman behavior and intellectual narrowness onto narrowness of experience. Nekayah finds "their *thoughts narrow*, their wishes low, and their merriment often artificial. Their *pleasures, poor as they were*, could not be preserved pure, but were embittered by petty competitions and worthless emulation. . . . With these girls she played as with *inoffensive animals*, and found them proud of her countenance and weary of her company" (55–56; my italics). Johnson prefigured for Wollstonecraft the alignment of stereotypical women in the harem with elite women of wealth and leisure. The inextricable meshing of intellectual development and moral education is put into sharp relief by the contrast between Pekuah (who learns to set a good example of courage when thrown on her own resources), the enervated women of the Arab seraglio, and the women of leisure who so bore the Astellian Nekayah.

But what of the Johnsonian bandit? In some ways, Pekuah's discussions with the Arab bandit stage a platonic version of the problematic courtship-as-attempted-seduction of Pamela and Mr. B. Indeed, Pekuah suggests that the bandit's lengthy delays in acquiring her ransom were due to his "suspense" between wanting money and wanting the intellectual companionship that only she could provide (87). For the bandit, the women of the harem are subhuman (they are like flowers "plucked and carelessly thrown away"; 86); they cannot offer the "pleasures . . . of society and friendship" (86). They lack intelligence, for since "they had no knowledge, their talk could take nothing from the tediousness of life" (86). The women of the harem have no experience, no knowledge, no intelligence—nothing to offer, except a love that is "only a careless distribution of superfluous time" (87). With them, the bandit is in the midst of an "intellectual famine" (87). Clearly, it is the Christian education that Pekuah has received from Nekayah that alone can provide the intelligent pleasure of "society and friendship." Like Richardson's heroines, Pekuah resists enclosed sexualized spaces because they degrade the mind.

I now turn from the philosophical tale with a conclusion in which nothing is concluded to meander back with the *Rambler* to Johnson's contributor—Samuel Richardson—before turning to Charlotte Lennox's *The Female Quixote*, a novel in which an English heroine's curiosity about Muslim contexts is definitely concluded.

RICHARDSON AMONG THE LADIES

As James Boswell observed in his *Life of Johnson* (1791), the only assistance that Johnson received in writing his voluminous periodical the *Rambler* was "four billets in No. 10, by Miss Mulso (now Mrs. Chapone); No. 30, by Mrs. Catherine Talbot; No. 97, by Mr. Samuel Richardson . . . ; and Nos. 44 and 100 by Mrs. Elizabeth Carter."[18] Further, both Johnson and Richardson assisted Charlotte Lennox's literary career; indeed, Johnson may have written the final, controversial, chapter of Lennox's novel *The Female Quixote* (1752). Each writer, with his or her own individual variations, made some commentary on women and Islam that reinforced the notion that Islam was a threat to women's intelligence and dignity.

In no. 4 of the *Rambler*, an issue on the new realist fiction of the novel, Johnson famously praised Richardson's fiction above Henry Fielding's. Richardson brought pain and pleasure, virtue and delight together, and it was for this reason Johnson included Richardson's essay on the modern lady in the *Rambler*. Richardson had, by the time of the *Rambler*, already achieved resounding success with two novels focused on highly literate and virtuous women: *Pamela* (1740, and its continuation, 1741) and *Clarissa* (1747–48). He was thus seen as an authority on the representation of virtuous women, and his words in the *Rambler* had great weight. This was a problem for Elizabeth Carter, as we shall see, but some analysis of Richardson's attention both to Islam and to the matter of women's immortality will help to show how his fiction was both valuable to women in their education arguments and relatively complex in its representation of religious toleration.

Richardson, who was familiar with popular fiction by women and with the representational tradition of the Ottoman despot, used a domestic arena to demonstrate the political, social, and moral import of the resistance of a woman's soul to tyranny. He was also unusually knowledgeable about the Ottoman Empire. As a successful printer, Richardson published in 1740 (the same year as *Pamela*'s publication) *The Negotiations of Sir Thomas Roe*. Detailing his time as ambassador to Constantinople in the 1620s, Roe's *Negotiations* includes accounts of threats posed by Tunisian and Algerian pirates and by rival European trading powers, like Spain and France.

Richardson was intimately familiar with Roe's material and compiled an index of summaries ("headings") of each letter. Richardson's correspondent, Aaron Hill, expressed great appreciation of Richardson's efforts, writing to him that "I owe most of the pleasure [Roe] gave me to the discovery I made, with astonishment, as I turned over the book, that your comprehensive and excellent index of heads had drawn every thing out of the body!"[19] It is clear from these extensive descriptive heads that Richardson was aware of Roe's belief that, by the 1620s, the Ottoman

Empire's superior power was declining but that the dissension between Christian European powers was impeding the decline.[20] Roe's letters show a concern with barbary pirates and the imprisonment of Englishmen (and other Europeans) in Turkey, as well as an awareness that various European powers (Dutch, English, French, Papal) were in competition for Ottoman favors regarding access to strategic locations for trade.

Apart from the *Negotiations*, Richardson was involved, after 1736, in the publishing of the multivolume *Universal History*. One of the authors of the section on ancient history, John Swinton, "evidently tried to use the History as religious polemic" in writing a life of "Mohammed" in which he intended to characterize him as an "impostor." Apparently, Swinton believed the Trinitarian Controversy had not exhausted this genre. But when George Sale, the most recent English translator of the Qur'an "reproved" Swinton, the latter accused those who sided with Sale of "not being Christians—'calling Deists and Atheists, Persons absolutely unknown to him'"[21] Richardson did not approve of Swinton's scurrilities and sided with Sale.

Richardson clearly did not support the Trinitarian Controversy rhetoric of castigating opponents as heretics, atheists, or Mahometans. Further, Richardson generally favored religious toleration, even toward Catholics. His tolerance for cultural differences figures interestingly in his understanding of gender relations. Perhaps the most succinct overview of gender relations in Richardson's oeuvre is the spirited discussion about the naturalness of women's subordination in *Sir Charles Grandison*. Mrs. Shirley, the elderly "moderatrix," reasons, "I think . . . women are generally too much considered as a species apart. . . . Why must women always be addressed in an appropriated language; and not treated on the common footing of reasonable creatures?"[22] She emphasizes the commonality of men and women—returning to the Lockean complication of "species"—and argues that they are equally part of a community of rational creatures. She believes that, while there is a difference in the social duties of men and women, and while, in general, women's sphere is the home and their educations are necessarily more limited, this should not be considered a natural hierarchy.

Men were much better educated than women, to be sure, but Mrs. Shirley insists, "Don't let them despise us for this, as if their superiority were entirely founded on a natural difference of capacity! Despise us as women, and value themselves merely as men: For it is not the hat or cap which covers the head, that decides of the merit of it" (3:243). This soul-body dualism (the belief that the socialized bodies of men and women are different, but that the souls are essentially uninvolved in this difference) is echoed in Sir Charles's response. Sir Charles historicizes female learning, observing that in the court of Queen Elizabeth I "the very Ladies of it, were more learned than any court of our English Sovereigns was before, or hath been since" (3:245). He avers that gendered bodies are unequal, adapted to the different (heterosexual) duties of men and women in society, but concedes that this difference could be "temporary." Like Pamela and Clarissa, Sir Charles believes that human identity is eternal, even if the machine of the body is transitory: "Supposing . . . that all human souls are, in themselves, equal; yet the very design of the different machines in which they are inclosed, is to super-induce a temporary difference on their original equality; a difference adapted to the different purposes for which they are designed by Providence in the present transitory state. When those purposes are at an end, this difference will be at an end too. When Sex ceases, inequality of Souls will cease; and women will certainly be on a foot with men, as to intellectuals, in Heaven" (3:250). For Sir Charles, women and men are originally and ultimately, but not socially, equal. He also avoids setting up "boundaries" for women's proper education, declaring "genius, whether in man or woman, will push itself into light" (3:251). Education becomes a divine duty for such individuals, and Sir Charles advises that "if it has a laudable tendency, let it, as a ray of the Divinity, be encouraged, as well in the one Sex as in the other: I would not, by any means, have it limited" (3:251). Sir Charles fully acknowledges the immortality and rationality of women and shows a marked interest in women's arguments, reasoning, and motivations.

Further, Sir Charles is stalwart in defending his own religion while evincing a marked (though perhaps, as Bonnie Latimer argued, nominal) acceptance of religious difference.[23] *Sir Charles Grandison* in part charts the conflicted romances between Sir Charles and two admirable women: the English rose, Harriet Byron, and the fervently Catholic Clementina della Porretta. Clementina, though she is enamored of Sir Charles, considers any Anglican to be a heretic to the Roman Catholic faith (like much of the Platonic Lady discourse, she equates the Catholic with the "Mahometan"; 2:167). Like Mary Astell, Sir Charles protests that Anglicanism is the religion of his choice, not an accident of birth. Further, he values virtuous members of any faith tradition. He assures her that "good manners will make me shew respect to the religion of the country I happen to be in, were it the Mahometan, or even the Pagan; and to venerate the good men of it: But I never will enter into debate upon the subject as a traveler, a sojourner" (2:155). His is a polite Anglicanism.

Sir Charles's tolerance contrasts with the bigoted zeal of Clementina and the Porretta family, a zeal that harms them more than it does Sir Charles. Mrs. Beaumont, an acquaintance of the Porretta family, finally discerns that Clementina's emotional distress is caused by the tension between her love for Sir Charles and her vehement rejection of the legitimacy of Protestantism. Mrs. Beaumont explains,

"I had little doubt that Clementina was in Love; and that religion was the apprehended difficulty. Zealous Catholics think not better of Protestants, than of Mahometans: Nor, indeed, are zealous Protestants without their prejudices. Zeal will be zeal, in persons of whatever denomination" (2:167). Richardson was obviously very aware of the various conflations that arose from the Trinitarian Controversy's creation of Islam as the negative ideal. He also saw its political application.

Richardson explicitly figured the problems that could result from a Catholic-Protestant marital union in political terms. Father Marescotti, an Italian priest and "a zealous Roman Catholic," seeks to distance Sir Charles from Clementina, instancing the marriage of England's Charles I and France's Henrietta Maria and the "unhappy consequences which followed" (2:219). Father Marescotti casts the alliance in political terms, invoking the specter of England's Civil Wars, but Sir Charles recontextualizes the historical event, focusing not on the marriage or the nation but on the executed king. Sir Charles points out that "the Monarch was the sufferer, by the zeal of the Queen for her religion, and not the Queen, any otherwise than as she was involved in the consequences of those sufferings which she had brought upon him. In short, Father . . . Protestants, some of us, have zeal; but let us alone, and it is not a persecuting one" (2:219). Dissenters might have disagreed with this Anglican assessment. In any case, Sir Charles manages not only to deflect the charge of religious violence away from Anglicanism but also to encompass an entire nation's suffering in the person of a persecuted authority figure. However, he does later admit that Roman Catholics in England suffer a "great deal" from "disqualifications" (2:531), such as being excluded from receiving university degrees and from holding political office.

Sir Charles Grandison is Richardson's only novel focused on a male protagonist, and it was Richardson's intention to paint the portrait of a "good" man, a new kind of hero. While the novel has been widely criticized for the static irreproachability of the central character, John Sitter cautions the reader to "turn from Richardson's failure with the character of Sir Charles to his intentions," which were to embody "the theme of true—and new—heroism."[24] The action of the novel hinges on the virtuous love triangle between Harriet, Clementina, and Sir Charles. Ultimately, he chooses Harriet, effectively registering that a flighty Catholic woman cannot be absorbed into the English body politic as a reproducing body. Indeed, as we will see in chapter 5, the possibility of Sir Charles and Clementina's marriage, and the negotiation of religious toleration and education that it would entail, distressed Richardson's Bluestocking readers. Though they admired the fervency of Clementina's faith, they balked at the notion that English daughters produced by a union of Sir Charles and Clementina would grow up as Catholics. This tension is part of what Carol Houlihan Flynn calls "the costs of the domestic reconciliation that Richardson exacts from his female characters and readers."[25] The problem of absorbing foreign, or "singular," women into English domesticity also haunted *The Female Quixote*, Charlotte Lennox's novel of an idiosyncratically educated young woman who interprets English reality according to the conventions of foreign romances.

ARABELLA IN THE DOCK

Succeeding Johnson's *Irene* by only a few years, Lennox's *The Female Quixote* (1752), according to Margaret Anne Doody, is the decisive turning point in the movement of the English novel away from the continental romance tradition and toward a more regulatory "prescriptive realism."[26] Lennox's heroine Arabella had led a sequestered life in the countryside estate of her aristocratic but widowed and politically embittered father. Bereft of maternal influence, Arabella devotes herself to reading her mother's French romances and constructs her own sense of feminine identity based on the belief that the elite heroines are portrayed in a historically accurate manner. Arabella's father wishes her to conform more closely to the conventional domestic ideal and so writes a condition in his will that if Arabella does not marry her cousin Glanville, she will forfeit one-third of her estate.[27] Glanville, an unimpressive but sentimental hero, tries to convince Arabella to abandon her romantic ideals. He is unsuccessful until he receives the help of two people: an unnamed countess, who almost convinces Arabella that her pagan heroines are too sanguinary an example for a modern Christian woman to follow, and the "Good Divine" (a character possibly written by and certainly modeled on Samuel Johnson), who reasons Arabella out of her heroic ideals after she has nearly drowned. Ultimately, Arabella identifies her feminocentric romantic ideals as unchristian and historically inaccurate, abandons them, and consents to be Glanville's wife. The English patriarchal estate is therefore kept intact by excising the feminocentric romance tradition. Arabella, though never a hypocrite, in every other way becomes a reformed Platonic Lady.

Doody points out that while Lennox's title is certainly an allusion to Miguel de Cervantes's more famous novel, usually taken to be a warning about the perils of taking romances too seriously, this "reading vastly oversimplifies the book itself, and pays no heed to the fact that, as well as having written an extensive pastoral romance, *La Galatea* (1584), Cervantes in his last work *Persiles y Sigismunda* (1617) created a new romance."[28] Lennox, like Cervantes, was keenly aware that the possibilities and pleasures of idealism and skepticism could be combined. Thus, while Arabella may be a sheltered, privileged, English country girl who is often the object of satire, her worldview is informed by the admirable feminocentric and international perspective of the continental romance tradition. This is not only because Arabella longs for adventure. The romances are all that remain of her mother's life in rural seclusion. The romances were written and read by women, and passed on to women. Prose romances were, as Doody observes, "virtually the only extensive genre which women had successfully practiced" (xvi). Indeed, for the formative years of her life they are the only female, and specifically maternal, influence that Arabella experiences apart from servants. That the romances are valorized by a young woman who wishes to live heroically might seem to be Lennox's contribution to the feminocentric tradition. But history was not on Lennox's side. The outward-looking adventures of romance gave way to the domestication of the English realist novel.

What Doody identifies as a "revised notion of probability" (xvii) converged with the burying of the possibilities of feminocentric platonic discourse. The globalized fiction of the 1720s, along with the Platonic Lady, was domesticated in the period between the early 1740s and the mid-1750s. Philips and Rowe may have seen themselves—or been seen—as the muses of a potentially united Great Britain, while Astell, Aubin, and Barker surveyed the world in theorizing national unity. But women of later generations learned to keep their views, at least in "realist" fiction, increasingly within the contours of Great Britain's coasts: from *The Female Quixote* to *Northanger Abbey* (1818), sensible English heroines learned not to make the mistake of using a critical lens to judge England in relation to what lay beyond Great Britain's shores. Their status in the United Kingdom became the standard of women's enlightenment.

The Female Quixote stages this domestication in microcosm and on the person of Arabella. Glanville refuses to share Arabella's reading, hoping that the woman he intends to marry will become less singular. Other characters—his sister, Miss Glanville, and his father, Sir Charles—see Arabella as, by turns, impressively well-read and laughably unworldly. They certainly reject her defenses of non-English cultures. When Arabella clarifies, after an impassioned defense of one of her romance heroines, that the character Cleonice was from Sardis, not England, Miss Glanville smugly concludes, "Oh! then it is not in our Kingdom. . . . What signifies what Foreigners do? I shall never form my Conduct, upon the Example of Outlandish People; what is common enough in their Countries, would be very particular here" (*The Female Quixote*, 184). Sir Charles, though perfectly comfortable dismissing Arabella's "histories" for the romances that they are, nevertheless shows himself to be neither particularly worldly nor well-informed about current geopolitics. Coinciding with Glanville, he wonders why Arabella would wish to visit "Turky, . . . so great a Distance from your own Country," confuses the territories of the Ottoman and Mogul Empires, and declares of the "Great Mogul's Country" that "the People are all Pagans . . . and worship the Devil." When Glanville points out that the Great Mogul does not, in point of fact, rule over Turkey, Sir Charles gruffly declares, "Well, . . . the Great Mogul, or the Grand Signior, I know not what you call him: But I hope my Niece does not propose to go thither" (260). Sir Charles clearly considers both Turkey and India to be "foreign and uninteresting" subjects. Further, it seems that neither Glanville nor Sir Charles has ever heard of Lady Mary Wortley Montagu or the fact that, as a lady of an even higher rank than Arabella, she had accompanied her husband on his embassy to Constantinople.

Glanville is more sympathetic than either his sister or his father, but he shares their cultural chauvinism and avoids reading Arabella's books (50–51). Even though he knows how much discussing them means to her and that reading them would be the best way of sharing an intellectual interest, he cannot bring himself to do it. This is a significant refusal on Glanville's part. He frets at the embarrassment that Arabella's beliefs cause him, but he makes little effort to enter into her thoughts, her interests, her worldview, or how she evaluates reality. He wants what she has (beauty, wit, money), but not what she thinks. Further, there is a dark economic subtext to Glanville's and his father's interest in Arabella. She is independently wealthy after her father's death; but one-third of her inheritance will be forfeited to Glanville if she does not marry him. Arabella does not need the extra money, but her uncle raises a more ominous possibility for controlling a woman's wealth. Confused by what he considers to be Arabella's ludicrous behavior, Sir Charles (her guardian between the death of her father and her marriage to Glanville) bursts out that perhaps he should "bring a Commission of Lunacy against her" (339). There is nothing in the text to suggest that Sir Charles is a gothic villain who might actually imprison Arabella in order to get his hands on the entirety of her money. But the possibility of abusing the gendered inequality in the legal system is there.

The problem of institutionalized sexism went beyond the Glanville family. At one point Sir Charles declares that Arabella is so talented an orator that she would shine in Parliament. But, of course, women could not be members of Parliament in the eighteenth century. They had no access to the official levers of power. Within this historical reality the attractions of the feminocentric romance become clear: losing them unmasks women's lack of any real political, legal, financial, or physical power. Arabella is meant to produce—domestic stability and children—and romances interfere with her functioning as a productive member of English society, properly subordinate to her cousin's (and later husband's) authority.

Arabella's escapism is a product not only of her constraints as a woman but also of the constraints she experienced in the enforced parochialism of her father's estate. The romances furnish a transnational world of possibilities, and Arabella defends non-English heroines ardently. Others see her defense of other cultures as a product of her own outsider status and, perhaps, as evidence that she is not entirely rational. Not all assessments of Arabella are so extreme as to consider the possibility of lunacy, but various characters describe her in terms clearly meant to associate her with dangerous religious alterity. Miss Glanville both echoes her father and recalls Astell's female monastery when she dismisses one of Arabella's speeches by observing "that it was a Pity there were not such Things as Protestant Nunneries; giving it as her Opinion, that her Cousin ought to be confin'd in one of those Places, and never suffer'd to see any Company" (314). And at one fashionable gathering, Arabella's unusual appearance causes "the wiser Sort" to take her "for a Foreigner; others, of still more Sagacity, supposed her a Scots Lady, covered with her Plaid; and a third Sort, infinitely wiser than either, concluded she was a Spanish Nun, that had escaped from a Convent, and had not yet quitted her Veil" (263). The references to textile markers of difference—the plaid and the veil—situate Arabella symbolically as a religiopolitical other. The Scottish Highlanders had only a few years before been brutally defeated by the Duke of Cumberland in the Battle of Culloden (1746), the decisive battle of the second major Jacobite rebellion. Plaid tartans were textile signifiers of clan identity, and the Dress Act of 1746 banned male Highlanders from wearing them unless they were members of the British army.[29]

That romance had political import is made clear in an interchange between Arabella and Glanville toward the conclusion. Arabella upholds her own authority by seeing herself as a romantic heroine with "absolute Power" over her professed lovers. Glanville informs her that she can have no such power, since a lover "neither can give, nor you exercise an absolute Power over him; since you are both accountable to the King, whose Subjects you are, and both restrain'd by the Laws under whose Sanction you live." Arabella declares that the "Empire of Love . . . like the Empire of Honour, is govern'd by Laws of its own, which have no Dependence upon, or Relation to any other" (320). But it is these very empires that Arabella is expected to give up in order to be a (re)productive member of the British Empire. As the Doctor convinces her on her sickbed, "These books soften the Heart to Love, and harden it to Murder . . . they teach Women to exact Vengeance . . . to expect not only Worship, but the dreadful Worship of human Sacrifices" (380). He completes the domestic education that the Countess had begun. For in endeavoring to wean Arabella from her admiration of the heroes and heroines of romances, the Countess carefully distinguished them from the time, place, and religion of Arabella's own experience.

Of Arabella's noble heroes and heroines, the Countess had explained that "judging of them as Christians, we shall find them impious and base, and directly opposite to our present Notions of moral and relative Duties" (329). Weakened by near drowning, in love with Glanville, and persuaded by the combined forces of the Countess and the Doctor, Arabella finally "yields to the Force of Truth" and abandons her romances and their valorization of transnational heroism that she now identifies only with an unchristian and "unnecessary Bloodshed" (381). She is domesticated not only for Glanville, in other words, but for the Anglican state.

In sum, Arabella becomes a converted Platonic Lady. Lennox plays on the Platonic Lady riff that she knows her readers will recognize. Arabella is a "fair Visionary" with an "Imagination" that is "always prepossessed with the same fantastic Ideas" (21). She resents her father's high-handed declaration that he intends to bestow her "together with all his Estates" on Glanville, a cousin whom she has not seen "since she was eight Years old," and rejects the command, declaring that she prefers to "live single" (30, 27, 41). Her imperious father insists that she entertain Glanville as a suitor, and Glanville, in a notable adaptation of the rake seduction method, "resolved to accommodate himself, as much as possible, to her Taste, and endeavor to gain her Heart by a Behaviour most agreeable to her: He therefore assumed an Air of great Distance and Respect; never mentioned his Affection, nor the Intentions of her Father in his Favour" (46). Lennox converts the libertine seduction of the Platonic Lady into an earnest and sincere courtship by a sentimental lover. But the end result is the same: the Platonic Lady learns that her proper sphere is the home. The heroic, transnational model of womanhood is domesticated.

Despite the possibility of reading *The Female Quixote* as a gentle satire of feminine foibles, I would like to suggest a somewhat darker interpretation. Glanville, Arabella's future husband, only demonstrates a less huffy version of his father's chauvinistic ignorance. Just as Sir Charles conflates the leaders of the Mogul and Ottoman Empires—because he could not care less about the particulars of either—so, too, Glanville fails to realize that Oroontes and Oroondates are the same person because he could not care less about the books he so faithfully promised Arabella to read. Lennox is clearly critiquing all three reading practices as misguided, so why should Arabella's bad reading practices be more condemned than Sir Charles's or Glanville's? Hers, after all, were produced by a rural seclusion enforced by patriarchal authority *and* a genuine interest in what she took to be the particularities of other cultures and other women. The bad reading practices of the Glanville family were produced by sloppy data gathering, dismissiveness, and chauvinism (and often outright xenophobia). *The Female Quixote* nevertheless concludes that the foreign nation (and the foreign heroine) should be considered uninteresting to a properly domesticated English wife.

There is a real problem with historical reading here. Sir Charles at one point dismisses Arabella's belief that traveling in the Mediterranean might result in being captured and sold into slavery. It is disingenuous (or simply ignorant) of him to dismiss as ancient pagan history a European Christian reality: the enslavement on the high seas that Defoe, Rowe, Barker, and Aubin had been fictionalizing—and with much popular acclaim—only thirty years before. As Eve Tavor Bannet has pointed out, Aubin's narratives set in the Mediterranean and Atlantic were fictionalized ways of processing the real-life experiences of Barbary captives. Indeed, a group of 260 captives was released in 1720, arriving in England with much fanfare in 1721.[30] The elitism of Aubin's noble slaves—her heroes and heroines are always noble—is of course a violation of probability and sits uncomfortably within the conventions of formal realism. But, as Bannet points out, romance enabled Aubin "to introduce and foreground female protagonists, and to remind readers that women traveling in ships—whether as passengers, female tars, pirates, officers' wives, or nurses and laundresses on hospital ships—were captured, drowned and shipwrecked, too" (47). The experience of captivity was certainly in the realm of historical reality for eighteenth-century Englishwomen. It is Sir Charles who does not know enough about the rest of the world to separate historical fact from cultural fiction. Yet it is Arabella who must be regulated, disciplined, and humiliated so that her singularity, her queerness, her foreignness become safely domesticated. Her body can reproduce, but her reading practices should not. They cannot be allowed to influence other women's minds the way her mother's romances had influenced hers. The Platonic Lady and her attraction to the foreign are shut down in *The Female Quixote.*

The fate of Arabella's reading practices is born of the same cultural framework that produced the Bluestockings' displeasure with Richardson's hypothetical narrative in which English daughters are raised on English soil as Catholics. If Lennox reluctantly disciplined her heroine according to Johnsonian tenets of realism and probability in order to conform to the new prescriptive realism, the Bluestockings did not react so calmly to what they perceived as Richardson's portrayal of women's educational marginalization. Of particular concern were Richardson's portrayal of paternal authority in *Clarissa* (1747–48), his contribution to Samuel Johnson's periodical the *Rambler* (1750), and his portrayal of the marriage negotiations between his Anglican hero Sir Charles Grandison and the pious, emotionally traumatized Roman Catholic Clementina. The Bluestockings had strong objections to Richardson's characterization of women's education, and their correspondence, which I examine in the next chapter, registered the centrality of misogynistic mortalism to arguments for women's education in eighteenth-century England.

NOTES

1. Samuel Johnson, *Rambler*, 2nd ed., 8 vols. (Edinburgh: Printed by Sands, Murray, and Cochran; sold by W. Gordon, C. Wright, J. Yair, and the other booksellers, 1751).
2. Samuel Johnson, "A Journey to the Western Islands of Scotland," in *The Major Works*, ed. Donald Greene (Oxford: Oxford Worlds Classics, 2000), 638.
3. Weinbrot also notes the importance of pleasure in Johnson's theory of poetry. For Johnson, the poet "cannot legislate for man, since the poet's function is to instruct by pleasing not by fiat . . . the power of pleasing is essential." Howard D. Weinbrot, "The Reader, the General, and the Particular: Johnson and Imlac in Chapter Ten of *Rasselas*," *Eighteenth-Century Studies* 5, no. 1 (Autumn 1971): 85, 87. Srinivas Aravamudan suggests that demonstrating "the negation of particularities into an orientalist syncretism, *Rasselas* reconfirms agency (and its inverse, despotism) as *presentational* categories whose validity is determined by the adequacy of performance." Srinivas Aravamudan, *Tropicopolitans: Colonialism and Agency, 1688–1804* (Durham, N.C.: Duke University Press, 1999), 204.
4. Thomas Keymer, introduction to *The History of Rasselas, Prince of Abissinia*, by Samuel Johnson, ed. Thomas Keymer, Oxford World's Classics (Oxford: Oxford University Press, 2009), xix.
5. James Boswell, "Thursday, 10 April 1783," in *Life of Johnson, Unabridged*, ed. by R. W. Chapman, with an introduction by Pat Rogers, Oxford World's Classics (Oxford: Oxford University Press, 1998), 1218.
6. Boswell, "Thursday, 10 April 1783," in *Life of Johnson*, 1218.
7. Boswell, "Thursday, 10 April 1783," in *Life of Johnson*, 1218.
8. Boswell, "February 1749," in *Life of Johnson*, 142.
9. Boswell, "Monday, 6 February 1749," in *Life of Johnson*, 141.
10. Boswell, "1736," in *Life of Johnson*, 73.
11. David Nichol Smith, "Johnson's *Irene*," in *Essays and Studies*, vol. 14, collected by H. W. Garrod (Milford: English Association, 1929), 37–38.
12. Samuel Johnson *Irene: A Tragedy. As it is acted at the Theatre Royal in Drury-Lane. By Mr. Samuel Johnson* (London, 1749), 1.2.11. References are to act, scene, and page number.
13. Kathleen Nulton Kemmerer, *"A Neutral Being between the Sexes": Samuel Johnson's Sexual Politics* (Lewisburg, Pa.: Bucknell University Press, 1998), 39.
14. Elizabeth Singer [Rowe], *"Friendship in Death in Twenty Letters from the Dead to the Living" and "Letters Moral and Entertaining,"* ed. Josephine Grieder (New York: Garland Publishing, 1972), 61.
15. Kemmerer, *"Neutral Being,"* 57.
16. Keymer, introduction to Johnson, *History of Rasselas*, xxiv.
17. Nekayah informs Imlac, "I am resolved to retire from the world, with all its flatteries and deceits, and will hide myself in solitude, without any other care than to compose my thoughts and regulate my hours by a constant succession of innocent occupations, till, with a mind purified from earthly desires, I shall enter into that state, to which all are hastening, and in which I hope again to enjoy the friendship of Pekuah." Johnson, *History of Rasselas*, 76.
18. Boswell, "March 1750," in *Life of Johnson*, 144.
19. *The Correspondence of Samuel Richardson* (London: Printed for Richard Phillips, No. 71, St. Paul's Church-Yard, 1804), vol. 1. The quotation is on p. 43 of the section "Correspondence between Mr. Richardson and Aaron Hill" (the volume is not paginated continuously). Letter dated September 17, 1740.

20. *The Negotiations of Sir Thomas Roe* (London: Printed by Samuel Richardson, 1740). See Letters 24 (to the Prince) and 206 (to Sir Dudley Carleton) on the superiority of Ottoman power because of Christian disunity.
21. T. C. Duncan Eaves and Ben D. Kimpel, *Samuel Richardson: A Biography* (Oxford: Clarendon Press, 1971), 509.
22. Samuel Richardson, *The History of Sir Charles Grandison*, ed. with an introduction by Jocelyn Harris, 3 vols. (London: Oxford University Press, 1972), 3:243. For ease of reference I am citing according to modern volume number and page number. Harris provides the original volume numbers in text.
23. Bonnie Latimer, *Making Gender, Culture, and the Self in the Fiction of Samuel Richardson: The Novel Individual* (Farnham: Ashgate, 2013), 128–130.
24. John Sitter, *Literary Loneliness in Mid-Eighteenth-Century England* (Ithaca, N.Y.: Cornell University Press, 1982), 206.
25. Carol Houlihan Flynn, "The Pains of Compliance in *Sir Charles Grandison*," in *Samuel Richardson: Tercentenary Essays*, ed. Margaret Anne Doody and Peter Sabor (Cambridge: Cambridge University Press, 1989), 134.
26. See Margaret Anne Doody, *The True Story of the Novel* (New Brunswick, N.J.: Rutgers University Press, 1996), 288–289. More recently, Eugenia Zuroski Jenkins has provided an illuminating analysis of how Eastern cultures are marginalized in *The Female Quixote*. See Eugenia Zuroski Jenkins, "Disenchanting China: Orientalism and the English Novel," chap. 6 in *A Taste for China: English Subjectivity and the Prehistory of Orientalism* (Oxford: Oxford University Press, 2013), 188–213.
27. Charlotte Lennox, *The Female Quixote* [1752], ed. Margaret Dalziel, with an introduction by Margaret Anne Doody, Oxford World's Classics (Oxford: Oxford University Press, 1989), 64.
28. Doody, introduction to Lennox, *Female Quixote*, xiv.
29. The act reads: "That . . . no man or boy within that part of Britain called Scotland, other than such as shall be employed as Officers and Soldiers in His Majesty's Forces, shall, on any pretext whatever, wear or put on the clothes commonly called Highland clothes." Abolition and Proscription of the Highland Dress, 1746, 19 Geo. 2, c. 39, § 17.
30. Eve Tavor Bannet, *Transatlantic Stories and the History of Reading, 1720–1810: Migrant Fictions* (Cambridge: Cambridge University Press, 2011), 49.

5

THE "MAHOMETAN STRAIN"

BRITISH WOMEN INCREASINGLY RELIED ON misogynistic mortalism to criticize what they took to be bad education for women. Chapter 1 explored the production of Islam as the "negative ideal" in the Trinitarian and related controversies by which Christianity was aligned with intellectual pleasure and Islam with physical pleasure. Chapter 2 addressed women's understanding of the relationship between intelligence, the soul, and women's subordinate status to contextualize why misogynistic mortalism was useful to them from the 1690s forward. Chapter 3 explored women's increasing reliance on Addison's and Prideaux's juxtaposition of Christian spiritual pleasures and Muslim bodily pleasure and how this informed their imagining of the differences between Anglican and Muslim women. The Platonic Lady was a key trope used to contradistinguish British (but really Anglican) masculinity from the stereotypical representation of Muslim and Roman Catholic masculinities. Chapter 4 showed how the British heroine was domesticated by being ridiculed for her interest in "foreign and uninteresting" subjects. In this chapter I survey the use of misogynistic mortalism in women's education arguments from the 1730s to the 1790s, before concluding with an analysis of how it informed the cornerstone text of Western feminism: Mary Wollstonecraft's *A Vindication of the Rights of Woman* (1792).

"FROM A MUSSULMAN'S MOUTH"

The proto-feminist "Sophia" pamphlets, the first of which appeared in 1739 as "Woman Not Inferior to Man," have been variously attributed to Lady Mary Wortley Montagu or to Lady Sophia Fermor.[1] It is easy to see why Montagu would have been considered as a possible author: the wit and sharpness of style combined with the arguments regarding intelligence, education, and the pernicious influence of custom that run straight from Poullain through Astell (whose writing Montagu admired) are all characteristic of Montagu. However, given the Islamophobia embedded in the arguments for women's education, I find it unlikely that Montagu was the author.

Sophia begins her defense of women's intellectual ability with a critique of patriarchal power that is recognizable from Poullain, Astell, and Lady Chudleigh. Sophia questions how "those lordly creatures" can pretend to be masters of women when they cannot even master their own passions (*Woman Not Inferior* 1). In contrast, women "know we have reason, and are sensible that it is the only prerogative nature has bestow'd upon us, to lift us above the sphere of sensitive animals" (*Woman Not Inferior* 2). Using the Cartesian binaries of mind-body and human-animal to offset the specious "*great difference*" of the male-female binary, Sophia aligns women with the human intellect and men with the "passions they have in common with Brutes" (*Woman Not Inferior* 6, 2). Like Poullain, Astell, and Lady Chudleigh, she also targets "groundless custom" as the root of women's intellectual oppression (*Woman Not Inferior* 2).

Despite drawing so much from Poullain's Cartesian work, there is a sharp rejection of "blind followers of Des Cartes" who "are not ashamed to take upon religious trust from him, that the whole animal creation are but different kinds of automata, or self-moving clock-work; notwithstanding it's being pretty well known, that their master himself had too much sense to believe his own system, having invented it only to amuse and impose upon fools" (*Woman Not Inferior* 5). It is hard to say who looks worse in this description: Descartes or his simpleminded followers. The characterization suggests a complex acknowledgment of Descartes's influence, the burgeoning literature of sensibility (and its attentiveness to the vulnerable, including animals), and a distaste for philosophical freethinking.

Sophia seems to coincide with Poullain's position on the cross-cultural oppression of women when she insists that the "wild savages in the *Indies*" are capable of learning, too, and that they are of the "same species with our domestic ones at home" (*Woman Not Inferior* 4–5). But she soon moves into Islamophobic territory. After identifying "rectified reason" as the only "impartial judge" between men and women because it is "a pure intellectual faculty elevated above the consideration of any sex, and equally concern'd in the welfare of the whole rational species in general," she then turns to the question of men's interest in seeing women as *machines de plaisir* (*Woman Not Inferior* 8–9). As Sophia sees it, all men are secretly "unanimous" in seeing women as "made only for their use, that we are fit only to breed and nurse children in their tender years, to mind household affairs, and to obey, serve, and please our masters" (*Woman Not Inferior* 11). This is not Sophia's idea of an English kind of pleasure. As she says, "All this is very fine, and, amidst a seraglio of slaves, could not but sound mighty big from a mussulman's mouth. Yet I cannot help thinking it of a stamp with all those fantastical expressions which are more easily advanced than proved" (*Woman Not Inferior* 11). Sophia does not use misogynistic mortalism to reinforce her point, but the implication that Muslim pleasures are bodily while Christian pleasures are moral and intellectual is clearly in play. The version of *Woman Not Inferior to Man* published in 1751 as the first installment of the three-part collection *Beauty's Triumph*, would go even further, suggesting that Islamophobic misogynistic mortalism had calcified in the period between 1739 and 1751.

The title page of *Beauty's Triumph* proclaims the text to be a demonstration of women's superiority to men.[2] Yet while much of the 1751 version coincides with the 1739 text, there is a telling addition. In this version, a quotation from Thomas Seward's poem "The Female Right to Literature" (probably written and first circulated ca. 1735, but not published until 1782) is inserted between the sentence about pleasing "masters" and the comment about the "seraglio of slaves."[3] The 1739 "mussulman" is also changed to "Ishmaelite" (11). The quotation is sufficiently brief to include in its entirety, and, in Seward's original poem, the quotation is spoken by the "grand impostor Mahomet" (Seward, 2:310):

> *Women, the Toys of Men, and Slaves of Lust,*
> *Are but mere Moulds to form Man's outward Crust;*
> *The heavenly Spark, that animates the Clay,*
> *Of the prime Essence that effulgent Ray,*
> *Th'enobling Soul, is all to Man confin'd,*
> *Not meanly squander'd on weak Woman-kind.* (*Beauty's Triumph*, 11; italics in original)

This section of the poem obviously informed, or was informed by, Johnson's Mahomet-Irene seduction scene. There is also the conventional alignment of men with the divine, the intellectual, and the noble, and women with the earthly, the bodily, and the mean. Seward's poem in its entirety stages a survey of world history that begins in Asia ("the first-peopled East"; Seward, 2:309) and progresses both temporally and geographically to "happy BRITAIN, dear parental land, / Where Liberty maintains her latest stand" (2:312). Yet this is a gendered liberty for Seward, who asks a personified Britannia why "thy sons" do not dispense the "birth-right liberty" in "equal scales" but rather allow custom to "bind / In chains of Ignorance the female mind" (2:312). Seward imagines a truly enlightened England as one that has fully forsaken the example of humanity's Asiatic benightedness, a misogynistic intellectual darkness identified with Islam. Seward was a

Lichfield acquaintance of Samuel Johnson, and the inclusion of Seward's poem in the 1751 version of *Woman not Inferior to Man* recalls the possibilities for women's intellectual accomplishments in the writings of Johnson and Richardson and the Bluestockings' reaction to them.

THE MAHOMETAN RICHARDSON

One of Samuel Richardson's younger correspondents in the 1750s was Hester Mulso, later Mrs. Chapone and the author of *Letters on the Improvement of the Mind* (1773), an influential work on girls' education. Mulso wrote three extraordinary letters to Richardson (October 12, 1750; November 10, 1750; January 3, 1751) that would come to be known as the *Letters on Filial Obedience*.[4] Only twenty-three years old at the time of writing, Mulso challenged Richardson to rethink Clarissa's fearful sentiments regarding her father's power to influence her immortal life when he curses her, calling down God's vengeance on her in this life and the next.

In her first letter (October 12, 1750), Mulso's approach to Richardson as mentor emphasized the importance of reason and affection as integral parts of authority. She stated that her understanding would no doubt be rectified by his opinion and that she appreciated his permission to "oppose" her arguments to his until her reason could "give its free assent" (3:205) to Richardson's view of filial obedience as propounded in *Clarissa*. She thus established their mentoring relationship on a combination of affection and reason, which she maintained throughout her letters to Richardson.

In rejecting Mr. Harlowe's authority as abusive, Mulso drew an analogy between a king's and a parent's authority that drew on John Locke's political argument against patriarchal absolutism. Within a lengthy quote from Locke's chapter on paternal power, specifically the section in which he asserted that the maturity that makes a man free also makes his son free, Mulso inserted her own comment: "And if his son, I presume his daughter too; since the duty of a child is equally imposed on both, and since the natural liberty Mr. Locke speaks of arising from reason, it can never be proved that women have not a right to it, unless it can be proved that they are not capable of knowing the law they are under" (3:211). She positioned Richardson as the model of authority properly practiced, describing him as having "too much real dignity . . . to exact that deference to your *years* which is due to your wisdom and virtue" (3:217). For Mulso, affectionate and reasonable relational behavior, not mere status, confers authority. As Mulso asserted, in relation to Clarissa's father's curse, "I think a father who can be capable of solemnly imprecating divine vengeance on his child, has very little title to be looked upon in this awful light" (3:224). In other words, a father must be reasonable and affectively attentive to his child in order to be considered a father worthy of a child's obedience. Mr. Harlowe insisted on the absolute prerogatives of a father, but he hypocritically ignored the temporal will of Clarissa's grandfather and heretically ignored the divine will of God the Father.

Mulso rejected the notion of absolute obedience to parents and bluntly excluded from consideration the conduct writers and clergy who "talk of rational beings as the *property* and *possessions* of a fellow creature, like the cattle upon his estate" (3:228). She even recasts passages from Scripture that Richardson had cited to justify absolute obedience to parents: "They can only be understood to mean a reasonable obedience; such as is consistent with the liberty of a rational creature" (3:238). Mulso insists that Mr. Harlowe's unfatherly behavior would have made his curse have no effect, while Clarissa's rationality, which Richardson had taken pains to emphasize in the novel, would have made obvious to her the ineffectiveness of the curse. Furthermore, Clarissa's friend Anna had also comforted her with the assurance that a just God would not let malignant curses take effect. Mulso seems to echo Anna, exclaiming, "I would not make fathers nothing at all; but I would not make them gods!" (3:246). This exclamation has particular import for the relationship she has cultivated throughout the correspondence with Richardson, whom she refers to as "my dear papa Richardson" (3:247). It is God the Father, not Harlowe the father, who determines Clarissa's immortal fate. Fathers and their children are all equally children of God the Father.

Bluestockings Elizabeth Carter and Catharine Talbot must have known of Mulso's representation of the proper practice of authority in the *Letters on Filial Obedience*. Richardson circulated the letters, and their dates (the latest being January 3, 1751) coincide with Talbot's query to Carter about who Mulso was and Talbot's comment that she respected her writing (3:400n6). The letters might also explain why Carter reacted so emphatically to Richardson's *Rambler* article, for, as she later admits to Talbot, "I have given Mr. Richardson another reading, and confess myself to have been too much prejudiced . . . from some of his own notions which I had lately seen on another subject."[5] The ameliorative effect of Talbot's perspective might explain Carter's willingness to participate in Richardson's creation of the Protestant English hero, Sir Charles Grandison, an example for all English gentlemen. But what had Richardson said that initially offended her?

Richardson's contribution to the *Rambler* (no. 97) critiqued the behavior of modern ladies and set off a sharp debate about women, education, religion, and England's national identity between Carter and Talbot.[6] They were both members of a circle of women who applauded, critiqued, and scrutinized the work of Richardson and Johnson, work that furnished them with an opportunity to make their own literary contributions and served as a springboard for debating women's identities in eighteenth-century England. Examining their correspondence will show the power of Richardson's heroic women as well as the anxieties regarding Christian and Muslim pleasures that his fiction perpetuated.

Richardson's *Rambler* article is ostensibly, in part, an elegy for the way women used to be—a combination of "modesty and diffidence, gentleness and meekness" (242)—and, in part, a pointed criticism of the fashionable young ladies of contemporary London. Frivolous, dissipated, and not remotely domestic, these young women prowl the public places of London, rendering themselves "impolitickly cheap" (251) and making men "frighted at wedlock" (249). They are the proto–Female Coterie. Striving to valorize the domestic virtues for both men and women, Richardson longs (or claims to long) for the days when a young maiden would be "all resignation to her parents" (245) in the choice of a mate and when a husband was not *required* to bestow a private allowance on his wife, for this "makes a wife independent, and destroys love, by putting it out of a man's power to lay any obligation upon her, that might engage gratitude, and kindle affection" (249). He praises the time when a woman's "forward spirit" would be "exposed in print as it deserved" (242). Whether the views of Richardson's epistolary persona were his or not, the article certainly drew the attention of his Bluestocking acquaintances.

Carter and Talbot were both writers anxious about the difficulties women encountered as intellectuals and authors. They were keenly aware of the constant threat of a female intellectual's "forward spirit" being publicly maligned. Though they were as appalled as Richardson by what they saw as England's increasingly lax morals, they did not attribute the decline to women's "forward spirit." Significantly, Carter interprets what she sees as Richardson's disparaging remarks on women's modern behavior in terms of misogynistic mortalism. In a letter to Talbot of March 4, 1751, she fulminates against what she perceives as Richardson's dismissiveness toward women's spiritual and intellectual dignity: "I cannot see how some of his doctrines can be founded on any other supposition than that Providence designed one half of the human species for idiots and slaves. One would think the man was, in this respect, a Mahometan."[7] Carter falls back on Islamophobic misogynistic mortalism to categorize Richardson's views on women's education as foreign to English values.

English values were important to Carter and Talbot, who believed women could be agents of England's educational and moral improvement. In the winter of 1750, Talbot wrote to Carter about an acquaintance of theirs, Lady Grey, and her maternal prospects, continuing on to an argument for the importance of good mothers in the education of the nation's next generation. Lady Grey's children, Talbot believed, would receive an education "very different" from that of "the fine folks of this world" and would "consequently be of more use in it, and their beings more valuable. Alas! How many come into the world for no purpose at all, or indeed worse than none, only to be contemptible, wretched, and mischievous" (December 17, 1750). Talbot and Carter often framed their approval or disapproval of society by contrasting the superficially "fine folks of this world" with the example of admirable figures in real life or in fiction, whether Lady Grey or Clarissa. They saw women's education as foundational to the moral role of the mothers of future national leaders. Women's education was a national security concern for them. Talbot, for instance, was convinced that, without a moral reform, England soon would be "a nation of savages" (February 29, 1751). Thus, Carter's excoriation of Richardson as a "Mahometan" is not frivolous: she saw herself as a watchdog of English values. Talbot, more sympathetic to Richardson than Carter was, justified his article both in terms of women's education and his exemplary heroine. She exclaims, "I will answer your's in order, and first for the Mahometan Richardson. Fie upon you! . . . He does not pretend to give a scheme (not an entire scheme) of female education, only to say how when well educated they should behave. . . . How can you ever imagine that the author of Clarissa has not an idea high enough of what women may be, and ought to be?" (March 16, 1751; *sic*). Talbot's defense of Richardson indicates that she, like Carter, takes Islamophobic misogynistic mortalism as axiomatic. She recuperates Richardson for England by arguing that he, unlike a Mahometan, has a "high enough" idea of "what women may be," and she uses his anti-annihilationist heroine to defend his views on women and their capabilities.

Talbot's letter shows that the friends shared a deep familiarity with, and approval of, *Clarissa*. Talbot uses Clarissa's example as the *ne plus ultra* of womanly accomplishment: Richardson's heroine is the exemplar of what a virtuous, well-educated woman is and how she behaves. Both women agreed with the argument Richardson gave Clarissa—that the immortal soul is the basis of a woman's identity. What women are, apart from what Lovelace considered the "customary visibles" of material identity, is central to women's dignity, education, and status as humans rather than as sexualized objects in Richardson's "religious plan" for *Clarissa* and in all his novels. It is significant, then, that Carter criticizes Richardson's characterization of women's education by aligning him with his creation, the "Turk" Lovelace. Richardson's horror at his readers' approval of the libertine villain, whose behavior and motivations he had intended the audience to detest, resulted in his heavy revisions to the third edition of *Clarissa*. Carter could thus be seen as not only attacking Richardson's characterization of women's intellectual capacities but also challenging the sincerity of his entire moral project.

In reminding Carter that it was Richardson who created Clarissa, Talbot pointed out what she believed to be the impossibility of a single mind creating a female exemplar of virtue, religious conviction, and reason and simultaneously asserting that the education necessary to defend those characteristics could imperil female identity. The characterization of women in Richardson's final novel, *Sir Charles Grandison*, which he was writing at the time, would confirm or belie Talbot's faith in him. In writing *Sir Charles Grandison* (1753–54), Richardson solicited recommendations among his acquaintances, including Talbot and Carter, as to how his masculine ideal ought to be characterized. Talbot continues in her letter of March 16, "Mr. Richardson has been so good as to call on us twice. Pray send me in mere hints your idea of the good and agreeable man, whom every body wants him to draw, but he must resolutely refuse to fight a duel. . . . Pray who and what is Miss Mulso? She writes well, and corresponds with you and Mr. Richardson. I honour her, and want to know more about her." Talbot associates all four writers—Richardson, Mulso, Carter, and herself—in a network of intellectual and emotional support that develops from social visits, epistolary correspondence, professional advice, and personal criticism. Carter eventually puts aside her former misgivings about Richardson, and Talbot delightedly blends fiction and reality, asking her, "Do you know the Grandison family? If you do not you will to your cost. Oh! Miss Carter, did you ever call Pigmalion a fool, for making an image and falling in love with it—and do you know that you and I are two Pigmalionesses? Did not Mr. Richardson ask us for some traits of his good man's character? And did not we give him some? And has not he gone and put these and his own charming ideas into a book and formed a Sir Charles Grandison?" (December 23, 1751). Their mutual concern with national morality had found an outlet in collaboratively influencing the construction of Sir Charles Grandison as a rational, feeling, domestic hero. Opposed to dueling and attentive to the needs of others, he instantiates the national ideal as a public figure, but also as a private family man. Their collaboration on the idea of the good man reinforced relationships among the correspondents. The next year Talbot thanked Carter for lending her some of Mulso's verses, originally shown to her by Richardson, and she chides Carter for her former hostility to Richardson, describing him as "an excellent man, too, though you have not loved him as you ought, but when Sir Charles appears, he will make you pay for all" (April 22, 1752). For Talbot, Carter's accusation that Richardson's opinion of women's education was that of a "Mahometan" would be corrected by his creation of the good man, a moral exemplar for the home and nation.

Talbot continued to mend fences through epistolary mediation and by pointing out the social network of which Carter and Richardson were both a part. She teased Carter, "I heard with pleasure of the agreeable day you were to spend with Miss Mulso. I hope she has made you a perfect convert to a worthy man that you was [*sic*] too angry with, and who has the highest regard for you. Do not be frightened, I mean nobody more dangerous than Mr. Richardson."[8] By the autumn of 1753 Carter seems to have been perfectly reconciled to Richardson, just in time for the publication of the first few volumes of *Sir Charles Grandison*. She informs Talbot, "Mr. Richardson has been so good as to send me four volumes of his most charming work, and I heartily wish, for his sake as well as their own, that all the world may be as fond of it as I am. . . . How inimitably are all the characters supported, what an original, what a masterpiece is Clementina! But there would be no end to one's admiration of the whole" (September 21, 1753). Carter's comment is significant for two reasons. First, she seems entirely to have given over her exclusion of Richardson from English identity; he is no longer a "Mahometan" but a man who is "so good" as to deserve admiration from the whole world. Second, Carter directs her praise not, as she and Talbot had anticipated, toward the eponymous hero, but rather to a figure of religious and national alterity: the fervently (one could say fanatically) Catholic love interest of Sir Charles, Clementina.

Clementina, though a Catholic heroine, met with almost universal approval among Richardson's female readers. It is this positive reaction to a woman depicted in primarily spiritual terms—Carter approvingly calls her "a saint and a martyr" (March 18, 1754)—that brings the issue of women's education and Richardson's representation of women full circle. Richardson's acquaintance Mary Granville Pendarves Delany exclaimed to Anne Granville Dewes, "What a divine creature, Clementina! What a madness is hers! Was ever Xtian fortitude put to a greater trial considering her religion! And great as Sir Charles is, Clementina has a superiority over him. . . . The style is better in most places than that of 'Clarissa,' but nothing can ever equal that work" (December 3, 1753).[9] Carter echoes Delany's assessment of Clementina: "I have read only four volumes . . . but I am persuaded Mr. Richardson will think even a Sir Charles Grandison too inconsiderable a reward for Clementina, who like Clarissa, can be properly recompensed by nothing less than heaven" (December 10, 1753).

Readers sympathized with Clementina, who believed she must reject the possibility of marrying Sir Charles because the difference in their religions would imperil one or even both of their souls. She insists she would prefer the life of a convent. Clementina writes to Sir Charles of her family's pressuring her to marry rather than to join a convent: "They pretend to leave me free to choose through the world. They plead, that, so zealous as they are in the Catholic faith, they were *so* earnest for me to enter into the state, that they were desirous to see me the wife even of a Protestant, rather than I should remain single: And they remind me, that it was owing to my scruple only, that this was not effected."[10] She explains to Sir Charles that her refusal was based on three considerations, including the "sense of my own unworthiness, after my mind had been disturbed; The *insuperable* apprehension, that, drawn aside by your Love, I should probably have ensnared my own Soul; and that I should be perpetually lamenting the certainty of the loss of his whom it would be my duty to love as my own" (3:7). Clementina sacrificed her heart and, temporarily, her head in order, as she believed, to save Sir Charles's soul and her own.

Richardson's readers applauded this noble preference of religious conviction to romantic attachment, but there was a shadow cast over *Sir Charles Grandison*, and it was none other than the treatment of women's religious education, discussed in the marriage negotiations between Sir Charles and the Porretta family. As Sir Charles recounted the negotiations to Harriet, the modest Anglican girl he ultimately marries, "I proposed to leave her [Clementina] entirely at her liberty, in the article of religion; and, in case of children by the marriage, the daughters to be educated by *her*, the sons by *me*" (2:130). But for Richardson's readers, this was to ignore the very objection Clementina made to the marriage: souls are imperiled when people remain tied to a heretical faith. Since Sir Charles and Clementina were of different religions, Sir Charles was necessarily suggesting that his daughters' souls would be of less importance than his sons'. Richardson's female readers felt strongly about this prevarication regarding a religious "other," but this time the target was Catholicism, not Islam. The fact that the Bluestockings could use two distinct kinds of religious alterity to criticize the Anglican gentleman (or his author) underscores the arbitrariness of the Islam-as-negative-ideal rhetoric. Certainly, there was a long chain of Islamophobic thought in England, but there were also alternatives—Islamophilia, for one, or choosing another negative ideal to regulate Anglican identity. Obviously, Roman Catholicism was just such an alternative. Yet the exclusion of Islam and Roman Catholicism continued to be used in concert: they were two pincers used to mold and enforce the contours of Anglican identity.

Delany assures Dewes, "You asked me what I thought of 'Sir Charles Grandison' consenting to have his daughters bred papists? Why I think it the only blot in Sir Charles's character. Had a woman written the story, she would have thought the daughters of as much consequence as the sons, and when I see Mr. Richardson I shall call him to an account for that *faux-pas*" (December 21, 1753). In Delany's privileging of female authorship, she argues along the same lines as Mulso's criticism of Richardson's conception of the daughter-parent bond. A woman author, Delany pointed out, would put all children, male and female, on the same level in relation to parents; a child, Mulso observed, whether male or female, would be able to exercise reason independently once an adult. Education, not gender, explains the differences in men's and women's rational capabilities.

Delany was generally sympathetic to Richardson. But one reader of *Sir Charles Grandison* was not, and this was none other than Lady Mary Wortley Montagu. She also took exception to Sir Charles's concession to educate any potential daughters of a union with Clementina as Catholics. In a letter to her own daughter, Montagu declares, "There must be a great indifference as to religion on both sides, to make so strict a union as marriage tolerable between people of such distinct persuasions. He seems to think women have no souls, by agreeing so easily that his daughters should be educated in bigotry and idolatry. You will perhaps think this last a hard word; yet it is not difficult to prove, that either the papists are guilty of idolatry, or the pagans never were so" (October 20, 1752). Montagu had no qualms in condemning Catholicism on the same charge from which she defended Islam—that it imperils women's souls. That different women could alight on the same problem in his representation of women's education yet criticize Richardson by associating him with entirely distinct religious others shows that Islamophobia and anti-Catholicism were intimately related and structurally interchangeable.

There was a peculiar tension for women readers in engaging Richardson's texts: on the one hand are his creations, Clarissa and Clementina, all that a woman "may be, and ought to be," and, on the other, his approving descriptions of daughters who quiver at the parental frown as if before God and of a Protestant national hero who seems to consider a daughter's religious belief—indeed her spiritual welfare—to be not as important as that of a son's. Delany, like Carter, ameliorates Sir Charles's institutionally supported injustice by having recourse to an immortal identity for the heroine: "Clementina is indeed a most divine creature; she is too refined for a wife to anything less meritorious than Sir C. G. and *his* she must *not* be!" (January 21, 1754). Richardson later defended his hero, pointing out that Sir Charles's decision was not without precedent and resulted from much consideration. It is significant, though, and demonstrates the importance of the immortal soul to women's self-conceptions, that several well-read women (Montagu, Carter, Delany) would censure him on the grounds that proper education is crucial to the cultivation of the soul. Sir Charles's decision to separate the moral education of girls and boys is another instance of his values being "essentially at one" with those of society.[11] Focusing their criticism through the exemplary case of Sir Charles, these women were really critiquing society's values.

What is clear in women's responses to Richardson's influential fiction is that his heroes and heroines were explicitly figured as national examples and thus his representations of women's education carried great weight with them. In response to his *Rambler* article, Carter hit back with Islamophobic misogynistic mortalism at the first hint that women's intellectual abilities were being questioned; Lady Mary Wortley Montagu, more familiar with Islamic doctrine, nevertheless reacts similarly by using a version of misogynistic mortalism that equally excludes pagans and papists in reaction to Sir Charles's thoughts on educating his daughters as Roman Catholics. Finally, Hester Mulso, Richardson's correspondent in the 1750s, provides a complicated example of Bluestocking views on Islam in the 1770s.

Having married and taken the name Mrs. Chapone, she argued, in her popular *Letters on the Improvement of the Mind* (1773), that young women ought to take an interest in Islam.[12] Nevertheless, she framed Muhammad as an impostor of interest to English women because of his Luciferian bravado. Like Johnson, her commentary on Islam arose when discussing history ("Letter X: On the Manner and Course of reading History"). Chapone was clearly influenced by anti-Muhammad seventeenth-century discourse, for she situated the "successful imposture" of "Mahomet" in terms of Christian disunity (3:344). She also participated in the generalizing trend of Enlightenment learning by arguing that the earliest part of "more modern" history is "too much involved in obscurity to require a very minute knowledge of its history" and that "two or three of the most singular circumstances" will suffice for a young lady's knowledge (3:343). Nevertheless, she included the rise of Islam as one of those circumstances, because in those "dark ages, you will find no single character so interesting as that of Mahomet—a bold impostor, who extended his usurped dominion equally over the minds and properties of men" (3:349). Chapone describes Muhammad as a gothic villain with an almost supernatural ability to control minds. Yet there is also, in a familiar gesture, a sense of competition with Muslim imperial power in the desire to situate it in the past. Indeed, there is more than a hint of imperialist pride in Chapone's description of the island of Great Britain, which, though small, is "the throne, from which we rule the world" (3:350). Charlotte Lennox, another woman who benefited from Richardson's professional mentorship, took up the problem of what kinds of education for women could be characterized as "English" or "Mahometan." We have seen Lennox's complex criticism of xenophobic reading practices among English characters in her novel of 1752; in her didactic periodical of 1760–61, she was decidedly reliant on Islamophobic misogynistic mortalism.

ENDEARING PLEASURES

In *The Lady's Museum* (1760–61), Charlotte Lennox included in her essay "OF THE STUDIES proper for WOMEN" a translation of a French essay devoted to showing that the study of "history and natural philosophy alone" are the proper studies for a woman even though "something more than beauty" is "necessary to rivet the lover's chain."[13] In other words, the motive to support female education is the desire to make women more attractive romantic and domestic partners. Women are to "avoid all abstract learning, all thorny researches," for who "would wish to see assemblies made up of doctors in petticoats, who will regale us with Greek and the systems of Leibnitz. . . . There is nothing more disgustful than those female theologians, who, adopting all the animosity of the party they have thought fit to join, assemble ridiculous synods in their houses, and form extravagant sects" (1:11). Predictably, the Platonic Lady trope is trotted out to reinforce heterosexual conformity. Yet the (presumably male) author begins his essay by assuring readers that to "prohibit women entirely from learning is treating them with the same indignity that Mahomet did, who, to render them voluptuous, denied them souls; and indeed the greatest part of women act as if they had really adopted a tenet so injurious to the sex" (1:9). By including this essay, Lennox criticizes moral and intellectual inadequacies in the education of Englishwomen while linking these inadequacies to what is constructed as a "tenet" of Islam.

Lennox was not alone. The evangelical reformer Hannah More laments in her chapter "ON DISSIPATION," in *Essays on Various Subjects* (1777), "How much . . . is it to be regretted, that the British ladies should ever sit down contented to polish, when they are able to reform, to entertain, when they might instruct, and to dazzle for an hour, when they are candidates for eternity."[14] More's defense of women's learning is premised on Astell's substance-shadow binary: women should not limit themselves to cultivating physical attractiveness, when their real interest is to rejoice in a glorious eternal reward. Unlike Astell, More immediately relied on Islamophobic misogynistic mortalism to reinforce her point. She continued, "UNDER the dispensation of Mahomet's law, indeed, these mental excellencies cannot be expected, because the women are shut out from all opportunities of instruction, and excluded from the endearing pleasures of a delightful and equal society" (19–20). Here is the conventional alignment of Christian pleasures with the intellect and Mahometan pleasures with the body that was established by Addison and Prideaux and that influenced Elizabeth Singer Rowe, Penelope Aubin, and Eliza Haywood. From a modern point of view it is of course astonishing to see eighteenth-century English society described as "equal" for all its members. But particularly relevant for discussing More's description in terms of Islam is her investment in treating a clearly fictionalized account of Islam as fact. She proceeds to quote "a charming poet" (20) to reinforce her point about Muslim doctrine. The poet is Samuel Johnson and the passage is the selection from Mahomet's misogynistic mortalist speech in *Irene*. More associates Mahomet's argument with women who "lighten the intolerable burden of time, by the most frivolous and vain amusements. They act in consequence of their own blind belief, and the tyranny of their despotic masters; for they have neither the freedom of a present choice, nor the prospect of a future being" (20). More's defense of women's education is premised on the exclusion of Muslim doctrine, but it does not characterize Muslim women as essentially inferior to Christian women. The implication of her argument is that, once freed from "Mahomet's law," these currently superficial women would have the freedom of a "present choice" and the "prospect of a future being." More does not deny that Muslim women have immortal, intelligent souls; she denies that "Mahomet's law" acknowledges them. As was the case in earlier prose fiction, in More's didactic work Muslim women *could* be brought into the fold of Western intelligence since the assumption is that they, like European women, have immortal, improvable souls. But only if they abandoned Islam could they save those souls through the development of their intelligence. The primary target of misogynistic mortalism was not Muslim women but rather the presumed despotism of Muslim law as it mapped onto Muslim military power. Yet in this distinction, the beginning of the mentality that Gayatri Chakravorty Spivak famously summed up as "white men saving brown women from brown men" was clearly emerging: removing Muslim women from a Muslim context and giving them a Christian education will civilize, free, and intellectualize them.[15]

Indeed, More makes this assumed connection between Christianity and enlightenment explicit in the succeeding paragraph, when she rejoices "in this land of civil and religious liberty, where there is as little despotism exercised over the minds, as over the persons of women, they have every liberty of choice, and every opportunity of improvement; and how greatly does this increase their obligation to be exemplary in their general conduct, attentive to the government of their families, and instrumental to the good order of society!" (21). Like the Bluestockings of Richardson's circle, More saw women as agents of national morality through their proper domestic government. As opposed to Elizabeth Johnson in 1696 and Sarah Chapone in 1735, More asserted that English society was entirely unlike the presumed despotism of Ottoman society. This being so, she reasoned, women had only themselves to blame if they failed to contribute to the moral fabric of the nation. Dissipation is a choice, and "she who regrets being doomed to a state of dark and gloomy ignorance, by the injustice, or tyranny of the men, complains of an evil which does not exist" (21). More ignores the systemic inequalities of current educational options—even women with the leisure and financial means to do so would not be allowed to attend English universities for many more decades—in favor of a valorization of the moral and political superiority of English society. Compared to More, Wollstonecraft was in one way actually returning to an older, less imperialistic strain of Islamophobic misogynistic mortalism when she included English society within her criticism of women's education. Nevertheless, Wollstonecraft contributed to an Islamophobic representational tradition just as much as Haywood, Lennox, More, and historian Catharine Macaulay.

Macaulay's brief but denigrating reference to Islam occurs in the chapter "Flattery—Chastity—Male Rakes" in *Letters on Education* (1790).[16] Asserting a heterosexual imperative by claiming that "the happiness and perfection of the two sexes are so reciprocally dependant [*sic*] on one another that, till both are reformed, there is no expecting excellence in either" (135), she reasons that the "candid [Joseph] Addison has confessed, that in order to embellish the mistress, you must give a new education to the lover, and teach the men not to be any longer dazzled by false charms and unreal beauty" (135). Female education is underwritten by a companionate marital ideal. Macaulay finds that "the most difficult part of female education, is to give girls such an idea of chastity, as shall arm their reason and their sentiments on the side of this useful virtue" (137). Macaulay argued that chastity could not be a "sexual virtue" (specific to one sex) and that teaching girls that it is would simply teach them not to trust their instructors. According to the "principles of religion, morals, and the reason of things" (137), chastity is a moral duty common to both sexes.

A girl ought to be trained to see the "reason" of chastity rather than to accept it uncritically, as Jean-Jacques Rousseau would have her do. Macaulay saw Rousseau, at least in regard to his position on female chastity, as "being as great a fanatic in morals, as some are in religion" (138). In an argument that echoes Astell's valorization of the moral foundation of reason and anticipates Wollstonecraft's, Macaulay affirms, "I intend to breed my pupils up to act a rational part in the world, and not to fill up a niche in the seraglio of a sultan, I shall certainly give them leave to use their reason in all matters which concern their duty and happiness, and shall spare no pains in the cultivation of this only sure guide to virtue" (138). Macaulay figured Englishwomen's education in terms of freedom and capaciousness, while Muslim women are characterized by narrowness of space and intellect—their bodies can "fill up" a "niche," but their minds can act no "rational part" in the wider world.

Further, in a scathing but conservative indictment of the sexual double standard, she asserts that "the great difference now beheld in the external consequences which follow the deviations from chastity in the two sexes, did in all probability arise from women having been considered as the mere property of the men; and, on this account had no right to dispose of their own persons" (138). Macaulay's argument hearkens back to Elizabeth Johnson's claim that, while Turkish wives could expect to be treated as if they were "without properties, or sense, or souls," only the most egregious religious hypocrisy enabled English men to deny women's intellectual abilities. In her view this attitude of Englishmen to Englishwomen is both a relic of the benighted past and a characteristic of contemporary Muslim contexts.

WOLLSTONECRAFT AND FEMINIST ORIENTALISM

Wollstonecraft followed Haywood and Johnson in mapping a hierarchized binary of pleasures onto Christian and Muslim women. As mentioned in the introduction, Joyce Zonana identified Mary Wollstonecraft's *A Vindication of the Rights of Woman* (1792) as the foundational text of feminist orientalism within the context of Western feminism as a politically theorized movement. But Wollstonecraft's text, however foundational, was not original in its use of Islamophobic misogynistic mortalism.

Mary Wollstonecraft is often identified as the mother of Western feminism. Like the Bluestockings, she had a complex and problematic attitude to Muslim women born of the centrality of women's immortality to her defense of women's rights, her view of historical progress and social evolution, and her misapprehension of Muslim doctrine. Before turning to her arguments about women's education, a brief look at how the immortal soul functioned in her fiction will show that Wollstonecraft was aware of the Platonic Lady trope and sought to distinguish her heroine from it (and from the members of the fashionable Female Coterie). This distinction was important because, in her privileging of the immortal soul, Wollstonecraft risked being identified herself with the Platonic Lady as a figure of religious and cultural otherness.

Lyndall Gordon explains that some aspects of Wollstonecraft's life and theory have caused "embarrassment to late-twentieth-century feminists": some "discovered signs of prudery, and others saw in her domesticity a betrayal of her case for independence. The aim of her critics was not necessarily to kill her cause, but to appropriate it in limited terms."[17] This reluctance to acknowledge Wollstonecraft's full complexity particularly informed the slow recognition of the enormous impact of Wollstonecraft's religious imagination on her educational theory.[18] Scholars like Virginia Sapiro, Eileen Hunt Botting, and Barbara Taylor have argued for a richer understanding of the fundamental importance of Wollstonecraft's religious imagination to her political theory. According to Taylor, "The religious basis of Wollstonecraft's radicalism is its least-explored aspect, yet it is impossible to understand her political hopes, including her hopes for women, outside a theistic framework. . . . Most interpretations of the *Rights of Woman* simply obliterate its religious underpinnings. But to secularise Wollstonecraft's radical vision is not only to tear it from its eighteenth-century context but also to lose its utopian thrust: that unwavering faith in divine purpose."[19] Taylor describes Wollstonecraft's solution to her conflicting motivations—to excoriate the failings of the frivolous contemporary woman while asserting the nobility of women's potential—as the construction of a "female self redeemed by transcendent fantasy" (21). Though Taylor has little sympathy for the direction Wollstonecraft's "fantasy" takes (the pieties of Wollstonecraft's fiction make her long for the "fresh air" of Fielding or Austen), she perceives that the same impetus behind political change is at work in fantasy: the desire for a better world. The association of social and literary vision connects the works of Wollstonecraft with those of Cavendish and Philips, writers interested in intellectual friendship that transcends the boundaries of the body, space, and time, and with those of moral writers interested in the potential of literature to inspire social reform, like Astell, Barker, Rowe, Aubin, Richardson, and the Bluestockings. As Taylor observes, feminism, "it is worth recalling, has for most of its history been deeply embedded in religious belief" (99). The relationship between feminism and religion had a specifically political meaning in Wollstonecraft's thought, according to Taylor, since, influenced by the Rational Dissenting community of Newington Green, she compared the political marginalization of Dissenters to that of women (104). Wollstonecraft believed that the private judgment of individuals should be respected in the liberal Protestant nation that England professed to be.

Wollstonecraft believed that because women have immortal souls, they have a direct connection to God, which they must be allowed to develop like men, their fellow creatures. All humans, regardless of gender, must aim for a universal moral standard. Wollstonecraft balanced an acknowledgment of the power of temporal authority with the recognition that all human beings share physical and moral frailties and are equal in the eyes of divine authority. As Virginia Sapiro describes Wollstonecraft's hierarchy of temporal and divine authority, the "distinction between religion and church is critical . . . one is an aspect of natural virtue ultimately defined by God, the other is a human institution . . . defined by human corruption."[20] Understanding the individual in relation to the divine was crucial to Wollstonecraft's thought, but that thought was not static. Wollstonecraft's later fiction demanded an ethic of female community much more urgently than the solitary spirituality celebrated in her earlier fiction. Lasting, fulfilling friendship between women seems impossible in *Mary, a Fiction* (1788); it is a sociopolitical imperative in *The Wrongs of Woman; or, Maria* (published posthumously in 1798).

That friendship did not extend to Muslim women, however. Wollstonecraft believed that they were too narrowly educated to have developed intelligence. Wollstonecraft saw this narrowness as endemic to Muslim contexts. If education enabled humans to improve, then miseducation (force, superstition, or prejudice) would necessarily stunt human development. Wollstonecraft used the stereotypical despotism of non-Western authority to underscore the importance of education as well as the contingency of all political regimes. Invoking the specter of the Crusades as well as the Ottoman encroachments into Europe during the early modern period, Wollstonecraft argued in *A Vindication of the Rights of Men*, "We should be aware of confining all moral excellence to one channel, however capacious; or, if we are so narrow-minded, we should not forget how much we owe to chance that our inheritance was not Mahometism, and that the iron hand of destiny, in the shape of deeply rooted authority, has not suspended the sword of destruction over our heads."[21] Wollstonecraft saw Muslim dominance as a path that European history could have taken. Further, as Wendy Gunther-Canada has pointed out, Wollstonecraft's anti-Islam critique of Rousseau and the narrowness of mind that he encouraged in women is almost verbatim the same critique offered by Macaulay.[22] Before turning to Wollstonecraft's excoriation of the "Mahometan strain" in the *Vindication*, an analysis of the "soul" in her fiction will show its relevance to her understanding of women's education and personal growth.

Wollstonecraft claims in the "Advertisement" to *Mary, a Fiction*, that the following fiction will display the soul of an author and the character of a heroine with a "mind," "thinking powers," her "own faculties," and a voice. She explains her aesthetic theory in a statement that shows the connection Wollstonecraft made between fiction, originality, identity, and the soul:

> Those compositions only have power to delight, and carry us willing captives, where the soul of the author is exhibited, and animates the hidden springs. Lost in a pleasing enthusiasm, they live in the scenes they represent; and do not measure their steps in a beaten track . . . according to the prescribed rules of art.
>
> These chosen few, wish to speak for themselves, and not to be an echo—even of the sweetest sounds—or the reflector of the most sublime beams. The paradise they ramble in, must be of their own creating.[23]

Both author and heroine, who share the same first name, wish to "speak for themselves, and not to be an echo—even of the sweetest sounds." Those sweetest sounds include the voices of Richardson's and Rousseau's heroines, and Wollstonecraft declares that her Mary "is neither a Clarissa, a Lady G——, nor a Sophie" (3). It is not, however, these representations of womanhood per se that Wollstonecraft is rejecting, but rather the act of choosing to imitate rather than to create. The conviction of "how widely artists wander from nature, when they copy the original of great masters" prompts Wollstonecraft to veer from the "beaten track," even a track established by "great masters" (3). Her rejection of imitation is part of her rejection of mediated identity. The individual genius can participate in the divine activity of creation without relying on previous authorities. Nevertheless, Wollstonecraft saw literary predecessors as constituting an intellectual community that assisted individual education and improvement.

Mary is in some ways the "artless tale" (3) that Wollstonecraft claims it to be, for though the author readily includes quotations from canonical dramatists and poets (especially William Shakespeare, John Milton, Edward Young, and James Thomson), she echoes without acknowledgment several of her novelist forebears, suggesting that she had, perhaps unconsciously or indirectly, absorbed their influence. Wollstonecraft was indeed the "first of a new genus," as she proclaimed herself, but she did not arise in a creative vacuum.[24] This vexed relationship to literary history and authority helps to explain the startling power of a formally flawed text. For *Mary*, while a novel, is also a spiritual biography of sorts, an inner pilgrimage mapped onto physical wandering. Mary, like Clarissa, is an alien in a temporal world, a sojourner learning to apprehend the divine through a glass darkly. Both heroines prize education, but they gain education by very different routes. Clarissa receives good principles from her parents, but must learn that parental authority does not always set the example it expects its children to follow. Mary is entirely left to her own devices, morally and intellectually, by a brutish, appetitive father and a venal, weak mother. Mary's self-education leads her to the divine: she explores nature fervently and, as her mind develops through sensation and reflection, she becomes convinced that there must be a superior Being of "wisdom and goodness" (*Mary*, 8) that created it all.

From the novel's outset, the narrator structures the heroine's identity in opposition to the unthinking appetite, brutishness, machinelike unconsciousness, and social conventions embodied by her parents. Eileen Hunt Botting describes *Mary* as a "theological novel, not a political novel" and argues that, given Wollstonecraft's "pessimism regarding the possibility of the wide-scale reform of the family, society, and politics, it is not surprising that the early Wollstonecraft, animated by a deep Christian faith, devotes her attention instead to the reform of the individual soul."[25] This concern for the individual woman's soul explains the many echoes of *Clarissa* in *Mary*, despite Wollstonecraft's explicit intention to diverge from the example of Richardson's heroine. Mary is not Clarissa, but her preoccupation with death, eternity, and alienation from the temporal world and her solace in the concept of a divine Father who alone can satisfy her deepest yearnings for comfort and companionship all indicate that Richardson's work was a central influence. As the narrator says, "Could she have loved her father or mother, had they returned her affection, she would not so soon, perhaps, have sought out a new world" (*Mary*, 8). Mary's turn to the divine hearkens back to Clarissa's struggles with temporal authority. It also indicates that her education will be a self-directed one, an ascent toward the divine mediated only by the providential beauty of the natural world.

Mary's father's character is registered in his "brute, unconscious gaze," and her mother is "a mere machine . . . a mere nothing" (5). Mary's mother is the first in a series of women throughout the novel whose intellectual (and moral) torpor makes them unfit companions for Mary. Her mother is not exceptional, as the narrator declares, for "many such noughts are there in the female world!" (5). She has at best a "negative good-nature" that prompts her to attend "to the *shews* of things" (5). Her moral obtuseness clearly has eternal consequences, though the narrator sidesteps the issue of the mother's damnation while raising its possibility: "She dreaded that horrid place vulgarly called *hell*, the regions below; but whether hers was a mounting spirit, I cannot pretend to determine. . . . I have nothing to say to her unclothed spirit" (5–6).

Mary, on the other hand, is characterized by intense sentimentalism throughout the novel. The representation of the mother's cold indifference to Mary and preference for Mary's older brother contributes to the novel's privileging of an intellectual, spiritualized, solitary female identity. As the narrator says of the mother's occupations, "A rational [soul] can find no employment in polite circles. The glare of lights, the studied inelegancies of dress, and the compliments offered up at the shrine of false beauty, are all equally addressed to the senses" (6). Mary's mother may read novels such as *The Platonic Marriage*, but her unthinking sensual sentimentalism ("had she thought while she read, her mind would have been contaminated"; 6) could never cultivate the tenderness Mary feels for animals or give her a sense of the maternal duties of which her daughter so keenly feels the deprivation. Wollstonecraft was clearly distinguishing her heroine from the fashionable women of the Female Coterie and its association with platonic love—*Mary* is not a novel that Mary's mother would read.

Denied parental affection and attention, as well as a formal education, Mary examines the world around her voraciously, looking for love and companionship. The narrator describes the young Mary: "As she had learned to read, she perused with avidity every book that came in her way. Neglected in every respect, and left to the operations of her own mind, she considered every thing that came under her inspection, and learned to think. She had heard of a separate state, and that angels sometimes visited this earth. She would sit in a thick wood in the park, and talk to them; make little songs addressed to them, and sing them to tunes of her own composing" (7). It is the fictive realm of imagination and possibility that leads Mary to contemplate futurity and the divine. The pathos of her thoughtful childhood solitude combined with the restless activity of trying to understand herself and her surroundings characterizes the rest of Mary's journey, her struggle to live life on earth. Like Clarissa, Mary longs for heaven. Later, coerced into a loveless marriage and robbed of intellectual and emotional companionship by the death of her friend and mentor, Henry, Mary feels herself "hastening" toward "that world *where there is neither marrying*, nor giving in marriage" (53). Mary's biblical allusion to heaven concludes a novel saturated with a melancholic preoccupation with the frustrations experienced by an individual soul yearning for sustenance. Yet Mary's misery is itself an indication that the world is not enough for her, that she is connected to something greater.

Barbara Taylor, who describes Mary as "an irritating little saint," nevertheless recognizes that she "embodies a powerful pro-woman dimension of the Christian tradition."[26] *Mary* may be maudlin and self-indulgent in places, but it is an earnest (indeed, elegiac) endeavor to explore the agency and subjectivity of an individual woman who longs for friendship of the heart and mind. The idea of a divine Father and Mary's belief in her soul's connection to Him enables her to articulate her unsatisfied longings and to give her activities meaning. The concept of the soul gives her a framework within which to understand herself outside of temporal constraints like marriage; it enables her to exercise agency in living her life with purpose, if not happiness. This power—to access the divine without mediation—is at the heart of her political and educational theories, too.

THE "STAMEN OF IMMORTALITY"

Wollstonecraft declared, in a statement that both identifies her allegiances and distinguishes her from what she feels to be their excesses, "Rousseau exerts himself to prove that all *was* right originally: a crowd of authors that all *is* now right: and I, that all will be right" (*Rights of Woman*, 82). Examining *A Vindication of the Rights of Woman* in relation to *A Vindication of the Rights of Men* will provide a more holistic understanding of Wollstonecraft's description of education as the necessary starting point of historical progress for men and women than reading her more famous text alone. Addressed to the orator, aesthetic theorist, and member of Parliament Edmund Burke, *A Vindication of the Rights of Men* (1790) is a vitriolic attack on what Wollstonecraft perceives as Burke's hypocritical privileging of property rights and hereditary hierarchy over the shared natural rights of mankind. She argues for a revolution of social and political organization that is based on the acknowledgment that God created all men essentially equal, declaring, "It is necessary emphatically to repeat, that there are rights which men inherit at their birth, as rational creatures, who were raised above the brute creation by their improveable faculties; and that, in receiving these, not from their forefathers but, from God, prescription can never undermine natural rights" (*Rights of Men*, 13). In Wollstonecraft's political theory any kind of arbitrary authority—hereditary, monarchal, sexual—is anathema to her vision of the theocentric character of human nature. All humans are equal because each is endowed with an immortal soul that is rational and therefore capable of improvement. As she says, "Brutes hope and fear, love and hate; but, without a capacity to improve, a power of turning these passions to good or evil, they neither acquire virtue nor wisdom.—Why? Because the Creator has not given them reason" (*Rights of Men*, 31). Without reason man is not capable of improvement, nor is he capable of wisdom or virtue. Any creature capable of virtue or wisdom must therefore be allowed to be human, possessed of the reason that distinguishes man from beast.

For Wollstonecraft, the current state of affairs in England, an officially Christian and therefore ostensibly theocentric nation, belies this belief that all humans are raised above the brute creation by the reason that enables them to change their circumstances. Enshrined in prejudice and self-interested hierarchies, the privileged assert the naturalness of their superiority, attributing it to intrinsic merit rather than to systemic injustice ossified by time. Wollstonecraft's is a progressive political theory, stemming from her utter dissatisfaction with current dispensations, for men as for women. It is no affront to "nature" to reject unjust social hierarchies, argues Wollstonecraft, for men, not God, have set the boundaries: "The virtues of man are not limited by the Being who alone could limit them . . . he [man] may press forward without considering whether he steps out of his sphere by indulging such a noble ambition [of imitating God]" (*Rights of Woman*, 120). Like Poullain, she saw custom and prejudice as accretions of time, not natural categories. Arbitrary authority refuses to recognize the intrinsic equality of all humans and must rely on a variety of means, especially "luxury and superstition" (*Rights of Woman*, 86), to bulwark its power. Thus, the "indolent puppet of a court first becomes a luxurious monster, or fastidious sensualist, and then makes the contagion which his unnatural state spread, the instrument of tyranny" (*Rights of Woman*, 86). This description is Wollstonecraft's portrait of the modern European monarch, and it suggests her equal antipathy to the stereotypical Muslim despot.

In Wollstonecraft's view, the harem may be a specifically Eastern cultural site, but it is not a unique experience for women—it is simply the most extreme manifestation of the oppression of women that she sees in operation everywhere. Yet there are several reasons why Wollstonecraft considered the harem to be the extreme case: she had a marked antipathy to physical confinement, believing that "a girl, whose spirits have not been damped by inactivity . . . will always be a romp";

indeed, "most of the women . . . who have acted like rational creatures, or shown any vigour of intellect, have accidentally been allowed to run wild" (*Rights of Woman*, 115). She equally disliked all-female environments such as "nurseries, schools, or convents" (*Rights of Woman*, 215). Finally, she invested uncritically in the Islamophobic version of misogynistic mortalism. Thus, in Wollstonecraft's view, while European practices also institutionalized women's debility, it was Muslim doctrine (or what she took to be Muslim doctrine) that legitimized it. Significantly, however, she was as vehemently opposed to the convent as to the harem.

Wollstonecraft's understanding of Islam placed it in direct conflict with her political theory and her educational philosophy. Without a soul, there could be no ability to improve, no wisdom, no reason, no virtue in Wollstonecraft's view. Without a soul, creatures are not human and therefore not capable of improving either themselves or society. Islam and the harem were therefore beyond the pale of political or social acceptability in Wollstonecraft's vision of historical progress, which included "the improvement and emancipation of the whole sex" (*Rights of Woman*, 272).

Of course, Wollstonecraft was incorrect about Islamic doctrine. It was the "mussulman's creed" (*Rights of Men*, 47)—the *stereotype* of Islamic doctrine that Wollstonecraft had received—that in her view made the harem so insidiously destructive to women's development. But for Wollstonecraft, there was no essential difference between Christian and Muslim women, in the English home or the Muslim harem: women were treated everywhere as if they did not have intelligent souls. The difference, as Wollstonecraft incorrectly believed, was that women in a harem were treated as if they did not have souls because Muslim doctrine taught that they did not. In England, women were allowed to have souls, but, Wollstonecraft asserted, they were treated just as if men believed they did not. The "mussulman's creed" gave Wollstonecraft rhetorical leverage in pointing out the inconsistency between professed doctrine and actual practice in a Christian country. Since the possession of a soul indicated the necessity of having a rational education—the "stamen of immortality . . . is the perfectability of human reason" (*Rights of Woman*, 125)—the "mussulman's creed," whether practiced by Muslim or Christian men, was the primary impediment to that education for women.

Wollstonecraft was ideologically compelled to reject Islam based on the stereotype she uncritically received that nevertheless gave her rhetorical leverage in arguing against the treatment of women in a European Christian context. But what can be said of Wollstonecraft's denigrating references to the women of the harem? Did she indeed rely on a cultural binary opposition by which Muslim "teachings are accurate in their representation of Eastern women: their souls are barely 'animated.' In the West, however, women are made of sterner stuff, and the seraglio—or anything that resembles it—has no place"?[27] Did Wollstonecraft assert that Muslim women have lesser souls than Christian women? To answer this question, let us first look at Wollstonecraft's characterization of Englishwomen.

For Wollstonecraft, there were few things more unjust than teaching human beings to focus only on the temporal world, for it is "a comparatively mean field of action" (*Rights of Woman*, 101) that "yields not the felicity which can satisfy an immortal soul" (*Rights of Woman*, 95). Yet women are systematically trained "only to provide for the present" rather than for "a future state" (*Rights of Woman*, 103). She believed that women had been trained this way to render them pleasing to men. Women were taught to focus only on physical beauty and superficial graces rather than to cultivate talents and virtues that would withstand the ravages of time. Beauty, like wealth, was for Wollstonecraft an arbitrary authority that vitiated the possessor: women "have been duped by their lovers, as princes by their ministers, whilst dreaming that they reigned over them" (*Rights of Woman*, 93). In criticizing women's and princes' gullibility Wollstonecraft did not claim that it stemmed from intrinsic debility. Rather, the power that beauty and hereditary status gave individuals, in Wollstonecraft's view, trained them not to cultivate their own faculties. They became dehumanized because they never exercised their reason independently.

Wollstonecraft realized, however, that her progressive vision of social justice would take time to achieve: "For this epoch we must wait—wait, perhaps, till kings and nobles, enlightened by reason, and, preferring the real dignity of man to childish state, throw off their gaudy hereditary trappings: and if then women do not resign the arbitrary power of beauty—they will prove that they have *less* mind than man" (*Rights of Woman*, 90). The nature and limits of temporality, for women and for princes, were crucial to Wollstonecraft's holistic theory of politics, social progress, history, education, and gender. Human potential cannot be discerned in the current state of affairs: we cannot determine what could be by what has been. Logically, women cannot be categorized as ignorant, weak, and passive until they have failed to succeed under circumstances that would render a rational creature an independent thinker. Thus, "till it is proved that the courtier, who servilely resigns the birthright of a man, is not a moral agent, it cannot be demonstrated that woman is essentially inferior to man because she has always been subjugated" (*Rights of Woman*, 107–108). Woman has the potential to develop her rational autonomy, her human identity, fully; it is the social demand that she keep young and beautiful that prevents her from attaining it.

Wollstonecraft spent a great deal of time surveying conduct literature in *Rights of Woman*, showing that it furnishes women with no idea of how they are "to exist in that state where there is to be neither marrying nor giving in marriage"

(*Rights of Woman*, 103).[28] Women are not taught to prepare for the time when they are neither young, nor beautiful, nor alluring, and this has consequences for women as well as for the rest of society. In contrast, the figure of womanhood Wollstonecraft promotes is that of the "rational old woman" of the *Rights of Men* who objects to Burke's gendered theory of aesthetics in *A Philosophical Enquiry into the Origin of our Ideas of the Sublime and Beautiful* (1757). Burke had envisioned the sublime, the experience of awe-inspiring grandeur, as masculine; beauty, the experience of the diminutive and pleasing, he gendered as feminine. Wollstonecraft challenged this gendered binary by describing the inhumanity of women who cultivate the Burkean notion of beauty. Such women, the mistresses of slave plantations in Wollstonecraft's vignette, "after the sight of a flagellation, compose their ruffled spirits and exercise their tender feelings by the perusal of the last imported novel" (*Rights of Men*, 46). These "fair ladies" have "laboured to be pretty, by counterfeiting weakness" (*Rights of Men*, 47), yet they remain unresponsive to the curses of the "captive negroes . . . for the unheard of tortures they invent" (46). The privileging of physical beauty over emotional and intellectual depth has moral as well as aesthetic consequences.

Burke, in Wollstonecraft's view, has confined "truth, fortitude, and humanity, within the rigid pale of manly morals," arguing that "woman's high end and great distinction" is merely, passively, to be loved (*Rights of Men*, 47). Burke's fair ladies, according to Wollstonecraft, do not act as if they or the fellow human beings whom they torture have immortal souls. In contrast, Wollstonecraft envisioned a "rational old woman" who "might chance to stumble at this doctrine, and hint, that in avoiding atheism you had not steered clear of the mussulman's creed. . . . Nor would it be necessary for you to recollect, that if virtue has any other foundation than worldly utility, you have clearly proved that one half of the human species, at least, have not souls" (*Rights of Men*, 47). Women who focus only on "worldly utility" rather than immortal dignity will degenerate into monsters, and this, in Wollstonecraft's view, was the consequence of Burke's theory of gender. To focus women's attention narrowly on beauty while monopolizing truth, fortitude, and humanity for men was equivalent to denying women immortal souls. Wollstonecraft very specifically identified this denial of women's moral agency as the "mussulman's creed"—one step removed from atheism, but certainly not acceptable in an English context.

Atheism would deny immortal souls to all humans, undermining Wollstonecraft's theory of education and social progress for men and women alike; the "mussulman's creed" denied immortal souls only to women. In the *Rights of Woman*, the focus being on women as a group rather than humanity in total, it is logically the "mussulman's creed" that she attacks rather than atheism, though atheism was a far more pernicious doctrine in Wollstonecraft's view. Atheism would put all humans on the level with animals, trapping them in an unending cycle of instinct and training, preventing personal or social progress; the "mussulman's creed" refused full humanity only to women.

Thus, when Wollstonecraft censured John Milton's representation of Eve as a being formed only for "softness and sweet attractive grace" in *Paradise Lost* (1667), she did so by placing him in the tradition of men who espouse the "mussulman's creed": "I cannot comprehend his meaning, unless, in the true Mahometan strain, he meant to deprive us of souls, and insinuate that we were beings only designed by sweet attractive grace, and docile blind obedience, to gratify the senses of man when he can no longer soar on the wing of contemplation" (*Rights of Woman*, 87). Milton located women's value to society in beauty and passivity; in doing so, he denied them, in Wollstonecraft's view, an opportunity to develop their full human identity through the improvement of their reason. Here the "mussulman's creed" is synonymous with the "Mahometan strain," and it was entirely antithetical to everything for which Wollstonecraft stood as a philosopher and as a woman. Milton's praise of women in effect reduced them to animals, and Wollstonecraft rejected it accordingly: "They insult us who thus advise us only to render ourselves gentle, domestic brutes" (*Rights of Woman*, 87). Of women who conform to Milton's model of female identity, a femininity that "governs by obeying," Wollstonecraft exclaimed, "What childish expressions, and how insignificant is the being—can it be an immortal one? who will condescend to govern by such sinister methods" (*Rights of Woman*, 87–88). Like the mistress of the slave plantation, the Miltonic Eve is weak as well as sinister. Such a woman ignores the immortal life of the soul in order to enjoy the temporal gratifications of power and beauty.

Wollstonecraft specifically criticized Christian women and the conditions by which they were dehumanized. Wollstonecraft believed that women in England and women in the harem were subject to the same debilitating conditions. Thus, if education would make a difference for European women, it would have the same effect for Muslim women, too. The difference between an English context and a Muslim context, according to Wollstonecraft's faulty understanding, was that the doctrinal basis for restricting women was embedded in Muslim doctrine. The "Mahometan strain" was *officially* absent in England but was practiced anyway, in Wollstonecraft's view. In other words, Wollstonecraft used the "Mahometan strain" to throw into relief English hypocrisy—its misogynistic practices belied its insistence that all humans, regardless of gender or sex, were images of God.

Wollstonecraft did not claim that Christian women were immune to cultural conditioning; she claimed that all humans are influenced by it and that therefore education is the only means by which humanity, across cultures, could achieve historical progress. She repeatedly stated that all women who are trained to focus on beauty will fail to develop the intelligence—the human identity—that the soul guarantees. She criticized the treatment of women in a Christian context by aligning enforced ignorance with the "mussulman's creed," claiming that "in the true style of Mahometanism," women "are treated as a kind of subordinate beings, and not as part of the human species, when improveable reason is allowed to be the dignified distinction which raises men above the brute creation" (*Rights of Woman*, 74–75). But to believe that Muslim men denied the existence of women's immortal souls was not the same as believing that Muslim women actually did not have them or that, if they had them, they were inferior to the souls of Christian women. Indeed, to assert any original inequality among immortal souls would undermine the entire system by which Wollstonecraft justified her political and educational philosophies. However, because Wollstonecraft believed that there was a *doctrinal* difference between Christianity and Islam on the question of women's souls, she assumed Christianity would help all women. She thus reproduced the Eurocentric evangelistic impulse of Aubin's and Barker's fiction while integrating it with Islamophobic misogynistic mortalism.

Further, though she relied on this Islamophobic trope, cultural essentialism of any kind was antithetical to Wollstonecraft's belief in the transformative power of education. Her belief in women's responsiveness to education was inextricable from her belief in social progress. She saw the emancipation of women and of the common people as analogous, declaring, "Let not men then in the pride of power, use the same arguments that tyrannic kings and venal ministers have used, and fallaciously assert that woman ought to be subjected because she has always been so. . . . If men be demi-gods—why let us serve them! And if the dignity of the female soul be as disputable as that of animals—if their reason does not afford sufficient light to direct their conduct whilst unerring instinct is denied—they are surely of all creatures the most miserable!" (*Rights of Woman*, 117). Immortal souls render all humans fundamentally equal; that is, equally endowed with the ability to improve themselves by the independent exercise of their own reason. If arbitrary authority—whether in despotic France (*Rights of Woman*, 136), in "unfruitful" Turkey (*Rights of Woman*, 116), or in the "libertine" harem—had dehumanized certain groups, education could rescue them.

Belief in the existence of the immortal soul enabled Wollstonecraft to argue that men and women should be held to the same moral standard regardless of gender, that women are capable of reason, and that this capability requires development through education. This is true of Eastern and Western peoples, regardless of the culture, for women "are every where in this deplorable state" (*Rights of Woman*, 116). Like the wealthy, women have all been "*localized* . . . by the rank they are placed in, by *courtesy*" (*Rights of Woman*, 133). The arch-villain of Wollstonecraft's discourse was the arbitrary authority that privileged certain social groups or individuals at the expense of their spiritual equals. However, her cultural bias mapped Islamic doctrine onto Christian hypocrisy rather than acknowledging that both Islamic and Christian doctrines are vulnerable to misogynistic interpretation.

Thus, when she criticized the "libertine notions of beauty" with which Englishwomen have been raised, trained to think it the only way to attain marriage, she does so by claiming that with "this desire making mere animals of them, when they marry they act as such children may be expected to act. . . . Surely these weak beings are only fit for a seraglio!" (*Rights of Woman*, 77). For Wollstonecraft, the desire instilled in Englishwomen by a faulty education has made them animals, just as the conditions of the harem dehumanized Muslim women. For women, in Wollstonecraft's view, human identity had been reduced to the sexual character by the locality of custom, and that locality extended across all cultural borders. Yet, as Felicity Nussbaum has pointed out of Wollstonecraft's Enlightenment ideal of "the public consensual discussion from which commonsensical reason derives," this "rational exchange is bound to conserve and consolidate the hegemonic class and race."[29] Wollstonecraft's ignorance of life in the harem and of Muslim doctrine meant that her emphasis on how courtesy localizes women actually collapsed all knowledge into a false universal, collapsing the real, specific localized knowledge of Muslim women. Because misogynistic mortalism had been mapped onto Islam since the 1690s, Wollstonecraft was able to imagine that she knew what life must be like for Muslim women. Because she believed she knew what their life was like, she was able to dismiss their intelligence, unique perspective, and possible differences from herself without ever inquiring about them.

To be sure, consciously to oppress other women's perspectives would not have been consistent with Wollstonecraft's investment in the intellectual freedom of education. The goal of education and, consequently, of social progress is to achieve union with the divine, for "the powers of the soul that are of little use here, and, probably, disturb our animal enjoyments, even while conscious dignity makes us glory in possessing them, prove that life is merely an education, a state of infancy, to which the only hopes worth cherishing should not be sacrificed. I mean, therefore, to infer, that we ought to have a precise idea of what we wish to attain by education, for the immortality of the soul is contradicted by the actions of many people who firmly profess the belief" (*Rights of Woman*, 192–193). This passage encapsulates Wollstonecraft's educational theory and places it firmly and centrally on the foundation of human immortality. Wollstonecraft's theocentric framework of human identity—the primary relationship of all individuals is to the divine, not to other gendered individuals—enabled her to dispute the relevance of the corporeal distinction of the sexes by arguing that the noblest part of human identity, the immortal soul, is undifferentiated. Men and women should value themselves and each other because all humans are an image of God. "What," she demands, "can make us reverence ourselves, but a reverence for that Being, of whom we are a faint image?" (*Rights of Men*, 40). Wollstonecraft wanted to demystify and demonize the institutionalization of arbitrary authority, whether that authority was Christian or Muslim, European or Ottoman. Angered at the compliments showered on women to encourage them in their "slavish dependence" (*Rights of Woman*, 76), Wollstonecraft admonishes each woman to "obtain a character as a human being, regardless of the distinction of sex" (*Rights of Woman*, 77). If women believe marriage is the highest achievement a woman can hope for, and if they believe that marriage is primarily attained by adhering to "libertine notions of beauty," then women will be "mere animals . . . only fit for a seraglio" (*Rights of Woman*, 77). The crucial question is whether Wollstonecraft believes the women in the seraglio are—essentially—animals, or simply that they are *treated* like animals by being denied an education.

Wollstonecraft believed European women could be reduced to what she believes is an animallike state themselves. She puts little faith in the intrinsic merit of particular cultural groups. Proper education alone is conducive to a distinctively human identity. For instance, when Wollstonecraft excoriates the "woman of fashion, who was more than commonly proud of her delicacy and sensibility," for her cruelty to "a worthy old gentlewoman" (*Rights of Woman*, 115–116), she does so by comparing and contrasting Roman tyranny, modern European monarchy, and Turkish despotism: "Such a woman is not a more irrational monster than some of the Roman emperors, who were depraved by lawless power. Yet since kings have been more under the restraint of law, and the curb, however weak, of honour, the records of history are not filled with such unnatural instances of folly and cruelty, nor does the despotism that kills virtue and genius in the bud, hover over Europe with that destructive blast which desolates Turkey, and renders the men, as well as the soil, unfruitful" (*Rights of Woman*, 116). The target of her criticism was arbitrary power in any manifestation, whether that power derives from physical beauty, wealth, or political despotism. She emphasizes the historical evolution of all human authority. The logical consequence of her argument is that if the West has shed its despotism "since kings have been more under the restraint of law," then so may Turkey once its "virtue" and "genius" are no longer blighted by despotism. Despotism, though an abusive power that may "hover" over nations and deliver a "destructive blast," is not essential to the people themselves, nor is there any indication she believes that the despotism she associates with Turkey will necessarily continue in the future. If anything, Wollstonecraft is aware that former victims of oppression *can* recover, though slowly. As she says, comparing women and slaves: "Man, taking her body, the mind is left to rust; so that while physical love enervates man, as being his favourite recreation, he will endeavour to enslave woman:—and, who can tell, how many generations may be necessary to give vigour to the virtue and talents of the freed posterity of abject slaves?" (*Rights of Woman*, 155). Education is the key to all human flourishing. Indeed, Wollstonecraft argues that without cultivating women's reason it is useless to take them out of their "harams," since education alone teaches women to "love with reasonable subordination their whole family, from their husband to the house-dog" (*Rights of Woman*, 269).

Wollstonecraft believed that the "power of generalizing ideas, of drawing comprehensive conclusions from individual observations" is the only "acquirement, for an immortal being, that really deserves the name of knowledge" (*Rights of Woman*, 128). But this is to assert that it is possible to draw "comprehensive" conclusions from one perspective, one set of observations. In trying to rescue women from the localization of custom, Wollstonecraft failed to see that inquiring into localized knowledge different from her own might broaden her perspective. Curiosity about the localized knowledge of Muslim women would certainly have corrected Wollstonecraft's misunderstanding of Muslim doctrine and, likewise, the writing of what became the cornerstone of Western liberal feminism.

NOTES

Parts of this chapter previously appeared in Samara Anne Cahill, "'Powers of the Soul': Mary Wollstonecraft, Islam, and Historical Progress," *Assuming Gender* 1, no. 2 (2010): 22–43.

1. [Anon.], *Woman not Inferior to Man: or, a Short and Modest Vindication of the Natural Right of the Fair-Sex to a Perfect Equality of Power, Dignity and Esteem with the Men. By Sophia. A Person of Quality* (London: Printed for John Hawkins, at the Falcon in St. Paul's Church-Yard, 1739).
2. [Anon.], *Beauty's Triumph or, the Superiority of the Fair Sex invincibly proved. Wherein The Arguments for the natural Right of Man to a Sovereign Authority over the Woman are fairly urged, and undeniably refuted; and the undoubted Title of the Ladies, even to a Superiority over the Men both in Head and Heart, is clearly evinced; Shewing Their Minds to be as much more beautiful than the Mens as their Bodies; and that, if they had the same Advantages of Education, they would excel their Tyrants as much in Sense as they do in Virtue. In Three Parts. The Whole interspers'd with a delightful Variety of Characters, which some of the most celebrated* Heroes *and* Heroines *of the present Time have had the Goodness to sit for* (London: Printed and sold by J. Robinson at the Golden Lion in Ludgate-Street, 1751).
3. Thomas Seward, "The Female Right to Literature, in a Letter to a young Lady from Florence," in *A Collection of Poems in Six Volumes. By Several Hands. With Notes* (London: Printed for J. Dodsley, in Pall Mall, 1782), 2:309–315. For the influence of the poem on Seward's daughter, the poet Anna Seward, see Teresa Barnard, *Anna Seward: A Constructed Life; A Critical Biography* (Farnham: Ashgate, 2009), 34–35.

4. Hester Mulso, *Letters on Filial Obedience*, in *Bluestocking Feminism: Writings of the Bluestocking Circle, 1738–1785*, vol. 3, *Catherine Talbot & Hester Chapone*, ed. Rhoda Zuk (London: Pickering & Chatto, 1999).
5. Elizabeth Carter and Catherine Talbot, *A Series of Letters between Mrs. Elizabeth Carter and Miss Catherine Talbot from the Year 1741 to 1770* (London: F. C. & J. Rivington, 1808). Letter dated March 24, 1751.
6. Samuel Johnson, *Rambler*, no. 97, in *Rambler* (London: Printed for J. Payne and J. Bouquet, 1752), 3:240–251. The submission is dated February 19, 1751. Although anonymous, it is attributed to "an author . . . who has enlarged the knowledge of human nature, and taught the passions to move at the command of virtue" (240). The date of the article corresponds well with Talbot and Carter's March 4, 1751, interchange referring to Richardson's article on women published in the *Rambler.*
7. Carter and Talbot, *Series of Letters*. Letter dated March 4, 1751.
8. The date of this letter is uncertain, but appears to be sometime in July 1752.
9. *The Life and Correspondence of Mary Granville, Mrs. Delany: with Interesting Reminiscences of King George the Third and Queen Charlotte. Edited by the Right Honourable Lady Llanover*, 3 vols. (London: Richard Bentley, New Burlington Street, 1861), vol. 3.
10. Samuel Richardson, *The History of Sir Charles Grandison*, ed. with an introduction by Jocelyn Harris, 3 vols. (London: Oxford University Press, 1972), 3:7. For ease of reference I am citing according to modern volume number and page number. Harris provides the original volume numbers in text.
11. Morris Golden, *Richardson's Characters* (Ann Arbor: University of Michigan Press, 1963), 180.
12. Hester Chapone, *Letters on the Improvement of the Mind*, in Zuk, *Bluestocking Feminism*, vol. 3.
13. Charlotte Lennox, *The Lady's Museum. By the Author of "The Female Quixote,"* 2 vols. (London, 1760–61), 1:12, 1:9–10.
14. Hannah More, *Essays on Various Subjects, Principally Designed for Young Ladies* (London, 1777), 19.
15. Gayatri C. Spivak, "Can the Subaltern Speak?," in *Colonial Discourse and Post-Colonial Theory: A Reader*, ed. Patrick Williams and Laura Chrisman (Hemel Hempstead: Harvester, 1993), 93.
16. Catharine Macaulay, *Letters on Education. With Observations on Religious and Metaphysical Subjects* (Dublin: Printed for H. Chamberlaine and Rice, L. White, W. Mc. Kenzie, J. Moore, Grueber and Mc. Allister, [and two others in Dublin], 1790).
17. Lyndall Gordon, *Vindication: A Life of Mary Wollstonecraft* (New York: HarperCollins, 2005), 5.
18. For the crucial importance of the "soul" to Wollstonecraft's thought, see Barbara Taylor, *Mary Wollstonecraft and the Feminist Imagination*, Cambridge Studies in Romanticism 56 (Cambridge: Cambridge University Press, 2004). See especially chapter 3, "For the Love of God" (95–142), which places Wollstonecraft in a Christian feminine tradition that borrows from Christian Platonism and Rational Dissent. Eileen Hunt Botting also analyzes the use of the "soul" in Wollstonecraft's political theory of the relationship between individual, family, and state. Eileen Hunt Botting, *Family Feuds: Wollstonecraft, Burke, and Rousseau on the Transformation of the Family* (Albany: State University of New York Press, 2006). See especially chap. 4, "The Family as Cave, Platoon, and Prison: The Three Stages of Wollstonecraft's Philosophy of the Family," 131–187.
19. Taylor, *Mary Wollstonecraft*, 3–4.
20. Virginia Sapiro, *A Vindication of Political Virtue: The Political Theory of Mary Wollstonecraft* (Chicago: University of Chicago Press, 1992), 45.

21. Mary Wollstonecraft, *"A Vindication of the Rights of Men" and "A Vindication of the Rights of Woman,"* ed. by Sylvana Tomaselli (Cambridge: Cambridge University Press, 2001), 19.
22. According to Gunther-Canada, Wollstonecraft "repeats almost word for word Macaulay's charges against Rousseau's sexually differentiated education in the *Rights of Woman*." Wendy Gunther-Canada, "Cultivating Virtue: Catharine Macaulay and Mary Wollstonecraft on Civic Education," *Women and Politics* 25, no. 3 (2003): 64.
23. Mary Wollstonecraft and Mary Shelley, *"Mary," "Maria" and "Matilda,"* ed. Janet Todd (London: Penguin Classics, 1992), 3. All quotations from *Mary* and *The Wrongs of Woman; or, Maria* are taken from this volume.
24. Wollstonecraft, quoted in Gordon, *Vindication*, 2.
25. Botting, *Family Feuds*, 141, 145.
26. Taylor, *Mary Wollstonecraft*, 98.
27. Joyce Zonana, "The Sultan and the Slave: Feminist Orientalism and the Structure of *Jane Eyre*," *Signs: Journal of Women in Culture and Society* 18, no. 3 (Spring 1993): 602.
28. The description of heaven as a place in which marriage does not occur can be found in Matthew 22:30, Mark 12:25, and Luke 20:35. The conclusion of the passage in Matthew is "in the resurrection they neither marry, nor are given in marriage, but are as the angels of God in heaven." This passage, which Wollstonecraft also uses in the conclusion of her semi-autobiographical novel *Mary, a Fiction* (1788), suggests that she sees human identity as essentially genderless (like the angels in heaven) despite the local, temporal, material conditions of the sexed body.
29. Felicity Nussbaum, *Torrid Zones: Maternity, Sexuality, and Empire in Eighteenth-Century English Narratives* (Baltimore: Johns Hopkins University Press, 1995), 201.

EPILOGUE

Save Our Souls?

ENGLISH WOMEN DID NOT CLAIM that Muslim women did not have souls; they believed that Islam taught women that they did not have souls and that therefore women's education was a peculiarly Christian affair. From this perspective, Muslim women could develop their intelligence, but not within a Muslim framework. The roots of Western "savior" feminism originate in this assumption that Muslim women must reject Islam in order to be educated. Further, because women's intelligent (human, immortal) souls were so central to women's education arguments, it became imperative for English women—in fiction and in their real-life correspondence—to distinguish their beliefs from what they took to be Muslim doctrine and to make sure that English men followed suit. The alignment of Islam with physical pleasure and Christianity with intellectual pleasure—a polemical argument that achieved special force during the Trinitarian Controversy—enabled English women to displace the stereotype of women as *machines de plaisir* onto Muslim women while appealing to men to envision an intellectual heterosociability. The fate of the Platonic Lady—whose deviant intellectualism masked a deviant sexuality that hankered for stereotypical Muslim despotism in the bedroom—shows that anti-Muslim sentiment had little to do with Muslims or Muslim doctrine and everything to do with consolidating Anglican patriarchy and carving out an intellectual space for women within it. Women authors continued to use the soul in education arguments after Wollstonecraft's death.

Wollstonecraft's nineteenth-century reception was thorny because her husband, William Godwin, in his forthright *Memoirs* (1798) detailed Wollstonecraft's perceived sexual improprieties. Whether acknowledging Wollstonecraft's contribution or not, the most significant nineteenth-century advocates for women's education (including Emily Davies and Emily and Maria Shirreff) also relied on the importance of the immortal soul. Framing women's identity in terms of their immortal connection to a benevolent and all-power deity enabled them to argue that men and women should, as equal images of God, aim for the same rational education.

Edward W. Ellsworth notes that Emily Shirreff and her sister Maria "laid the foundation of a national educational system for girls at the secondary level," among other educational innovations. But he acknowledges that the Shirreff sisters were not alone in their goals: "The Shirreffs set forth in their writings the basic educational goals that had been agreed upon by many of the most influential women educators and women's rightists of the last third of the century."[1] Emily Shirreff grounded her educational theory on the belief that all human beings have the same objective: "Now, the fundamental truth to start from appears to me to be this—that education . . . has one and the same purpose for every human being; and this purpose is the systematic and harmonious development of his whole moral and intellectual nature. . . . The human creature, whether man or woman, a peasant or a prince, is born with the germ of certain faculties, capable in some degree of moral feeling, of responsibility, of forethought, of reason, of judgment, and it is the business of education to train those faculties for use."[2] Shirreff's position coincided with Wollstonecraft's argument that reason is the capacity for improvement and that all immortal, rational creatures must cultivate themselves spiritually and intellectually. Indeed, Shirreff explicitly identified immortality as the incentive to pursue a liberal education, declaring that "it is a duty as well as a privilege to every creature born to the inheritance of immortality to cultivate all the powers God has given, and to cherish the love of truth in every form" (15). She distinguished between a liberal education and a vocational one, exclaiming, "How far the worship of Mammon has dimmed our spiritual perceptions, how the cravings of the body have silenced the 'still small voice' that speaks from God's wide creation to His noblest work—the soul of man; how utterly the music of the spheres is lost to us amidst the noisy babblings of the market-place" (18). For Shirreff, the contemplation of goodness and beauty for its own sake was the aim of a true education because this contemplation enables individuals "to feel the craving after truth, the perception of the beautiful, the love of the purely good and great, which give our souls an earnest of immortality" (21). The immortal soul and its potential for improvement enable Shirreff to base education not on mere utilitarian, materialist concerns but on the desire for rational and moral improvement, to train a girl "as God's creature, not as man's subordinate" (29).

Shirreff, like Wollstonecraft, based women's need for education on their direct relationship to God. Staunchly resisting the claims of materialism, Shirreff insists that women value themselves on the personal identity that they have cultivated through education. Rationally developed women, especially if remaining unmarried and poor, will "need that spirit loftier than ambition, which will keep the mind active and aspiring without the spur of worldly motive; and that true appreciation of life which maintains, against all false associations, the conviction how superior what we *are* is to what we *do*" (399). And, like Wollstonecraft, Shirreff has a deep suspicion of organized religion. She sternly remarks on the "establishment of nunneries under a thin Protestant disguise" and bitterly notes the effects of "ecclesiastical despotism" (407). Deprived of an education, women will fall under the sway of religious leaders who convince them to "renounce Protestant freedom of conscience as a burden too heavy to bear" (407). Shirreff's antipathy to Catholicism reminds us that an investment in the dignity with which women believed an immortal soul endowed them does not preclude the suppression of other women's localized knowledge, especially if that knowledge might conflict with one's national investments. It is no surprise, then, that misogynistic mortalism continued, even in the secularized public sphere of the twentieth and twenty-first centuries, to be associated with both Catholicism and Islam. Indeed, Kathleen Sprows Cummings has discussed how the anti-Catholic use of the soulless woman trope was deployed as late as 1905, while Leila Ahmed has described a conversation in the early 1980s with an "American feminist" who claimed that "women, according to Islam, had no souls and were thought of simply as animals."[3] The trope of misogynistic mortalism and the wider problem of feminist orientalism is not just feminist prehistory, or even history; it has informed the lives and discourses of feminists and feminisms still living or existing today.

As Eileen Hunt Botting has argued, Wollstonecraft produced a "feminist liberalism with both humanist and imperialist sides" that enjoyed approval on both sides of the Atlantic.[4] The influence of *The Rights of Woman* on the "young liberal democracy" of the United States led to Wollstonecraft's "Orientalist metaphors" influencing not just nineteenth-century British women like Mary Robinson, Emily Brontë, Harriet Martineau, and Millicent Fawcett but also nineteenth-century American women's rights advocates like Hannah Mather Crocker and Sarah Grimké.[5]

Muslim feminists have been protesting this narrative for some time. In her 1982 analysis of the imbrication of orientalism and global feminism, Leila Ahmed called on Western feminists to recognize the "prehistory" that conditions perceptions of Muslim women in the Middle East.[6] Citing Western perceptions of the harem, polygamy, and the veil, Ahmed argued that, just as "Americans 'know,' that Arabs are backward, they know also with the same flawless certainty that Muslim women are terribly oppressed and degraded" (522). More recently, Jasmine Zine and Lisa K. Taylor have argued that an orientalist "image repertoire," a "ready archive of Orientalist and Islamophobic images," "shape[s] popular sentiments and practices of common sense."[7] This orientalist archive has become particularly powerful among responses to the 9/11 attack on the Pentagon and the World Trade Center. In the wake of the post-9/11 U.S. campaign to "save" the women of Afghanistan, Lila Abu-Lughod cautioned against a secular recapitulation of "colonial feminism," arguing that as "anthropologists, feminists, or concerned citizens, we should be wary of taking on the mantles of those 19th-century Christian missionary women who devoted their lives to saving their Muslim sisters."[8]

In 2014, feminist blogger Zara Bennett was still compelled to point out "a trend among feminists, which is the idea that a Western society is the ideal that other cultures should strive to duplicate. . . . These statements [about the backwardness of non-Western cultures] not only alienate a huge portion of the feminist population, but also create divides among feminists that really shouldn't exist in the first place."[9] The mapping of misogynistic mortalism onto Islam, as a root of feminist orientalism, is an influential strand of the thinking that represents Western society as the "ideal" that other societies ought to replicate.

My concurrence with Ahmed, Abu-Lughod, Bennett, and others is not meant to excoriate the West or Western secular feminism but rather to open up a space of dialogue by unearthing a prehistory that has long divided women (and men) of different cultures and religions. *Intelligent Souls?* is, in part, an analysis of the English analogue of what Isobel Coleman has observed of Islamist movements: "Linking feminism with the 'heresy' of the West is good politics, and helps turn patriarchy into patriotism."[10] The "heresy" of Islam was used for the same purpose in seventeenth- and eighteenth-century England. Today we need to share intelligence, in all senses of the word, to understand why women's spaces—the harem, the convent, the privacy within the veil—continue to be objects of either popular satire or militarized anxiety.

NOTES

1. Edward W. Ellsworth, *Liberators of the Female Mind: The Shirreff Sisters, Educational Reform, and the Woman's Movement* (Westport, Conn.: Greenwood Press, 1979), 4–5.
2. Emily Shirreff, *Intellectual Education, and Its Influence on the Character and Happiness of Women* (London: John W. Parker and Son, West Strand, 1858), 7.
3. Kathleen Sprows Cummings, "Do Women Have Souls? Catholicism, Feminism & the Council of Mâcon," *Commonweal*, September 11, 2009, 20–23; Leila Ahmed, "Western Ethnocentrism and Perceptions of the Harem," *Feminist Studies* 8, no. 3 (Autumn 1982): 522.
4. Eileen Hunt Botting, *Wollstonecraft, Mill, and Women's Human Rights* (New Haven, Conn.: Yale University Press, 2016), 168.
5. Botting, *Wollstonecraft*, 168–172.
6. Ahmed, "Western Ethnocentrism," 526.
7. Jasmin Zine and Lisa K. Taylor, "Introduction: The Contested Imaginaries of Reading Muslim Women and Muslim Women Reading Back," in *Muslim Women, Transnational Femi-*

nism and the Ethics of Pedagogy: Contested Imaginaries in Post-9/11 Cultural Practice, ed. Lisa K. Taylor and Jasmin Zine (New York: Routledge, 2014), 7.

8. Lila Abu-Lughod, "Do Muslim Women Really Need Saving? Anthropological Reflections on Cultural Relativism and Its Others," *American Anthropologist*, n.s., 104, no. 3 (September 2002): 789.
9. Zara Bennett, "Dear Feminists: I'm One of You! Please Don't Save Me," editorial, *Feminspire*, July 29, 2014, http://feminspire.com/dear feminists-im-one-please-don't-save/. See also Anthea Taderera, "'Standing in Solidarity' Doesn't Mean Becoming a Messiah," editorial, *Feminspire*, July 3, 2014, http://feminspire.com/standing-in-solidarity-doesnt-mean-becoming-a-messiah/. See also the objection to Western support of controversial secular Egyptian performance art activist Aliaa Magda Elmahdy's criticism of the Islamic State in Iraq and Syria (ISIS), in Briana Urena-Ravelo, "Why I Disagree with the Western Support of Aliaa Magda Elmahdy's Jab at ISIS," editorial, *Feminspire*, August 27, 2014, http://feminspire.com/disagree-western-support-aliaa-magda-elmahdys-jab-isis/.
10. Isobel Coleman, *Paradise beneath Her Feet: How Women Are Transforming the Middle East* (New York: Random House, 2010), xxii.

BIBLIOGRAPHY

ABC News. "'This Week' Transcript: Donald Trump, Vice President Joe Biden, and Ret. Gen. John Allen." July 31, 2016. http://abcnews.go.com/Politics/week-transcript-donald-trump-vice-president-joe-biden/story?id=41020870.

Abu-Lughod, Lila. *Do Muslim Women Need Saving?* Cambridge, Mass.: Harvard University Press, 2013.

———. "Do Muslim Women Really Need Saving? Anthropological Reflections on Cultural Relativism and Its Others." *American Anthropologist*, n.s., 104, no. 3 (September 2002): 783–790.

Addison, Lancelot. *The First State of Mahumedism*. London: Printed for Will Crook, 1687.

Ahmed, Leila. "Western Ethnocentrism and Perceptions of the Harem." *Feminist Studies* 8, no. 3 (Autumn 1982): 521–534.

———. *Women and Gender in Islam*. New Haven, Conn.: Yale University Press, 1992.

Akalin, Esin. *Staging the Ottoman Turk: British Drama, 1656–1792*. Stuttgart: ibidem-Verlag, 2016).

Akkerman, Tjitske, and Siep Stuurman. Introduction to *Perspectives on Feminist Political Thought in European History: From the Middle Ages to the Present*, edited by Tjitske Akkerman and Siep Stuurman. London: Routledge, 1998.

Alvarez, David P. "Reason and Religious Tolerance: Mary Astell's Critique of Shaftesbury." *Eighteenth-Century Studies* 44,, no. 4 (Summer 2011): 475–494.

Andrea, Bernadette, ed. *Delarivier Manley and Mary Pix: English Women Staging Islam, 1696–1707*. With an introduction by Bernadette Andrea. The Other Voice in Early Modern Europe: The Toronto Series, 17. Toronto: Iter Inc. and Centre for Reformation and Renaissance Studies, 2012.

———. *The Lives of Girls and Women from the Islamic World in Early Modern British Literature and Culture*. Toronto: University of Toronto Press, 2017.

———. *Women and Islam in Early Modern English Literature*. Cambridge: Cambridge University Press, 2007.

Andreadis, Harriette. "Re-configuring Early Modern Friendship: Katherine Philips and Homoerotic Desire." *Studies in English Literature, 1500–1900* 46, no. 3 (Summer 2006): 523–542.

[Anon.]. *Beauty's Triumph or, the Superiority of the Fair Sex invincibly proved. Wherein The Arguments for the natural Right of Man to a Sovereign Authority over the Woman are fairly urged, and undeniably refuted; and the undoubted Title of the Ladies, even to a Superiority over the Men both in Head and Heart, is clearly evinced; Shewing Their Minds to be as much more beautiful than the Mens as their Bodies; and that, if they had the same Advantages of Education, they would excel their Tyrants as much in Sense as they do in Virtue. In Three Parts. The Whole interspers'd with a delightful Variety of Characters, which some of the most celebrated* Heroes *and* Heroines *of the present Time have had the Goodness to sit for*. London: Printed and sold by J. Robinson at the Golden Lion in Ludgate-Street, 1751.

[Anon.]. *Gazetteer and New Daily Advertiser* (London). No. 12 (Saturday, May 19, 1770).

[Anon.]. *Gazetteer and New Daily Advertiser* (London). No. 12 (Thursday, May 24, 1770).

[Anon.]. *Gazetteer and New Daily Advertiser* (London). No. 12 (Monday, May 28, 1770).

[Anon.]. *Gentleman's Magazine, and Historical Chronicle.* By Sylvanus Urban. Vol. 21. Printed for Edw. Cave, at St. John's Gate, London, 1751.

[Anon.]. *Gentleman's Magazine: Or, Monthly Intelligencer.* By Sylvanus Urban. No. 1 (January 1731). 4th ed. Printed and sold at St. John's Gate; by F. Jefferies in Ludgate-street, and most booksellers in Town and Country, London, 1732.

[Anon.]. *Gentleman's Magazine or Monthly Intelligencer.* By Sylvanus Urban. Vol. 5 (1735). Printed by Edward Cave, at St. John's Gate, London, 1735.

[Anon.]. *Hoey's Dublin Mercury* (Dublin). No. 613 (September 25–27, 1770).

[Anon.]. *Lloyd's Evening Post* (London). Friday, May 25, 1770.

[Anon.]. *The Macaroni and Theatrical Magazine, or Monthly Register, of the Fashions and Diversions of the Times.* London: Printed for the Authors, and sold by John Williams, next the Mitre Tavern, Fleet Street, 1772.

[Anon.]. *Morning Chronicle and London Advertiser* (London). No. 1513 (Wednesday, March 30, 1774).

[Anon.]. *The polite repository; or, amusing companion: a selection of tales, histories, adventures, and anecdotes from the best modern publications.* Vol. 1. London: Printed for William Lane, at the Minerva, Scadenhal Street, 1791.

[Anon.]. Preface to *Poems By the most deservedly Admired Mrs. Katherine Philips The matchless ORINDA. To which is added Monsieur Corneille's POMPEY & HORACE, Tragedies. With several other Translations out of FRENCH.* London: Printed by J. M for H. Herringman, at the Sign of the Blew Anchor in the Lower Walk of the New Exchange, 1667.

[Anon.]. *Public Advertiser* (London). No. 11097 (Friday, July 3, 1770).

[Anon.]. *Public Advertiser* (London). Friday, May 29, 1772.

[Anon.]. *St. James's Chronicle; or, The British Evening Post* (London). No. 2856 (July 3–6, 1779).

[Anon.]. *Town and Country Magazine.* Vol. 5 (1773).

[Anon.]. *Town and Country Magazine; or Universal repository of knowledge, instruction, and entertainment.* Vol. 2. London: Printed for A. Hamilton, Junr. near St. John's-Gate, 1770.

[Anon.]. *Woman not Inferior to Man: or, a Short and Modest Vindication of the Natural Right of the Fair-Sex to a Perfect Equality of Power, Dignity and Esteem with the Men. By Sophia. A Person of Quality.* London: Printed for John Hawkins, at the Falcon in St. Paul's Church-Yard, 1739. http://digital.library.upenn.edu/women/sophia/woman/woman.html.

Aravamudan, Srinivas. *Enlightenment Orientalism: Resisting the Rise of the Novel.* Chicago: University of Chicago Press, 2012.

———. *Tropicopolitans: Colonialism and Agency, 1688–1804.* Durham, N.C.: Duke University Press, 1999.

[Astell, Mary]. *Bart'lemy Fair: Or, An Enquiry after Wit; In which due Respect is had to a Letter Concerning Enthusiasm, To my Lord ***. By Mr. Wotton.* London, Printed for R. Wilkin, at the King's Head in St. Paul's Church-Yard, 1709.

———. *The Christian Religion, As Profess'd by a Daughter of the Church of England.* London: Printed by S. H. for R. Wilkin, at the King's-Head in St. Paul's-Church-Yeard, 1705.

———. *A Fair Way With The Dissenters And Their Patrons. Not Writ by Mr. L——y, or any other* Furious Jacobite, *whether Clergyman or Layman; but by a very Moderate Person and Dutiful Subject to the QUEEN.* London: Printed by E. P. for R. Wilkin, at the King's-Head, in St. Paul's Church-Yard, 1704.

———. *A Serious Proposal to the Ladies, For the Advancement of their True and Greatest Interest. In Two Parts. By a Lover of her Sex.* London: Printed for Richard Wilkin at the King's-Head in St. Paul's Church-Yard, 1697.

———. *Some Reflections Upon Marriage*. 2nd ed. London: Printed for R. Wilkin, at the King's Head in St. Paul's Church-Yard, 1703.

Astell, Mary, and John Norris. *Letters Concerning the Love of God*, edited by E. Derek Taylor and Melvyn New. Aldershot: Ashgate, 2005.

Aubin, Penelope. *A Collection of Entertaining Histories and Novels, Designed to Promote the Cause of Virtue and Honour*. 3 vols. London: Printed for D. Midwinter, A. Bettesworth and C. Hitch, J. and J. Pemberton, R. Ware, C. Rivington, A. Ward, J. and P. Knapton, T. Longman, R. Hett, S. Austen, and J. Wood, 1739.

Aydin, Cemil. *The Idea of the Muslim World: A Global Intellectual History*. Cambridge, Mass.: Harvard University Press, 2017.

Backscheider, Paula R. *Elizabeth Singer Rowe and the Development of the English Novel*. Baltimore: Johns Hopkins University Press, 2013.

Backscheider, Paula R., and John J. Richetti, eds. *Popular Fiction by Women, 1660–1730: An Anthology*. Oxford: Clarendon Press, 1996.

Badran, Margot. *Feminism in Islam: Secular and Religious Convergences*. Oxford: Oneworld Publications, 2009.

Ball, Bryan W. *The Soul Sleepers: Christian Mortalism from Wycliffe to Priestley*. Cambridge: James Clarke, 2008.

Ballaster, Ros. *Fabulous Orients: Fictions of the East in England, 1662–1785*. 2005. Reprint, Oxford: Oxford University Press, 2007.

———. *Seductive Forms: Women's Amatory Fiction from 1684 to 1740*. Oxford: Clarendon Paperbacks, 1992.

Bannet, Eve Tavor. *The Domestic Revolution: Enlightenment Feminisms and the Novel*. Baltimore: Johns Hopkins University Press, 2000.

———. *Transatlantic Stories and the History of Reading, 1720–1810: Migrant Fictions*. Cambridge: Cambridge University Press, 2011.

Barash, Carol. *English Women's Poetry, 1649–1714: Politics, Community, and Linguistic Authority*. 1996. Reprint, Oxford: Oxford University Press, 2002.

Barbour, Reid. *John Selden: Measures of the Holy Commonwealth in Seventeenth-Century England*. Toronto: University of Toronto Press, 2003.

Barker, Jane. *Exilius: Or, The Banish'd Roman*. Edited by Josephine Grieder. New York: Garland Publishing, 1973.

———. *The Galesia Trilogy and Selected Manuscript Poems of Jane Barker*. Edited by Carol Shiner Wilson. Oxford: Oxford University Press, 1997.

Barnard, Teresa. *Anna Seward: A Constructed Life; A Critical Biography*. Farnham: Ashgate, 2009.

Bayle, Pierre. *Dictionnaire historique et critique*. Rotterdam: R. Leers, 1697.

Beach, Adam. "Aubin's *The Noble Slaves*, Montagu's Spanish Lady, and English Feminist Writing about Sexual Slavery in the Ottoman World." *Eighteenth-Century Fiction* 29, no. 4 (Summer 2017): 583–606.

Bennett, Zara. "Dear Feminists: I'm One of You! Please Don't Save Me." Editorial, *Feminspire*, July 29, 2014. http://feminspire.com/dear feminists-im-one-please-don't-save/.

Berland, Kevin. "The Paradise Garden and the Imaginary East: Alterity and Reflexivity in British Orientalist Romances." *Eighteenth-Century Novel* 2 (2002): 137–159.

Berry, Helen. *Gender, Society and Print Culture in Late-Stuart England: The Cultural World of the Athenian Mercury*. Women and Gender in the Early Modern World. Aldershot: Ashgate, 2003.

Berti, Silvia, Françoise Charles-Daubert, and Richard Popkin, eds. *Heterodoxy, Spinozism, and Free Thought in Early-Eighteenth-Century Europe: Studies in the "Traité des trois imposteurs."* International Archives of the History of Ideas 148. Dordrecht: Kluwer Academic Publishers, 1996.

Bevilacqua, Alexander. *The Republic of Arabic Letters: Islam and the European Enlightenment.* Cambridge, Mass.: Belknap Press of Harvard University Press, 2018.

Bisaha, Nancy. *Creating East and West: Renaissance Humanists and the Ottoman Turks.* Philadelphia: University of Pennsylvania Press, 2004.

Blackstone, Sir William. *Commentaries on the laws of England* [. . .] *By William Blackstone, Esq. Vinerian Professor of Law, and solicitor general to her Majesty.* 4 vols. Oxford: Printed at the Clarendon Press, 1765–69.

Boswell, James. *Life of Johnson, Unabridged.* Edited by R. W. Chapman. With an introduction by Pat Rogers. Oxford World's Classics. Oxford: Oxford University Press, 1998.

Botting, Eileen Hunt. *Family Feuds: Wollstonecraft, Burke, and Rousseau on the Transformation of the Family.* Albany: State University of New York Press, 2006.

———. *Wollstonecraft, Mill, and Women's Human Rights.* New Haven, Conn.: Yale University Press, 2016.

Bowers, Toni. *Force or Fraud: British Seduction Stories and the Problem of Resistance, 1660–1760.* Oxford: Oxford University Press, 2011.

Brehaut, Ernest. Introduction to *History of the Franks,* by Gregory Bishop of Tours. New York: W. W. Norton, 1969.

Britland, Karen. *Drama at the Courts of Queen Henrietta Maria.* Cambridge: Cambridge University Press, 2006.

Broad, Jacqueline. *Women Philosophers of the Seventeenth Century.* Cambridge: Cambridge University Press, 2004.

Bulman, William J. *Anglican Enlightenment: Orientalism, Religion and Politics in England and Its Empire, 1648–1715.* Cambridge Studies in Early Modern British History. Cambridge: Cambridge University Press, 2015.

Burnet, Gilbert. *An Exposition of the Thirty-nine Articles of the Church of England. Written by Gilbert Bishop of Sarum. The Third Edition Corrected.* London: Printed for Ri. Chiswell, at the Rose and Crown in St. Paul's Church-Yard, 1705.

Burton, Jonathan. *Traffic and Turning: Islam and English Drama, 1579–1624.* Newark: University of Delaware Press, 2005.

Bywaters, David. *Dryden in Revolutionary England.* Berkeley: University of California Press, 1991.

Cahill, Samara Anne. "Madonella's Other Convent: 'Platonic Ladies,' Randy Rakes, and the 'Mahometan' Paradise." *Religion in the Age of Enlightenment* 4 (2013): 55–79.

———. "Novel 'Modes' and 'Indian Goods': Textilic Nationalism in *A Patch-Work Screen for the Ladies* and *The Lining of the Patch Work Screen.*" *Studies in Eighteenth-Century Culture* 44 (2015): 163–184.

———. "'Powers of the Soul': Mary Wollstonecraft, Islam, and Historical Progress." *Assuming Gender* 1, no. 2 (2010): 22–43.

———. "Realist Latitudes: Textilic Nationalism and the Global Fiction of the 1720s." *Digital Defoe: Studies in Defoe & His Contemporaries* 7, no. 1 (2015): 66–91.

[Carter, Elizabeth]. *All the works of Epictetus.* London: Printed by S. Richardson: and sold by A. Millar; John Rivington; and, R. and J. Dodsley, 1758.

Carter, Elizabeth, and Catherine Talbot. *A Series of Letters between Mrs. Elizabeth Carter and Miss Catherine Talbot from the Year 1741 to 1770.* London: F. C. & J. Rivington, 1808.

Cartwright, Kent. *Theatre and Humanism: English Drama in the Sixteenth Century.* Cambridge: Cambridge University Press, 2004.

Castle, Terry. *Masquerade and Civilization: The Carnivalesque in Eighteenth-Century English Culture and Fiction.* Stanford, Calif.: Stanford University Press, 1986.

Cavendish, Margaret. *The Blazing World, and Other Writings.* Edited by Kate Lilley. London: Penguin Classics, 1994.

Chaber, Lois. "'Sufficient to the Day': Anxiety in *Sir Charles Grandison*." In *Passion and Virtue: Essays on the Novels of Samuel Richardson*, edited by David Blewett, 268–294. Toronto: University of Toronto Press, 2001.

Chalmers, Hero. *Royalist Women Writers, 1650–1689*. Oxford: Clarendon Press, 2004.

Champion, J. A. I. *The Pillars of Priestcraft Shaken: The Church of England and Its Enemies, 1660–1730*. Cambridge Studies in Early Modern British History. Cambridge: Cambridge University Press, 1992; first paperback ed., 2014.

Chapone, Hester. *Letters on the Improvement of the Mind*. In *Bluestocking Feminism: Writings of the Bluestocking Circle, 1738–1785*, vol. 3, *Catherine Talbot & Hester Chapone*, edited by Rhoda Zuk. London: Pickering & Chatto, 1999.

———. *Miscellanies in prose and verse by Mrs. Chapone*. London: Printed for E. and C. Dilly, and J. Walter, 1775.

Chapone, Sarah. *The hardships of the English laws. In relation to wives. With an explanation of the original curse of subjection passed upon the woman. In an humble address to the legislature*. London: Printed; Dublin: Reprinted by and for George Faulkner, 1735.

Chatterjee, Kumkum, and Clement Hawes, eds. *Europe Observed: Multiple Gazes in Early Modern Encounters*. Aperçus: Histories Texts Cultures. Lewisburg, Pa.: Bucknell University Press, 2008.

Chew, Samuel C. *The Crescent and the Rose: Islam and England during the Renaissance*. New York: Octagon Books, 1965.

Christine, de Pizan. *The Book of the City of Ladies*. Translated by Rosalind Brown-Grant. London: Penguin Books, 1999.

[Chudleigh, Lady Mary]. *The Ladies Defence: Or, The Bride-Woman's Counsellor Answer'd: A Poem. In a Dialogue Between Sir John Brute, Sir William Loveall, Melissa, and a Parson. Written by a Lady*. London: Printed for John Deeve at Bernard's-Inn-Gate in Holborn, 1701.

Clark, Donald B. "The Source and Characterization of Nicholas Rowe's *Tamerlane*." *Modern Language Notes* 65, no. 3 (March 1950): 145–152.

Clarke, Norma. *The Rise and Fall of the Woman of Letters*. London: Pimlico Press, 2004.

Cockburn, Catherine Trotter. *A Letter to Dr. Holdsworth*. London: Benjamin Mott, 1726.

Cohen-Vrignaud, Gerard. *Radical Orientalism: Rights, Reform, and Romanticism*. Cambridge: Cambridge University Press, 2015.

Coleman, Isobel. *Paradise beneath Her Feet: How Women Are Transforming the Middle East*. New York: Random House, 2010.

A Collection of Divine Hymns and Poems on Several Occasions by the E. of Roscommon, John Dryden Esq; *Mr Dennis, Mr Norris, Mrs. Kath. Phillips, Mrs. Singer, & others. Most of them Never before Printed*. London: Printed for R. Burrough, and J. Baker, at the Sun and Moon, near the Royal-Exchange in Cornhill, 1707.

Colley, Linda. "Britishness and Otherness: An Argument." *Journal of British Studies* 31, no. 4 (October 1992): 309–329.

———. *Britons: Forging the Nation, 1707–1837*. Rev. ed. New Haven, Conn.: Yale University Press, 2014.

Cooke, Miriam. "Deploying the Muslimwoman." In "Roundtable Discussion: Religion, Gender, and the Muslimwoman." *Journal of Feminist Studies in Religion* 24, no. 1 (Spring 2008): 91–119.

Cummings, Kathleen Sprows. "Do Women Have Souls? Catholicism, Feminism & the Council of Mâcon." *Commonweal*, September 11, 2009, 20–23.

Darling, Linda. "Ottoman Politics through British Eyes: Paul Rycaut's *The Present State of the Ottoman Empire*." *Journal of World History* 5, no. 1 (1994): 71–97.

Davies, Paul C. "The Debate on Eternal Punishment in Late Seventeenth- and Eighteenth-Century English Literature." *Eighteenth-Century Studies* 4, no. 3 (Spring 1971): 257–276.

Davis, Rose Mary. *The Good Lord Lyttelton: A Study in Eighteenth Century Politics and Culture.* Bethlehem, Pa.: Times Publishing Company, 1939.

De Bellaigue, Christopher. "Turkey's Hidden Past." *New York Review of Books* 48, no. 4 (March 8, 2001).

Defoe, Daniel. "The True-Born Englishman." In *Satire, Fantasy and Writings on the Supernatural by Daniel Defoe*, vol. 1, edited by W. R. Owens, 77–122. London: Routledge, 2003.

Delany, Mary. *The Life and Correspondence of Mary Granville, Mrs. Delany: with Interesting Reminiscences of King George the Third and Queen Charlotte.* Edited by the Right Honourable Lady Llanover. 3 vols. London: Richard Bentley, New Burlington Street, 1861.

Descartes, René. *Sixth Meditation.* In *Meditations on First Philosophy = Meditationes de prima philosophia*, edited and translated by George Heffernan. Bilingual ed. Notre Dame, Ind.: University of Notre Dame Press, 1990.

Dimmock, Matthew. *New Turkes: Dramatizing Islam and the Ottomans in Early Modern England.* Aldershot: Ashgate, 2005.

Dixon, Philip. *"Nice and Hot Disputes": The Doctrine of the Trinity in the Seventeenth Century.* London: T & T Clark, 2003.

Dolan, Frances. *Whores of Babylon: Catholicism, Gender, and Seventeenth-Century Print Culture.* Paperback ed. Notre Dame, Ind.: University of Notre Dame Press, 2005.

———. "Why Are Nuns Funny?" *Huntington Library Quarterly* 70, no. 4 (2007): 509–534.

Donne, John. *LXXX Sermons.* 1640.

———. "To the Countess of Huntingdon" [ca. 1610]. In *The Complete Poetry and Selected Prose of John Donne*, edited by Charles M. Coffin. New York: Modern Library, 2001.

Doody, Margaret Anne. "Identity and Character in *Sir Charles Grandison*." In *Samuel Richardson: Tercentenary Essays*, edited by Margaret Anne Doody and Peter Sabor, 110–132. Cambridge: Cambridge University Press, 1989.

———. *A Natural Passion: A Study of the Novels of Samuel Richardson.* Oxford: Clarendon Press, 1974.

———. *The True Story of the Novel.* New Brunswick, N.J.: Rutgers University Press, 1996.

Dryden, John. *Aureng-Zebe: A Tragedy.* In *The Works of John Dryden*, vol. 12, *Plays: "Amboyna," "The State of Innocence," "Aureng-Zebe,"* edited by Vinton A. Dearing. Berkeley: University of California Press, 1994.

———. *Don Sebastian* [1689, published 1690]. In *The Works of John Dryden*, vol. 15, *Plays: "Albion and Albanius," "Don Sebastian," "Amphytrion,"* edited by Earl Miner and George R. Guffey. Berkeley: University of California Press, 1976.

———. *Don Sebastian, King of Portugal a tragedy, acted at the Theatre Royal, written by Mr. Dryden.* London: Printed for Jo. Hindmarsh, 1690.

Dryden, John, Thomas Shadwell, and John Crowne. "Notes and Observations on *The Empress of Morocco*" [1674]. In *The Works of John Dryden*, vol. 17, *Prose 1668–1691*, edited by Samuel Holt Monk and A. E. Wallace Maurer. Berkeley: University of California Press, 1971.

Dzielska, Maria. *Hypatia of Alexandria.* Translated by F. Lyra. Revealing Antiquity 8. Cambridge, Mass.: Harvard University Press, 1995.

Eagleton, Terry. *The Rape of Clarissa: Writing, Sexuality and Class Struggle in Samuel Richardson.* Minneapolis: University of Minnesota Press, 1986.

Eaves, T. C. Duncan, and Ben D. Kimpel. *Samuel Richardson: A Biography.* Oxford: Clarendon Press, 1971.

El Feki, Shereen. *Sex and the Citadel: Intimate Life in a Changing Arab World.* London: Chatto & Windus, 2013.

Ellsworth, Edward W. *Liberators of the Female Mind: The Shirreff Sisters, Educational Reform, and the Woman's Movement.* Westport, Conn.: Greenwood Press, 1979.

Elmarsafy, Ziad. *The Enlightenment Qur'an: The Politics of Translation and the Construction of Islam*. Oxford: Oneworld Books, 2009.

Farquhar, George. *The Beaux' Stratagem*. In *British Dramatists from Dryden to Sheridan*, edited by George H. Nettleton and Arthur E. Case, revised by George Winchester Stone Jr. Carbondale: Southern Illinois University Press, 1969.

Feingold, Mordechai. "Learning Arabic in Early Modern England." In *The Teaching and Learning of Arabic in Early Modern Europe*, edited by Jan Loop, Alastair Hamilton, and Charles Burnett, 33–56. Leiden: Brill, 2017.

Fielding, Henry. *An Apology for the Life of Mrs. Shamela Andrews*. In *"Anti-Pamela" and "Shamela,"* edited by Catherine Ingrassia, 229–276. Peterborough, Ont.: Broadview Literary Texts, 2004.

———. *Joseph Andrews with Shamela and Related Writings*. Edited by Homer Goldberg. Norton Critical Editions, 1st ed. New York: W. W. Norton, 1987.

———. *Tom Jones*. Edited by Sheridan Baker. Norton Critical Editions, 2nd ed. New York: W. W. Norton, 1995.

Fisher, Michael H. *Counterflows to Colonialism: Indian Travellers and Settlers in Britain, 1600–1857*. Delhi: Permanent Black, 2004.

Fleischer, Manfred P. "'Are Women Human?'—the Debate of 1595 between Valens Acidalius and Simon Gediccus." *Sixteenth Century Journal* 12, no. 2 (Summer 1981): 107–120.

Flynn, Carol Houlihan. "The Pains of Compliance in *Sir Charles Grandison*." In *Samuel Richardson: Tercentenary Essays*, edited by Margaret Anne Doody and Peter Sabor, 133–145. Cambridge: Cambridge University Press, 1989.

Fox, George. *A JOURNAL, or Historical Account of the Life, Travels, Sufferings, Christian Experiences and Labour of Love in the Work of the Ministry Of That Ancient, Eminent and Faithful Servant of George Fox; Who departed this Life in great Peace with the LORD, the 13th of the 11th Month, 1690. The First Part*. London: Printed and sold by J. Sowle in White-Hart-Court in Gracious-street, 1709.

Garcia, Humberto. *Islam and the English Enlightenment, 1670–1840*. Baltimore: Johns Hopkins University Press, 2012.

Gardner, Helen L. "Notes on Donne's Verse Letters." *Modern Language Review* 41, no. 3 (July 1946): 318–321.

Goffman, Daniel. *The Ottoman Empire and Early Modern Europe*. Cambridge: Cambridge University Press, 2009.

Golden, Morris. *Richardson's Characters*. Ann Arbor: University of Michigan Press, 1963.

Goldie, Mark. "John Locke, Jonas Proast and Religious Toleration 1688–1692." In Walsh, Haydon, and Taylor, *Church of England*, 143–171.

Gollapudi, Aparna. "Virtuous Voyages in Penelope Aubin's Fiction." *Studies in English Literature, 1500–1900* 45, no. 3 (Summer 2005): 669–690.

Gordon, Lyndall. *Vindication: A Life of Mary Wollstonecraft*. New York: HarperCollins, 2005.

Gregg, Stephen H. "'A Truly Christian Hero': Religion, Effeminacy, and Nation in the Writings of the Societies for Reformation of Manners." *Eighteenth-Century Life* 25 (Winter 2001): 17–28.

Greig, Martin. "Heresy Hunt: Gilbert Burnet and the Convocation Controversy of 1701." *Historical Journal* 37, no. 3 (1994): 569–592.

Grelot, Guillaume-Joseph. *Relation nouvelle d'un voyage de Constantinople*. Paris: en la boutique de Pierre Rocolet. Chez la veuve de Damien Foucault, impr. & libr. ordin. du roy & de la ville, au Palais en la gallerie des Prisonniers, aux Armes du Roy et de la Ville, 1680.

Grenby, M. O. "Orientalism and Propaganda: The Oriental Tale and Popular Politics in Late-Eighteenth-Century Britain." *Eighteenth-Century Novel* 2 (2002): 215–237.

Griffin, Martin I. J., Jr. *Latitudinarianism in the Seventeenth-Century Church of England.* Annotated by Richard H. Popkin. Edited by Lila Freedman. Brill's Studies in Intellectual History 32. Leiden: Brill, 1992.

Grosrichard, Alain. *The Sultan's Court: European Fantasies of the East.* Translated by Liz Heron. London: Verso, 1998.

Gunther-Canada, Wendy. "Cultivating Virtue: Catharine Macaulay and Mary Wollstonecraft on Civic Education." *Women and Politics* 25, no. 3 (2003): 47–70.

Haakonssen, Knud. "Enlightened Dissent: An Introduction." In Haakonssen, *Enlightenment and Religion*, 1–11.

———, ed. *Enlightenment and Religion: Rational Dissent in Eighteenth-Century Britain.* Cambridge: Cambridge University Press, 1996.

Haleem, M. A. S. Abdel, trans. *The Qur'an.* Oxford: Oxford University Press, 2010.

Hammond, Brean, and Shaun Regan. *Making the Novel: Fiction and Society in Britain, 1660–1789.* Houndmills: Palgrave Macmillan, 2006.

Hart, Clive. *Treatise on the Question Do Women Have Souls and Are They Human Beings? "Disputatio Nova," with Translation, Commentary and Appendices by Clive Hart*, expanded and rev. ed. Lewiston, N.Y.: Edwin Mellen Press, 1998.

Haywood, Eliza Fowler. *Female Spectator.* 4 vols. London, 1744–46.

Hedley, Douglas, "Persons of Substance and the Cambridge Connection: Some Roots and Ramifications of the Trinitarian Controversy in Seventeenth-Century England." In Mulsow and Rohls, *Socinianism and Arminianism*, 225–240.

Henry, John. "A Cambridge Platonist's Materialism: Henry More and the Concept of Soul." *Journal of the Warburg and Courtauld Institutes* 49 (1986): 172–195.

Higgins-Biddle, John C. Introduction to *The Reasonableness of Christianity* (1695), by John Locke, xv–cxv. Edited by John C. Higgins-Biddle. Oxford: Clarendon Press, 1999.

Hill, Bridget. "A Refuge from Men: The Idea of a Protestant Nunnery." *Past and Present* 117 (November 1987): 107–130.

Hobby, Elaine. *Virtue of Necessity: English Women's Writing, 1649–88.* Ann Arbor: University of Michigan Press, 1989.

Holt, P. M. "The Study of Arabic Historians in Seventeenth Century England: The Background and the Work of Edward Pococke." *Bulletin of the School of Oriental and African Studies* 19, no. 3 (1957): 444–455.

———. "The Treatment of Arab History by Prideaux, Ockley and Sale." In *Historians of the Middle East*, edited by Bernard Lewis and P. M. Holt. London: Oxford University Press, 1962; reprint, London: Oxford University Press, 1964.

Hossain, Mary. "Women and Paradise." *Journal of European Studies* 19 (1989): 293–310.

Hughes, Derek. "Dryden's *Don Sebastian* and the Literature of Heroism." *Yearbook of English Studies* 12 (1982): 72–90.

Hutton, Sarah. "Platonism and the Trinity: Anne Conway, Henry More and Christoph Sand." In Mulsow and Rohls *Socinianism and Arminianism*, 209–224.

———. "Platonism in Some Metaphysical Poets: Marvell, Vaughan and Traherne." In *Platonism and the English Imagination*, edited by Anna Baldwin and Sarah Hutton. Cambridge: Cambridge University Press, 2005.

Inalcik, Halil. *The Ottoman Empire: The Classical Age 1300–1600.* 1973. Reprint, London: Phoenix Press, 2000.

Ingram, Robert G. *Religion, Reform and Modernity in the Eighteenth Century: Thomas Secker and the Church of England.* Studies in Modern British Religious History. Woodbridge: Boydell Press, 2007.

Isom-Verhaaren, Christine. "Royal French Women in the Ottoman Sultans' Harem: The Political Uses of Fabricated Accounts from the Sixteenth to the Twenty-First Century." *Journal of World History* 17, no. 2 (2006): 159–196.

Jacob, James R. *Henry Stubbe, Radical Protestantism and the Early Enlightenment.* Cambridge: Cambridge University Press, 1983; first paperback ed., 2002.

Jenkins, Eugenia Zuroski. *A Taste for China: English Subjectivity and the Prehistory of Orientalism.* Oxford: Oxford University Press, 2013.

Johnson, Carina L. *Cultural Hierarchy in Sixteenth-Century Europe: The Ottomans and Mexicans.* Cambridge: Cambridge University Press, 2011.

Johnson, Claudia. *Equivocal Beings. Politics, Gender, and Sentimentality in the 1790s: Wollstonecraft, Radcliffe, Burney, and Austen.* Chicago: University of Chicago Press, 1991.

Johnson, Elizabeth. "Preface to the Reader." In *Poems on Several Occasions. Written by Philomela* [Elizabeth Singer (Rowe)]. London: Printed for John Dunton at the raven in Jewen-Street, 1696.

Johnson, Samuel. *The History of Rasselas, Prince of Abissinia* [1759]. Edited with an introduction and notes by Thomas Keymer. Oxford World's Classics. Oxford: Oxford University Press, 2009.

———. *Irene: A Tragedy. As it is acted at the Theatre Royal in Drury-Lane. By Mr. Samuel Johnson.* London, 1749.

———. "A Journey to the Western Islands of Scotland." In *The Major Works,* 593–641. Edited by Donald Greene. Oxford: Oxford Worlds Classics, 2000.

———. *Rambler.* 2nd ed. 8 vols. Edinburgh: Printed by Sands, Murray, and Cochran; sold by W. Gordon, C. Wright, J. Yair, and the other booksellers, 1751.

———. *Rambler.* London: Printed for J. Payne and J. Bouquet, 1752.

Jones, Tod E. *The Cambridge Platonists: A Brief Introduction with Eight Letters of Dr. Antony Tuckney and Dr. Benjamin Whichcote.* Edited by Tod E. Jones. With translations by Sarah E. Phang. Lanham, Md.: University Press of America, 2005.

Jones, Wendy S. *Consensual Fictions: Women, Liberalism, and the English Novel.* Toronto: University of Toronto Press, 2005.

Kahf, Mohja. *Western Representations of the Muslim Woman: From Termagant to Odalisque.* Austin: University of Texas Press, 2002.

Kelleher, Paul. *Making Love: Sentiment and Sexuality in Eighteenth-Century British Literature.* Lewisburg, Pa.: Bucknell University Press, 2015.

Kemmerer, Kathleen Nulton. *"A Neutral Being between the Sexes": Samuel Johnson's Sexual Politics.* Lewisburg, Pa.: Bucknell University Press, 1998.

Keymer, Thomas. Introduction to Johnson, *History of Rasselas,* ix–xxxiv.

———. *Richardson's "Clarissa" and the Eighteenth-Century Reader.* Cambridge: Cambridge University Press, 1992.

Khalidi, Tarif, trans. *The Qur'an.* London: Penguin Classics, 2009.

Khan, Ghazala. "Ghazala Khan: Trump Criticized My Silence. He Knows Nothing about True Sacrifice." *Washington Post,* July 31, 2016. https://www.washingtonpost.com/opinions/ghazala-khan-donald-trump-criticized-my-silence-he-knows-nothing-about-true-sacrifice/2016/07/31/c46e52ec-571c-11e6-831d-0324760ca856_story.html?utm_term=.baa37472b458.

Klein, Dietrich. "Hugo Grotius' Position on Islam as Described in *De veritate religionis Christianae, Liber VI.*" In Mulsow and Rohls, *Socinianism and Arminianism,* 149–173.

Knolles, Richard. *The Generall Historie of the Turkes.* London: Printed by Adam Islip, 1603.

Kozaczka, Edward J. "Penelope Aubin and Narratives of Empire." *Eighteenth-Century Fiction* 25, no. 1 (Fall 2012): 199–225.

Kugler, Emily M. N. *Sway of the Ottoman Empire on English Identity in the Long Eighteenth Century.* Leiden: Brill, 2012.

Lake, Peter. "Anti-popery: The Structure of a Prejudice." In *Conflict in Early Stuart England: Studies in Religion and Politics, 1603–1642,* edited by Richard Cust and Ann Hughes, 72–106. London: Longman, 1989.

———. "Anti-Puritanism: The Structure of a Prejudice." In *Religious Politics in Post-Reformation England*, edited by Kenneth Fincham and Peter Lake, 80–97. Sussex: Boydell & Brewer, 2006.

Latimer, Bonnie. *Making Gender, Culture, and the Self in the Fiction of Samuel Richardson: The Novel Individual.* Farnham: Ashgate, 2013.

Lennox, Charlotte. *The Female Quixote* [1752]. Edited by Margaret Dalziel. With an introduction by Margaret Anne Doody. Oxford World's Classics. Oxford: Oxford University Press, 1989.

———. *The Lady's Museum. By the Author of "The Female Quixote."* 2 vols. London, 1760–61.

Lewis, Jayne Elizabeth. Introduction to *Religion in Enlightenment England: An Anthology of Primary Sources*, edited by Jayne Elizabeth Lewis, xi–xxx. Waco, Tex: Baylor University Press, 2017.

Lindsay, A. D. Introduction to *A Discourse on Method*, by René Descartes, vii–xxiii. Translated by John Veitch. London: J. M. Dent & Sons, 1957.

Linker, Laura. *Lucretian Thought in Late Stuart England: Debates about the Nature of the Soul.* New York: Palgrave Macmillan, 2013.

Locke, John. *An Essay Concerning Human Understanding.* Clarendon Edition. Edited and with a foreword by Peter H. Nidditch. Oxford: Oxford University Press, 1975; first paperback edition, reprinted (with corrections) from the Clarendon Edition, 1979.

———. *Two Treatises on Government.* Edited by Peter Laslett. Cambridge: Cambridge University Press, 1997.

Loop, Jan. "Johann Heinrich Hottinger (1620–1667) and the 'Historia Orientalis.'" *Church History and Religious Culture* 88, no. 2 (2008): 169–203.

———. *Johann Heinrich Hottinger: Arabic and Islamic Studies in the Seventeenth Century.* Oxford-Warburg Studies. Oxford: Oxford University Press, 2013.

Looser, Devoney. *British Women Writers and the Writing of History, 1670–1820.* Baltimore: Johns Hopkins University Press, 2005.

Loscocco, Paula. Introduction to *Katherine Philips (1631/2–1664): Printed Poems 1667.* Selected by Paula Loscocco. The Early Modern Englishwoman: A Facsimile Library of Essential Works and Printed Writings, 1641–1700: Series 2, Part 3, vol. 2. Edited by Betty S. Travitsky and Anne Lake Prescott. Aldershot: Ashgate, 2007.

Lowenthal, Cynthia. *Performing Identities on the Restoration Stage.* Carbondale: Southern Illinois University Press, 2003.

Luria, Gina. Introduction to *Appeal to the Men of Great Britain on Behalf of Women*, by Mary Hays [1798], 5–15. New York: Garland Publishing, 1974.

Lyttelton, George Lyttelton, Baron. *Letters from a Persian in England, to his Friend at Ispahan.* 2nd ed. London: Printed for J. Millan, Buckingham-Court, near the Admiralty-Office, 1735.

Macaulay, Catharine. *Letters on Education. With Observations on Religious and Metaphysical Subjects.* Dublin: Printed for H. Chamberlaine and Rice, L. White, W. Mc. Kenzie, J. Moore, Grueber and Mc. Allister, [and two others in Dublin], 1790.

MacCarthy, B. G. *The Female Pen: Women Writers and Novelists, 1621–1818* [1944–47]. New York: New York University Press, 1994.

Mack, Ruth. *Literary Historicity: Literature and Historical Experience in Eighteenth-Century Britain.* Stanford, Calif.: Stanford University Press, 2009.

Malebranche, Nicolas. *The Search after Truth.* Translated and edited by Thomas M. Lennon and Paul J. Olscamp. Columbus: Ohio State University Press, 1980.

Manley, Delarivier. *Almyna: Or, The Arabian Vow. A Tragedy.* In Andrea, *Delarivier Manley and Mary Pix.*

[Marana, Giovanni Paolo]. *Letters Writ by a Turkish Spy, Who live Five and forty Years, Undiscovered, at PARIS: Giving an Impartial Account to the Divan at Constantinople, of the most*

Remarkable Transactions of Europe; And discovering several Intrigues and Secrets of the Christian Courts, (especially that of France) from the Year 1637, to the Year 1682. Written Originally in Arabick, first Translated into Italian, afterwards into French, and now into English. London: Printed by J. Leake, and are to be sold by Henry Rhodes, next door to the Swan-Tavern, in Fleet-street, 1687.

[Marana, Giovanni Paolo?]. *The Third Volume of Letters Writ by a Turkish Spy, Who lived Five and forty Years, Undiscovered, at PARIS: Giving an Impartial Account to the Divan at Constantinople, of the most Remarkable Transactions of Europe; And discovering several Intrigues and Secrets of the Christian Courts, (especially that of France) continued from the Year 1645, to the Year 1682. Written Originally in Arabick, Translated into Italian, and from thence into English by the Translator of the First Volume.* London: Printed by J. Leake, for Henry Rhodes, near Bride lane, in Fleet street, 1691.

Marshall, John. *John Locke, Toleration and Early Enlightenment Culture.* Cambridge Studies in Early Modern British History. Cambridge: Cambridge University Press, 2006; digitally printed version, 2009.

Masham, Damaris. *A Discourse Concerning the Love of God.* London: Printed for Awnsham and John Churchil, 1696.

Matar, Nabil, ed. *Henry Stubbe and the Beginnings of Islam: "The Originall & Progress of Mahometanism."* With an introduction by Nabil Matar. New York: Columbia University Press, 2014.

———. *Islam in Britain, 1558–1685.* Cambridge: Cambridge University Press, 1998.

———. "Muslims in Seventeenth-Century England," *Journal of Islamic Studies* 8, no. 1 (1997): 63–82.

[Maurus, Andreas] I. N., trans. *THE CONFUSION OF MUHAMED'S SECT, OR A Confutation of the Turkish ALCORAN. Being a Discovery of many secret Policies and practices in that Religion, not till now Revealed. Written Originally in Spanish by Johannes Andreas Maurus, who was one of their Bishops and afterwards turned Christian. Translated into English by I. N.* London: Printed for h. Blunden, at the Castle in Cornhill, 1652.

McDowell, Nicholas. "Tales of Tub Preachers: Swift and Heresiography." *Review of English Studies* 61, no. 248 (August 4, 2009): 72–92.

McJannet, Linda. *The Sultan Speaks: Dialogue in English Plays and Histories about the Ottoman Turks.* New York: Palgrave Macmillan, 2006.

Meggitt, Justin J. *Early Quakers and Islam: Slavery, Apocalyptic and Christian-Muslim Encounters in the Seventeenth Century.* Studies on Inter-religious Relations 59. Uppsala: Swedish Science Press, 2013.

Mello, Patrick. "'Piety and Popishness': Tolerance and the Epistolary Reaction to Richardson's *Sir Charles Grandison*." *Eighteenth-Century Fiction* 25, no. 3 (Spring 2013): 511–531.

Mijuskovic, Ben Lazare. *The Achilles of Rationalist Arguments.* International Archives of the History of Ideas, Series Minor, 13. The Hague: Martinus Nijhoff, 1974.

Milton, Anthony. *Catholic and Reformed: The Roman and Protestant Churches in English Protestant Thought, 1600–1640.* Cambridge: Cambridge University Press, 1995; paperback ed., 2002.

Milton, John. *"Paradise Lost" & "Paradise Regained."* Edited by Christopher Ricks. With a new introduction by Susanne Woods. New York: Signet Classic, 2001.

Mirabeau, Gabriel-Honoré Riquetti, comte de. *Lettres originales de Mirabeau.* Paris: Garnery; Strasbourg: Treuttel; London: De Boffe, 1792.

Montagu, Lady Mary Wortley. *The Complete Letters of Lady Mary Wortley Montagu.* Edited by Robert Halsband. 3 vols. Oxford: Clarendon Press, 1965.

———. *The Turkish Embassy Letters.* Edited and annotated by Malcolm Jack. With an introduction by Anita Desai. 1994. Reprint, London: Virago, 2009.

Montesquieu, Charles de Secondat. "Letter 141." In *Persian Letters*. Translated with an introduction by C. J. Betts. Penguin Classics. 1973. Reprint, London: Penguin Books, 2004.

More, Hannah. *Essays on Various Subjects, Principally Designed for Young Ladies*. London, 1777.

More, Henry. *An Antidote Against Atheisme, or An Appeal to the Natural Faculties of the Minde of Man, whether there be not a God. By Henry More Fellow of Christ Colledge in Cambridge*. London. Printed by Roger Daniel, at Lovell's Inne in Paster-noster-Row, 1653.

Mortimer, Sarah. *Reason and Religion in the English Revolution: The Challenge of Socinianism*. Cambridge Studies in Early Modern British History. Cambridge: Cambridge University Press, 2013.

Mounsey, Chris. "'. . . bring her naked from her Bed, that I may ravish her before the Dotard's face, and then send his Soul to Hell': Penelope Aubin, Impious Pietist, Humourist or Purveyor of Juvenile Fantasy?" *British Journal for Eighteenth-Century Studies* 26 (2003): 55–75.

———."Conversion Panic, Circumcision, and Sexual Anxiety: Penelope Aubin's Queer Writing." In *Queer People: Negotiations and Expressions of Homosexuality, 1700–1800*, edited Chris Mounsey and Caroline Gonda, 246–260. Lewisburg, Pa.: Bucknell University Press, 2007.

Mulso, Hester. *Letters on Filial Obedience*. In *Bluestocking Feminism: Writings of the Bluestocking Circle, 1738–1785*, vol. 3, *Catherine Talbot & Hester Chapone*, edited by Rhoda Zuk. London: Pickering & Chatto, 1999.

Mulsow, Martin. "The 'New Socinians': Intertextuality and Cultural Exchange in Late Socinianism." In Mulsow and Rohls, *Socinianism and Arminianism*, 49–78.

Mulsow, Martin, and Jan Rohls, eds. *Socinianism and Arminianism: Antitrinitarians, Calvinists and Cultural Exchange in Seventeenth-Century Europe*. Leiden: Brill, 2005.

Myers, Sylvia Harcstark. *The Bluestocking Circle: Women, Friendship, and the Life of the Mind in Eighteenth-Century England*. Oxford: Clarendon Press, 1990.

Nolan, Michael. "The Myth of Soulless Women." *First Things* 72 (April 1997): 13–14.

Norris, Richard A., Jr., trans. and ed. *The Christological Controversy*. With supplemental material by Robert C. Saler. Minneapolis: Fortress Press, 1980.

Noue, Jean-Baptiste Sauvé de la. *Mahomet Second: tragédie*. Paris: Prualt, 1739.

Nussbaum, Felicity. *Torrid Zones: Maternity, Sexuality, and Empire in Eighteenth-Century English Narratives*. Baltimore: Johns Hopkins University Press, 1995.

O'Brien, Karen. *Women and Enlightenment in Eighteenth-Century Britain*. Cambridge: Cambridge University Press, 2009.

Orr, Bridget. *Empire on the English Stage, 1660–1714*. Cambridge: Cambridge University Press, 2001.

Pateman, Carol. *The Sexual Contract*. Stanford, Calif.: Stanford University Press, 1988.

Patrides, C. A. Introduction to *The Cambridge Platonists*, edited by C. A. Patrides. 1969. Reprint, Cambridge: Cambridge University Press, 2007.

Perera, Suvendrini. *Reaches of Empire: The English Novel from Edgeworth to Dickens*. New York: Columbia University Press, 1991.

Perkins, Franklin. *Leibniz and China: A Commerce of Light*. Cambridge: Cambridge University Press, 2004.

Perry, Ruth. *The Celebrated Mary Astell: An Early English Feminist*. Chicago: University of Chicago Press, 1986.

Pfizenmaier, Thomas C. *The Trinitarian Theology of Dr. Samuel Clarke (1675–1729): Context, Sources, and Controversy*. Leiden: Brill, 1997.

Pix, Mary. *Ibrahim, The Thirteenth Emperor of the Turks: A Tragedy* [1696]. In Andrea, *Delarivier Manley and Mary Pix*.

Pope, Alexander. *The Correspondence of Alexander Pope*. Vol. 1, *1704–1718*, edited by George Sherburn. Oxford: Clarendon Press, 1956.

Porter, Roy. "Enlightenment and Pleasure." In *Pleasure in the Eighteenth Century*, edited by Roy Porter and Marie Mulvey Roberts, 1–18. Houndmills: Macmillan Press, 1996.

Poullain de La Barre, François. *Three Cartesian Feminist Treatises*. With introductions and annotations by Marcelle Maistre Welch. Translated by Vivien Bosley. The Other Voice in Early Modern Europe. Chicago: University of Chicago Press, 2002.

Prescott, Sarah. "Penelope Aubin and *The Doctrine of Morality*: A Reassessment of the Pious Woman Novelist." *Women's Writing* 1, no. 1 (1994): 99–112.

Prest, Wilfrid. "Law, Lawyers and Rational Dissent." In Haakonssen, *Enlightenment and Religion*, 169–192.

Prideaux, Humphrey. *The True Nature of Imposture Fully Display'd in the Life of Mahomet with A Discourse annexed, for the Vindicating of Christianity from this Charge; Offered to the Consideration of the Deists of the present Age.* 2nd ed., corrected. London: Printed for William Rogers, at the Sun against St. Dunsten's Church in Fleetstreet, 1697.

Pritchard, Penny. "Studies in English Protestant Dissent and Literature after 1662." *Literature Compass* 15, no. 5 (2018): e12469. http://doi.org/10.1111/lic3.12469.

Quataert, Donald. *The Ottoman Empire, 1700–1922*. 2nd ed. Cambridge: Cambridge University Press, 2009.

Rabin, Dana. "The Jew Bill of 1753: Masculinity, Virility, and the Nation." *Eighteenth-Century Studies* 39, no. 2 (2006): 157–171.

Radcliffe, Mary Anne. *The Female Advocate; or An Attempt to Recover the Rights of Women from Male Usurpation* [1799]. Anglistica & Americana 183. Hildesheim: Georg Olms Verlag, 1980.

Rees, Emma L. E. "Triply Bound: Genre and the Exilic Self." In *Authorial Conquests: Essays on Genre in the Writings of Margaret Cavendish*, edited by Line Cottegnies and Nancy Weitz, 23–39. Cranbury, N.J.: Associated University Presses, 2003.

Richards, Jennifer. Introduction to *Elizabeth Singer [Rowe]*, ix–xvi. Selected by Jennifer Richards. The Early Modern Englishwoman: A Facsimile Library of Essential Works and Printed Writings, 1641–1700: Series 2, Part 2, vol. 7. Edited by Betty S. Travitsky and Anne Lake Prescott. Aldershot: Ashgate, 2003.

Richardson, Samuel. *Clarissa, or, The History of a Young Lady*. Edited by Angus Ross. London: Penguin Classics, 1985.

———. *Clarissa. Or, the history of a young lady* [1747–48]. 3rd ed. 8 vols. London: Printed for S. Richardson, 1750–51.

———. *The Correspondence of Samuel Richardson*. Vol. 1. London: Printed for Richard Phillips, No. 71, St. Paul's Church-Yard, 1804.

———. *The History of Sir Charles Grandison*. Edited with an introduction by Jocelyn Harris. 3 vols. London: Oxford University Press, 1972.

———. *Pamela; or, Virtue Rewarded* [1740–41]. Edited by Thomas Keymer. With notes by Alice Wakely. Oxford: Oxford University Press, 2001.

———. *Pamela in Her Exalted Condition* [1742]. Edited by Albert J. Rivero. The Cambridge Edition of the Works of Samuel Richardson. Cambridge: Cambridge University Press, 2012.

Richetti, John J. "Mrs. Elizabeth Rowe: The Novel as Polemic." *PMLA* 82, no. 7 (December 1967): 522–529.

———. *Popular Fiction before Richardson: Narrative Patterns, 1700–1739*. Oxford: Clarendon Press, 1969.

Rivers, Isabel. *Reason, Grace, and Sentiment: A Study of the Language of Religion and Ethics in England, 1660–1780*. Vol. 1, *Whichcote to Wesley*. Cambridge: Cambridge University Press, 1991.

———. "Religion and Literature." In *The Cambridge History of English Literature, 1660–1780*, edited by John J. Richetti, 445–470. Cambridge: Cambridge University Press, 2005.

Roberts, Marie Mulvey. Preface to *Pleasure in the Eighteenth Century*, edited by Roy Porter and Marie Mulvey Roberts, ix–xv. Houndmills: Macmillan Press, 1996.

Robinson, Benedict S. *Islam and Early Modern English Literature: The Politics of Romance from Spenser to Milton*. Early Modern Cultural Studies, 1500–1700. New York: Palgrave Macmillan, 2007.

Roe, Sir Thomas. *The Negotiations of Sir Thomas Roe*. London: Printed by Samuel Richardson, 1740.

[Ross, Alexander]. *The Alcoran of Mahomet, Translated out of Arabick into French BY THE Sieur du Ryer, Lord of Malezair, and Resident for the French King, at ALEXANDRIA. And Newly Englished, for the satisfaction of all that desire to look into the Turkish Vanities*. London: Printed, and are to be sold by Randal Taylor, near Stationers Hall, 1688.

[Rowe], Elizabeth Singer. *"Friendship in Death in Twenty Letters from the Dead to the Living" and "Letters Moral and Entertaining."* Edited by Josephine Grieder. New York: Garland Publishing, 1972.

[Rowe, Elizabeth Singer]. *Poems on Several Occasions. Written by Philomela*. London: Printed for John Dunton at the Raven in Jewen-street, 1696.

Rubenhold, Hallie. "The New Female Coterie" and "Variety." In *The Lady in Red: An Eighteenth-Century Tale of Sex, Scandal, and Divorce*, 171–203. New York: St. Martin's Press, 2008.

Rusch, William G., trans. and ed. *The Trinitarian Controversy*. Minneapolis: Fortress Press, 1980.

Russell, Gillian. *Women, Sociability and Theatre in Georgian London*. Cambridge: Cambridge University Press, 2010.

Russell, Gül A., ed. *The 'Arabick' Interest of the Natural Philosophers in Seventeenth-Century England*. Leiden: Brill, 1994.

Rycaut, Sir Paul. *The present state of the Ottoman Empire*. London: Printed for John Starkey and Henry Brome, 1668.

Said, Edward. *Culture and Imperialism*. New York: Vintage Books, 1993.

———. *Orientalism*. New York: Vintage Books, 1979; reprint, with a new afterword, New York: Vintage Books, 1994).

Sale, George. *The Koran*. London: Printed by C. Ackers, for J. Wilcox, 1734.

Sapiro, Virginia. *A Vindication of Political Virtue: The Political Theory of Mary Wollstonecraft*. Chicago: University of Chicago Press, 1992.

Sardar, Ziauddin. *Orientalism*. Concepts in the Social Sciences. Buckingham: Open University Press, 1999.

Schiebinger, Londa. *Nature's Body: Gender in the Making of Modern Science*. Boston: Beacon Press, 1993.

Scott, Joan Wallach. *The Politics of the Veil*. Princeton, N.J.: Princeton University Press, 2010.

Sell, Alan P. F. *John Locke and the Eighteenth-Century Divines*. Cardiff: University of Wales Press, 1997.

Seward, Thomas. "The Female Right to Literature, in a Letter to a young Lady from Florence." In *A Collection of Poems in Six Volumes. By Several Hands. With Notes*, 2:309–315. London: Printed for J. Dodsley, in Pall Mall, 1782.

Shagan, Ethan. Introduction to *Catholics and the "Protestant Nation": Religious Politics and Identity in Early Modern England*, edited by Ethan Shagan. Manchester: Manchester University Press, 2005.

Shakespeare, William. *Othello*. The Alexander Shakespeare. Gen. Ed. R. B. Kennedy. With additional notes and editing by Mike Gould. Collins Classics, Harper Press paperback edition. London: Harper Press, 2011.

Sheehan, Jonathan. *The Enlightenment Bible: Translation, Scholarship, Culture*. Princeton, N.J.: Princeton University Press, 2005.

Sherburn, George, ed. *The Correspondence of Alexander Pope*. Vol. 1, *1704–1718*. Oxford: Clarendon Press, 1956.

Shirreff, Emily. *Intellectual Education, and Its Influence on the Character and Happiness of Women*. London: John W. Parker and Son, West Strand, 1858.

Sirota, Brent. *The Christian Monitors: The Church of England and the Age of Benevolence, 1680–1730*. New Haven, Conn.: Yale University Press, 2014.

———. "The Trinitarian Crisis in Church and State: Religious Controversy and the Making of the Postrevolutionary Church of England, 1687–1702." *Journal of British Studies* 52 (January 2013): 26–54.

Sitter, John. *Literary Loneliness in Mid-Eighteenth-Century England*. Ithaca, N.Y.: Cornell University Press, 1982.

Smith, David Nichol. "Johnson's *Irene*." In *Essays and Studies*, vol. 14, collected by H. W. Garrod, 35–53. Milford: English Association, 1929.

Smollett, Tobias. *The Adventures of Roderick Random*. Edited with an introduction and notes by Paul-Gabriel Boucé. Oxford World's Classics. Oxford: Oxford University Press, 1999; reissued 2008.

———. *The Miscellaneous Works of Tobias Smollett, M.D. with a Life of the Author. In Twelve Volumes*. London, 1824.

Sorkin, Amy Davidson. "What Donald Trump Doesn't Get about Ghazala and Khizr Khan." *New Yorker*, August 1, 2016. http://www.newyorker.com/news/amy-davidson/what-donald-trump-doesnt-get-about-ghazala-and-khizr-khan.

Sorkin, David. *The Religious Enlightenment: Protestants, Jews, and Catholics from London to Vienna*. Princeton, N.J.: Princeton University Press, 2008.

Souers, Philip. *The Matchless Orinda*. Cambridge, Mass.: Harvard University Press, 1931.

Spencer, Jane. *The Rise of the Woman Novelist: From Aphra Behn to Jane Austen*. Oxford: Blackwell, 1986.

Spivak, Gayatri C. "Can the Subaltern Speak?" In *Colonial Discourse and Post-Colonial Theory: A Reader*, edited by Patrick Williams and Laura Chrisman, 66–111. Hemel Hempstead: Harvester, 1993.

———. "Three Women's Texts and a Critique of Imperialism." *Critical Inquiry* 12, no. 1 (Autumn 1985): 243–261.

Springborg, Patricia. *Mary Astell: Theorist of Freedom from Domination*. Cambridge: Cambridge University Press, 2005.

Sprint, John. *The Bride-Woman's Counseller: Being a Sermon Preach'd at a Wedding, May the Eleventh 1699, at Sherbourn in Dorsetshire*. London: Printed and sold by H. Hills, in Black-Fryars, near the Water-side, for the Benefit of the Poor, 1699.

Stafford, William. *English Feminists and Their Opponents in the 1790s: Unsex'd and Proper Females*. Manchester: Manchester University Press, 2002.

Staves, Susan. *A Literary History of Women's Writing in Britain, 1660–1789*. Cambridge: Cambridge University Press, 2006.

Steele, Richard. *The Lucubrations of Isaac Bickerstaff Esq; Revised and corrected by the author*. Vol. 1. London: Printed and sold by Charles Lillie, at the Corner of Beauford Buildings in the Strand; and John Morphew, near Stationers-Hall, 1710.

Steinsaltz, Adin. *The Essential Talmud*. 30th anniversary ed. New York: Basic Books, 2006.

Stewart, Dustin. "Dunton and Singer after the *Athenian Mercury*: Two Plots of Platonic Love." In *Women's Periodicals and Print Culture in Britain, 1690–1820s*, edited by Jennie Batchelor and Manushag N. Powell, 87–100. Edinburgh, Edinburgh University Press, 2018.

Stillingfleet, Edward. *The Doctrine of the Trinity*. In *Three Criticisms of Locke*. Hildesheim: George Olms Verlag, 1987.

Stuurman, Siep. *François Poulain de la Barre and the Invention of Modern Equality*. Cambridge, Mass.: Harvard University Press, 2004.

Sullivan, Robert E. *John Toland and the Deist Controversy: A Study in Adaptations*. Harvard Historical Studies. Cambridge, Mass.: Harvard University Press, 1982.

Taderera, Anthea. "'Standing in Solidarity' Doesn't Mean Becoming a Messiah." Editorial, *Feminspire*, July 3, 2014. http://feminspire.com/standing-in-solidarity-doesnt-mean-becoming-a-messiah/.

Taliaferro, Charles, and Alison J. Teply. Introduction to *Cambridge Platonist Spirituality*, edited by Charles Taliaferro and Allison J. Teply. New York: Paulist Press, 2004.

Tankard, Paul. Introduction to *Facts and Inventions: Selections from the Journalism of James Boswell*, edited by Paul Tankard, xxiii–xlviii. New Haven, Conn.: Yale University Press, 2014.

Taylor, Barbara. *Mary Wollstonecraft and the Feminist Imagination*. Cambridge Studies in Romanticism 56. Cambridge: Cambridge University Press, 2004.

Teo, Hsu-Ming. *Desert Passions: Orientalism and Romance Novels*. Austin: University of Texas Press, 2012.

Thomson, Ann. *Bodies of Thought: Science, Religion, and the Soul in the Early Enlightenment*. Oxford: Oxford University Press, 2008.

Toenjes, Christopher. *Islam, the Turks and the Making of the English Reformation: The History of the Ottoman Empire in John Foxe's "Acts and Monuments."* Frankfurt am Main: Peter Lang, 2016.

Tomlinson, Sophie. *Women on Stage in Stuart Drama*. Cambridge: Cambridge University Press, 2005.

Toomer, G. J. *Eastern Wisedome and Learning: The Study of Arabic in Seventeenth-Century England*. Oxford: Oxford University Press, 1996.

Urena-Ravelo, Briana. "Why I Disagree with the Western Support of Aliaa Magda Elmahdy's Jab at ISIS." Editorial, *Feminspire* (August 27, 2014), http://feminspire.com/disagree-western-support-aliaa-magda-elmahdys-jab-isis/.

Veevers, Erica. *Images of Love and Religion: Queen Henrietta Maria and Court Entertainments*. Cambridge: Cambridge University Press, 1989.

Vitkus, Daniel. *Turning Turk: English Theater and the Multicultural Mediterranean, 1570–1630*. New York: Palgrave Macmillan, 2003.

Wadud, Amina. *Qur'an and Woman: Rereading the Sacred Text from a Woman's Perspective*. New York: Oxford University Press, 1999.

Wager, Lewis. *A new enterlude, never before this tyme imprinted, entreating of the life and repentaunce of Marie Magdalene not only godlie, learned and fruitefull, but also well furnished with pleasaunt myrth and pastime, very delectable for those which shall heare or reade the same. Made by the learned clarke Lewis Wager*. Imprinted at London: By Iohn Charlevvood, dwelling in Barbican, at the signe of the halfe Eagle and the Key, 1566.

Walker, Robert G. *Eighteenth-Century Arguments for Immortality and Johnson's "Rasselas."* English Literary Studies Monograph Series, 9. Victoria, B.C.: University of Victoria, 1977).

Walsh, John, Colin Haydon, and Stephen Taylor, eds. *The Church of England c. 1689–c. 1833: From Toleration to Tractarianism*. Cambridge: Cambridge University Press, 1993; first paperback ed., 2002.

Walsh, John, and Stephen Taylor. "Introduction: The Church and Anglicanism in the 'Long' Eighteenth Century." In Walsh, Haydon, and Taylor, *Church of England*, 1–64.

Ware, Henry, ed. *Christian Disciple and Theological Review*, n.s., vol. 2 (1820). Boston: Wells and Lilly, Court-Street, 1821.

Warner, William Beatty. *Reading "Clarissa": The Struggles of Interpretation*. New Haven, Conn.: Yale University Press, 1979.

Waterman, A. M. C. "The Nexus between Theology and Political Doctrine." In Haakonssen, *Enlightenment and Religion*, 193–218.

Webb, R. K. "The Emergence of Rational Dissent." In Haakonssen, *Enlightenment and Religion*, 12–41.

Weinbrot, Howard D. "Johnson's *Irene* and *Rasselas*, Richardson's *Pamela Exalted*: Contexts, Polygamy, and the Seraglio." *Age of Johnson* 23 (2015): 89–140.

———. "The Reader, the General, and the Particular: Johnson and Imlac in Chapter Ten of *Rasselas*." *Eighteenth-Century Studies* 5, no. 1 (Autumn 1971): 80–96.

Welham, Debbie. "The Particular Case of Penelope Aubin." *Journal for Eighteenth-Century Studies* 31, no. 1 (2008): 63–76.

———. "The Political Afterlife of Resentment in Penelope Aubin's *The Life and Amorous Adventures of Lucinda* (1721)." *Women's Writing* 20, no. 1 (February 2013): 49–63.

Williams, George Huntston. *The Radical Reformation*. 3rd ed. Kirksville, Mo.: Truman State University Press, 2000.

Williamson, George. "*The Ephesian Matron* versus the Platonic Lady." *Review of English Studies* 12, no. 48 (October 1936): 445–449.

Wilson, Brett. "Jane Shore and the Jacobites: Nicholas Rowe, the Pretender, and the National She-Tragedy." *ELH* 72, no. 4 (2005): 823–843.

———. *A Race of Female Patriots: Women and Public Spirit on the British Stage, 1688–1745*. Lewisburg, Pa.: Bucknell University Press, 2012.

Wollstonecraft, Mary. *A Vindication of the Rights of Woman*. In *"A Vindication of the Rights of Men" and "A Vindication of the Rights of Woman,"* edited by Sylvana Tomaselli. Cambridge: Cambridge University Press, 2001.

Wollstonecraft, Mary, and Mary Shelley. *"Mary," "Maria" and "Matilda*. Edited by Janet Todd. London: Penguin Classics, 1992.

Woolhouse, Roger. *Locke: A Biography*. Cambridge: Cambridge University Press, 2007.

Yeazell, Ruth Bernard. *Harems of the Mind: Passages of Western Art and Literature*. New Haven, Conn.: Yale University Press, 2000.

Yolton, John W. *Thinking Matter: Materialism in Eighteenth-Century Britain*. Minneapolis: University of Minnesota Press, 1983.

Young, B. W. *Religion and Enlightenment in Eighteenth-Century England: Theological Debate from Locke to Burke*. Oxford: Clarendon Press, 1998; reprint, Oxford: Clarendon Press, 2001.

Zhulkeflee, Bin Haji Ismail. "Principles in Tafsir al-Qur'an in the Name of Allah, the Most Compassionate, Most Merciful. How the Qur'an Explains Itself regarding Interpretation of Its Verses." Slides presented in clarifying questions posed by Samara Anne Cahill, School of Humanities and Social Sciences, Division of English, Nanyang Technological University, Singapore, October 19, 2016. @ Wisma Inda, SlideShare.

Zine, Jasmin, and Lisa K. Taylor. "Introduction: The Contested Imaginaries of Reading Muslim Women and Muslim Women Reading Back." In *Muslim Women, Transnational Feminism and the Ethics of Pedagogy: Contested Imaginaries in Post-9/11 Cultural Practice*, edited by Lisa K. Taylor and Jasmin Zine, 1–22. New York: Routledge, 2014.

Zonana, Joyce. "The Sultan and the Slave: Feminist Orientalism and the Structure of *Jane Eyre*." *Signs: Journal of Women in Culture and Society* 18, no. 3 (Spring 1993): 592–617.

INDEX

Abu-Lughod, Lila, 202
Acidalius, Valens, 7, 24, 25, 47–48n39
Act of Toleration (1689), 16–17, 38
Act of Uniformity (1662), 16, 27, 43–44n9
Adam, 21, 61, 126
Addison, Joseph, 122, 181
Addison, Lancelot, 10, 30–31, 37, 49n70, 76, 92, 105, 152, 167, 179
Afghanistan, 202
Ahmed, Leila, 201, 202
Aikenhead, Thomas, 2, 18
alterity, religious, 6, 100, 110, 114, 134, 136, 162, 175, 176
amatory fiction, 87, 91, 94, 100, 101, 110, 113
Anabaptists, 24, 27, 46n25
Andrea, Bernadette, 9, 96n35
Andreadis, Harriette, 97n45
Anglican Church/Anglicanism, 27, 28, 157, 158, 176; and British masculinity, 117, 122, 123, 137, 167; centrality of Trinitarian orthodoxy to, 2, 15; global, welcoming to converts, 66, 87, 89; the importance of the immortal soul in the doctrine of, 22, 65; tension in, between High Church and Latitudinarians, 29–30, 77, 80; and the Trinitarian Controversy, 7, 10, 15–21, 84, 87, 102
Anne I of England, 68
annihilationism, 23, 102, 104, 107, 108, 109, 173
Arabia/Arabians, 38–39, 152. *See also* Ottoman Empire; Turkey
Arabic history: study of in England, exemplified by Edward Pococke the elder, 29, 34–35; use of, to debunk Roman Catholic authority, 38
Aravamudan, Srinivas, 165n3
Arbuthnot, John, 122
Aristotle, 22
Astell, Mary, 53, 55, 69, 95n14, 105, 140n39, 160, 162, 181, 183; absence of Islamophobic misogynistic mortalism in work of, 58–60, 78–80, 179; as an advocate for women's education, 56, 58–60, 101, 106, 123, 168, 179; correspondence of, with John Norris, 56, 77, 79, 104; criticism of John Locke by, 56, 79; global Anglicanism of, 66, 77, 157; satire of in the *Tatler*, 121, 124–125
Athanasian Creed, 18, 46n19
atheism, 8, 61, 156; apparent encroachment of, due to Christian disunity, 36–37, 79, 87, 105; Christian mortalism viewed as, 23; Locke accused of, 65, 77; viewed as similar to Islam, 35; Wollstonecraft on, 191–192
Aubin, Penelope, 68, 86–89, 116, 164, 193; global stage used by, 91, 160; reliance of, on Islamophobic misogynistic mortalism, 4, 11, 53, 66, 85, 88, 94, 107, 179; and the use of fiction to inspire social reform, 89, 183
Austen, Jane, 183; *Northanger Abbey*, 160
Awbrey, Mary, 70

Backscheider, Paula R., 81, 82
Ballaster, Ros, 31
Bandello, Matteo, 148
Bannet, Eve Tavor, 63, 164
Barker, Jane, 86, 110, 129, 160, 164, 183, 193; influences on, 68, 69, 116, and Jacobite transnationalism, 89–94; reliance of, on Islamophobic misogynistic mortalism, 11, 53, 66, 85, 107
Bayle, Pierre, 25, 47–48n39
Beckford, William, 135–137
Behn, Aphra, 41, 91, 101
Bennett, Zara, 202
Berland, Kevin, 12–13n4
Bernier, François, 51–52n102
Bérulle, Pierre de, 69

Bevilacqua, Alexander, 13n15
"Bickerstaff, Isaac" (*Tatler* persona), 124–125, 127
Blackstone, William, 124
Blasphemy Act, 2, 18
Blazing World, The (Cavendish), 56, 74, 75–76
Bluestockings, 11, 83, 102, 142, 183; efforts of, to distinguish themselves from the Platonic Lady stereotype, 116, 118, 138, 142; and Samuel Johnson's writing, 4, 144, 170, 171–172; and Samuel Richardson's fiction, 4, 110, 158, 164–165, 170, 171–175, 176, 180; views of, on Islam, 176, 178, 182
Boaistuau, Pierre, 148
Book of Common Prayer, 16, 17, 45n16, 112
Book of Genesis, 21–22
Boswell, James, 11, 145–146, 147, 155
Botting, Eileen Hunt, 182, 185, 197n18, 201
Bowers, Toni, 112
Broad, Jacqueline, 55
Brontë, Emily, 201
Brook, Nathaniel, 56
Bulman, William J., 28
Bunyan, John, 16
Burke, Edmund, 187, 191
Burnet, Gilbert, 7, 18, 19–20, 38, 42–43, 112
Bury, Arthur, 46n19
Butler, Joseph, 20, 46n22, 102
Bywaters, David, 41, 42

Calvinism, 29
Cambridge University, 2, 18; Cambridge Platonists, 55, 56, 77, 79
Carter, Elizabeth, 116, 155, 171–175, 177–178
Cartesianism, 54, 55–56, 57, 101, 105, 106, 168
Castle, Terry, 131
Catholic Church. *See* Roman Catholic Church/Roman Catholicism
Cavendish, Margaret, 10, 53, 66, 73, 74–77, 97n47, 110; and Astell, 78; death of, 41; and Descartes, 55–56; and Henrietta Maria, 69, 70; and Philips, 68, 69; and Rowe, 81; and Wollstonecraft, 183
Centlivre, Susannah, 122
Cervantes, Miguel de, 159
Chapone, Hester, 178. *See also* Mulso, Hester
Chapone, Sarah, 117, 170, 178, 180
Charles I of England, 10, 55, 69, 118, 158
Charles II of England, 16, 69, 76, 108
Chew, Samuel C., 29
China, 29, 57, 110, 138n7
Christianity, 2, 8, 29, 93–94, 138, 202; alignment of, with intellectual rather than physical pleasures, and assumed superiority of over Islam, 6, 9, 10, 11, 27, 32, 35–40, 80, 85–86, 92, 94, 100, 101, 106, 107, 119, 142, 167, 169, 172, 179, 182, 199; immortality as central tenet of (contrasted with mortalism), 23–24, 27, 65; disunity in, including the Trinitarian Controversy, 7, 16–21, 26, 28, 29, 30, 35, 36, 63–64, 156, 178; Eastern Christian Church, 35, 36, 37, 38, 153; and a proper Christian education, 85, 88, 118, 147, 151, 180, 189, 192–193, 199; and the Trinity, 2, 7, 15, 23, 24, 28, 37, 38, 80; as a unifying force, shoring up English identity, 68, 87, 89, 91, 94, 106; and women's immortality, 3, 21–23, 25, 114, 117. *See also* Anglican Church; Roman Catholic Church; Protestantism
Christian mortalism, 23–27. *See also* misogynistic mortalism
Chudleigh, Mary, 58, 60, 61–62, 105, 106, 168
Church of England. *See* Anglican Church
Clarendon (Edward Hyde, 1st Earl of Clarendon), 143
Clarendon Code, 16
Clarissa (Richardson), 100, 110, 112–115, 129, 157, 177; heroine of, as exemplar of virtuous womanhood, 173; heroine of, compared to heroine of *Mary, A Fiction*, 184, 185–186, 187; heroine of, compared to hero of *Sir Charles Grandison*, 157, 175; paternal authority in, 164, 170–171; and platonic love as a set of rules used in seduction, 122–123, 131; success of, 155
Clarke, Norma, 66
Clarke, Samuel, 123
Clinton, Hillary Rodham, 1
Cockburn, Catharine Trotter, 55, 56, 77
Coleman, Isobel, 202
Collier, Regina, 70
communion, 17
Conquest of Granada, The (Dryden), 40–42
Constantine (Roman emperor), 19, 23, 46n25

Constantinople, 32, 148, 155, 161; conquest of, 19, 26, 147; Ottoman court at, 31
convents, 93, 175, 189, 202; "Protestant nunneries," 123, 125, 126, 162, 201
Convocation, 17, 27, 44n10
Conway, Anne, 50n77, 55
Cooke, Miriam, 3
Cooper, Anthony Ashley (1st Earl of Shaftesbury), 41
Cooper, Anthony Ashley (3rd Earl of Shaftesbury), 95n14
Corneille, Pierre, 69
Corporation Act (1661), 16, 17
Cotterell, Charles, 97n46
Council of Chalcedon, 19, 45n16
Council of Nicaea, 19, 45n16
Countess of Huntingdon, 21, 22
Cowley, Abraham, 72–73
"criminal conversation," or *crim. con.* (adultery) cases, 133–134
Crocker, Hannah Mather, 201
Cromwell, Oliver, 51–52n102
Crowne, John, 41
Crusades, 54, 184
Crusius, Martinus, 148
Cudworth, Ralph, 55, 77
Cummings, Kathleen Sprows, 201

Darling, Linda, 48n47
Davies, Emily, 199
Davies, Paul C., 28
Davis, Rose Mary, 139n25
Defoe, Daniel, 16, 79, 164
deism, 10, 18, 19, 20, 46n22; women's anti-mortalist writing as a defense against, 87, 102, 105, 109, 117; Locke accused of, 65–66; Prideaux refutes beliefs of, 35–40
Delany, Mary Granville Pendarves, 175, 176–177
Descartes, René, 53, 55–56, 61, 64, 77, 168. *See also* Cartesianism
despotism and Muslim males, stereotype of, 61, 66, 114, 117, 121, 122, 123, 133, 137, 147, 155, 165n3, 179–180, 184, 188, 195
Dewes, Anne Granville, 175, 176
didacticism, in fiction, 110, 147, 149, 178, 180; in Aubin, 85, 86, 94; in Barker, 85, 91, 94; in Haywood, 101; and the misogynistic mortalism trope, 4; in Richardson, 100–101; in Rowe, 80–81, 82
Disputatio Nova Contra Mulieres (anon.), 10, 23–26, 34, 47n29
Dissenters, 15, 16, 17, 18, 79, 80, 158, 183
Dixon, Philip, 15, 29–30, 44n10, 45n16
Dodwell, Henry, 77
Don Sebastian (Dryden), 40–42, 67
Donne, John, 21–22
Donnellan, Anne, 129
Doody, Margeret Anne, 82, 86, 115, 128, 159–160
Dryden, John, 40–43, 51–52n102, 67, 98n57, 140n39
du Ryer, André, 31
Dunton, John, 81, 98n60
d'Urfé, Honoré, 69, 97n40
Dzielska, Maria, 127

Eagleton, Terry, 112
education, women's. *See* women's education
Edwards, John, 66
Egerton, Sarah Fyge, 56
Elizabeth I of England, 36, 156
Ellsworth, Edward W., 200
Elmahdy, Aliaa Magda, 203n9
Elmarsafy, Ziad, 27, 48n45
England: emergence of, as modern political state, 55, 62; and formation of the United Kingdom, 17; marriage and divorce laws in, 67, 117, 124; moral laxness in, 172–173; and the Ottoman Empire, 8, 36; and Wales, 71, 72, 90. *See also* Church of England; English Civil Wars; Glorious Revolution; Trinitarian Controversy; *and specific monarchs, historical events, movements, and institutions*
English Civil Wars, 16, 35, 70, 79, 158
English novel: and the continental romance tradition, 69, 159; domestication of, by excluding the foreign, 82, 128; and imperialism, 3–4; influences on, 69; and the misogynistic mortalism trope, 5, 10, 86; platonic love and, 133; pleasures of, 100; realism in, 155, 159, 160, 164; contributions of Elizabeth Singer Rowe to development of, 81. *See also* specific novels, novelists, and literary movements
Enlightenment, 26, 28, 30, 44n10, 45n15, 127, 178, 194
Erastianism, 36, 44n10
Eutychius, 36, 51n87

Eve, 21, 22, 32, 61, 126
Exclusion Crisis, 35, 41
Exposition of the Thirty-nine Articles, An (Burnet), 7, 19–20, 112

Fawcett, Millicent, 201
Female Coterie, 116, 133, 134, 135–138, 141n54, 172, 182, 186
Female *Quixote, The* (Lennox), 11, 123, 142, 146, 154, 155, 159–165, 166n26
Female Spectator, 101–110, 145
feminism: relationship between religion and, 183; Wollstonecraft as mother of Western, 2, 5, 167, 182, 196. *See also* feminist orientalism
feminist orientalism, 29, 96n35, 109–110, 117; in Astell's work, 78; counter discourse to, 10, 68; origins of, 3, 4–5, 8, 9, 12, 34, 35, 67; in Aubin's work, 86; and the Platonic Lady stereotype, 11, 116; and Prideaux's marks of imposture, 37; in Wollstonecraft's work, 5, 182–187. *See also* Islamophobia; misogynistic mortalism
Fermor, Lady Sophia, 167
Fielding, Henry, 101, 127, 128, 134, 155, 183; *Joseph Andrews*, 101, 130–131; *Shamela*, 101, 118, 136; *Tom Jones*, 118, 130, 131
Filmer, Robert, 62, 63
Fleischer, Manfred P., 25
Flynn, Carol Houlihan, 158–159
Fox, Charles James, 2
Fox, George, 47n35
France, 31, 66, 72, 90, 127, 155, 156, 193; Henrietta Maria of, 11, 69, 158; literature of, 47–48n39, 54–55, 69, 148; the Stuart court in exile in, 91, 92
freethinking, 19, 29, 47n27, 168; fiction as a defense against, 84, 87; Islam as stand-in for, 8, 20; texts, 30; and the Trinitarian Controversy, 18, 19, 10, 38, 102
Freind, William, 117
Friendship in Death (Rowe), 81, 82, 84–85
friendship: between women, 70, 71, 74, 75, 76, 97n45, 183; between women and men, 130, 132

Garcia, Humberto, 9
Garrick, David, 147
Garrick, Peter, 147
Gay, John, 122
Gediccus, Simon, 25, 47–48n39
Generall Historie of the Turkes, The (Knolles), 26, 50–51n81, 143–144, 147, 148
Gentleman's Magazine, 129, 130
George I of England, 17, 66
Gibbon, Edward, 127
Glorious Revolution (1688), 9, 17, 40, 41, 42, 92. *See also* Revolution Settlement
God: belief that all humans are equal before, 59, 187; belief that humans should love only, 79; Christ as consubstantial with, 23, 24, 33; Descartes on, 55; as the only true Father, 171; rights granted to humans by, at birth, 188; humans in image of (*imago Dei*), 3, 21, 22, 192, 195; Islam viewed as scourge of, on a disunited Christianity, 19, 26, 35, 36; Locke on, 63–65; women's direct connection to, through their immortal souls, 183, 187, 200. *See also* Christianity; Jesus Christ; soul, immortal; Trinity
Godwin, William, 199
Goldsmith, Oliver, 139n25
Gordon, Lyndall, 182
Gournay, Marie de, 54
Grand Signior (Ottoman sultan), 39, 76–77, 161
Great Britain, 2, 178; concept of, 66, 86, 90, 160. *See also* England; Scotland; United Kingdom; Wales
Gregg, Stephen H., 117
Gregory of Tours, 25
Greig, Martin, 29, 43n4
Grenby, M. O, 12–13n4
Grimké, Sarah, 201
Grotius, Hugo, 46n18
Gunther-Canada, Wendy, 184, 198n22
Gwinnett, Richard, 140n39

Hadith, 13–14n18
Hammond, Brean, 4, 5
harem(s), 32, 66, 201; scene of, in *Rasselas*, 145, 146, 151, 152–154; stereotype/imagined space of, 3, 9, 14n19, 145; Wollstonecraft's view of, as a manifestation of women's oppression everywhere, 188–189, 192–194
Hart, Clive, 22, 25
Hawes, Frances Anne, 128
Haywood, Eliza, 56, 94, 105, 106, 107, 152, 179, 181, 182; and the *Female*

Spectator, 101–103; feminist orientalism of, 109–110; and Johnson, 144, 145; and the platonic tradition, 116; on women's education, 101, 102, 103, 105, 106
Hedley, Douglas, 43–44n9
Hegel, Georg Wilhelm Friedrich, 29
Henrietta Maria (queen of England and consort of Charles I), 10, 11, 55, 69–70, 118, 158
Hill, Aaron, 155
Hill, Bridget, 123
Hobbes, Thomas, 55
Holt, P. M., 35
Holy Spirit (or Holy Ghost), 2, 24, 33
Hottinger, Johann Heinrich, 36–37, 38
Hughes, Derek, 40
Hypatia of Alexandria, 127

immateriality, 56, 60, 63–65, 75, 77, 82, 116, 121. *See also* women's souls
immortality. *See* women's souls
imperialism: British, 86, 152, 178; and the novel, 4; and the Platonic Lady stereotype, 133, 135, 151; Turkish, 152, 178; and Wollstonecraft, 180, 201
India, 133, 138n7; exoticized, 38–39, 109–110; Mogul, 42, 51n102, 107, 110, 137, 161, 163
Ingram, Robert G., 20, 46n22
intelligence, 11–12, 23, 56, 79, 102, 133, 138, 147, 167–168, 202; apparitional, 85, 108, 138n6; associated with the soul, 3, 5, 53, 56, 70–73, 82, 193; British women's, as foundational to national identity, 2, 10; development of, by abandoning Islam, 180, 199; sensual pleasure as an obstacle to, 107–110, 145, 153; trope that Islam denies women's, 1–3, 5–6, 8–9, 15, 101, 142, 153–155, 183, 194
Ireland, 66, 90–91
Irene (Johnson), 145, 146–151, 152, 159, 169, 179
Islam, 20, 41, 88, 169, 179; alignment of, with sensuality and violence, 37–40, 66, 76, 78, 82, 85–86, 92, 94, 106, 119, 142, 167; alignment of, with tyranny, 43, 53–54, 66, 106; associated by critics with non-Trinitarian Christianity and Roman Catholicism, 38, 176, 177; associated with denial of women's immortal souls (misogynistic mortalism), 2–12, 31, 155, 189, 193, 194, 199, 201, 202; Bluestocking views on, 178; conversion to, 85, 91, 123, 147; conversion from, 8, 180; and the harem, 3, 9, 14n19, 145, 151, 152–154, 188–190, 192, 194, 201; military power of, 19, 20, 26, 34, 35–36, 39; as a "negative ideal," 2, 10, 12, 26, 27, 38, 48n47, 58, 86, 94, 105, 117, 158, 167, 176; rejection of the Trinity by, 7, 16; as stand-in for Socinianism, freethinking, Catholicism, and other heterodox belief systems, 8, 16, 19, 20, 26–27, 29–30, 35–36, 58, 65–66, 176, 177; sympathetic portrayals of, 67, 71, 72, 73, 74, 80; and the veil, 3, 201, 202; view of Jesus Christ in, 16. *See also* Islamophobia; Muslim(s)
Islamic State (ISIS), 203n9
Islamophobia, 2, 5, 39, 41, 74, 181; history of, in articulating vision of pro-British unity, 66, 176. *See also* feminist orientalism; misogynistic mortalism
Italy, 57, 78, 120; Catholic masculinity in, 119, 121, 122

Jacobites, 41, 83, 112–113, 162; Jane Barker as, 89–92
James I of England, 66
James II of England, 16, 18, 41, 42, 90, 108
Jenkins, Eugenia Zuroski, 166n26
Jesus Christ: and the Eucharist, 20, 26; as an imposter, 30; in Islam, 16; Socinians' view of, 23, 24, 30, 47n27; and the Trinity, 2, 22, 23, 34
Jew Bill of 1753, 114
Johnson, Elizabeth, 66–67, 68, 180, 181
Johnson, Samuel, 4, 84, 138, 142, 159, 178, 179; Boswell on, 155; Islam used as a foil by, 11, 105–106, 142, 152–154; and the *Rambler*, 142, 144, 146, 154, 155, 164; on the value of curiosity and attention to the foreign, 144–147; scrutinized by the Bluestockings, 4, 144, 164, 170, 171–172; and women's education, 101, 147–151, 170; on the writing of history, 143
Judaism, 21, 26, 37, 93, 100, 114; and the belief in women's mortality, 34, 47n29, 114

Kant, Immanuel, 29
Kelleher, Paul, 112
Kemmerer, Kathleen Nulton, 148, 151

Keymer, Thomas, 145, 152
Khan, Ghazala, 1, 12n (epigraph), 38
Khan, Humayun, 1
Khan, Khizr, 1, 12n (epigraph), 38
Klein, Dietrich, 46n18
Knolles, Richard, 26, 35, 37, 46n18, 87, 147, 148; influence of, on Sir Paul Rycaut, 10, 50–51n81; Samuel Johnson on, 143–144, 146, 147
Kozaczka, Edward J., 86
Kugler, Emily, 14n21

Lake, Peter, 27
Latimer, Bonnie, 4, 123, 157
Latitudinarians, 28, 42, 43n4, 43–44n9, 105; beliefs of, 7, 18–20; dominance of, 17, 27; influential, 7, 18, 19, 64, 123; and the Trinitarian Controversy, 29–30
Lennox, Charlotte, 11, 123, 138, 154, 159–165, 179, 181; effort of, to distinguish work from Platonic Lady stereotype, 116, 142, 163; and Johnson, 155; and Richardson, 155, 178
Letter on Filial Obedience (Mulso), 170–171
Letters from a Persian in England, to his Friend in Ispahan (Lyttelton), 116, 118–122, 128, 139n25
Letters Writ by a Turkish Spy (Marana), 31–34
libertinism, 23; Islam as a stand-in for, 8, 84, 121, 122, 133, 138; and the Platonic Lady stereotype, 11, 121, 163
Lindsay, A. D., 64
Locke, John, 29, 53, 55, 61, 62–66, 114, 156; critics of, 56, 65–66, 78, 79; defenders of, 56, 63–65, 77, 80; on patriarchal absolutism, 62, 170
Loscocco, Paula, 69
Lowenthal, Cynthia, 67–68
Luther, Martin, 46n18
Lutheranism, 29, 46n25
Lyttelton, George Lyttelton, 1st Baron, 116, 118, 121–122, 128, 133, 134, 139n24

Macaulay, Catharine, 138, 181–182, 184, 198n21
"Magisterial Reformation," 21, 23, 46n25
Mahomet II, 147, 148
Mahomet. *See* Muhammad
Malebranche, Nicolas, 54, 79, 94n3
Manley, Delarivier, 67, 101
Marana, Giovanni Paolo, 31
Martineau, Harriet, 201
Mary Beatrice of Modena, 90
Mary II of England, 16, 17, 41, 68
Mary Magdalene, 47n29
Mary, A Fiction (Wollstonecraft), 183, 184–187, 198n28
Masham, Lady Damaris, 55, 56, 66, 77, 79–80
Matar, Nabil, 44–45n14, 44–45n17, 50n77, 91
Maurus, Johannes Andreas, 30–31, 37
McDowell, Nicholas, 139n21
Mijuskovic, Ben Lazare, 28
Milton, John, 16, 124, 185; and Eve, 192; and Satan, 115, 151
misogynistic mortalism, 10, 27, 73, 76, 169, 179–180; in Astell's work, 78, 80; in Aubin's and Barker's work, 85, 94; authors who avoided, 68, 71, 77; in contemporary feminist dialogue, 12, 201–202; defined, 2; in the *Disputatio*, 24; and the English novel, 5, 10; in the *Female Spectator*, 104–105, 110; Islamophobic transition of, 26, 30–32, 34, 41, 53, 58; in Johnson's work, 148–150, 179; misunderstood as Muslim doctrine, 7–8; origins of, 3, 9, 15, 25; in plays, 40–43, 67; in the responses to Richardson's work, 172, 173, 177–178; and Roman Catholicism, 25; in Rowe's work, 84–85; in Wollstonecraft's work, 180–181, 182, 189, 193–194; in women's education arguments, 11–12, 60, 165, 167, 192–196
Mogul Empire. *See* India: Mogul
Muhammad, 6, 10, 19, 30, 32, 34, 37, 39, 93, 156, 178
Montagu, Elizabeth, 117, 118, 128
Montagu, Lady Mary Wortley, 5–7, 50–51n81, 58, 67, 146, 161, 167–168, 177
Montesquieu, Charles de Secondat, 31, 118
Moors, 26, 42
More, Hannah, 148, 179–181
More, Henry, 50n77, 55, 79–80
mortalism, Christian. *See* Christian mortalism
Moses, 30
Mounsey, Chris, 87
Muhammad (the prophet), 32; character assassination of, and view of as an imposter, 10, 30, 34, 37, 93, 178; dates of, 19

Mulso, Hester, 155, 170–171, 174–175, 176, 178
"Muslimwoman," 3
Muslim(s): and castration, 120; feminists, 201–202; men, portrayed as despots and libertines, 61, 66, 106, 114, 117, 118, 122, 123, 133, 137, 147, 188; and otherness, 10, 66, 83–84; and polygamy, 36, 93, 201; portrayed as preferring physical to spiritual pleasures, 38–39, 76, 78, 84, 88, 107, 121, 152, 167, 172, 182; sympathetic portrayals of, 42, 68, 80; welcomed in Christian Europe, but only after conversion, 8, 91, 93–94, 180; women, portrayed as oppressed by Muslim men, 1, 2, 3, 54, 61, 91, 117, 188, 201; women, question of intelligence and immortality of, 8–9, 32–33, 41–42, 67, 101, 114, 142, 153, 181, 183–184, 189–190, 192, 193, 194, 199. *See also* harems(s); Islam; Turk(s)

Nicene Creed, 19
9/11 terrorist attacks, 3, 202
noncomformists. *See* Dissenters
Norris, John, 56, 77, 79, 98n57, 104, 124, 140n39
novels. *See* English novel
nunneries. *See* convents
Nussbaum, Felicity, 194
Nye, Stephen, 27, 29, 30, 34, 38, 44n10

O'Brien, Karen, 102
Occasional Conformity Act (1711), 17, 79
orientalism. *See* feminist orientalism
Orinda (or the "matchless Orinda"). *See* Philips, Katherine
Orr, Bridget, 96n35
Ottoman Empire, 34, 71, 133, 195; lack of curiosity about, 11, 145, 161, 163; presumption of barbaric despotism in, 61, 66, 114, 117, 121, 122, 123, 133, 137, 147, 155, 165n3, 179–180, 184, 188, 195; presumption that women are denied immortal souls in, 5–7, 8, 50–51n81, 114; rise of, as a world and military power (often associated with Christian disunity), 19, 26, 33, 54, 119, 155–156, 184; and rise of Islamophobia in the West, 34–40, 84, 88, 117, 149; writers who portrayed without resorting to Islamophobia, 10, 74–77, 92–93, 94. *See also* Turkey
Owen, Anne, 70
Oxford University, 2, 18

Painter, William, 148
Pamela (Richardson), 87, 100, 101, 110–115, 128, 155
Pamela in Her Exalted Condition (Richardson), 131–132
Parliament (English), 17, 46n25, 69, 87, 136, 187; women in, 161
Patch-work Screen for the Ladies, A (Barker), 91, 129
Patrick, Simon, 18
Perkins, Franklin, 28
Pfizenmaier, Thomas C., 45n16
Philips, James, 69
Philips, Katherine, 10, 53, 69–74, 97n47, 104, 110; and Astell, 77; and Aubin, 68; and Barker, 68, 90, 91; and Cavendish, 68; death of, 41; and the nature of friendship, 116; and Rowe, 68, 81, 82; on the unity of England and Wales, 66, 90, 160; and Wollstonecraft, 183
Pix, Mary, 67
Pizan, Christine de, 53–54
Plato, 76. See also Platonism
"Platonic Lady," 110, 115, 133, 135, 147, 149, 150, 151, 157, 159, 179, 199; Bluestockings distance themselves from, 116, 118, 138, 142; in the *Female Quixote*, 160–165; and the Mahometan paradise, 116–129; shift in satirical emphasis away from, and toward platonic love, 128–129
platonic love, 69, 76, 81, 116, 129–133, 154, 186
platonism, 29, 76, 68, 81–82, 91, 124, 130; Cambridge Platonists, 43–44n9, 55, 56, 77, 79; feminocentric, 110, 116, 123, 128, 129, 133, 160. *See also* "Platonic Lady"
Pococke, Edward (the elder), 29, 34–35, 36, 50n77
Pococke, Edward (the younger), 50n77
Poems on Several Occasions (Rowe), 80, 81, 83
polygamy, 32, 36, 100, 131, 132, 201
Pope, Alexander, 5–7, 122, 128, 140n39
Porter, Roy, 100
Poullain de La Barre, François, 54, 56–58, 59, 60, 71, 105, 106, 168, 188

précieuses, 118, 127
Presbyterianism, 36, 44–45n14, 58
Prideaux, Humphrey, 10, 35–40, 76, 92, 105, 167, 179
Protestantism: continental, 25; disunity of in England, after the Civil Wars, 16–20, 27; and ecumenism, 7, 16; and Islam, 29, 34; and "Protestant nunneries," 123, 125, 126, 162, 201; and Roman Catholicism, 93, 94, 157–158, 175; and toleration, 80. *See also* Anglican Church; Trinitarian Controversy
Public Advertiser, 136, 137

Quakers, 36, 50n77
querelle des femmes (Renaissance debate), 9, 25, 53–55
Qur'an, 37, 46n19, 85; translations of, 10, 26–27, 31, 34, 48n45, 156; on the afterlife, and whether women have souls, 7–8, 13–14n18, 31, 32

Rabin, Dana, 117
"Radical Reformation," 21, 46n25
Raleigh, Walter, 143
Rambler (Samuel Johnson's periodical), 142–147, 154, 155, 164, 171–172, 177–178
Rasselas (Johnson), 12–13n4, 105, 144, 145, 146, 147, 151, 152–154, 165n3
realism, in fiction, 4, 100, 155, 159, 160, 164
Rees, Emma L. E., 97n48
Reformation, 19, 23, 25, 26, 40. *See also* "Magisterial Reformation"; "Radical Reformation"
Regan, Shaun, 4, 5
Renaissance: the *prisca theologia* of, 29; and the *querelle des femmes*, 9, 25, 53
Restoration England, 66, 81, 121
Revolution of 1688. *See* Glorious Revolution
Revolution Settlement, 18, 42, 44–45n14
Richards, Jennifer, 81
Richardson, Samuel, 4, 87, 101, 123, 147, 154, 155–159, 183; importance of immortal soul in works of, 110–111, 112, 115; influence of, on Wollstonecraft, 184, 185; influences on, 69, 84, 86, 116; Islam used as a foil by, 11, 122; Mulso's correspondence with, 170–171, 178; scrutinized by the Bluestockings, 4, 110, 158, 164–165, 170, 171–175, 176, 180; sublimation of Platonic Lady trope in fiction of, 115, 116, 128, 130, 131
Richetti, John J., 81, 86
Roberts, Marie Mulvey, 100
Robinson, Benedict S., 29
Robinson, Elizabeth. *See* Montagu, Elizabeth
Robinson, Mary, 201
Roe, Sir Thomas, 155–156
Roman Empire, 20, 35, 66, 73
romance tradition, in fiction, 12–13n4, 69, 70, 159–165
Roman Catholic Church/Roman Catholicism, 6, 40, 89–90, 93, 94, 116–117, 127, 138, 158; alignment of, with other dissenters, 58, 79; and castration, 119, 120; conflation of, with Islam, 11, 34, 38, 41, 116–117, 176, 201; conflicts of, with Latitudinarian Anglicans (including the Trinitarian Controversy), 7, 15–21, 29–30, 34; corruption in, 19, 20; and the English monarchy, 66, 69; in Italy, 119, 120, 121; and nunneries, 123, 126, 153; and the Platonic Lady stereotype, 11, 121–122, 139n24, 167; and the question of the immortal soul, 21–22, 23, 24, 25; in Richardson's *Sir Charles Grandison*, 157–159, 164, 175, 176, 177, 178; and the Virgin Mary, 124
Ross, Alexander, 31
Ross, Angus, 114
Rousseau, Jean-Jacques, 181, 184, 187, 198n22
Rowe, Elizabeth Singer, 80–86, 87, 104, 107, 110, 149, 160, 164, 183; influences on, 68, 69, 116, 179; reliance of, on Islamophobic misogynistic mortalism, 4, 11, 53, 66
Russell, Gillian, 117, 138
Rycaut, Sir Paul, 10, 35, 50–51n81

Said, Edward, 3–4, 5
Sale, George, 8, 156
Sales, St. François de, 69, 97n40
Sapiro, Virginia, 182, 183
Saracens, 20, 44–45n14, 54
Schiebinger, Londa, 54
Scotland: Thomas Aikenhead's execution in, 2, 18; and the Dress Act of 1746, 162, 166n29; and ESFI, 66; Johnson on, 146; and the United Kingdom, 17
Selden, John, 36, 51n87
seraglio. *See* harem(s)
Serious Proposal to the Ladies, A (Astell), 58, 78, 80, 123

Settle, Elkanah, 41
Seward, Thomas, 169–170
Shadwell, Thomas, 41
Shakespeare, William, 54, 185
Sheehan, Jonathan, 26
Sherlock, William, 44n10
Shirreff, Emily and Maria, 199–201
Singer, Elizabeth. *See* Rowe, Elizbeth Singer
Sir Charles Grandison (Richardson), 110–111, 156–159, 174–177; hero of, as exemplar of English manhood, 111, 123, 158, 171, 174; treatment of women's education in, 164–165, 176–177
Sirota, Brent, 28, 43n4
Sitter, John, 158
Smith, David Nichol, 147
Smollett, Tobias, 128, 129, 134
Socinianism, 7, 15, 34–35, 44–45n14, 45–46n17, 47n27, 87, 117; Astell attacks, 58, 78; demonized in the *Disputatio*, 10, 23–26, 34; Islam as stand-in for, 8, 19, 20, 27, 34; Latitudinarians charged with, 16, 18; Locke accused of, 56, 65–66; Prideaux on, 36–37, 38; texts, 30. *See also* Trinitarian Controversy; Unitarianism
Socinus, Faustus, 23
"Sophia" pamphlets, 11, 56–57, 167–169
Souers, Philip, 116
souls. *See* immateriality; women's souls
Spain, 26, 41, 78, 155
Spencer, Jane, 86, 128
Spivak, Gayatri Chakravorty, 4, 11, 180
Sprint, John, 60–62
Staves, Susan, 83
Steele, Richard, 122, 124
Stillingfleet, Edward, 18, 36, 43n4, 64, 65
Stuart, James Francis Edward (Prince of Wales), 90
Stuart, William, 146
Stuarts (Scottish/British royal family), 61, 66, 68, 73, 83, 90–91. *See also* individual monarchs
Stubbe, Henry, 29, 34, 38, 45–46n17
"Sturdy, Charles" (*Tatler* reader), 124, 125, 127
Stuurman, Siep, 54–55
Swinton, John, 156

Talbot, Catherine, 83, 116, 171–175, 197n6
Tankard, Paul, 133
Tarabotti, Arcangela, 25
Tatler, 116, 121, 122, 123, 124
Taylor, Barbara, 182, 187, 197n18
Taylor, Jeremy, 97n45, 104, 116
Taylor, Lisa K., 201
Taylor, Stephen, 28, 30
Tenison, Thomas, 18
Test Act (1673), 16, 17
Thirty-Nine Articles of Religion, 2, 7, 16, 18, 27, 30
Thomas, Elizabeth, 140n39
Thomson, Ann, 14, 43
Thomson, James, 185
Tillotson, John, 18, 123
Tindal, Matthew, 30, 103, 105
Toland, John, 20, 30, 38, 46n19, 103, 105, 127
toleration (of non-Anglican Protestants), 9, 18, 27, 42, 58, 78–80; in Richardson's work, 155, 156, 158. *See also* Act of Toleration; Latitudinarians
Tomlinson, Sophie, 70
Town and Country Magazine, 133, 134, 138
transubstantiation, 7, 20, 26, 50–51n81, 90
Trinitarian Controversy, 9, 10, 11, 15, 19, 29–30, 33, 34, 35, 43n4, 54, 116, 117, 199; Astell on, 77, 80; Aubin as bridge between domestic fiction of the 1740s and, 87; in the *Female Spectator*, 108; Haywood on, 103; and the Latitudinarians, 18; Locke on, 63–64; Richardson on, 156; Rowe on, 81–82, 84; threat of deism (or freethinking) as continuation of, 102; William III asked to intervene in, 18; women's education implicated in, 85
Trinity/Trinitarian orthodoxy, 2–3, 7, 10, 15, 18, 24, 28, 36, 37, 38, 80; rejected by Islam, 10, 19, 33, 54; rejected by Socianism, 8, 10, 16, 19, 23, 38. *See also* Trinitarian Controversy
True Nature of Imposture Fully Display'd in the Life of Mahomet, The (Prideaux), 35–40
Trump, Donald J., 1, 2, 12n (epigraph), 38–39
Turk(s), 87; substituted for "Jew," in *Clarissa*, 114, 122, 173; used by theologians against theological opponents within Christianity, 44–45n14; used as insult in Shakespeare's *Othello*, 54
Turkey, 161; castration in, 120; endorsed by Boswell as a place to visit, 146; false belief that women in lack souls,

Turkey (cont.)
6, 66, 67, 103, 114, 181; imprisonment of Europeans in, 156; Johnson on, 144, 152; Knolles on, 26; Lennox on, 160–161; Luther on, 46n18; Poullain on, 56–57; used as example to call for greater unity among Christians (and Britons), 87–88, 91; Wollstonecraft on, 106, 193, 195. *See also* Ottoman Empire
Turk plays, 6, 89

Unitarianism, 27, 38, 47n27. *See also* Socinianism
United Kingdom, 160; formation of, 17

van Schurman, Anna Maria, 54
Vindication of the Rights of Men, A (Wollstonecraft), 184, 187–189, 191, 195
Vindication of the Rights of Woman, A (Wollstonecraft), 2, 3, 12, 68, 167, 182–184, 187–196, 198n22
Virgin Mary, 112, 124, 125
Voltaire, 127
Von Ruville, Albert, 139n25

Wadud, Amina, 8
Wager, Lewis, 47n29
Wales, 69; and the United Kingdom, 17; unity of, with England, 66, 71, 72, 73, 90
Walker, Roger G., 65
Walpole, Robert, 118
Walsh, John, 28, 30
Waterman, A. M. C., 45n16
Watt, Ian, 3–4
Weinbrot, Howard D., 144–145, 165n3
Whigs, 2, 14n21, 27, 44–45n14, 65, 81
Whiston, William, 30
Wilkes, John, 136
William III of England (William of Orange), 2, 17, 40, 41, 42–43, 66, 68, 83, 90
William of Orange. See William III of England
Williams, George Huntston, 21, 46n25
Wilson, Carol Shiner, 90
Wollstonecraft, Mary, 11, 56, 116, 138, 181; and Islamophobic misogynistic mortalism, 4–5, 12, 180, 182–187, 193–196; and *Mary, A Fiction*, 183, 184–187, 198n28; as the mother of Western feminism, 2, 5, 167, 182, 196; religious faith of, 182, 185; and *A Vindication of the Rights of Woman*, 2, 3, 12, 68, 167, 182–184, 187–196, 198n22; and women's education, 101, 106, 154, 180, 187
Woman not Inferior to Man (Anon.), 167–170. *See also* "Sophia" pamplets
women playwrights, 2, 9, 67. *See also specific playwrights*
women's education, 56, 170; academy for, proposed by Mary Astell, 123; arguments for, from Poullain and Astell, 57, 58–60, 101; arguments for, related to theories of Descartes and Locke, 61–62; arguments for, reliant on misogynistic mortalism, 2, 5, 9, 11, 12, 22, 54, 58, 78, 85, 86, 151, 167, 168, 178–180, 181; arguments for, seeking to adapt to a more modern, enlightened concept, 101, 103–107; at the center of Samuel Johnson's fiction, 147–151, 155; for Muslim women, 8, 118, 180, 183–184; nineteenth-century advocates for, 199–201; in Samuel Richardson's work, and Bluestocking objections to theories of, 155, 156, 157, 158, 164–165, 171, 172–174, 175, 176, 177–178; Wollstonecraft on, 180, 182–187, 189, 190, 191, 192–196
women's souls, 11, 177; in the *Disputatio*, 24–25, 34; existence of, aligned with intelligence, 2–3, 10, 12, 56–57, 58, 59, 63, 68, 72–74, 82, 123, 142, 147, 157, 189, 193; existence of, and a direct connection to God, 183; and female friendship, 70–71, 74; in Islam, 7–8, 31, 32–33, 41; and necessity of education for women, 58–60, 61, 103–104, 117–118, 142, 147, 180, 189–190; and platonism, 81–82; presumption that Muslim women lack, or have inferior ones, 5–8, 15, 34, 42, 67, 103, 114, 122, 180, 183–184, 188–189; in the public realm, 75–76; scriptural grounds for, 21–23. *See also* misogynistic mortalism
Wroth, Lady Mary, 40–41
Wycherley, William, 121

Yeazell, Ruth Bernard, 14n19
Yolton, John W., 65
Young, B. W., 28
Young, Edward, 129, 185

Zhulkeflee, Ustaz Bin Haji Ismail, 13–14n18
Zine, Jasmine, 201
Zonana, Joyce, 3, 41, 182

ABOUT THE AUTHOR

SAMARA ANNE CAHILL is an assistant professor of eighteenth-century English literature at Nanyang Technological University in Singapore. She received her dual BA from the University of Texas at Austin and her PhD from the University of Notre Dame. She co-edited (with Kevin Cope) *Citizens of the World: Adapting in the Eighteenth Century* (2015). She is editor of the journal *Studies in Religion and the Enlightenment* and book review editor of *1650–1850: Ideas, Aesthetics, and Inquiries in the Early Modern Era*. She has published articles on Jane Barker, Mary Wollstonecraft, anti-Catholic and anti-Muslim rhetoric, earthquake jeremiads, and feminist orientalism.

TRANSITS:
LITERATURE, THOUGHT & CULTURE, 1650–1850

Recent titles in the *Transits* series:

Fire on the Water: Sailors, Slaves, and Insurrection in Early American Literature, 1789–1886
Lenora Warren

Community and Solitude: New Essays on Johnson's Circle
Anthony W. Lee, ed.

The Global Wordsworth: Romanticism Out of Place
Katherine Bergren

Cultivating Peace: The Virgilian Georgic in English, 1650–1750
Melissa Schoenberger

Intelligent Souls? Feminist Orientalism in Eighteenth-Century English Literature
Samara Anne Cahill

The Printed Reader: Gender, Quixotism, and Textual Bodies in Eighteenth-Century Britain
Amelia Dale

For a full list of *Transits* titles, go to https://www.bucknell.edu/script/upress/series.asp?id=33.